E. M. NICHOLSON has twice accepted invitations for government service, in wartime for shipping control and after World War II for economic planning as Secretary of the Lord President's Office, in intimate contact with the Cabinet Office, the Treasury and other key sections of the central administration. He is also a leader of the British nature conservation movement and a distinguished ornithologist. His book *Birds and Men* is a classic in its field.

Max Nicholson was born in Ireland of English parents. He read Modern History at Oxford, but at the same time was much occupied there with exploration and with biological investigations. He then worked as a journalist on *The Weekend Review* and later became General Secretary of the pioneer economic and social research group PEP (Political and Economic Planning). His war work in shipping gave him direct responsibility for the London Pool of dry cargo tonnage, and he attended the Cairo, Quebec, Yalta and Potsdam conferences as a senior adviser of the Anglo-American Combined Shipping Adjustment Board. From 1945 to 1952 he was senior official adviser to the then Deputy Prime Minister, Herbert Morrison, and to his successors as Lord President down to Lord Woolton. His contacts with journalism have remained close and from 1952 until 1966 he was a Trustee of *The Observer*. From 1951 to 1965 he also organized the development of the Nature Conservancy and traveled widely both within Great Britain and abroad in the cause of conservation.

The System

THE SYSTEM

The Misgovernment of Modern Britain

by Max Nicholson

Introduction by Max Lerner

McGraw-Hill Book Company   New York

Foreword for American Readers

If we could recall for further testimony that eighteenth-century witness, Bishop Berkeley, we might find him somewhat more disposed to hedge about identifying as "Time's noblest offspring" the inhabitants of the United States. He would certainly reaffirm that "Westward the course of Empire takes its way," but he might quizzically speculate whether it is an unmixed blessing to have an unruly secondhand empire dumped into one's lap. He might further inquire how diligently its latest heirs are studying the sad faults and errors which proved the downfall of their predecessor farther east. After all, staying a millionaire is child's play compared with the cares of empire.

It is on this account that I venture to suggest, as we say when we stretch our necks out in England, that this book may have some message for American readers, as well as for the British to whom it was primarily addressed. Americans may justly experience some glow of satisfaction at having successfully avoided the four cardinal errors which are traced in Part One as having done so much to pull Britain down throughout the past century. But one sobering conclusion to which this analysis points is that once the kind of status that Bishop Berkeley termed "Empire" is acquired, decisive errors are more likely to occur, less easy to perceive, and more difficult to correct afterwards. A nation saddled with the obligations of "Empire" is a much more rigid and less adaptable organism than the kind of carefree, informal, loose-boundary frontier society and economy to which Americans not unnaturally look with some nostalgia.

For this there are several clear reasons. "Empire" imports a much greater complexity into the sphere of political and economic decision-making, and uncovers nightmarish situations in which a commonsense decision to follow an evidently sound course in an apparently uncomplicated situation can suddenly transform itself into an imperative for going through with agonizingly different measures in an unrecognizably changed scene.

The decision-makers need far more data in order to know what they are doing, and this means training new types of decision-makers who must be more remote from ordinary men and women. It also tends to centralize far more power at fewer points, and to leave the grass roots with little to do more interesting than growing grass. As the book shows this creates a dangerous and unpleasant alienation between government and governed—a gulf no less pronounced in America than in Britain. As ever more powerful agencies are built up to take care of certain fields a stronger resistance arises to change and adaptation. Agencies become both possessive and empire-building, with a vested interest in continuing such distortions and maladjustments as are enshrined in them. The steering mechanism of the body politic thus stiffens at the same time that its owner, the sovereign nation, is losing control of the hired driver and is becoming agonizingly aware of simply being taken for a ride. If this disturbing situation is to be corrected, citizens must get to work on it. One of the more promising ways of making progress is to exchange experiences and ideas with citizens who are similarly placed elsewhere. Such exchange between the British and Americans can be all the more fruitful because their lines of development have contrasted and each has been exposed to more experience in some fields and to less in others. British mistakes in world affairs look horribly like being repeated from Washington. For example, Vietnam developed unbidden from small, unperceived beginnings to enmesh the United States, just as the Boer War enmeshed Britain seventy years ago. In the same way it has driven a wedge in domestic politics between those who think in terms of world responsibility and its unpleasant imperatives, and those who prefer to maintain at all costs liberal values learned at home.

Inevitably this book includes a good deal of detail about the British record, which American readers may choose to skip. Nevertheless, I make no apology for including it, since such a work would be worthless without documentation and evidence to enable a skeptical reader to judge for himself what conclusion he will accept and what inferences he may wish to draw, perhaps in quite different contexts of his own. Also, beyond any conventional interpretation of the historical record, we are concerned here to begin developing a new approach based on ecological principles and flow processes, to enable us to look from a fresh angle at government and governed, and at the subtle evolution of their often unhappy mutual relationships. To apply such a new approach to American insitutions could be fully as rewarding as applying it to British, and it is to be hoped that to some extent this book may form a do-it-yourself kit for that purpose. All the ingredients of national loss of identity and group alienation, of institutional distortions and excessive power concentrations, and of a disharmony between people, land and government are as clearly discernible in the United States as in Britain, even though the patterns and manifestations are so different.

In case I may seem biased towards magnifying the potential of such an Anglo-American exchange of experience, I should perhaps explain that I have over many years personally learned much from it in several fields. Before World War II, I gained from frequent contacts with pioneers of resources planning in America, and I have always felt a little embarrassed that after giving a small dinner in my honor, President Roosevelt's National Resources Planning Board was abolished the next day!

During World War II, I frequently came to Washington and New York to co-ordinate shipping movements. It was here that the immense importance of framing the right questions and organizing the right flow of information for current decision-making was demonstrated to me. In the fifties my American colleagues in conservation gave me a similar stimulus to rethinking and to new lines of action, which I attempted to sum up in my Albright lecture at the University of California at Berkeley in March, 1964. More recently I have begun to participate in linked studies by Resources for the Future and PEP of some of the repercussions of our respective megalopolises between Boston and Washington and between Preston and Dover. To me, therefore, it comes very naturally to adopt a mid-Atlantic standpoint, scanning each side for material relevant to the other, and I have never yet come back to land empty-handed. The many thorough and illuminating studies of British institutions and trends produced by American writers confirm the fruitfulness of such interchanges.

In grappling with this vast mass of material and attempting to hack out a sound and coherent model corresponding nearly enough to the facts, I have obviously obtained at most only a partial success. Others who follow up may contrive to do better. At any rate, I have found the experience illuminating in many indirect ways. For example, the love-hate relation between the United States and Britain has often been re-marked upon, but now it emerges that many of the features which fuel the hate element in this are identical with features which arouse quite similar reactions among large numbers of the British themselves against the system under which they are, as I contend, misgoverned. Remedying these features could therefore at the same time greatly change both the image of Britain in America and the character of rela-tions between the two nations. The process is bound to be painful in both directions. A quarter of a century ago, during World War II, I often encountered in Washington the clear-cut view that the British had no business in the Far East and that the sooner they quit or were expelled from Asia the better. When at last in the New Year 1968 this wish was largely fulfilled the British, who had so long stoutly resisted it, gave a sigh of relief, but were Americans satisfied by the achieve-ment of their ambition? The simultaneous abandonment of equality of benefit in favor of selectivity in the British Welfare State also implied a change in the British image in North America. No longer either im-perialist or socialist, the new Britain is still keenly concerned with world affairs and deeply attentive to the well-being of the underprivi-leged, abroad as well as at home. The means of working out these in-terests in practice and of harmonizing British and American policies need much fresh thinking.

My analysis of the peculiar and perennial practices and results of the System reached only up to 1966, but connoisseurs will observe that its characteristic pattern of bias towards certain types of blunders and failures has been amply maintained since then. The inept and futile gestures for preventing or influencing the 1967 Middle East War, or for remedying even such unpalatable results as the extended closure of the Suez Canal, the bitter domestic controversies over the high-handed actions of the System regarding the choice of London's third airport site at Stansted, the attempt to override civic rights in the case of plans for new comprehensive schools, and the arbitrary reversal without consultation of governmental decisions regarding the future of the British Museum helped to open many eyes to what goes on.

A much more spectacular example of the failure of the System to anticipate impending events, to prepare the obvious contingency plans for them, or to handle their immediate repercussions with any sem-blance of grip or understanding, was duly furnished when its inepti-tudes and miscalculations brought on the national disaster of enforced devaluation of the pound sterling in November, 1967. This bitter blow to Britain and to Britain's friends has been aggravated by the inadequate and belated remedial measures produced by the government and their clumsy improvisation without any coherent philosophy or plan. The accompanying disclosures and the national and international debates which followed indicated that this book had been at fault in failing to make clear the extent to which the System had already lost control of events. The scale of repercussions on American policies and interests confirmed the sad fact that Britain's troubles have become troubles for everyone else too.

While much—in my view too much—of the inquest within Britain has been devoted to transitory issues of policies, personalities and party tactics, the obvious cluelessness of the Opposition and their large share of responsibility for the evolution of the long-term situation have at last begun to direct attention to and to discredit the System itself. As the System is so much a mirror image of the foibles and daydreams of Britain's traditional ruling groups and of her backward-looking educators this process is intensely difficult and painful. The cuts and adjustments are not merely external. People are being forced to amputate long-cherished parts of their own beliefs and assumptions. The ivy weighs heavily on Britain and clings hard, but its cutting away and replacement is now much nearer than when this book was written. The pace of modern change makes us all prisoners of our past and it is only in disaster and frustration that new voices can make themselves heard, and new attitudes and styles can begin to assert their healing role. In some ways it is agonizing to endure these processes, but it is also an exciting and stimulating experience to be overtaken by an irresistible drive for national renewal, even through national discomfiture. I hope, therefore, that the American readers will bear with many faults of this book and its inevitable irrelevancies for them. They may be able to extract from it some material which will help to advance understanding of the ills under which we both labor.

Contents

Diagrams

[1] Based on a map compiled by Dr T. H. Hollingsworth and published in *The Reader's Digest Complete Atlas of the British Isles.*

Introduction by Max Lerner

This is a radical book on British government and society. I use "radical" in the sense of a sustained effort to cut to the effective heart of the matter, past the foliage and branches, straight at the root.

A reader of the brilliant close-packed pages that follow had better prepare himself for one of the most devastating demolition jobs he is likely to encounter. This is more than an attack on a government or a ruling group. It is a taking-apart of a whole society and power-structure, done by a man with learning, wit and style, to see why its historic role has been lost, its power-mass has suffered a decline, and so much of its splendid human resources have been wasted.

Only an Englishman who knows England could dare capture the whole sweep of its history and its present functioning, to probe insistently for where it took the wrong-turnings. Only an Englishman who loves England could afford thus to see England plain, confident that his love can survive his truth.

From the rich abundance of Nicholson's material one could carve out several short textbooks that any university teacher would covet for his classes: one on British government—and misgovernment; one on British economic and administrative history in the past forty years; one on governmental and policy reform. The chapters that would be included—especially "Leading and Lagging" and "Britain's Performance"—furnish a hard factual base for the entire analysis. It is an analysis by a man who not only draws upon his own administrative experience in depth, but who also draws on the resources of the modern social sciences and uses the frame of a liberal man-of-the-world for perspective.

The themes in the book which hit me hardest are, of course, those that affect my own concerns: first, for what is happening in our American civilization as well as in the British, and consequently for the "British sickness" as a melancholy case-history in the inquiry about great civilizations and how they flourish and fall.

When Dean Acheson was once asked what was the American "national purpose," his answer was a no-nonsense one: "Our purpose, Sir, is to survive—and perchance to flourish." High among the factors that decide whether a nation survives and flourishes is the capacity and training of its directing elites. The education of Britain's rulers—at "Oxbridge" for Whitehall—is a leading theme in Nicholson's account of what went wrong. A system of higher education must in the end be judged not only by how it shapes character and personality style, but also by what direction it gives to the national society as an energy system. Judged in these terms the British system did badly by stressing the value of the gifted amateur as against the professionally competent craftsman and innovator.

This leads to a related theme of the attitude of the elites toward technology, science and work. The inventors and pioneers of the seventeenth and eighteenth centuries took pride in their craft and work. But the British abandoned their commanding world lead in technology and science, and they failed to consolidate that role. Thorstein Veblen, comparing the case of Britain with that of Germany in his *Imperial Germany and the Industrial Revolution,* spoke of the British "penalty for taking the lead," and argued that the British were held back by the encumbrances of their democratic institutions which the Germans had the luck to lack. Nicholson puts the burden of guilt not on democracy but on class education, especially on the Victorian educational ideal of the "gentleman," who is broadly trained in leisure-class dead languages but remains unspecialized for the nitty-gritty tasks of technology or science or business management. The gentleman has a lofty condescension for messing around with "work" which falls outside the approved sphere. Nicholson notes also how the discriminations and resentments at the other end of the class spectrum have left the manual workers alienated from the general society. More recently, the mental workers also have become estranged from the mainstream.

The Americans today, who are wrestling with their own problems of education and alienation, may well ponder such an analysis of the "British sickness." There can be little question that America has maintained itself as an energy system. But the question is where the energies are being channeled, and how they can be contained without an explosive destructiveness. The problem is at once that of over-reaching and that of rigidity. Nicholson works both veins in his analysis of the British, who conquered an empire that spent their energies fruitlessly, and developed a rigid power-structure at home that became the "system" within which their imagination was imprisoned and their creativeness smothered. The British "imperialist deviation" was a deviation not only from national social and moral health but from simple good sense, whether measured by economic or military or political tests. What made the wrong-turning even more ironic was that it came at the height of middle-class power in Great Britain, when the possibilities of British life seemed to be boundless. "The hour was golden," said G. M. Trevelyan of the British middle class, "and it was theirs."

The American imperium today is not a territorial one, and its overreaching is not for meaningless real estate. Its power-base at home is also vastly greater than the British, and if anything it suffers not from amateurism but overspecialization. Yet its over-reaching, in a distant and distracting war and in ideological obsessiveness, can be no less dangerous for the health of the society.

Whatever excursions Nicholson takes, into whatever by-paths—and they are many and rewarding—he keeps coming back to his main theme of the rigidity and idiocy of "the system." However one defines it—amateurism and an Oxbridge-to-Whitehall in-group exclusiveness plus the cult of how-things-are-done and the throttling of the innovative—it remains somewhat mistier than one might wish. Similarly his agenda for reform, much as one identifies with their good sense, strike one reader as less rewarding than the mordant analysis of what is wrong.

Yet these may be peckish criticisms. The American reader will feel grateful for the hard-bitten analysis itself, and for the whole context of British history in which it is imbedded, and for the insights into the British national character, and not least for the spicy—and sometimes spiteful—language the author knows how to use. We are carried along on its stream. And when, at the end, he holds out some hope that the creativeness of young Britons in films and theater and TV, in the arts and design, in popular music and fashions needs only a new frame to be released, one is carried along with the hope as well.

PART ONE
THE BRITISH INHERITANCE

CHAPTER I

From the Origins to the Conquest

Britain means a subtle mixture of facts, of ideas, of emotions. Geographically it is simply an island, the eighth largest on earth, flanked to the west and north by many other islands, one fairly large, the rest much smaller, lying close off the western shores of Eurasia, the earth's greatest and most populous land-mass. The English, who have in recent history won for themselves the largest, most fertile and most accessible part of this island group, share the rest, not always easily, with lowland and highland Scots, Welshmen, Cornishmen and Irishmen who are also British. A great world language and literature, mature systems of law and politics, immense developments in science and technology, movements or trends of thought and fashion, sport and leisure, landscape and drama, and much else was born of these islands and became a part of all civilization. Britain has been the scene of struggles for liberty and the rule of law and has contributed principles of tolerance and fair play, the pattern of the gentleman, the archetype of the capitalist, the strivings for brotherhood and against exploitation, the passion for reform and for social justice, the vulgarity and vanity of imperialism, the class-consciousness and race-consciousness, the "finest hour" after Dunkirk, and the apparent self-indulgence and ineptitude which have lately made it necessary for other nations, who order their affairs better, to come economically to the rescue of these same British. It has produced endless triviality, mediocrity, misconduct and incompetence; as well as inspiring adventure, bold leadership and initiative, and talented innovations and creative achievements, half hidden among a mass of evasions, of neglects and of manifestly outdated clutter from the past.

What is to be made of it all? This is a question which today urgently confronts not only the British themselves, but the much more numerous other human beings with whom they share this crowded planet. It will be the function of this book to discuss the main facets of this problem factually but critically, with special reference to the choices open to the British people, the desirability of making certain choices rather than others, and the channels for reaching and carrying through such decisions and actions.

For mainly technological reasons, the world is today undergoing a rapid movement towards unification. In earlier ages attempts at extensive political unification were often made, as in the conquests of Alexander the Great and the Romans, but once standards of leadership and drive declined such empires collapsed. Those early civilizations which endured longest tended, as in the Nile Valley, Mesopotamia and the Indus and Yellow River basins, to depend on a fairly compact base whose productivity was geared to efficient systems of irrigation or other technology. These demanded strong and stable government. Indeed modern government may be regarded as an activity first brought into being only about 5000 years ago in order to make it possible to operate complex large-scale irrigation schemes. Fortunately they needed further to solve many other problems of social organization, in which they largely succeeded. Unfortunately they also required immunity from attack by aggressors of superior strength, and could therefore last only in conditions of limited mobility for their enemies. The advent of the horse, as much later of the automobile, proved very upsetting to comfortable government. Growth of mobility, especially through the breeding and breaking-in of horses, and through the design of larger ocean-going ships, brought a long period of insecurity to settled civilizations. It affected least those which were best served by natural early defensive barriers.

In this way the balance tipped against the early big-river civilizations of the Near, Middle and Far East, not only because looting them proved too tempting to fiercer and more mobile aggressors, but also because they were not able in the long run to conserve their natural environment successfully against their own destructive pressures upon it, or to resist major alterations in river flow or land level which rendered untenable some of their most impressive urban centers.

The great Mediterranean civilizations of Greece and Rome, which succeeded them, collapsed after only a few centuries under somewhat similar pressures, but not before having posed intellectually and passed on to posterity the fundamental issues concerning man's capacity for governing men, and its limitations. These partly seaborne civilizations were less sedentary and more adventurous. In their expansionist days traders, and later soldiers and administrators, from the Mediterranean stretched their influence to include parts of Britain. When they proved unable to maintain the contact they left a legacy of enlightened tradition, which in some obscure way clung on thinly through succeeding periods of conflict and anarchy.

The confused origins of the British nation occurred upon an isolated, cool and rainy offshore island, only recently freed from a great ice-cap, gradually becoming exposed to a trickle of immigration from successive waves of continental peoples driven to colonize it either as pioneers of expansion or as refugees from oppression. This immigration brought with it three elements which were to dominate the subsequent history of the island—trade with overseas territories, budding ideologies, including religions, and armed conflict, triggered off by requirements of defense against further invaders.

No doubt some of the waves of human immigrants following withdrawal of the ice had themselves been displaced by climatic changes and their consequences elsewhere in Europe. They could not have known the nature and scale of the geographic vicissitudes from which their new homeland was emerging. The earlier of the settlers, from about 5500–2500 BC, enjoyed a climate very comfortably warmer than any of their successors so far. It was during this period, after 4000 BC, that the first agriculturalists reached Britain from the Mediterranean, people probably resembling most of the modern Welsh in physical type. (The Cymric Celts, who became credited with being the ancestors of the Welsh, were actually much later immigrants, arriving only a few generations before the Romans, and they seem never to have become more than a powerful minority among the Welsh stock.) They found favorable opportunities for settlement on the chalk uplands of southern England, where their earthworks and monuments still dominate landscapes.

They were the first to apply technology on a large scale in Britain, and on parts of the chalk effective technology for cropraising disappeared with them, to return only in the latest tractor age. They were also the first to develop settlements sufficiently populous for large-scale social activity, and to cut down time required for food production sufficiently to leave a useful margin for inessential activities such as religious ceremonies and the erection of impressive structures. For that they were evidently able to move large blocks over long distances, presumably by the organized use of water transport and of manpower equipped with rollers.

They evidently had developed a form of government which was efficient and acceptable within its limits. The great stone monuments of Avebury and Stonehenge bear testimony to the competence and power of their administration nearly 4000 years ago. They are also evidence that the long and checkered relationship between government and governed in Britain had by then already begun its course, and that the role of an established church invoking supernatural sanctions was already filled. Contemporary British politics, therefore, deal with processes which in one form or another have been taking shape over fully 120 generations. Among present-day counties Kent is traceable under approximately the same name for 2300 years back, until just after the death of Aristotle.

During this evolution there have frequently been rises and declines of constructive activity, new departures, abandonments of projects and ways of life, fresh impacts from outside, welcome or imposed, and a continuous hybridization, not only genetically between the various human stocks, but in ideas and practices. The sum of these developments is all-important in the creation of the British nation as it now exists, but the capacity to trace them is still very limited. Nevertheless, the knowledge that they have taken place, and that if we were more aware of them they might throw light on much that is still obscure about the British and their habits of mind, is in itself of some value. Everywhere in Britain there is the sense of a varied, vigorous, conflicting human heritage and of unending interplay of stubborn groups who, even literally, do not speak the same language. The half-forgotten unspoken things still count for much.

In terms of geopolitics the nature and location and size of a nation's homeland is not only of decisive significance to its history, but needs to be freshly assessed at frequent intervals as technology develops and as history marches on. Of no country is this more true than of Britain. Almost everything of importance about Britain's role and status in the world depends on geographical factors, some obvious, some widely overlooked.

Britain as it is known today is physically a very young country, compared with which only the Scandinavian lands, and a few others, have been more unrecognizably transformed during the past 10,000 years. This brief period has seen the disappearance of a large ice-cap and its neighboring cold zone, great changes in land levels, the breakthrough of the seas to surround the newly made island through the Straits of Dover, sweeping changes in the coastline and in the larger wetlands, and the rapid covering of most of the surface with forest and the resulting fertile brown soils, followed by climatic deterioration and the formation of vast layers of deep peat.

The changing and changeable physical environment has played a large part in shaping the complex peculiarities of the changing British peoples. A summer day in mid-Scotland can be seventeen and a half hours long from sunrise to sunset, while a winter's day shrinks to only seven. The climate of the higher Pennines is close to that of Iceland, while sheltered spots on the Atlantic coasts, from Scilly to as far north as Wester Ross (in the same latitude as Sitka in Alaska), will support subtropical trees and shrubs in the open. In July nearly all of England and Wales and the southeastern half of Ireland enjoy the comfortable mean maximum temperature of 20° C (68° F), while in January virtually all lowland Britain, unlike much more southerly parts of continental Europe and North America, is at least above freezing point throughout the average day. In the extreme west of Scotland and Wales, and the west and south of England, the average frost-free period lasts eight months or more. In the northeast Highlands it may scarcely last three, and snow may be lying on a hundred mornings in the year, compared with under five in the west and south.

Perhaps the best-known characteristics of the British climate are its deficiency of bright sunshine and its high frequencies of rain, gales and fog. Bright sunshine averages around four hours daily in England and rather under three and a half hours in Scotland, with the best months running up to between five and eight hours in different years. In the worst month on record London had only six minutes of sunshine. While there are mountainous areas with rainfalls up to 250 cm (100 inches) or more, the sites of nearly all the main towns are below the forty-inch mark, and many are below thirty, with a few below twenty-five. The most intense summer rains yield up to eleven inches (275 mm) in twenty-four hours. These figures do not compare so badly with many lands whose inhabitants complain less. In terms of human experience the worst faults are perhaps the erratic and unreliable nature of the weather from day to day, the spread of moderate amounts of precipitation over too many and too long periods of rainfall, and the frequency of cloud or a chilly breeze or both.

Every day brings its new uncertainty and its new challenge out of doors, molding the characters of the natives as much as of their landscape. That they secretly enjoy this is confirmed by the changes and extremes of temperature which they choose to live in indoors. Contrary to common belief overseas there are now very few and very small areas in Britain where thick fog occurs at all often—say on twenty or more days a year—the frequency over most of the country being less than ten days annually. The longest fogs recorded have gone on for less than five days in London. Gale-force winds, exceeding thirty-eight mph, occur on from twenty to thirty or more days on exposed coasts, but on fewer than two in most of the Midlands and southeast, while such destructive winds as hurricanes and tornadoes are virtually unknown. Moderate winds however are frequent, and in the Hebrides the annual average wind-speed can exceed seventeen mph. The frequency of thunderstorms is also fairly low, the worst areas experiencing them on about twenty-one days a year. The height of tides affects coastal dwellers; their average vertical range is from about eleven and a half feet at neap tides to fifteen at springs, but extremes can be as low as four feet or as high as forty-two feet, which is surpassed at few other points on earth. Apart from certain foreshores and estuaries the seas surrounding Britain are never frozen over. Volcanic and destructive earthquake activity does not occur.

No point in Great Britain is more than seventy-five miles from tidal water, and with a coastline of about 5000 miles the influence and proximity of the sea is very marked. By contrast the rivers are relatively short. The longest, the Severn and Thames, only just exceed 200 miles. The Scottish river Tay can carry down at least twice as much water as the Thames, which is nearly twice as long. Except in the Scottish Highlands there are no lakes as large as six square miles (just under sixteen square km). Scotland has a dozen of this size and upwards. Only twelve summits in Great Britain rise above 4000 feet and these are all in the central Scottish Highlands. Apart from Ireland, the Low Countries and Denmark, every country of western and Mediterranean Europe rises to a greater height. A substantial part of Great Britain is however above 1000 feet, and gradients of surprising steepness are frequent on British roads. Nearly all the high land lies towards the west, except in Northern Britain. The communications within most of England, and between England and the Continent, are therefore much easier than, say, those within Norway or those between France and either Italy or Spain. Moreover both Wales and Scotland are awkwardly shaped compared with England, Wales having no natural center while Scotland is heavily dissected by mountains and arms of the sea. In both, therefore, geography favors centrifugal politics, whereas for England the opposite is true. In all three countries, however, the intense variety of geology, scenery, aspect, soil and even climate within short distances makes for strongly marked local differences of character, landscape and production. Each, and therefore Britain as a whole, is conspicuously heterogeneous, in landscape as in people.

The situation, however, has not been static. During the period when Avebury and Stonehenge were erected the climate was already deteriorating gradually. (At its best, about 6000 BC the mean summer temperature had reached about $67°$ F—about $6°$ F higher than now.) Five thousand years later, (*c.* 800 BC) rainfall increased and average temperature fell rather suddenly. This was the time when the earliest Celtic invasions began, bringing with them a much more advanced technology even than that which had already been developed through the warlike bronze-age invaders during the preceding thousand years. It was the expressive Celts also who, observing, no doubt with distaste, the native fashion of coloring themselves with woad, first called the people of this country "painted," the word for which in their language was, as we now pronounce it, "Britain."

There is evidence that the combined effect of unsuitable agricultural practices and climatic change was by that time forcing the gradual abandonment of the open uplands as the main base for food production in Britain. Much of the lowland was however clothed in denser woodland, with wetter and heavier soils than could be faced by contemporary manpower and equipment. A redistribution of population took place, in which the settlers seem to have been squeezed between the increasingly inhospitable uplands and the largely impenetrable low-lying forests and wetlands.

During this uncomfortable transition, which lasted until the Roman invasion in AD 43, the population seems to have undergone a drastic melting-pot process. Iron-age weapons led to the formation of the earliest traceable tribal kingdoms. While the earlier Celts, driven out from the Rhineland, had been peaceful farmers, bringing two-ox ploughs and iron ploughshares, the main (Iron Age B) wave from northern France was more warlike, and brought in interests in mining and horse-rearing which gave an increased war potential. Just in advance of the Romans, other Celts in better organized and more military Belgic tribes, retreating before the Roman conquest of Gaul, came in and created fortified towns with a money economy. From such bases they fought both the earlier established peoples of Britain and the Roman invaders of Gaul and later of Britain itself. Suddenly Britain began to be parcelled up into roughly organized political units.

The Roman occupation, and the *Pax Romana* which it brought, may therefore be looked upon as a timely deliverance from chaos which might otherwise have become chronic. It superimposed lightly but efficiently on the confused and conflicting political structure of all except Northern Britain a concept of orderly and peaceful development on a national scale, buttressed above all by the magnificent system of Roman roads. It gave the opportunity of creating a Romano-British nation at a high level of civilization. Unfortunately this opportunity was largely wasted, since whatever may have been the gains under Roman rule were in the main destroyed by the ensuing anarchy. A Count of the Saxon Shore was appointed to command a south and east coast defense system for keeping the English out of England, but he failed. It was instead the Romans who were forced to withdraw by the outset of the fifth century AD, after being increasingly harassed from the east and north, and finally cut off by the loss of Gaul. In the ensuing twilight there flickered on for a time a precarious relict civilization whose dimly recalled glories were to be nostalgically perpetuated in the Arthurian legend, and to become a persisting glimmer in the folk-memory of Britain.

By this time Saxon tribes were already settling Kent and East Anglia, and within a century they were in possession of all eastern Britain from the Forth to beyond the Solent. They were late-comers, however, in world history: the English have been in England for even less time than the Polynesians have been in Hawaii. Within two centuries virtually the entire remains of all the previous populations of Britain south of the Solway were corralled in the southwestern penin-

sula, and in Wales and its Marches, apart from a large pocket in the
Lake District and North Lancashire, and an unknown number who
stayed to be absorbed among the invaders.

There remained three centuries yet before the Norman Conquest.
These were redeemed chiefly by the scholarship and devotion of bands
of monks, led and inspired by the tradition of Celtic Christianity, who
gradually pervaded Saxon Britain and Frankish central Europe, and
by the resistance to Viking invasion personified by Alfred, King of
Wessex, whose grandson Athelstan became the first King of England
around AD 925. By now, however, the Scandinavians (Danes and
Norsemen) and the Britons (Welsh, Cornish, Scots and Picts) each occupied regions of the same order of size as the Anglo-Saxons. These
were concentrated mainly in a large triangular region between Chester, the Tamar and the Straits of Dover, and a smaller block between
the Forth and the Tees. From Shetland and Orkney down to the Moray
Firth in the east, and much farther down the whole west coast of
present-day Scotland and England to Flint and Anglesey, were important Norse settlements, including nearly all the offshore islands from
the Hebrides to Man. Parts of this region remained in Norse hands
until late in the Middle Ages; Orkney and Shetland retain a predominantly Norse character to this day.

Blending of races has been most marked between the Anglo-Saxons
and the Danes, but the core of the former Danelaw between the Hum-
ber and Suffolk is still characterized by the highest ratio of fair hair
(15–20 percent) and one of the highest ratios of red hair in the modern
population a thousand years afterwards. A map of blood-groups still
shows up the area of the Danelaw as that in which more than half the
population fall in blood-group A. Such counties as Norfolk still wear
an aspect conspicuously distinct from the Anglo-Saxon shires to the
west. Blending of "Celtic" and Saxon elements has been perhaps less
widespread, but there is growing evidence of it, especially in Devon
and in southwestern Scotland (the former kingdom of Strathclyde) and
in Cumberland, in all of which the Saxon infiltration was long delayed
and apparently gradual.

Since the population of England by the time of the Norman Conquest was already at least one and a half million, and the Norman infiltration, although socially and politically dominant, was not very

numerous, it can be broadly assumed that the major redistribution and physical mingling of the original elements in the British population was largely complete by about a thousand years ago, and has only in relatively modern days again become much disturbed in its pattern. Cultural mingling has been a different story, as anyone can witness who watches the English singing *Auld Lang Syne* and the Scots playing cricket.

In a sense, and looking only at a few recent centuries, Britain has enjoyed a relative immunity from invasion by foreign peoples, but on a rather longer view the opposite would be true. From the end of the last glaciation, only some 10,000 years ago, successive tribes came in, first by the remaining land bridge over the channel and North Sea and later across the water. The Romans, arriving 2000 years ago, were already about the tenth major distinguishable wave of new invaders, and they were soon followed by Frisians, Jutes, Saxons, Angles, Danish, Swedish and Norwegian Vikings and finally the Norman-French in 1066. Although military and political take-overs then came to an end important genetic infiltrations continued, especially from France and Flanders in the Middle Ages, and from France again, Central Europe, Italy, Asia and the Caribbean in most recent times. The Pakistanis and the Jamaicans are the latest followers of the Belgae and the Jutes, and no doubt the feelings they arouse are similar.

What has been somewhat peculiar about the British experience of invasions is that even when they have been uninvited and opposed they have, with the sole exception of the earlier Vikings, been primarily interested in achieving peaceful permanent settlement. They have therefore in most cases exhibited a conciliatory interest in coexistence, and a reluctance to indulge in destruction for destruction's sake, or to compel unnecessary change, especially in matters of custom and belief. Irrupting hordes which have passed quickly across continental territories have been sobered by the logistic difficulties of Britain since it became an island. On arrival those who, in limited numbers, have surmounted the test have had, as the alternative to turning back, or being exterminated, to come to terms with their new neighbors and their new environment. Tolerance was enforced by circumstances.

Internal warfare has been frequent, at times almost chronic, but it has rarely been totalitarian, and it has been compatible with the survival of many distinct ethnic groups and of their language and outlook. The desire to settle down in peace has been strong and widespread in most parts of the country, the main exceptions being on both sides of the Scottish Border and in the Highlands, where strong local vested interests in disorder persisted for centuries. From this fairly general desire have come many benefits. The varied genetic composition of the people, drawn from so many different adventurous and pioneering stocks, has been able to work itself out in tolerant and settled surroundings, sustained by a sense of continuity and confidence and by a gradually accumulating economic, social, and intellectual capital endowment which has opened out increasing opportunities. Perhaps the first remarkable, although short-lived, manifestation of this was the successful conservation of many Christian cultural traditions in the British Isles after the departure of the Romans, and the missions to what are now the Low Countries, Germany and Switzerland of Boniface, Willibald, and others. Alcuin of York assisted Charlemagne in his civilizing work on the continent nearly three hundred years before the Norman Conquest. Thus a significant two-way communication between Britain and mainland Europe is discernible in ideological and cultural relations long before it emerges in terms of trade and of political and military exchanges, after the union of England with Normandy had at last created a continuing entanglement with continental affairs. The virtual annihilation of Celtic Christian culture by the Vikings, and the resulting impoverishment of Irish and Gaelic culture, is the great exception to the main tradition.

Descended from many distinct strains of early immigrants, whose only common characteristic was that they had been ready to travel far and pioneer hardily in times when living must already have been in some ways easier and pleasanter in southern Europe, our forefathers must have exhibited some of the conflicting traits of the early American settlers, especially in a strong attachment to their new homeland pulling against a restless urge to travel farther. Ancient and changeless as it may look to the tourist, England has been the scene of perpetual unrest and displacement during more than a couple of hundred of the three hundred or so human generations who have made it their home. The more the urge to achieve security and stability has been satisfied the more the opposite urge to wander adventurously through the world has made itself felt. The manifestations of these opposite urges, and the tensions between them, recur strongly in British history.

It is therefore possible to pick out three main stages in the origins of the British inheritance. First, from very roughly 8000 BC to about 2000 BC, very gradual beginnings in the build-up of a human population and its confrontation with a raw, fresh, rapidly changing and largely intractable, even frightening environment. Secondly, from about 2000 BC to after AD 1000, a vastly increased scale of impact by far more people of diverse and conflicting human types jostling one another to establish their own territorial claims, ideologies, technologies and social, economic, and political systems, in intense and often brutal rivalry, under massive interference from overseas. Thirdly, from the eleventh to the twentieth century, a virtual cessation of successful armed invasions, and a unified effort to compose internal strife and to enforce law and order, hampered by great and increasing diversions of effort to conducting military operations elsewhere. During the first period capital formation and the improvement or use of the island's natural resources were negligible. During the second they were from time to time impressive, but the net gain was disappointingly small, owing largely to destruction and insecurity. During the third they became a dominant factor.

The Normans had been compelled by their overseas campaigning to become expert in planning and in practical execution, combining mobility and opportunism with a capacity to learn quickly and to adapt even their ways of life and thought to their new surroundings. They produced masterful types, with outstanding organizing ability, full of energy and initiative. As they came in at the top level and were able to set the tone of society their influence to this day can safely be taken as out of all proportion to their numbers. Their simultaneous conquest of Sicily and successful blending there of Norman, Greek, and Saracen elements confirms their potency.

Through the Norman invasions Britain became exposed around the first millennium AD to no less than three distinct and major Scandinavian influences—that of the Norsemen from Norway, especially in Orkney, Shetland, northern and western Scotland and the coasts of the Irish Sea; that of the Danes directly from Denmark (and southern Sweden) in southeast Scotland and eastern and southern England; and that of the partly gallicized Normans, themselves originally from Scandinavia, who were initially confined to England, but later seeped into Scotland, Wales and Ireland. These three influences were superimposed on the three previous Anglo-Saxon immigrant groups, the Angles and Jutes who though Germanic were also from Denmark, the Saxons from what is now northwest Germany and the Frisians from present-day Holland. Under the drive and stimulus of the Normans these six or seven stocks, together with what remained in England of the pre-existing Celtic and pre-Celtic populations, became at least to some extent blended, and a similar process occurred in southern Scotland, but not in the Scottish Highlands and islands, nor in Wales.

Consequences very important for the future flowed from this early partial blending. If we date conscious and effective national feeling from the fourteenth and fifteenth centuries onwards (and an earlier dating would be difficult to sustain) the English peoples had six or seven generations' experience of government as a unity before modern national feeling began to emerge. In contrast, the constituent elements of the French, Germans, Spaniards, Swiss and other earliest nation-states were already accustomed to a more or less fragmented autonomous existence and regional self-consciousness as separate princely domains until centuries later. The new Norman earls and barons never acquired strong enough territorial roots or separate jurisdictions to be able to develop in their struggles against the monarchy an effective regionalism in England, like that of Burgundy or Brittany or Navarre. English regionalism became and has remained rather an underdog movement, expressed not infrequently in earlier days in regional rebellions such as that of the North in the Pilgrimage of Grace, and those of Wat Tyler and Robert Ket.

As the defeated English represented for many years a standing opposition party their chroniclers made the most of largely technical grievances such as the creation of the New Forest, actually on an infertile and almost uninhabited tract of southwest Hampshire, as well as of the more plausible but very poorly documented harrying of the North. Only in the Scottish Highlands, and until more modern times in Ireland, did an intense regional patriotism retain effective support at a high level as well as among the rank and file. For many generations this lack of an effective rival to national organization proved largely a source of strength, but as efforts to decentralize government regionally become more advisable it emerges increasingly as a weakness.

It is extremely fortunate that William the Conqueror should have carried out the Domesday survey of his new kingdom, and thus left a fairly comprehensive and trustworthy record of its population and assets. This provides a yardstick by which the subsequent increase of national wealth can be measured. Despite the many great troubles which loom large in the history of Norman England there remains plenty of tangible and indisputable evidence of a sharp upturn in the output of durable capital assets, notably stone buildings such as castles, bridges, cathedrals and churches, which had been far scarcer and on a much smaller scale under the Saxons. From about 1100 onwards capital construction in England began for the first time to exceed the highest previous rates achieved by the Romans nearly a thousand years earlier. Other clear signs of expanding economic output are seen in the enlarged military establishment provided by the Norman feudal system and its demonstrated capacity, within four generations, to support operations in the Crusades, more than two thousand miles distant and continuing over many years. It is no accident that the advent of a strong government, acceptable as an alternative to chronic wars, raids and pillage, despite its great faults and misdeeds, should have been reflected in the immediate release of constructive effort in these and other directions. Nonetheless the first four centuries after the Norman Conquest were curiously barren of new British invention —technological improvements up to the invention of printing were largely of foreign origin, and the leading English export was a raw material—wool.

CHAPTER 2

From Feudalism to Imperialism

Once embarked on the path of a continuing national relationship between government and governed England passed through a series of stages decisive in the growth of Britain's modern world influence. These stages may be roughly listed as:

1. The feudal-clerical, during roughly the first century after the Conquest, in which the Crown backed the feudal lords and the bishops as its main agents in pacifying the country.

2. The second stage of feudalism in which such new factors as a judiciary and embryo administration, a merchant class organized in boroughs, unbeneficed clerics in monastic and itinerant orders and intellectuals in incipient universities sought crown support in carving out a niche for themselves. This was partly at the expense of the feudal and ecclesiastical hierarchies, thereby triggering off trouble with the church and the barons and giving an opening for a Parliament and an eventual middle class, while prolonging the depressed state of the serfs. It is perhaps from this stage that the chronic English obsession with social class originates as an articulate and dominant problem, and that the alienation of the "lower orders" has grown.

3. The crown-based nation-state, devised by the Tudors to fill the power vacuum created by the suicide of the leading feudal barons in the Wars of the Roses, and by the debacle of the church at the Reformation. Once more the opportunest and only dimly understood way out of the immediate difficulty opened the doors to new men and tapped a spectacular vein of unsuspected talent in Elizabethan and Shakespearean England.

4. The Parliament-based nation-state, hastily and brutally substituted,

following the succession to the English throne of Stuart kings, who did not understand, and rashly sought to reverse the Tudor compromise. This sweeping transfer of power, which was confirmed by the Act of Settlement and by the inability of the Hanoverians to rule as well as reign, once more released great untapped national energies and talents.

5. The Victorian opportunist-expansionist nation-state in which Parliament gradually ceased to be master and became reluctantly the agent of the new manufacturing, speculative, professional and inventive classes—a double agent, as it continued doggedly to represent their landed and titled predecessors, whose power of veto and review remained great.

6. The radically and socialistically-inspired, bureaucratic and vote-centered welfare state of the early twentieth century, uneasily administered by a still largely Gladstonian Civil Service.

By looking at such a skeleton analysis—and equally valid alternative series could be defined from differing standpoints—certain clear implications emerge. First, the progress from less advanced to more advanced stages which is the function of social evolution in mankind has occurred in England during the past thousand years with for most of the time a remarkably fortunate rapidity and consistency of direction. This consistency has been most marked in the preservation, by often changing devices, of a fair balance between acceptability and consultation on the one hand and executive efficiency and political leadership on the other. Another constantly recurring theme has been the progressive widening of opportunity for new hitherto unprivileged elements to participate in power and in changing standards and ways of life. A third has been the often interrupted but always successfully reasserted requirement for consent to be given peacefully to change when it is sufficiently demanded.

Whether because of a folk-memory of the condition of peaceful co-existence upon which the successive immigrant groups had been admitted to the club, or whether because of the tradition of negotiation which even William the Conqueror had to observe before securing his coronation, it early became accepted that the nation is an organism which should not tear itself to pieces. Hateful as Norman rule must have felt for several generations, it not only ended a millennium in which hardly any century had been immune from some destructive external onslaught on Britain, but it also quite unmistakably released many talents and energies which had hitherto never had a fair chance, and so provided on the whole a safety-valve for the feelings of the conquered. The rapid development of the King's justice, and the expansion of career opportunities in the church must have helped to give a sense of progress and opportunity for the active and ambitious. To these, on the whole, the new ruling class was complementary rather than competitive, except of course as regards the Anglo-Saxon landowners who were so largely dispossessed.

From the Conquest onwards it is possible to discern an irregular cycle swinging between support for strong centralized government with a definite agenda and program and a reaction responsive to sectional or local inhibiting forces. To some extent no doubt this represents a genuine swing of the pendulum between the attractions and irritations of effective government and the joys and frustrations of weak or stalemated government.

What has been peculiar to English history has been the recurrent tendency to force conflict into peaceful ritualized confrontations (e.g. between King and Parliament, King and Church, King and Barons, Protestants and Catholics, landed interests and manufacturers, the well-to-do and the Chartists) where in many other countries resort would almost automatically have been made to force. This was not for lack of aggressive feelings, of military instincts and drives, or of a stomach for cruelty and brutality (compare the killing of the French prisoners at Agincourt, the torture and murder of several kings and the savage penal law).

Partly this tendency perhaps arose from the uncertainty and insecurity of a Norman-French ruling class in an English land, and the unwisdom both for king and barons of alienating the lesser tenants. Partly also it was eased by the incipient constitutional channels resulting from the uneasy dialogue begun after Hastings and continued at Runnymede and with Simon de Montfort. There were exceptions in the Wars of the Roses and the Civil War, but Charles II remarking that he did not want to go on his travels again was as much in the tradition as his father invoking the divine right of kings was out of it.

The slow, often stupid, boring dialogue between rival interests, leading sometimes quite mysteriously to a solution, is central to the English tradition of government and governed. Perhaps there is some affinity between this tradition and the English addiction to the equally

slow and boring game of cricket, which somehow also displays mysterious binding and solvent qualities. In both examples quite different
emotions and experiences are involved for the protagonists, who confront each other, and the great amorphous, often silent mass of followers of the game, some with seats round the field, some standing, or removed at second or third hand from it. Yet both protagonists and followers share something and exchange some influence each upon the
other in a tacit and almost mystical manner which creates deep
impressions long remembered. In both examples also the rules of the
game change almost insensibly as new ways are devised of exploiting
them and new limits of tolerance are set, yet in both there are certain
types of conduct which are not permissible, or in other words, not
cricket, and which if indulged in will result in a massive moral victory
for the other side.

The formation and acceptance of such idea-systems, or moral or intellectual stereotypes, and the part which they have played in history
and still play in public affairs is a neglected subject of the first importance. The record shows that the English, in contrast to the Scots,
Welsh, Irish and other nations, have exhibited over several centuries
an astonishing capacity to convert vague or abstract general thoughts
and feelings, or mixtures of both, into sufficiently concrete ideograms
to be digested in their inner consciousness and to assume a powerful
hierarchical position in guiding or censoring their conduct. Among
examples which come immediately to mind are the ideas of the rule of
law, fair play, the gentleman and his standards, sportsmanlike behavior, the weekend, the country house and its peculiar life, the amateur
and the club. Some of these are purely abstract, others express themselves in institutions, but all have shown immense durability in adverse circumstances and changing conditions, and most have sooner or
later even demonstrated their capacity to permeate other cultures.

No doubt a case could be made for a similar capacity in other
peoples, but perhaps the peculiarity of the English contribution is that
it has been so consistently vital and that it touches so deeply on the two
key areas, politics and leisure, where other guidelines are so inadequate. Above all, it is surprisingly abstract, not depending upon
superficial points of conformity. This English system of idea-systems
has however severe shortcomings; it has little to say about work or
learning or research or other equally important aspects of life, and it is
subject to a very long timelag in responding to change. It safeguards
those who share it against a good deal of destructive and foolish behav-

ior, but it does not positively lead them to doing the right thing, especially if the right thing is something they have never done before.

The coverage and the intensity of acceptance of these idea-systems at any one time imposes overriding if invisible limits on the course of British politics and social evolution. To flout them too openly or in the wrong way at the wrong time can mean political suicide or the destruction of a career. How exactly they emerged and how they are so vigorously maintained is largely a mystery.

It is possible, however, to speculate that, while they arose from a native poetry, their peculiar grip is in some way a by-product of the dialogue of interests. Where direct understanding proved impossible they furnished a series of symbolic stereotypes which helped to avert collisions, and to encourage restraint against pushing controversy too far or too hotly. The nation was thus enabled to arrive at broad judgments or to assume attitudes adequate for handling and reconciling the big interests. Often also they might open escape routes through which political and economic tensions could be relieved in more congenial contests during leisure. If this is so, it would go far to explain the frustration and bewilderment felt by so many in recent years who had implicitly relied upon idea-systems which they now find to have lost their relevance and their sovereign powers of guiding, healing and reconciling. That idea-systems, like ships and railways, simply wear out in time and need to be replaced by different kinds of new ones is not the kind of concept that occurs to them at all readily. In fact nothing much more painful or unpalatable could be imagined.

Perhaps the very sharpness of the mental differences between the Anglo-Saxon governed and the Norman-French rulers compelled the elaboration of an ideological super-language, hierarchically dominating and neutralizing the endless semantic and psychological misunderstandings destined to arise in daily communication. (The sort of situation demanding such a solution can perhaps best be visualized from the example of the similar almost total communication blocks between the Europeans and the Africans in Rhodesia, and between both and the British, during 1964–68.) Perhaps also the English richness in poets, and readiness to resort to poetic imagery, made it easier to coin and give circulation to such an ethereal and compulsive substitute for normal speech, in which each symbol is itself a whole chapter, if not an entire book. Proverbs and allegories, now so unfashionable that their former currency and force is difficult to appreciate, had a similar function.

One of the most remarkable and important parts of the British inheritance is the English language itself. Pre-Conquest Britain spoke a series of Anglo-Saxon, Celtic and Scandinavian tongues, among which Northumbrian and Wessex were of special political and literary significance. The new line of kings found all of these too difficult, and they continued to use French as the court language for over 250 years before finally resigning themselves to coming to terms with something that their subjects could understand. When they did this they rejected the scholarly claims of Northumbrian and Wessex and chose in preference that rather low and mongrel form of Anglo-Saxon known as Mercian. The Mercians were sandwiched between the Danelaw on the east, the Welsh beyond Offa's Dyke on the west, the Northumbrians whose southern linguistic boundary oddly cuts Yorkshire in half about along the line of the Aire, and the Wessex folk south of the Thames. They had no firmly fixed feeling for language and borrowed words so freely from their neighbors that, as the influence of the Norman court and of Oxford and Cambridge universities became absorbed, they developed a new hybrid tongue which in modern terms might be classed as the earliest form of Franglais. Not only were the words all mixed up, but the old complicated inflections and the rules of scholarly Anglo-Saxon went overboard in favor of a loose and flexible new structure. This kind of neo-Mercian evolution into what we know as English seems to have happened rather quickly during the thirteenth and fourteenth centuries, culminating in the writings of Chaucer and Langland, who demonstrated for the first time that you can do anything you like with English. The words will flow briskly to tell a tale, or to sum up a situation lucidly. They can mock and tease with irony or satire. They roll like thunder from the lips of a Churchill, but they are just as apt to dance in the air, sparkling with wit and spirit. They can picture far countries or explain precisely how some kind of machinery works, or illuminate the most hidden processes of nature. They can measure out laws or form themselves into lyrics. Or, issuing from some dreary Department, they can drag and congeal in clumsy and slipshod circumlocution, replacing the true means to inform, to instruct or to admonish. For the tool is no better than its user, and if the user is a pedant or a clot the liveliness and clarity of English can soon vanish.

Yet this English tongue, with its many and great debts to its different ancestors, is too much taken for granted. It is not just the language of Shakespeare; it is also the language of science, the language of travel and now ever more dominantly the language of international intercourse. It is not a language that stands still; it is always changing and expanding, yet as it grows and unfolds in ever more complex ways to embrace new thought, new knowledge and new conduct it remains one, no more subdivided into separate tongues than it was two centuries ago, and still nursed and guided from its original fourteenth-century homeland. One of the facts about the English is that they created this language and that they are still creating it today, as its rival tongues recede into subordinate and regional roles in the world. If it is beginning to decay the signs are singularly hard to detect.

But with all its merits and properties English can, no more than other languages, break down the barriers between those whose fixed prejudices and mental limitations confine them as if in a strait-jacket. The dominance in British education of traditional scholastic, pedagogic lines of thought and habits of mind closes many doors which must be opened in order that the modern world may be understood and kept up with. Latinity, logic and often stale book-learning are no help in grasping the moving patterns, the evolving structures and the flows of energy and information in which we live and to which we must adapt. For help in this we need to return to the plane of idea-systems, which can show the way and make it acceptable.

In the social evolution of a nation such a capability for making idea-systems may well be as decisive a break-through as the development of a capability for tool-making in human evolution. The idea-system is in effect a social tool for cracking open otherwise intractable problems and for harmonizing the efforts of otherwise chaotically conflicting groups. Where positive harmonization is unattainable it can at least ritualize the different roles and substitute a kind of game for something more lethal or destructive. The existence of such stereotypes and their dominance over human beings had for many years a disastrous fascination for British dramatists, some of whom seemed powerless to win through to the individual personalities underneath. It is at least arguable that some of the wilder manifestations of British attire and manners which currently horrify and bewilder other nations represent a desperate effort by the younger generation in Britain to fight its way out of this sociological cocoon. Idea-systems, as we have seen, are not immune from the problem of obsolescence, or worse still of partial obsolescence, affecting an otherwise serviceable and indeed still essential mechanism, from which the obsolete element has to be surgically disentangled and removed.

One of the functions and special values of this British, but particularly English, fertility in coining stereotypes and recognized idea-systems is that it confers an accepted identity and a respected if not approved status on a large number of otherwise unidentifiable or un-acceptable types. For example, the local landowner or *rentier* may be personally disliked and politically anathema to many who will never-theless to some extent accept and respect his efforts to live up to the stereotype of a gentleman. Conversely the stereotype of the common man as a good chap and of Judy O'Grady and the colonel's lady being sisters under the skin confers a valuable kind of quasi-status on per-sons who otherwise have virtually none under the British class system. The hunger for some kind of identity, nationally and individually, and its political significance, is a factor for further consideration.

This aspect of British evolution which, as Marx himself recognized, deftly if quite unfairly sidesteps the Marxist analysis and defeats Marxist ambitions in Britain. In other European capitalist nations stratification seems to have gone lower and become frequently more rigid, with less social mobility. The proletarian had a more or less cut-and-dried place in the scheme of things, from which in principle he could not rise without upsetting that scheme which, again in principle, he could only manage to do by violent revolution. In Britain, how-ever, despite such egregious backslidings as the hymn about the rich man in his castle, the poor man at his gate, for whom God "ordered his estate," there has not, since the messy and gradual collapse of serfdom six hundred years ago, been any clear-cut or logical status for the poor. The centuries of floundering and inconsistent poor-law legislation amply demonstrate that. The weakness, perhaps the capital weakness, of British political and social evolution has been this centuries-old un-imaginative and irresponsible refusal to bring the ordinary worker in among the interests which participate as of right in the national dia-logue. That refusal compelled the workers to resort to organizations designed to assert their right to a voice, such as the consumer's cooper-atives and the Chartist movement, and above all the trade unions and the Labour Party of the present century. While both these last have won an enviable degree of power and recognition, they have been forced through lack of understanding to do it by methods, especially strike methods, inimical to a national consensus and to the national interest. Oddly enough, they have nevertheless largely failed to per-suade their presumed constituency interest group to identify with them except partially and spasmodically, and they have developed a grave We/They division within their own ranks. Locally Cockneys and Geordies attained a marked type of identity, but the proletariat as a whole has remained as poor in identity as in income, and lately much poorer.

How far was this unhappy division into Disraeli's "two nations" foreordained as a result of the Norman Conquest and the colonization of England which it established? Certainly there is visible through most of English history a sharp division of attitude, interest and power between the rather small active ruling class and the alienated and often sullen subject masses—the readers, nowadays, of *The Times* and *Daily Telegraph* on the one hand and the *Sun* and *News of the World* on the other. These masses are psychologically in a state much as if they were under alien colonial administration. They do not feel, and in fact do not have, any real voice in what goes on or in what is done to them by their central or local government, nor do they regard these acts as anything other than external and foreign to them. While any racial distinction between Normans and Anglo-Saxons has long since disappeared, it may well be that the earlier built-in They/Us caste division established by Norman feudalism has continued to provide a more clear-cut and persistent regular underdog niche for the less successful or fortunate in Britain than in certain other countries, particularly the newer overseas English-speaking countries which never knew any such system. Apart from the main mass of unskilled wage-earners there have been large numbers of depressed sub-professional groups, including many schoolteachers, clergymen, technicians and clerks, whose attitude has been soured by a sense of alienation, and of not belonging, or being excluded. Unfortunately social mobility has been adequate to waft away upwards most of the obvious potential leaders who have emerged in these circles, while leaving the majority to stew in their own juice, too well-behaved to fight and too unorganized and leaderless to join in the national dialogue and talk themselves into a more tolerable status.

Sometimes, notably during the two world wars, it has seemed that this rift might soon be healed. That hope was encouraged by the development of the welfare state and by the progress of the affluent society in rapidly reducing differences of dress, appearance and basic standards of life, in the later 'fifties and early 'sixties. Unfortunately, however, it is only too clear that the fundamental alienation and lack of will and interest to join in the responsibility of shaping the future have hardly been touched. Is this, as many believe, due to the memory of the dole and the unemployment queues and hunger marches of the 'thirties, or is there a more serious organic gulf?

Every nation continues to suffer from traumas of the past and Britain has a varied list of them. Two of the earlier ones—the murder of Becket and its aftermath, and John's surrender to the barons at Runnymede over Magna Carta—were fortunately first-class public rebuffs for a monarch at the pinnacle of the feudal system, in both cases accepted as bringing an adjustment in his sovereign powers, and in both cases presenting the mass of the governed with a dramatic and unforgettable free spectacle by which their status and their sense of participation were enhanced without their actually having to take risks, or indeed any action. It is possible that from this has grown the peculiar tradition, so often commented on by foreign observers, that even the lowliest Englishman felt, and was accepted as being, quite at liberty to comment most candidly on the sovereign, the state of government and any other national issue, centuries before he possessed any voting power or other civic right to do so, or could expect his views to be taken seriously.

The subsequent confrontation between De Montfort and the Crown was most notable in convincing the greatest interests of the capacity of each to make life impossible for the others, and of the advisability of setting up more formal arrangements for continuing their dialogue and reaching a fresh *modus vivendi,* which took shape as Parliament. Looking back on it, however, it is possible to overstress the importance of the institutional aspect, and underrate the significance of this first decisive step in providing for a regular dialogue between the great interests, and for a basis of responsible and stable deals between them. Thus regarded the issue is a live one today, when considering what is wrong with Parliament. Is it that the quality of the Parliamentarians is too low, or their procedure outmoded? Or is it perhaps at least partly that the great interests, such as the trade union leadership, which can make life impossible for the nation, are not so represented in Parliament that a searching and conclusive dialogue can be carried on with them there, and a responsible settlement arrived at?

The next landmarks to be noted are two battles fought almost exactly a hundred years apart—Bannockburn in 1314 and Agincourt in 1415. At Bannockburn the Scots under King Robert the Bruce decisively and permanently defeated the efforts of the English under King Edward II to do to them what had just been successfully done to the less numerous and united Welsh, in converting them into an English-occupied dominion. Bannockburn, like the following year's Swiss victory at Morgarten over the Hapsburg forces, effectively made a new nation. The new force of nationalism was released in its full vigor and has continued unabated in Scotland to this day. It rendered inevitable the union, nearly 300 years later, of England and Scotland as two kingdoms of equal status, and the subsequent evolution of a United Kingdom and thus indirectly of a Commonwealth, rather than of a unitary nation-state like France. Agincourt, although it achieved nothing beyond an ephemeral English hegemony over France, was psychologically no less important. The astonishing and total defeat of the much larger and more heavily-armed French forces under Constable Charles d'Albret was achieved by nearly 5000 English archers with fewer than 1000 knights and men at arms, against odds of nearly five to one. But for this victory King Henry V and his men would probably have been trapped and destroyed; their triumphant deliverance, as Professor R. B. Mowat pointed out, gave the English a calm confidence in their luck and eventual success which has turned the tide of many dubious conflicts since.

Politically the common people gained from the demonstration that great knights and princes were no match for yeomen with longbows; feudal armies were now visibly obsolete. Ironically enough the longbow as a battle-winner had been developed neither by the Normans nor the English but by the less bellicose and chronically oppressed Welsh who, as usual, were unable to exploit their own asset effectively. On the other hand, the fact that even so spectacular a victory so soon and so utterly failed to bring to fruition English ambitions for conquests in France demonstrated convincingly and in an acceptable form the need to renounce these ambitions in favor of something more constructive. As usual the time lag in fully facing these realities was long, but within about fifty years of Agincourt serious attempts at expansion on the Continent were dropped, although it was nearly a further century before the last English outpost, Calais, was surrendered, with bitter regret, by Mary I.

The directions in which the inhabitants of Britain have looked abroad have often changed since early times: southwards towards Gaul and the Atlantic and Mediterranean coasts until late Roman days; then eastwards to the Low Countries and Denmark for some three centuries, and northeastwards to Scandinavia as a whole for about three centuries more. From the Norman Conquest until final defeat in France in 1453 their gaze had been turned southwards over the

Channel and the Bay of Biscay as far as Provence and Portugal. Now it was to extend across the oceans.

The immediate effect of final defeat in France was the reimportation of hordes of troublesome ex-warriors who helped to trigger off and to fight the Wars of the Roses against their own countrymen. The Crown was now forced to learn how to govern more effectively both in England and in Wales and Ireland. Thus deprived of their domestic spoiling opportunities, the restless elements were ready for the great age of exploration and expansion overseas. They resumed the already long-established English tradition that the best thing to do with the restless and discontented is gently to export them, to make such trouble as they seek elsewhere. A sufficient outlet was thus provided, with occasional interruptions, from 1190 to 1815, by the Crusades, the French wars, the seafaring, colonizing and merchant-adventuring enterprises of the sixteenth to eighteenth centuries and the century and a half of war with the Netherlands, France and Spain which began with Cromwell and ended with Wellington. The interruptions, the longest of which were during most of the thirteenth century, the second half of the fifteenth and the first half of the seventeenth, were, perhaps by coincidence and perhaps not, all periods of civil war in England. Fortunately during the century from 1815 the vast expansion of the British overseas empire and the mass emigration to North America made foreign and domestic peace less incompatible, but at a high cost in permanent loss of enterprising types.

During the later Middle Ages, the semi-monopolies in trade of the Hanseatic League, the Rhenish Town League and the Flemings severely limited opportunities for English merchants. The domination by foreign headquarters of religious orders, and other similar factors, also tended to canalize in England the ambitious and enterprising types rather excessively into military employment, apart from the small but influential minority of mobile clerks and scholars and craftsmen.

Thus during the great period of the moulding of the modern English character, from 1066 for roughly the next four centuries, strong forces combined to mould it into a peculiar and inconsistent form which still endures. The reaction to centuries of successful foreign invasion gave top priority to soldierly capacity and to efficient military organization. The Anglo-Saxons already had the first but they needed the Normans to provide the second; and the two never fully blended. This meant a division of labor between full-time tough farmers and semiprofessional soldiers. It incidentally encouraged such technological advances as the heavy mouldboard plough and improvements in administration. These enabled and impelled England, more than any other country, to develop as an agrarian-based, solidly progressing, outward-looking and expansionist nation-state, with a regrettable taste and flair for overseas military adventure. "The English," wrote Froissart in a famous passage, "will never love or honour their king, unless he be victorious and a lover of arms and war against their neighbours . . . Their land is more fulfilled of riches and all manner of goods when they are at war than in time of peace. They take delight and solace in battles and slaughter . . . The King of England must needs obey his people and do all their will." The English aggression, with the massive eager and skilful participation of common men as well as feudal knights and barons, forced a similar deformation on the neighboring Scots and French. No doubt the same ambitions also existed there, but it was the need to match the English which dictated their growth to dominance in other nations.

The dynamic thus generated rapidly found additional outlets overseas, first in exploration and opportunist exploitation and later in systematic colonization and development of bases. This, together with many ancillary developments which were stimulated in science and technology, education, finance and administration, rapidly carried the Western world, warring and divided as it was, to a point where after nearly a thousand years of threats the danger of a successful Moslem invasion no longer needed to be taken seriously. After the repulse of the Turkish army from the gates of Vienna on September 12, 1683, little Europe emerged with a commanding lead in power and wealth over all the rest of mankind, which faced the prospect of three centuries of submission. The West was now supreme, owing to developments in the arts of peace and war in which the English had had a large share.

Unfortunately for the English the powerful dynamic which they had stumbled upon and unwittingly transmitted to their neighbors would not now be damped down, but gave rise to incessant chain reactions both within England and abroad. The needs of navigation, of medicine and of agriculture created among the livelier intellects a scientific curiosity to delve deeper into natural phenomena, which during the seventeenth century launched modern science and technology on their course, and during the eighteenth initiated in England the industrial and the agricultural revolutions. The creative forces which during the Middle Ages had been successfully harnessed to institutions such as the church, the boroughs and the guilds now ran wild, leaving the universities, the municipalities, the churches and all the corporate institutions except Parliament in a dormant or moribund state. Profound changes in society and politics paralleled these developments. The Reformation and the dissolution of the monasteries in the early sixteenth century had already cut many of the most important links with the Continent and redeployed much capital in the hands of ambitious and energetic new men identified with the Tudor monarchy. Another potentially traumatic experience, which after much suspense followed the Agincourt pattern, was the defeat of the Spanish Armada. But just as Agincourt had soon led on to the chastening experience of the Wars of the Roses, so the deliverance from Spanish invasion was followed within a lifetime by the Civil War and the beheading of Charles I. Clarendon, who lived through that era, and had a ringside seat, attributed the origin of the trouble to the intriguing and quarrelsome Scots influence imported under James I and VI, upon the union of the two crowns in 1603. At that time the monarchy in Scotland was in much the same state of harassment by the undisciplined magnates as the English monarch had been during the Wars of the Roses. While the partly Welsh Henry Tudor and his son Henry VIII had contrived to develop a role and image for the monarchy which was in tune with English feelings and led to the triumphant outburst of English identity under Elizabeth, the Scots Stuarts sought to convert it into something cold, remote and pedantic, which could hardly have been less congenial to the English outlook. By so rashly and arbitrarily seeking to turn the clock back they temporarily lost the throne itself, and thus accelerated the transfer of power from the monarch and his personal servants to the representatives of Parliament and to a slowly but surely expanding bureaucracy.

The violent death of Charles I, the joyful restoration of Charles II, the abject flight of James II, the welcome dullness of William and Mary and of Queen Anne and her Hanoverian successors made the transition from traditional to modern constitutional monarchy possible. Thus emerged for the first time an objective basis for that feeling of age-old stability, order, and moderation which the modern visitor to England so strongly feels, but for which the earlier history of this fickle and protean nation gives so little warrant.

The political and social settlement was accompanied by a surprisingly keen and effective desire to achieve a harmony between the English and their landscape. This was so transformed in the seventeenth and eighteenth centuries that it remains one of the great English contributions to civilization, and the basis of much of the best English painting, poetry and architecture. This landscape, and its accompanying Queen Anne and Georgian buildings, composed an unforgettable picture on the grand scale of essential English characteristics. The abrupt discontinuance of efforts to force nature into the geometrical patterns which strait-jacketed the trees and herbs in French and Dutch gardens, and the deliberate adoption of the flowing naturalistic patterns in which natural and man-made elements became reconciled, was more than a brilliant aesthetic. It was also a confident statement of the English belief in the possibility of successful coexistence of everybody and everything under the benevolent and indirect guidance of a human, and preferably of an English, ruler imbued with tolerance and moderation and common sense. Country-house civilization dominated not only land use, land management, agriculture and rural sports, but also politics, administration, the arts and even much of banking and commerce. Above all the new landscape made a visible, agreeable and distinctive niche in which the Englishman's identity could confidently unfold. Well-managed land, and plenty of it, became the supreme status symbol.

The most urban of nations, except perhaps for the Netherlands, looked most fixedly and most widely to the land for inspiration. The ownership of a landed estate became incomparably the favorite ecological niche of an Englishman. The growing eighteenth-century towns were laid out with well-planned and well-planted squares and gardens and parks to import some feeling of the countryside. The clubs, which arose from the coffee-houses, sought to reproduce something of the atmosphere of a country houseparty in permanent session, and in doing so they created a remarkably well-knit society with a high measure of social mobility, and much interchange between men of differing vocations and interests, in contrast to the functional isolation of some other élites overseas.

Great strains and risks developed, however, as the more populous French nation with its greater natural resources emerged under an efficient centralized monarchy as an implacable rival, to be fought decade after decade on continent after continent. The Bourbon monarchy was gradually undermined in the eighteenth century, like the British Empire in the twentieth, largely with the help of political ideas imported from England. But any hope of a *détente* was rudely removed after the French Revolution by a course of totalitarian egalitarian imperialism which under Napoleon threatened the interests and even the existence of Britain. It also outraged the increasingly conservative feelings of Britain's partly sated and now stability-loving rulers. Trafalgar and Waterloo maintained the Agincourt theme of surprise deliverance (as in a different way did the Battle of Britain in World War II), and they ushered in the most British of all centuries — the nineteenth. Even France now came increasingly under British influence in politics, economics, and even for a time in art, through Constable and his contemporaries.

The nineteenth century was that in which the industrial revolution came to full fruition with the creation of the network of railways and steamship lines, of telegraphs and sanitation, of a disciplined police force and the opening up of great new sources of supply and new markets overseas. As Britain so largely pioneered in these developments the world looked often to her for guidance and help, but the duration of genuine British industrial and economic supremacy was much briefer than is often supposed. Potentially it began after Waterloo, when London replaced Amsterdam as Europe's chief financial center, but owing to the postwar slump and other factors it was only twenty years later that Britain really began to cash in on her advantages. Between 1819 and 1834 the volume of British exports doubled, but their value increased only slightly. By 1845 however it was about 50 percent up, the volume having now almost quadrupled. By 1869 it had more than trebled the 1845 level, and the volume was now over ten times higher than in 1819. The years 1834–69 were about the only really good expansion period that British exports have ever had, and the centenary of its ending is now near at hand.

Here is a point at which history most intimately touches present-day thoughts and feelings. There is a widespread belief that Britain during the nineteenth and early twentieth century was a kind of almost omnipotent Great Power, ruling much of the world and policing the rest with an iron hand inside a velvet glove. Uncritical and exaggerated beliefs of this sort can give a misleading picture of the nature, extent and direction of recent changes in the situation of Britain, and thus give rise to misleading inferences for the future. How then should the difference between Britain's world situation now and Britain's nineteenth-century world situation be realistically assessed?

The concept of a Great Power is highly subjective, vague, and difficult, if not incapable, of exact definition. In recent days especially, popular imagery has dwelt upon vast numbers of bomber and fighter aircraft, fleets of battleships, cruisers and destroyers, regiments of tanks, divisions of infantry and far-flung military bases or nuclear missiles capable of distant delivery by various means. Armed with such big battalions and ironmongery the Great Power of popular fancy has only to make menacing movements or to send threatening notes to ensure that all lesser powers incurring its displeasure hasten abjectly to do its bidding. It can readily be shown that in such a sense Britain's enjoyment of Great Power status has been at best occasional and fleeting at any period.

A second more sophisticated view might be expressed in terms of resources and potential. On such a view the actual construction and maintenance of vast superior forces would be rather a mark of insecurity and of the likelihood of decline through overstrain. The truly Great Power on this view is sufficiently wealthy, progressive and wisely led to be able to shape a course in the world primarily by diplomatic, economic and geopolitical means, thus creating a climate and environment in which all powers to some extent and a number to a very large extent find themselves led consciously or unconsciously to shape parallel or compatible courses themselves. Given ample and manifest potential no more than token military forces need be maintained, except in periods of dangerous tension. This was until recently the posture of the United States and it corresponds fairly well to the British attitude after the Napoleonic Wars.

A third view might distinguish between passive powers, however large and strong, which keep themselves to themselves more or less within their own borders, and more activist powers which reach out over more extensive or even worldwide spheres of influence or intervention, either by military means or simply commercially and diplomatically, or by settlement and annexations. Variants within this class extend at one extreme to undertaking considerable responsibilities which are, at least ostensibly, on behalf of international interests, or of an alliance, ideology, or political league, while at the other extreme they may be confined to narrowly self-regarding objectives. Britain throughout modern history has shown strong activist leanings.

On a fourth, slightly different, approach, Great Powers might be regarded rather as those which, judged by the test of results, have earned and maintained what may be considered first-class status in relation to such critical matters as being included in or left out of decisive conferences or confrontations leading to possible major changes in the international situation. On this view there is something like a Great Power club, with the implication, vividly illustrated by Chiang Kai-shek and the UN Security Council, that once admitted it may be fairly easy to defy or postpone exclusion after the qualification has been lost. Britain has usually been jealous of such status and successful in exacting it, but that can simply call attention to the gulf between pretensions and power.

All this assumes, without clear justification, that similar criteria for Great Power status can meaningfully be adopted for the mid-nineteenth and the mid-twentieth centuries. Indeed it begs the question whether the age of Great Powers may not be just about at an end. With this preamble and caution we may consider the case of Britain in detail.

It is of course true that the admitted importance of sea power reached a new high level after Trafalgar, and that, according to the fashionable political-strategic thinking emanating from Britain, sea power must ultimately be decisive. It is also true that, by in effect underwriting the Monroe Doctrine, Britain with her sea power incidentally and tacitly guaranteed the United States against invasion or threat throughout the vital generations of her development. But, as was clearly shown in both the Napoleonic and the two twentieth-century World Wars, British sea power at a showdown was capable of doing little more than safeguarding the British base. It was at best an extremely indirect and long-winded means of trying to bring down any first-class military dictator on the Continent, or even of putting much pressure on a hostile associate or unhelpful neutral. The contrary continental opinion on the value of navies was vividly demonstrated in 1853, when the German fleet was sold by auction. On land after Waterloo, when the small British army, with much indirect Prussian help, only just managed to defeat a scratch French force improvised by Napoleon, there were no major engagements between major powers for half a century, except for those in the Crimean War. Then, even in alliance with France and Turkey, the ill-administered and ill-led British army had great difficulty in discouraging Russian designs on Constantinople.

In the Italian Wars of Independence British support was only moral and diplomatic. Although it undoubtedly helped Cavour to get the better of Napoleon III in the final maneuvers for a united Italy it was the French, not the British, who pushed the occupying Austrians out. It was Palmerston's interventionist spirit and colorful language which probably did most to promote the popular image of Britain as the arbiter of Europe at that time. Yet in 1863–64, when Prussia threatened Denmark over Schleswig-Holstein (just after the heir to the British throne had married a Danish Princess) Palmerston and his Foreign Secretary Russell suffered a bitter public humiliation in finding themselves unable to lift a finger to prevent the dismemberment of Denmark, after having warned that in case of such an attack it would not be Denmark alone who would contest it. A decade with this as its ending, the Crimean War as its beginning and the Indian Mutiny as its centerpiece is hardly what one would expect to find in the middle of the supposed era of British world supremacy. It is also difficult to picture a dominant Great Power without a clear and successful foreign policy. The inability of British Victorian leaders to produce any such thing is notorious. Bagehot expressed the contemporary verdict in 1867: "The foreign policy of England has for many years been . . . inconsequent, fruitless, casual; aiming at no distinct pre-imagined end, based on no steadily concerned principle." What kind of Great Power was this?

During the American Civil War neither side showed much respect for or readiness to conciliate Great Britain, as was shown by the embarrassing and dangerous incident over the *Trent* and the *Alabama*. On the latter the British Government continued to be pressed hard for several years, and was eventually obliged to accept arbitration by a third party on the amount of damages due. At the Berlin conference of 1878 Disraeli attained a certain much-advertised measure of success, but the dominant figure here was Bismarck (who also became the arbiter in conciliating the dangerous rivalries in the heart of Africa a few years later). In the Franco-Prussian War of 1870 Gladstone announced that Britain would intervene against a violator of Belgian neutrality, but in view of the previous deployment of both armies far to the south the relevance of this warning is dubious.

At the time Britain was not regarded in Europe as having the role of a Great Power but as pursuing a policy of "spendid isolation." It does not appear that calculations about the British attitude, or fear of British intervention, exercised among the sovereign states of the nineteenth century any great and continuous influence, in the way that consideration of the attitude of the USA or the USSR would now, or that the attitude of Louis XIV or Bismarck would have in their day.

This may readily be confirmed from the well-documented record of the condition and performance throughout this period of the British army and the Royal Navy. Even after the spectacular exposure of maladministration and incompetent leadership in the Crimean War, the army remained the last happy hunting ground of corrupt patronage and of promotion by seniority. What it cost to preserve "Buggins's turn next" was vividly described by Wolseley, Commander-in-Chief in Egypt after the Gordon fiasco, in a personal letter to the Liberal leader Lord Hartington demanding a system of promotion by merit. There were, he said, now serving under his command, senior officers who were "entirely unfit for their positions . . . these officers are a source of constant anxiety . . . I have often on active service seen splendid battalions kept in the rear or broken up for work along the line of communications whilst others of inferior quality were sent to the front, because the commanding officer did not dare employ against the enemy, corps whose commanding officers were manifestly incompetent."

The whole performance of the British army from 1815, until its administration was at last drastically overhauled by the German-educated Secretary of State Lord Haldane nearly a century later, gives no ground to assume that the thought of having it deployed against them would have given much anxiety even to governments of smallish advanced nations. Its wonderful human material was chronically sacrificed by muddling through under officers who, even when sufficiently intelligent to fulfil their duties, were quite untrained to do so. The futile and tragic Charge of the Light Brigade at Balaclava in the Crimea was unhappily characteristic of an approach still influential in Britain. Such an approach scorns thorough preparation and staff work and tries to compensate by rash and ill-considered action at the last moment.

The story of the Royal Navy after 1815 is equally inconsistent with the "Great Power" legend. The ninety-nine ships of the line in commission at the end of the Napoleonic Wars were cut to twenty-three by Queen Victoria's accession. Naval estimates were more than halved between 1816 and 1834. During the Venezuelan crisis in 1896 it proved impossible to send extra ships to the West Indies because the margin of naval superiority in Europe was so narrow.

Professor G. S. Graham in *The Politics of Naval Supremacy* (Cambridge, 1965) writes of "The Illusion of Pax Britannica" in these illuminating terms:

> . . . it was this general desire to avoid war that made the so-called age of Pax Britannica possible. It is true that men-of-war were used on occasion to effect specific ends whether in Greece, Latin America or China, but it would be wrong to suggest that the British Navy imposed a British peace on the world . . . the general quiescence of the European Powers gave Britain the opportunity to use her navy, not only as a means of conducting anything from a demonstration to a local war, but as an effective restraining force in the interests of a European balance . . .

Looking at the record from the naval angle Professor Graham has come to an identical conclusion with that independently developed here. A peculiar conjunction of circumstances following the Napoleonic Wars left an international vacuum in which Great Britain could for some time function as if she were a dominant Power. Unfortunately the illusion spread and gained strength at home simultaneously with the vanishing of what flimsy basis there was for crediting it. As the changing world situation and the blunders of British policy swept away the last vestiges of objective justification for it, more and more resources, which could ill be spared, were thrown in to enable the British, at least, to go on clinging to the illusion.

At the time when British worldwide freedom of action was least inhibited and efforts to check or counter British policy were least frequent, the armed power of Britain was in fact at a singularly low ebb, around the mid-century. Although many territories and places fell into British hands with no more than slight opposition, colonialism involved also a whole alphabet of military disasters from Afghanistan in 1839 to Zululand forty years afterwards. Later as British military force increased and the creed of imperialism was boasted the frequency of reverses and frustrations increased too. As Professor Graham states:

> At the beginning of 1896 Britain stood completely isolated. France, Russia, Turkey, Germany and the United States were openly hostile . . .

This was the state to which the great Victorians had brought their cherished British Empire. Its feebleness was soon to be exposed by the protracted Boer War—a multiple disaster because it at once demonstrated the incapacity of the British army against even a weak adversary, thus destroying any illusion of British imperial invincibility, and also showed how ill-fitted the British economy had become to carry the cost of even a minor war, while, by putting Britain in the role of an aggressor against a weaker nation, it split British public opinion and undermined what remained of British moral authority and goodwill in the world.

Mourners today over the final decline and fall of the British Empire like to forget the defeats and humiliations which it so frequently brought to Britain even in what is nostalgically regarded as its golden age. Contemporaries were under no such illusions. Even the swashbuckling Lord Palmerston as Prime Minister in 1857 could very reasonably declare:

> We do not want to have Egypt. We want to trade with Egypt and to travel through Egypt but we do not want the burthen of governing Egypt.

Yet only twenty-two years later, against the wishes of the French partners and still more of the Egyptians, who had first to be bombarded at Alexandria and crushed at Tel-el-Kebir under Arabi, that was just what the British insisted on doing. Disraeli, in the saner days of the mid-century, had expressed robust views on the folly and futility of imperialism. Gladstone fought the Midlothian campaign against it, and described British annexation of Cyprus as a breach of the public law of Europe. Yet as Prime Minister later he failed to stem the tide, and led Liberals into a situation inconsistent with their principles, involving the seizure of Egypt. On paper it appears that the late nineteenth-century drive which led to thirty-nine territories or protectorates being annexed to Britain within thirty-five years from 1870, had in principle remarkably little solid and respectable political backing. Some of the more volatile political leaders embraced it for a period, but Parliament, the political parties and the electorate showed very limited interest or enthusiasm. A revealing statement, worth quoting at length, was made by Lord Rosebery, recently Liberal Prime Minister, in a speech at Edinburgh on October 9, 1896:

> The British Empire . . . needs peace. For the last twenty years, still more during the last twelve, you have been laying your hands,

with almost frantic eagerness, on every tract of territory adjacent to your own, or desirable from any other point of view, which you thought it desirable to take. That has had two results. I daresay it has been quite right but it has had two results. The first result is this, that you have excited to an almost intolerable degree the envy of other colonizing nations, and that, in the case of . . . countries . . . which were formerly friendly to you, you can reckon—in consequence of your colonial policy, whether right or wrong—not on their active benevolence but on their active malevolence. And, secondly, you have acquired so enormous a mass of territory that it will be years before you can settle it or control it, or make it capable of defense, or make it amenable to the acts of your administration. In twelve years you have added to the Empire, whether in the shape of actual annexation or of dominion, or of what is called a sphere of influence, 2,600,000 square miles of territory . . . to the 120,000 square miles of the United Kingdom . . . You have added during the last twelve years twenty-two areas as large as the United Kingdom itself . . . You may be compelled to draw the sword—I hope you may not be; but the foreign policy of Great Britain, until its territory is consolidated, filled up, settled, civilized, must inevitably be a policy of peace.

Whoever may actually have been responsible for the policies thus characterized and the consequences so clearly and correctly predicted, it seems somewhat unfair to have blamed them so vividly on the Edinburgh electors! Indeed the key group who could have averted them and failed were the aptly named LIMPS—the vacillating but influential band of Liberal Imperialists. Yet Rosebery, who was one of them, may have had good reason to allude to some interests quite distinct from government. Some curious tacit alliance seems to have arisen between a high-minded Oxbridge-educated élite who fancied themselves as new Romans and a low-minded twilight fraternity of speculators and exploiters who saw quick profits here and there in the world, provided that the British government could be cajoled or maneuvered into coming in at the right moment to pull their chestnuts out of the fire. In the forefront were the adventurous travelers, the missionaries, the eccentrics, and the sheer misfits who pushed or drifted into fresh territories and opened them up. What seems quite clear is that no farsighted conspiracy, no coherent political program and no theoretical search for outlets for a surplus of capital can explain the messy, inarticulate, semi-conscious process by which this vast and ill-fated expansion of the British Empire was carried through. It was imposed on the

British, almost as much without their understanding or consent, as it was imposed on the growing number of territories which awoke one day to find themselves colored red on the map. Different schools within the British government scrapped with one another to defend the imperial lifeline to India by garrisoning the Suez Canal, by acquiring a naval base at the Cape and by bolstering up the tottering Turkish Empire to keep open the land route beyond the Bosphorus, all at the same time.

The conclusion which emerges is that in the popular sense, and in the sense that Lord Palmerston so eagerly desired, Great Britain has not during the past hundred years been a dominant Great Power. In retrospect many suppose, and some wish to believe, that there was a day when the world trembled at or at least respectfully heeded Britain's voice: if so the exact date when this was true is singularly difficult to trace. In fact after the Napoleonic Wars there was by tacit agreement a prolonged suspension of active Great Power politics, and for some time a "Concert" of five Powers, including Britain, settled major continental issues by diplomacy. But in the rest of the world as a whole there was a power vacuum, while ruling groups busied themselves with domestic politics or economics. In the peculiar circumstances of that vacuum Britain was able to a considerable extent to enjoy the more routine and passive attributes of a Great Power by dint of not claiming the riskier and more ambitious ones. From time to time a fortunate stroke could be brought off when other powers were otherwise preoccupied, or before most of them had become accustomed to think of colonial acquisitions as worthwhile. Until the second half of the century self-interest rarely led Britain to attempt objectives which were not fairly widely acceptable to other nations. There was thus some degree of built-in international support for British policy so long as it continued to embrace liberalism, free trade, freedom of the seas and of movement and support for down-trodden peoples. This relative freedom from clashes of policy, the general revulsion against European war after 1815, and the intense preoccupation with domestic change make it possible to interpret the first half of the nineteenth century as a period of British dominance, provided it is not overlooked that this dominance was fortuitous, not imposed. When after 1870 imperialism became an official creed, and contrary movements of opinion gathered strength, the real limits of British power became obvious.

The fiasco of the Crimean War and British impotence to discourage or check German territorial expansion proved that if British intervention overseas was to have any effect it would have to be based, not on governessy admonitions and bluff, but on skilful diplomacy, backed by genuine and immediately available superior force. A small number of ambitious men, misled by a false assessment of the nature and scale of British economic superiority, and tempted by dreams of a new Rome, led their unsuspecting fellow-countrymen down the imperialist path. So unfolded the fatal commitment to ambitious prestige policies, bolstered by the bogus claim to imperial destiny and backed by the building-up of expensive armaments. At the end of the nineteenth century the United Kingdom, which was already falling far behind the United States and also behind Germany in terms of national income, was spending more than any other nation on armaments and was doing at least as much as any other state to render the tragic twentieth-century armaments race inevitable.

A vicious spiral was beginning, in which efforts, often unskilful and misguided, to exert power ostentatiously throughout the world were making for tensions and rivalries which necessitated increasingly frequent and risky adventures in power politics. These tended to drain away resources and to distract attention from the maintenance and enhancement of the real bases on which British power rested. The illusion of being the greatest power led to mistaken attempts to act that part as it was conceived in the vulgar and debased atmosphere of the late nineteenth and early twentieth century. Thus again, as in the fourteenth and fifteenth centuries, England, by setting an aggressive example, stirred up in other nations reactions which would have been better left unstimulated, and which once more resulted, after decades of suffering, in these pretensions being cut down to size. The blunders, neglects and provocations of British policy during the Hundred Years' Peace almost matched in their political consequences those of the Hundred Years' War.

CHAPTER 3
The Economic Wrong-turning

One of the main reasons for the failure of British foreign policy was the growing disparity between the scale of commitments demanded by imperialism and the capacity of the British economy to support them. British national income and exports failed to keep pace not only with those of the Americans but with others. In the seventeenth century productive forces of surprising vigor had been released in Britain by the Cromwellian and Whig revolutions and by the Union with Scotland. These had led during the ensuing century and a half to many significant innovations in science and technology, financial and commercial organization, agricultural and manufacturing practice, transport, land management and professional training. It was largely the fruits of these innovations, coinciding with the exhaustion of Europe after the Napoleonic Wars and the rapid agricultural development in America, which brought the flood of Victorian material progress, so spectacularly demonstrated in London at the Great Exhibition of 1851. At that time, less than a hundred and twenty years ago, the income per head in the United States was probably much the same as in Britain, but a far smaller share of it was derived from industry. The total populations also were not very different, although it was already clear that the United States had an immensely greater potential in land and natural resources.

The record shows that from that time to now the United States has pulled ahead, but not at an even pace. At the outset the United States was highly dependent on British capital and also on British technology, particularly for much of its early railway development. The repeal of the Corn Laws in 1846, although not so viewed at the time, can now be seen as the first step towards placing the United Kingdom in a position of permanent dependence on the United States. The accompanying sacrifice of the landed and agricultural interest to that of urban manufacture and commerce changed the balance of political power in Britain, although perhaps not in full proportion to the extent of the economic shift which it brought about. The greatest national misfortune was that cheap imported food was used mainly to buy time in continuing to compete on a basis of relatively cheap semi-illiterate labor and amateurish management and technology in a series of industries already destined to fail in carrying on the impetus of national economic growth, particularly in the export markets. The opportunity for rapidly raising the national standards and numbers of educated and trained workers of all kinds, as the Prince Consort Albert had struggled heroically to ensure, was stolidly neglected.

As Conrad and Meyer show, in their penetrating *Studies in Econometric History:*

> The rate of growth of British industrial production clearly slowed down in the last quarter of the nineteenth century . . . The slowdown in the growth of production was accompanied by a significant drop in the rate of expansion of British export markets—explicitly from a figure of 4.5 per cent per year in the 1840–60 period to one of 1.5 in the period from 1905 to 1913.

For British industrial production, including construction:

> The actual growth rate from 1854 to 1872 was (on a compounded basis) 3.05 per cent, and from 1872 to 1907 it was 1.75 or 2 per cent.

After considering a number of possible explanations the authors incline to the view that the reduced rate of growth in exports was responsible for the slower industrial development of the last quarter of the nineteenth century in the United Kingdom.

It is instructive to compare this with the course of evolution in the US economy, as traced by the same authors. There the net national product rose from an annual average of $9·5 billion in 1869–78 to $142·7 billion in 1950–54—a growth rate of more than 4 percent per year, sustained over the better part of a century. As population increased from 44·6 million to 157·5 million the increase in real *per capita* product was about 2 percent annually or from $213 to $906 at 1929 prices. This growth did not occur evenly. The first surge took place during the two decades after the Civil War, when the annual growth rate maintained a level of about 9 percent and the net national product doubled in the ten years 1869–79. The second burst came in the last decade of that century and in the first decade of this, averaging nearly 6 percent annually. Up to this period much of American expansion had been based on British capital, but now, while Britain was entering "the first great stagnation of a modern industrial economy," the United States was experiencing a great new impetus to capital formation through the technological development of electric light and power, the electric street railway, the telephone and many other inventions such as the sewing machine and applications of natural gas, petroleum and coking. Linked with this were innovations in organization, such as the holding company, and behind it was the driving pressure of scarcity of labor which forced up the capital–labor ratio from $2,320 per worker in 1879 to $4,170 in 1909 (figures recalculated at 1929 prices). Agricultural prices came down over the period in almost exactly the same degree as all commodity prices, and this cheapening of food indirectly eased the course of British industry—without it British costs would have been higher and the decline in growth of exports would probably have been even more serious. Without it however the British obsession with cheap food and cheap labor would probably have been proved unworkable before 1900, and the long run consequences therefore were anything but beneficial.

Conrad and Meyer's analysis is far from complete, but it throws a flood of light on what went wrong with Britain's all-important economic power base after 1851. Up to then the genius of a smallish number of inventors, engineers like George and Robert Stephenson, Brunel and Paxton, and other technologists and scientists had unfolded vast possibilities of rapid economic expansion. Some of these had been vigorously and ably taken up by the early contractors and industrialists, who had a fairly free hand operationally and financially until the politicians, administrators and bankers began to catch up with them after the mid-point of the century. From then onwards, for reasons which are complex and obscure, the inventors and pioneers ceased to be able to command the necessary resources and power to keep Britain on the move into the newer industries, as they had done, for example, by ruthlessly and wisely superseding a nearly brand-new and expensive national canal system by the even newer railways in the eighteen-forties. A dead hand was now laid on the British economy, which has lain in its grasp ever since. How did this come about?

It was not merely a change of outlook and practice, but rather a replacement of outdated old institutions by unsuitable and ill-conceived new ones which fell into the hands of men themselves unequipped and unsuited to keep the British economy moving forward. The Victorians are often pictured as high-principled, earnest businessmen and triumphant devotees of material progress. On the record it would seem more correct to regard those who ran Britain between 1850 and 1900 as chronic bunglers who inherited the most commanding advantages ever bequeathed to any generation in Britain and who lost no time in throwing them to the winds.

The ruling groups who emerged in the seventeenth and gradually lost ground during the nineteenth century had included many inquiring, scholarly but ambitious and worldly characters, such as Townsend, Coke of Norfolk, Matthew Boulton and the Duke of Bridgewater. They were closely in touch with practice in estate management, construction, agriculture and commerce, and intent on developing improved methods of all kinds, with a characteristic Englishman's eye on the main chance. Without them the agricultural and possibly also the industrial revolution would not have succeeded as smoothly. By 1850 their successors had either lost touch with such experience, or had lost their influence in ruling circles to types who did not share it. The new professional administrators from the public schools and Oxbridge prided themselves, as their successors still do, on their total innocence and ignorance of the great technical and economic forces on which their ambitious policies depended.

While we cannot cross-examine them on the reasons, we find a useful clue in words penned at The Poplars, Wimbledon in June 1872 by Walter Bagehot, then editor of the *Economist,* and one of the most influential opinion-formers of the day. He writes:

> . . . besides what the Americans pay to the Government, they are paying a great deal to some of their own citizens, and so are rearing a set of industries which never ought to have existed, which are bad speculations at present because other industries would have paid better . . . probably industry will return to its natural channel, the artificial trade will be first depressed, then discontinued, and the fixed capital employed in the trade will all be depreciated and much of it be worthless.

This gloomy dogma is not easily reconciled with our present knowledge that in that very decade of which he wrote the United States net national product doubled, while the same year marked in Britain the watershed between a period of growth at one-third the then current

American rate and a new period in which average annual growth fell back to one-fifth of that rate over the ensuing thirty-five years.

If such a brilliant man as Bagehot could be so hopelessly misled by the dogma of his day, and could use his persuasive pen so to mislead others, we may find it easier to understand why the affluent descendants of the Americans, whose ruin he predicted, are now able so helpfully to step in to prevent the collapse of the pound sterling. It is sad, however, to reflect on how much Britain has sacrificed in order to prefer dogma to fact-finding, and empiricism to higher training.

The first-hand, first-class, first-generation leaders of technical and industrial expansion were superseded in the City and elsewhere in the business world by men who knew remarkably little in many cases about the principles and practices which had created the new British economy. The divorce was partly geographical, between London and the North and Midlands. The latter, after the great booms in constructing railways and mills, were increasingly cut off from effective access to new capital, much of which was channeled overseas by City men in close touch with the economies of almost every country but their own. In theory—and theory unsupported by facts was immensely popular among the Victorians, as it is among their present-day heirs—this immense overseas investment ought to have stimulated British exports, but as the figures quoted above clearly show, however, the expansion of exports actually fell back disastrously. For that there were two main reasons which should have been obvious, and were in fact often pointed out—failure to keep up with other countries in education and training, and failure to modernize British industries and to develop new growth. The disastrous change from triumphant economic expansion to stagnation was brought about, without any external difficulties to excuse it, in only a couple of decades, between 1860 and 1880. Relative stagnation has reigned in the British economy ever since, if world standards of comparison are employed. If we are to seek the true causes of the British sickness we need to take a look at what happened then.

Possible carriers of this sickness were the main institutions and groups which came to power around that time, and which have held or enlarged their power ever since. The list of suspects thus includes the new class of semiprofessional politicians beginning with Gladstone and Disraeli, the City, the élite produced by the Arnold-Jowett new model of public school/Oxbridge partnership, and the new Victorian Civil Service, derived from the Northcote–Trevelyan reforms of the mid-eighteen-fifties. We have to consider not only the direct effects of these elements, but such indirect consequences of their emergence as diversion of resources from essential requirements, gaps and stalemates in lines of communication and action between different parts of the British nation, and the souring or alienation of those who were deprived of status or of a share of national prosperity. As we shall find in later chapters these indirect consequences are of great importance.

All four of these elements in the British body politic had a long history of some sort before 1850, but for all of them the years immediately following that date brought changes amounting to a virtual transformation either institutionally or in the scale and nature of their role, or both. In all four, most of all in the Civil Service, least in politics and the City, there was a more or less far-reaching take-over of an existing institution by the new men owing their fortune to the industrial revolution and to the forces released by the Reform Act of 1832. In all four, too, identifiable institutional changes were played down, the main differences being in the nature and scale of the activities and the standards, methods and outlook with which they now came to be conducted. All four also came at this time under the influence or direction of men who were highly susceptible to, and were untiring exponents of, many of the most characteristic mid-Victorian brands of highly respectable dogma. The most articulate, naturally, were the politicians, while the most secretive was the City.

Four cardinal errors of British policy, all connected with these elements and coinciding in origin with them, are, to an overwhelming degree, responsible for Britain's subsequent and current troubles.

1. The decision in effect to retard the further growth of the British economy from about 1860 by declining to expand education, training, scientific research and the arts as Prince Albert rightly advocated, and by preferring to rely on cheap semi-illiterate labor, free trade and hopes of continued dominance of the then leading industries—railways, cotton and other textiles, shipbuilding, coalmining and iron and steel—rather than to develop on a mass scale new industries and techniques, as our chief competitors did.

2. The decision to give strong preference to investment of British savings overseas rather than in home industry, agriculture and utilities, and therefore to forgo the development of investment institutions

and channels in support of British industry and commerce at home.
3. The decision to embrace imperialism and to indulge in large-scale power politics, rather than to pursue internationalist liberalism of the type exemplified by the 1851 Great Exhibition.
4. The decision to replace the moribund corrupt and patronage-ridden public service by a new model Civil Service based on academic amateurism rather than on professional training.

Search where you will through the unhappy and copious record of British failures, humiliations and missed opportunities during the past century, it is difficult to find any in which at least one of these four cardinal errors was not prominently involved. While in each of the four cases it is clear that a decisive choice in the wrong direction was made, in only one case—the fourth—is it precisely documented.

After Parliament had captured from the Crown in the eighteenth century the effective control of government, the integrated administrative drive formerly arising from the monarch's conception of his duty to keep the country moving was for a period replaced by a political leadership antagonistic to almost any form of government activity other than getting into and waging foreign wars. After the middle of the eighteenth century the cost of these mounted so steeply that the rash attempt was made to pass on some of it to the British settlements in North America, which had, it is true, been among the principal beneficiaries of the recent victories. The accompanying complications led to an expansion of the small administrative service, whose loyalty was still partly to the Crown direct, and only partly to Ministers, some of whom nevertheless treated their departments as a kind of personal household. Changes of administration and reshuffles of Ministers, together with the growing complexity and volume of the work, were already increasing the power of the top officials and their departments, who colored:

> every major piece of colonial administration to emerge during the period: (1) They implemented policy by shaping into precise acts or proclamations the ministry's clearly outlined American proposals, and by enforcing whatever parts of the new legislation properly fell within their departmental jurisdictions; (2) They formulated vaguely planned or only dimly considered ministerial ideas into acts of Parliament or orders to colonial officials; most importantly on a few occasions they actually suggested the colonial measures the government adopted. (Franklin B. Wickwar, *British Subministers and Colonial America, 1763–1783*, Princeton UP, 1966, p. 86.)

Wickwar points out that whereas many earlier Ministers had had time to become competent administrators also, their eighteenth-century successors had not, since "pursuing office or holding it demanded relentless attention to matters of patronage, electioneering, factional maneuvering and parliamentary tactics." During the efforts of George III to recapture control these pursuits became even more demanding than earlier, and it was then that the long-deferred acceptance by Parliament of the necessity for an administrative service tacitly occurred. Lord Dartmouth, the Colonial Secretary, headed the new department belatedly established to deal with the restive settlers—as an American historian has written:

> The British constitution provided for no office with exclusive jurisdiction over the colonies until seven years before losing thirteen of them. (*Lord Dartmouth and the American Revolution,* by B. D. Bargar, pp. 61–62.)

Unfortunately neither the Colonial Secretary nor his office was consulted over the Tea Act of 1773, which led to the Boston Tea Party and the loss of the American colonies because "the Treasury regarded the measure as primarily a revenue Bill designed to rescue the East India Company from bankruptcy." This is perhaps the first instance of a real Treasury clanger. Lord North and the humane and considerate Lord Dartmouth, like plenty of Ministers then unborn, were left carrying the can, as politicians must.

A year before Lord Cornwallis surrendered at Yorktown Edmund Burke in his notable speech in the House of Commons on the Economical Reformation of the Civil and other establishments spoke in terms which are no less true today of the fundamental weakness of the Civil Service. Although his Economic Reform Act of two years later (1782) greatly reduced the scandals of patronage nothing was done to provide Britain with a trained public service of high caliber, such as Prussia had already possessed for half a century, and Britain does not possess yet.

As has so often happened the way to reform was opened through an unofficial and roundabout channel. In this case it was the East India Company, which set up its own administrative training college at Haileybury in 1813 with strict discipline and a high educational standard—one of its early masters was Thomas Malthus. Patronage however still played a part, and this was not abolished until 1853, when open competition for entry to the Indian Civil Service was substituted.

Meanwhile, as was later candidly confessed to the Playfair Committee of 1875 by Sir Charles Trevelyan, then Permanent Secretary to the Treasury, "The revolutionary period of 1848 gave us a shake, and one of the consequences was a remarkable series of investigations into public offices, which lasted for five years, culminating in the Organization Report." Trevelyan, however, being himself a fine product of the Haileybury training and of the Indian Civil Service, in which he had served with distinction during twelve years, did not personally need so much of a shake as his colleagues. Aided by the fear inspired by outbreaks of cholera Edwin Chadwick, the great secretary of the Poor Law Commission, had contrived, also in 1848, to get the first Public Health Act passed, but he made himself so unpopular by his zeal that he was forcibly retired in 1854 and the Board of Health was abolished in 1858. Meanwhile, however, the scandals of the Crimean War had so upset public opinion as to trigger off one of the lesser-known of the Victorian mass movements—the Administrative Reform Association, which by gathering as many as five or six thousand adherents at its meetings made it impossible to postpone the issue any longer.

The Association campaigned, apparently triumphantly, for the abolition of the patronage system in manning the Civil Service and its replacement by a trained public administration. But by one of the smartest confidence tricks in British history that did not happen at all. At the last moment, under the influence behind the scenes of Benjamin Jowett, later Master of Balliol, and others, there was substituted a totally different prescription for replacing the place-men by a band of newly-fledged amateurs qualified merely by scholastic examination-passing qualifications and by evidence of character, which secured a virtual monopoly in the upper ranks of the reformed service for products of Arnold's public schools and of Jowett's Oxbridge.

One astonishing feature of this episode was that both Oxford and Cambridge Universities were at this time themselves in such a deplorable state that Royal Commissions had to be appointed to reform them, on the instance of Fellows of the Royal Society. While Cambridge, whose then Chancellor was the Prince Consort, welcomed the Commissioners, Oxford, through the Duke of Wellington as Chancellor, resisted in terms which perfectly illustrate both the tone and the attitude of the University:

> Two centuries ago—in 1636—the University revised the whole body of its statues, and the academic system of study was admirably arranged at a time when not only the nature and faculties of the

human mind were exactly what they are still, and must, of course, remain, but the principles also of a sound and enlarged intellectual culture were far from being imperfectly understood.

It is not surprising, after this, that the Commissioners should have had to refer in their Report, which the university did its best to sabotage, to:

> an opinion which has long prevailed at Oxford with regard to the nature of a liberal education. It has been held to be the sole business of the University to train the powers of the mind, not to give much positive or any professional knowledge, and the study of classical books is regarded as the best means of refreshing and invigorating the mind.

The Report criticizes "the extent to which all separate branches of learning, both professional and preparatory to professions, have been suffered to decay" and adds the comment that even "learned theologians are very rare in the university". It was this university at this time which was selected to be the leading nursery of the new Civil Service, despite the Report of the Royal Commission which also, in very modern terms, stressed the national loss of trained minds resulting from the operation of college selection systems to exclude from the university—up to then one of only four in England and Wales—any but well-to-do candidates.

A further surprising sequel was that at the first competitive examination under the new regulations not a single university candidate was able to qualify for entry into the upper ranks of the Civil Service. This lack however was soon made good, and before long the system was proving as useful a "fresh avenue of employment" to the right products of the right schools and universities as it previously had been to the right protégés of the right noble patrons.

Not only the swindled adherents of the Administrative Reform Association but others of some weight felt by no means happy over this neat solution. Queen Victoria was much perturbed and consented most grudgingly in 1854, no doubt having ascertained from her Consort where the measure was likely to lead. Other critics were as diverse as Anthony Trollope and the Clerk of the Privy Council who gave caustic evidence to the Playfair Committee of 1875. Even more revealing is the fact that Gladstone, who sponsored this reform, was still a Tory Minister and did so in order to secure administrative power for the "higher classes", whom he considered, at least in 1854, to be superior in natural gifts and in their "insensible education" irrespective of booklearning.

The reader should bear in mind that this is the system, unchanged in any significant respects, by which higher civil servants are still being recruited in 1968. Apart from its far-reaching effects on the style and competence of British government the choice made in 1855 to base the reformed Civil Service on direct intake of bright amateurs from the universities without further training was disastrous in two other directions. Generally it lent the backing of high authority to the favorite English myth that a true amateur, provided of course that he is English, can usually beat the professional at his own game. More specifically, owing to the stiff class discrimination which, as the contemporary Royal Commission has pointed out, was so deeply built in to the universities from which recruits for the higher ranks were to be drawn, and owing to the contempt for science, technology, and many other branches of learning which was also endemic there, a mortal blow was struck at Prince Albert's movement to foster higher education in the arts and sciences and in technology, and to link it with design and the management of industry and commerce.

A number of wise and public-spirited men saw clearly that Britain was taking the wrong course. After all, they had before them the brilliant examples of such all-rounders as Stephenson, Brunel and Sir Joseph Paxton, who designed and built for the Great Exhibition of 1851 the largest building ever constructed. It covered nearly nineteen acres, and was erected in thirty-nine weeks—"the whole procedure from Paxton's piece of blotting paper to the Queen's opening of the building completely furnished with exhibits was only forty-six weeks." The building was so far ahead of its time that if re-erected today in modern materials it would need to fear no adverse comparisons. As the *Journal of the Royal Institute of British Architects* has lately recalled, "Paxton's other activities included formal gardening, romantic suburb and park design, hydraulic experiments, conventional architecture, railway promotion, operation and contracting, botany, journalism, politics, land agency, sanitary reform and the organization of a civilian construction corps for the Crimean War." Paxton, in other words, was a great English talent in the Wren tradition, but this was the type which the new masters in Whitehall were resolved to thrust into outer darkness, as indeed they have largely succeeded in doing ever since.

A quarter of a century later a Royal Commission on Technical Instruction was set up under Sir Bernhard Samuelson FRS, a liberal scientist-industrialist who had had an advanced education in Germany:

> as a result on the one hand of widespread concern about the capacity of English industry to stand up to European competition, and on the other hand of the unregulated growth of various forms of technical education in England. (J. Stuart Maclure, *Educational Documents*, 1965.)

After the required blah-blah that "our people still maintain their position at the head of the industrial world", the Royal Commission went on to plead that "a few well-equipped institutions of high rank are needed" to train for the highest industrial positions and justly added, "no portion of the national expenditure on education is of greater importance than that employed in the scientific culture of the leaders of industry." In other words Britain needed technological universities. Seventy years later the late Lord Cherwell and Sir Henry Tizard, who agreed upon little else, were still pushing at the highest levels for this recommendation to be implemented, but Oxbridge/Whitehall still said no, and it was still axiomatic that they knew best.

Besides this chronic sabotage of the development of British rivals for the great *Technische Hochschule*, which had arisen from Zurich to Delft and Stockholm and east to Berlin from the middle of the nineteenth century, Whitehall took half a century more to sort out the appalling chaos and confusion in educational jurisdiction and supporting structure. Once this was done it was possible for Sir Robert Morant's Education Act of 1902 to constitute the county councils and county boroughs as education authorities with State aid and to create through them a network of new State grammar schools. These, as L. C. B. Seaman has expressed it in *Post-Victorian Britain* "provided for the first time since before the Reformation an organized route by which persons of humble birth with no flair for making money could rise to positions of authority." Morant had entered the Civil Service by an unusual route, after unusual experience with the King of Siam. But for this such an Act would have been much longer deferred. Even so, as Seaman points out, these grammar schools were:

> too ready to assume that a traditional education, taking its spirit and aims from the public schools, was the only possible education to

give to the new pool of ability for which they catered. A much greater readiness to respond to the country's obvious need for improved technical education would have been more in keeping with the first decade of the century, let alone later decades. By 1902 it was already nearly forty years since a Royal Commission had first called attention to the inadequacy of English technical education, and already well over a decade since the foundation of the Polytechnic movement by Quintin Hogg had pointed a way to the future which, despite the Technical Instruction Act of 1889, the local authorities and the State tended to ignore. They continued to ignore it when the 1944 Act gave them another opportunity . . .

Of all the fruits of misgovernment in Britain this has been perhaps the most bitter, and the most productive of Britain's present ills. It also perhaps most perfectly illustrates the systematic nature of the misgovernment, which unfailingly reiterated the same wrong decisions in 1855, 1889, 1902 and 1951, because it is manipulated with the same attitudes, for the same bad reasons. And, of course, the "new pool of ability" catered for first in 1902 was actually the same old stagnating pool of neglected and excluded "poor scholars" for whose plight the Royal Commissioners had criticized Oxford colleges half a century earlier.

Underlying the four cardinal errors outlined before are two more fundamental and complex human standpoints or patterns around which some of the most vital forces in British life unaccountably and unfortunately began to revolve in those same fateful middle years of the nineteenth century.

The first of these was Thomas Arnold's vigorous and impressive but peculiar and narrow brand of authoritarian Graeco-Roman-Christian character-schooling, originating at Rugby in 1828–42 and later buttressed by Benjamin Jowett's only less peculiar, backward-looking, anti-creative classics-oriented brand of higher education at Oxford. Arnold, as J. B. Hope Simpson well says in his *Rugby Since Arnold* (1967) "aimed to produce, in his own words, 'first religious and moral principle; secondly gentlemanly conduct; and thirdly intellectual ability'. *In this order of priority lies the real revolution which he brought about.* Though he had no opinion of mere brilliance, he believed that intellectual excellence and moral quality were closely allied and that therefore it was *his duty to get rid of unpromising material, intellectual as well as moral."* (My italics.) As their art and literature show, the classes from which this movement drew its energy and funds were naïve, puritanical and intensely self-assured. Even so it remains a curiosity of history that the influence of so small a number of dedicated teachers should so rapidly and almost completely have swept the board, and should have left British education too stunned to get back on its feet and start thinking for itself for all of a hundred years afterwards, with such crippling effects on the national talents and character. Whatever else they may have been, these were certainly men of power.

The second critical pattern was that into which British politics became reshaped during the aftermath of the Reform Act of 1832. Once more, this pattern exhibited a high degree of improbability, a fantastic dominance and durability, and an immense capacity for injury to the nation, also for a century or more. The Whig government, which won power in 1830 after nearly half a century of almost unbroken Tory rule, enacted the Reform Act which gave votes to the manufacturing and professional classes and threatened the Tories with being permanently in a minority and on the defensive. During the following years the vast and varied impacts of the industrial revolution and of the liberal upheavals, especially of 1848 on the Continent created great political stresses, confusion and disorientation, with which contemporary political thought was unable to cope. Practical politicians were thus left to follow their instincts to make do and mend, and the task of sorting things out gradually passed into the hands of two younger Tories, Benjamin Disraeli and his junior by five years, William Ewart Gladstone. Disraeli set out to reform and reshape the Tory party while Gladstone, after communing anxiously with his soul, left it and soon reappeared as leader of the rival Liberals, who had annexed not only the new middle-class vote but the support of the politically articulate Left who rallied to the bright banner of liberalism. Disraeli made a virtue of the only tolerable course left open to him by wooing and in 1867 enfranchising the solid core of the working classes, partly under the rival bright banner of imperialism. Many workers had close relatives in Canada and Australia, and were slow to understand that imperialism now meant annexing such territories as Egypt and Cyprus and grabbing a mixed bag of possessions in Africa, Asia and the Pacific. Thus instead of emerging with a coherent Right and Right-center party opposing one of the Left and Left-center, Britain was saddled with a pair of hopeless mixtures of both, steeped in compromise, hypocrisy and confusion of thought.

The interests and instincts of the manufacturers and upper middle classes were basically with the Conservatives, but having been spellbound by Gladstone's eloquence it took them anything up to eighty years to find this out. Meanwhile their half-baked rationalizations, backed by their very genuine purses, and their protracted struggles of conscience over leaving the Party, effectively prevented British liberalism from being liberal in any coherent or effective way. The pitch was further queered by an influential minority, especially among the leaders with Whig traditions, becoming strongly infected with imperialism contracted from the Tories, while many conservative supporters succumbed equally embarrassingly to free trade, not merely as a matter of expediency but as a religious faith. Eventually, after around half a century of this, many of the radicals and other heirs to deep-seated British Left traditions had had enough of it, and found themselves obliged to move across to the embryonic Labour Party, which rapidly expanded as the twentieth century went on. Labour, however, was hagridden by doctrines derived from a former London correspondent of a New York newspaper, named Karl Marx, and to add to the general confusion it also caught the contagion of imperialism which still divides it. Thus the British electorate, although there is no evidence that it has ever included a majority definitely in favor of imperialism, was offered a choice between three rival imperialist parties, and no other.

While it is impossible to evaluate the repercussions of this appalling political muddle on the modern development of Britain they have clearly been of the utmost seriousness. The effort to weld and hold together within one party elements which simply would not mix has vexed and exhausted generations of party leaders, and has immensely aggravated the difficulties of getting agreement on coherent and effective policies. In some cases, as in the formulae produced by Balfour over the tariff reform issue, meaninglessness has been carried to the nth degree, and all to no avail as his party was shortly afterwards routed at the polls. Many of the most stubborn problems which have plagued the nation arose while party leaders were occupied in papering over the cracks within their discordant teams. Home Rule for Ireland is perhaps the worst of several obvious examples of the absurd waste of time and energy which this radically misguided and jerrybuilt structure of party politics created by Gladstone and Disraeli has involved. It could and should have been settled at least a quarter of a century earlier. A more honest and common-sense grouping of opinions and interests could undoubtedly have avoided much of this grief and waste. It could also have brought into constructive participation a number of politically interested elements of the intelligentsia which the nonsenses of the System virtually excluded from any significant role in British politics.

Such however has been the extent of complacency and self-delusion that a pattern condemned by its meager and pitiful fruits has been held up as a model to the world. It is a ground for hope for the future that many of the worst features of this heritage have at long last worked themselves through the nation's troubled political digestive tract.

Of the four cardinal errors listed on pp. 47–48 the second will be more fully discussed in Part Four. The others have been briefly reviewed here, together with the two broader underlying patterns indicated on pp. 54–55. The fourth of these errors and the first of the two patterns remain virtually uncorrected to this day, while the rest have been, or are being, to some extent neutralized or made good.

All six of these strategic wrong turnings took effect roughly within the dozen years between 1855 and 1867, or say a clear century ago. All six of them, far from being of historical interest only, are highly relevant to the "English sickness" of today. It was then that Britain got well and truly bent. It is for us now to put Britain straight again.

PART TWO
LEADING AND LAGGING

CHAPTER 4

Measuring Progress and Decline

It is customary for politicians in opposition to describe their adversaries in power, whenever a good opportunity arises for it, as the worst government ever known, and to attribute to their incompetence everything which goes wrong except the weather. Such ritual exchanges of party courtesies must be clearly distinguished from the task of assessing seriously an entire political system and the advance or decline of a nation. In this context, the concern is not with the ostensible or actual policies of one party or another, or with the abstract merits or demerits of particular principles or programs, but with the outcome of the workings of an entire system within which all these come and go in a somewhat random and inconclusive manner.

Two findings of recent investigations have some bearing on the matter; each is useful as a pointer and a caution. It has been demonstrated, contrary to widespread previous belief, that the capacity of any individual politician, however talented and energetic, to attract to himself a personal following of voters independently of his party's national fortunes is so limited as to make no difference at all except in the most closely run contests. It has also been shown that the traditional canvass of voters is a grossly unreliable method of ascertaining their voting intentions compared with any soundly conducted sample opinion poll. In these two instances at least it is now known that politicians generally have hitherto been misleading themselves and the nation on verifiable aspects of the political processes which are most closely within their own direct knowledge and experience.

The question to what extent giving "power" (whatever that may in practice mean) to different "programs" actually influences events and determines national progress has for obvious reasons not yet been similarly probed. At least we have now been warned that what politicians think and say on such problems may be very far from the realities. It is therefore possible, at least, that their opinions and efforts may play a part less significant than they fondly suppose. This caution is applicable to the day-to-day political game, but the same does not necessarily apply in terms of longer periods. It could be that, while the impact of particular groups of politicians at a particular period on the problems and events of that period is of rather slight significance, nevertheless their cumulative impact over a series of decades may be all-important. This may result not only from what they think and do, but even more through what they ignore, and what they do only too little and too late. We must beware of confusing conscious politics with unconscious or incidental politics, and of overrating the first while underrating or missing the second.

This book, therefore, is not based primarily on weighing up the sage but irrelevant orations of Mr. X, or the horrible fiasco perpetrated by Earl Y in their memorable conduct of the government of their unfortunate country. It charitably suspends judgment, not merely on their motives and merits, but on the question how far they were, whatever they may have imagined, effectively responsible for what occurred while they proudly presided over the nation's affairs. It seeks first to analyze, however crudely, what progress the nation actually made in which directions, and with what fluctuations and set-backs. That makes a basis for comparing the performance with that of other nations, in order to find how Britain's status and ranking in the world has actually changed under Britain's recent rulers. The question of how far these rulers, and which of their groups, can be held responsible for the successes or failures revealed can then be more usefully considered by the reader. He should bear in mind that one government may enjoy or suffer the delayed outcome of a predecessor's policies, and that skilful timing or merely being lucky may greatly influence the result of a policy or measure.

Many discussions about alleged national decline (or progress) are vitiated by failure to define what this means, how it can be objectively tested or measured, what evidence about it is available, and how far this evidence is open to different interpretations, or may support different conclusions. There is then the quite distinct question how far such progress or decline may have occurred because of, or in spite of, a particular system of government. That in turn raises the question how far a modern government should or can determine national progress, for example in terms of expanding national income. It also brings up the issue of how far within the confines of a given governmental system one government can be much better or much worse in the long run than its alternative from another party. There will no doubt be objections that it is inherently impossible to discover any valid means of measuring the performance of governments or systems of government, but this is what we have to find out. At worst we can roughly measure a number of the ingredients going to make up what is commonly regarded as national progress. We can thus demonstrate what kind of national progress has been achieved during periods when certain governments were "in power," and compare them with the simultaneous performance of other nations where other governments were presiding. There will thus be a basis for discussing how far the particular trends and events, which the record shows, are attributable to the recorded acts or inherent weaknesses and neglects of a particular government or system.

Ideally, in the computer age, students of this fascinating but intractable problem might envisage eventually constructing three basic series of data which would go far towards yielding valid answers. The first might be described as a World League Table of National Progress, taking a mixed "shopping basket" of all measurable ingredients in "progress," and including all countries for which a sufficient range of reasonably reliable information is available. The second might be based on a bogey curve of growth or national income which was, or could have been, expected at various past dates. Comparisons could be made with the estimated potential, with actual output, and with the output for other countries during similar periods. This would go far to show whether the nation has or has not kept pace with the rest of the world and with its own plans and expectations in total economic development. The third device might be an evaluation of the overall efficiency of a government as such, roughly comparable to measurements by independent management consultants of the overall efficiency of great industrial corporations, some of which approach the same order of magnitude. Such an evaluation would be able to do little in relation to such imponderables as acceptability and right choice of national policy objectives, but might do a good deal in relation to structure, performance and right use of manpower. The three series of findings together would show in which areas most and least progress was being made, what was the overall strength and resilience of the national economy, and how efficient was the mechanism of government in those aspects where efficiency rating is now practicable. On such a basis further advances towards the eventual more comprehensive and sophisticated assessment of good and bad government would become possible, not least because high-level attention and training would at last have been directed to these problems, and resources thus found for their more serious study.

A democratic party system purports to be a more efficient and a more advanced system of government than one-party rule or dictatorship, particularly because it allows at intervals for orderly and peaceful change involving the injection of new men, new ideas and alternative programs, and thus possesses a built-in capability for keeping abreast of the times. It has repeatedly been claimed that the British Parliamentary system and the British Civil Service represent the most advanced and successful system of modern democratic government. These claims need to be objectively assessed. Many imitations of these British institutions have been put into practice elsewhere on the strength of them, and the frequent failures have been attributed rather to lack of political maturity than to possible faults in the institutions themselves.

While critical or uncritical studies of one part or another of the system have been numerous its overall performance has received astonishingly little consideration. It is really important for Britain, and for the world, to know whether the not very modest claims for these British institutions are or are not justified in contemporary conditions. The approach, as has already been indicated, must be indirect, by first examining the actual scale and pace of national progress which results from, or at least coincides with, the maintenance of this particular system of government, in order to determine whether the performance is satisfactory or unsatisfactory, and, if it is unsatisfactory, by considering what grounds there are for supposing that the prevalent system of government is unsatisfactory too. Is it possible to have a good system of government which consistently gives bad results?

Historically, as Part I has broadly recalled, Britain during the past millennium has proved to be one of the most consistently and rapidly progressing countries of the world over a wide range of human effort, political, intellectual, scientific and cultural, commercial, industrial, military and sporting, and has also been outstandingly successful in expanding throughout the world its sphere of power and influence. Although much entangled and mutually supporting, these two great aspects of success are quite distinct. The second was largely a result of the first, but a result which was by no means inevitable, indeed largely accidental. It created interests and resources of quite different and partly inconsistent types. We must be careful not to confuse Britain the font of civil liberties and literature, of scientific and technological discovery, of industrial and agricultural enterprise and of adventuring in the imaginative use of leisure in country houses and travel, in sport and society, with Britain the colonizing, empire-building, policing and campaigning power.

The forces generated by the first of these Britains initially launched and sustained, but later conflicted with, and finally undermined, the spectacular achievements of the second. The first was there before the birth of the second and survives after its demise. Britain gave birth to the Empire, but also to many of the new ideas and forces which made its survival an impossibility. The past half century has seen the British Empire twice fiercely assailed from without, twice emerging victorious from the onslaught, and in the end quickly and quietly dismantled, not by any foreign power or by the adoption of alien concepts, but by the triumphant spread of political principles and ideals which Britain herself originated and disseminated through the world. In seeking to assess British progress or decline at this particular moment in history the interplay, formerly constructive but now destructive, of these two distinct and rival Britains needs to be borne constantly in mind.

It must also be recalled that, although over several centuries the British record in many fields has been impressive, there have been not only marked fluctuations in visible and tangible evidence of progress, but also periods when the fruits of inventiveness and innovation were retarded or concealed by failures in structural adaptation, political, social or economic. The season when there is most in the shop window may not necessarily be the time of greatest production, and vice versa. The indices necessary to rely upon reveal something that cannot be ignored, but they do not reveal all.

There are bound to be periods when even France is short of first-rate native painters, Germany of scientists, Russia of novelists, America of inventors and England of poets, perhaps through some mysterious fluctuation in the supply of creative talent, perhaps through failure to encourage and develop it. And what applies to such scarce and critically recorded activities may well apply to others, where the results of current effort can be more readily measured, even if the supply of special talents cannot. There is here an analogy with attempts to chart climatic changes. We can tell at any given period how many glaciers are retreating or advancing, whether winter months show higher or lower mean temperatures, and whether frosts begin earlier in autumn and continue later in spring, but no one can say whether such trends will continue for decades or for centuries or whether they will be checked or reversed next year. There is however one conspicuous difference. Glaciers do not reflect with anxiety that they are retreating, and thus perhaps worry themselves into retreating faster or whip themselves into advancing again. With nations nothing succeeds like success, but nothing undermines success like the expectation that it will not be maintained or repeated.

Experience of exposure to propaganda, and of the results on stock exchanges of publication of indices of market trends, or on politicians of the results of opinion polls, indicates that there is a middle area between innocence and sophistication over such devices. Within that transitional zone their repercussions can be highly unsettling, and they can become serious factors in falsifying the inferences on which they are based. Fear of such situations, added to the ingrained prejudices and misunderstandings, often leads to a demand for cessation of inquiry and discussion. Apart, however, from the strong arguments for improving our knowledge of relative national progress as a tool in human advancement there is undoubtedly a keen unsatisfied popular demand to know how the nation stands in relation to others. This cannot indefinitely be fobbed off with slipshod and piecemeal answers, usually of a subjective and most misleading character.

Among the earliest measurements relied upon in considering relative national progress and decline were those of population. The belief that the greater the population and the more rapid its increase, the greater must be the nation concerned, was based partly on a somewhat primitive association between fertility or virility and destiny, partly on the obvious connection between numbers of boys and numbers of rifles and bayonets, and partly on the much more complex relationship between growing labor forces, growing consumer markets and growing economic prosperity. All three of these arguments have lately been weakened, and it is being belatedly recognized that countries such as China and India with large and rapidly growing populations are, on the contrary, much handicapped relatively to more manageably expanding countries such as Japan and the USSR. The higher a nation's standard of life and the faster its population expands the larger share of its gross national product is pre-empted for investment in order to keep abreast of the field. Nevertheless, as administrative techniques and mobility have developed during the past three centuries, the threshold size under which a nation is too small to maintain a front-rank economic or military position has steadily increased from about a couple of million in the seventeenth century, when Sweden and the Netherlands could still compete, to around ten million in the Napoleonic period, around twenty-five million during the Victorian age, around forty to fifty million during the first half of the twentieth century, and around 100 to 200 million now.

The United Kingdom had sixteen million inhabitants in 1800, which was two million less than Italy, eight and a half million less than Germany, eleven million less than France and about twenty-one million less than Russia. Italy and Germany were, however, not yet unified while France, Germany and Russia were exhausting themselves in the Napoleonic Wars. In 1850 the UK, overtaking Italy, had reached twenty-seven and a half million, but was still eight and a half million behind both France and Germany and now nearly thirty million behind Russia.

In 1900 the United Kingdom, with some forty-two million people ranked seventh among the world's sovereign states in population, following China, Russia (111 million), USA (seventy-six million), Germany (fifty-six million), Austro-Hungary (fifty million) and Japan (forty-seven million). As however at that time the Indian Empire with 294 million and the rest of the British Empire with a further fifty million were effectively controlled from London, the British Empire could fairly be claimed to be the world's greatest political unit. Nevertheless the decisive theater of power politics was Europe, and in Europe the United Kingdom ranked only fourth of the Big Five in population and armed forces.

Today, except for the Federal Republic of Germany, and the Eurasian USSR, the United Kingdom is considerably the most populous nation in Europe, accounting for nearly 9 percent of its inhabitants, compared with only about 4½ percent two centuries ago. Currently, however, the significant comparison is no longer with Europe but with world population, of which the UK accounted for less than 1 percent two centuries ago, nearly 3 percent at the outset of this century, and has fallen again to about 1·7 percent now.

In terms of relative strength in the world Britain has, therefore, been lucky during the past three centuries in managing to keep well inside the current qualifying size-class for a first-rate economic and military power. But there is some reason to believe that the minimum size has risen during the past decade or so to a level which leaves Britain as a drop-out. In this geographically shrinking but demographically expanding world a nation of fifty million in 1967 is already effectively much smaller than one of that order in 1947. It is not simply a question of numbers of population, since levels of productivity, mobility and national cohesion, effectiveness of administration, access to markets and nature and scale of military commitments also affect the rating. The fact that, relative to other countries, British national income per head, British transport and communications systems and other significant elements have simultaneously shown a relative decline certainly helps to tip the balance adversely. Had the rate of British advance still been leading rather than lagging behind other countries the almost marginal population handicap might have been overcome. The coincidence of these changes within the UK with the dismantling of the overseas Empire has, of course, been a serious misfortune for Britain's current adjustment in status.

Even after the granting of independence to India and Pakistan the UK in 1951 still ranked tenth, and the British Empire fifth, in population. By 1965, however, with the independence and rapid population growth of so many Asian and African countries, Britain with the surviving dependent remnants of the British Empire had dropped to ninth place, the United Kingdom itself being eleventh, after China, India, USSR, USA, Indonesia, Pakistan, Japan, Brazil, West Germany and Nigeria. While there are no other states which, as presently constituted, are likely to overtake Britain in numbers in the near future, there are plenty which could do so before this century is out, if present trends continue. Most if not all of these are, however, developing countries whose power is rather small in relation to the size of their populations.

Mere weight of population, unaccompanied by advanced technology and ample social capital, counts for less and less in a highly equipped world. Some small or smallish countries such as Sweden, Switzerland and the Netherlands rank among the highest in standards of living, and have world importance in a number of fields. Canada, with a population just over one-third that of the UK, is in an intermediate position, as is the much more populous Japan, which has already in important respects surpassed Britain industrially and commercially, and shows signs of going ahead on a much broader front. Britain's status is thus threatened by a pincer movement, on the one hand of more populous developing countries which are rapidly industrializing and gaining strength on a localized or specialized basis, and on the other of often smaller, more rapidly advancing, technologically mature countries which, if they do no more, certainly reduce the scale and extent of British leadership in many fields. Japan is a peculiar hybrid between the first and the second of these groups.

The two acknowledged super-powers, the USA and USSR, currently have populations of just under 200 million and just over 230 million respectively. Given their degree of technological and economic development it seems indisputable that no single nation of less than one-third of those numbers can now compete with them in terms of military strength, or of such expensive prestige products as exploration of outer space. There is also increasing ground for concluding that a home market of the order of 200 million or more now brings decisive advantages of scale in terms of economic production. Industries not enjoying this advantage not only have increasing difficulty in competing in world markets, but are increasingly vulnerable to take-over bids from the bigger brethren. In a giant economy small percentage margins yield large absolute sums, the deployment of which at decisive moments can prove crushing to normally efficient competitors who do not dispose of such sums. Similarly small fluctuations in demand can prove a matter of life or death to suppliers who lack alternative outlets and adequate reserves of capital behind them. Aircraft and aerospace vehicle production, manufacture of electronic equipment such as computers, and even motor vehicle manufacture may be threatened in nations of under 100 million working independently.

Apart from scale of national populations, urban concentration is an important factor in the modern world, although its significance is very difficult to assess. Whatever else it may mean it is perhaps symbolically unfortunate for Britain that at this time Tokyo should have taken over London's previous place—long challenged by Greater New York—as the world's most populous city. The use of different bases for counting heads in conurbations can still give an answer putting Tokyo back in third place if effective administrative units are ignored. Be this as it may, Dr. Ryokichi Minoke, the Governor of Tokyo Metropolis, is the only man in the world who can claim personal responsibility for the welfare of over ten million citizens in a single municipality. Judging by the recent growth rate of several other challengers it may not be long before London falls to sixth place (after Tokyo, New York, Buenos Aires, Shanghai and Moscow). The question between the advantages of metropolitan scale and the strangulation and environmental deterioration of a modern megalopolis is however fast changing.

These are by no means all the respects in which population can significantly influence relative national status. In many countries today the scale of the population explosion is giving rise to severe strains and problems. It seems safe to assume that freedom from rapid population expansion will henceforward increasingly be regarded as an important element in sound national progress. According to current forecasts the growth even of British population during the three coming decades is likely to be uncomfortably large and the prospect in some respects very tight. Compared, however, with other large nations, except France and possibly Germany, the British population increase is quite modest in its rate. If not the most favorable of all for the future it is certainly close to it, and likely to win growing envy from many others. There are signs, still quite slight, that the end of the recent spurt of the British birth-rate may now be near. These are only worth mentioning on account of the known accelerating spread of birth-control methods, which, if effective, might make the position even more favorable over the next decades, in relation to other countries.

Britain again has serious problems of regional maldistribution of population, but these once more are relatively slight compared with the acute excess of population on the land in nearly all the other large countries, and with regional problems such as the Italian Mezzogiorno, and even expanding California.

After population itself the next most essential factors in rating the situation of a nation are the education and training of the people, and the capabilities and skills which they have acquired. For Britain especially this aspect is crucial, since a manifest shortage of natural resources and a population scale demanding heavy dependence on imports put a premium on the fullest development and use of brains as an ingredient in exports of all kinds, visible and invisible. Despite over thirteen centuries of unbroken traditions of learning, and of sending teachers overseas, the attitude towards education, particularly in England, has been markedly fitful and inconstant. Education anywhere is rarely encouraged for the right reasons, and in England it has been especially unfortunate that the modern movement in its support has been so bound up with, on the one hand, class privilege and an emphasis on "character training" at the expense of scholarship and a feeling for research, and on the other with excessive preoccupation regarding social justice for the underdog. Now that at last the problem of a truly all-embracing national education at all levels is having to be faced, it presents the nation with a jigsaw of twisted pieces which cannot fit together and which leave huge gaps in between.

England, Wales and Scotland have differing educational systems. In spite of large modernization campaigns all are over-burdened with a common legacy of too many obsolete, unsuitable school buildings, too many obligations or anomalies carried down from past voluntary initiatives, too few, undertrained, and over-worked teachers, and above all too many obsolete concepts regarding the processes of education and what they are for. In England and Wales in 1964 the *average* size of class in maintained schools was 32·6 children at junior level and 28·4 at senior. No more need be said about the quality of the education that can be given on this basis. The school-leaving age, at fifteen, is higher than in France or Germany but lower than Sweden (which, however, it is aimed to match by 1970 when the level will be raised to sixteen). In the United States the proportion continuing their schooling after this age is very much larger. The pace of progress is illustrated by grant-aided secondary schools, which had 161,000 pupils in 1910–11 and 1,060,000 in 1958. There is a drive to train more teachers, and to raise the standard of training. Some efforts are being made particularly to improve science teaching, although these are not on the scale or of the standard of recent American measures with the same aim. The standard of design of buildings erected since World War II is on the whole among the highest in Europe. Reforms such as the introduction of comprehensive schools, and attempts to reconcile the independent schools with the state system, add to the complexities and obstacles. Research on education is still almost negligible, although the cost of education is far the largest item of local authority expenditure, representing some 40 percent of it in England and Wales.

One of the most unhappy comparisons internationally for British education is the proportion of students who go on to take university courses. In 1900 the total university population of Great Britain was only 20,436, and in 1964 including those from overseas it was still only 126,000. West Germany with a population only 15 percent larger than Great Britain's had double as many university students. The ratio in New Zealand was double. American figures are not comparable, but the American total in university and similar higher educational institutions of all standards is about thirty-four times that of Great Britain while the United States population is rather more than three and a half times the British.

The low ratio of graduates in professions, already referred to for teaching, is a natural consequence. In even such an inherently advanced subject of study as town and country planning the campaign to raise the level of recruitment at least to first-degree standard is still not won, and the deficit of trained men is put at well over 3,000. In medicine the situation has become a national problem, with an alarming "brain drain" to the United States and the Commonwealth from among an already inadequate force of newly-trained doctors, who complain of "starvation pay," and lack of opportunities for advancing their professional experience in the conditions offered most of them for their work. Recent campaigns have opened what seem to be adequate opportunities for the training and employment of research scientists, but for technologists, and especially engineers, the position is much less satisfactory. The traditional professions of the armed services, the law and the church contrast in their relatively ample and excellent provision for training with most of the newer professions, on which the economic prosperity and social advancement of Britain largely depend. When it comes to numbers, quality and balance of postgraduate instruction the British performance shows up even worse. The proportion of Russians acquiring such third-stage education is around four times the British level, although in view of disparity of population the reverse of that ratio would make more sense.

At other levels provision for training and retraining remains inadequate. For example, government training centers to retrain redundant workers in fresh skills which are in short supply had only 6,000 places in 1966, rising to 8,000 in 1967. This was on a labor force of twenty-four and a half million.

Of the two great social requirements for enabling a nation to realize its full potential, education has been placed first only because, in terms of advanced European countries, progress in securing a minimum standard of health services has hitherto been relatively greater. This simply means that gross deficiencies in medical and environmental services are no longer involving mass epidemics, chronic deficiency diseases, or crippling levels of preventable illness. While further improvements in national education would undoubtedly and almost automatically produce substantial improvements in productivity and standards of life, it is much less certain that reductions, say, in sickness absence or incapacity might not be offset by increased wastage at other points. Looking back on the experience of the National Health Service it is difficult to avoid some sense of disappointment that so great an effort and expenditure has not manifestly produced greater dividends in national well-being, and in achievement. The nineteenth-century legacy of stunted growth and of such humiliating diseases as the *Englische Krankheit* (rickets) has been dealt with by measures which have placed the children of Britain over the past quarter-century among the best-tended and healthiest in the world. Average heights and weights have risen to levels comparing adequately with those of Scandinavian and other leading countries. The age of puberty has fallen steeply, bringing with it increased teenage problems. Diphtheria, poliomyelitis and other childhood scourges have been almost eliminated as normal risks.

As always, the removal of certain ills has merely enhanced the prominence of others which still confront us. The state of the nation's teeth, including children's teeth, is perhaps worsening rather than improving. Eyesight also gives serious concern. Problems arising from insufficient exercise at all ages are on the increase, and the heavy incidence of traffic casualties, coupled with increased urbanization, deprives many children of safe and healthy opportunities for carefree outdoor recreation on traditional patterns. Similarly water pollution limits opportunities for swimming, and air pollution taxes many towndwellers' health. The growth of lung cancer has been correlated with the mass habit of cigarette smoking. Epidemics of influenza and the common cold have proved disappointingly recalcitrant to medical research.

It is possible to measure not only the main deviations from good health, such as incidence of disease and shortfall below physical standards, but also the relative international position in such matters as intake of nutrients and provision of medical and paramedical services. Indeed the range of yardsticks internationally available in this area is almost embarrassingly large. In nearly all of them the leading place assumed by Britain during the second half of the nineteenth century has been fairly well maintained, but in view of recent trends in the staffing of the professions concerned, especially medicine and nursing, it would be rash to take a complacent view about future prospects. Indeed there are few instances where adverse effects of government intervention are more directly and clearly traceable than in the increasing difficulties of maintaining an adequate contemporary standard of provision for care of the nation's health.

Closely related problems are those of physical education, sport and recreation, in which government intervention is too recent for its effects to be assessed. In research and provision on mental health, and on family planning, the poorness of the state's record is evident.

It is important to note here a contrast between the cases of education and health. Especially in England, education has hitherto been something of vital concern only to a minority. Its mass provision to a high standard has never until very recently been generally accepted as an essential element in national priorities.

The discussion of educational aims has been highly subjective and inconclusive, and research on comparative methods of teaching and learning has been negligible. In the sphere of health, on the other hand, cholera and other potent educational forces convinced even the mid-Victorian individualists that health is indivisible, and that at least a minimum of sanitation, hygiene, preventive medicine and medicinal treatment is not a luxury for the privileged but a necessity for all. Nearly a hundred years later, at about the usual timelag, a strong research element was injected, with the result that, at least potentially, much of British medicine is now internationally advanced and respectably science-based, while education still has to reach a corresponding stage. On the other hand failures in economic growth have lately done for education something of what cholera last century did for health, in frightening ruling circles into spending quite a lot of money on it. In contrast the alarms about extravagances over the National Health Service have resulted in acute difficulties in obtaining the necessary money to bring obsolete hospitals and medical facilities and services abreast of the standards which application of modern knowledge would require. Particularly in the hospital service there is therefore the paradox that thousands of doctors and others from many countries are prepared to come and learn in Britain, and thus fill the gaps left by young British doctors who find the facilities and conditions too disheartening, and who prefer to emigrate on an increasing scale rather than put up with them. A similar situation might have arisen in the universities, but for the accident that the forced expansion of production of graduates coincided with a spell of unparalleled State generosity towards scientific research, of which the universities were main beneficiaries.

In both education and health the great professions which carry the main responsibilities have been embittered by recent governmental policies. This cannot fail to react on Britain's international position in these fields.

Consideration of Britain's role and status in science follows naturally at this point, and here the situation is even more confused and confusing. Although the individual credit for scientific discoveries becomes more and more difficult to assign, there is no room for argument that England was the main nursery of scientific pioneering during the formative generations of the seventeenth, eighteenth and early nineteenth centuries—the age of Newton, Faraday and Darwin, and that British achievement in scientific research still ranks among the highest. No doubt coincidentally, this is perhaps of all important activities the one in which administrators have been most consistently resolved to avoid intervention. It is also one in which the leading professional body, the Royal Society of London, has been conspicuously more concerned with the maintenance of scholarly standards and the advancement of knowledge than with defense of the material interests of scientists themselves.

Perhaps the most independent and authoritative international yardstick is the award of Nobel Prizes for Physics, Chemistry and Physiology or Medicine. In Physics since 1901 fifteen of these have come to Great Britain compared with twenty-three to USA and fourteen to Germany which is in third place. In Chemistry Germany tops the list with twenty-one, Great Britain being again second with fifteen, and USA third with thirteen. By an odd coincidence the British score and place is once more identical in Physiology or Medicine, the leader in this case being USA with twenty-eight and the third place being again taken by Germany with ten. Only in Physics is there any sign of a falling-off in British successes since 1950; in Chemistry successes in as many as six years out of fourteen and in Physiology or Medicine in five years out of fourteen seem to rule out any suggestion of relative decline. (Although not strictly relevant, at this point, it may be noted that while Great Britain has taken, after France, equal second place with the USA in numbers of Nobel Prizes for Literature since 1901, the only one of these won since 1950 was Sir Winston Churchill's in 1953. This, probably not unfairly, suggests a failure to maintain an outstanding role in that sphere.)

Scientific research generally is a field in which official financial support has been relatively most lavish since World War II, and expansion has been most rapid, wherever a strong base for it was already in existence, or had to be created for some powerful extraneous reason. The official Research Councils, like the University Grants Committee and the Arts Council, have on the whole been able to get the money without having too many strings attached to it, and to maintain a balance between giving some constructive leadership and avoiding undesirable intervention in detail. As the key role of science in modern civilization is ever more clearly and widely recognized, the excellence and vigorous growth of British science become an increasingly important national asset. They also, however, give rise to problems, both about the continuing rate of expansion and allocation of what is becoming a significant share of the Gross National Product, and about the effective harmonization with scientific principles and discoveries of a society and economy whose main beliefs and practices are still blissfully pre-scientific. This must be discussed later, but here we need to note that, while it is reassuring to find Britain still so strong in so essential a field of growth as science, the practical consequences of this to Britain are currently far less beneficial than they would be if the nation, and above all its leaders, really understood or cared about scientific principles and the scientific method.

This is well illustrated by the familiar and interminable story of British discoveries which have been handed over or left over for others to exploit, among the latest being the swept-wing aircraft. Pneumatic tires were patented in principle by R. W. Thomson, a Scot, in 1845, but the vital adaptation to the automobile was left to the Michelins in France in 1895. The chronometer was invented in 1735 by John Harrison, who received a handsome government prize in due course, but the commercial prize of selling chronometers in millions to the entire world has gone to the Swiss (who are thereby assisted to the position of being able to lend money to support the weakness of sterling). London in 1855 was the first place where steel was produced, by Sir Henry Bessemer, but superior American drive in exploiting this invention was one of the main factors in establishing the industrial leadership of the United States during the last third of the nineteenth century. The tank was first built in 1915 at Leicester as a weapon during World War I: the fact that the German, not the British army was effectively equipped with them in 1940, and was trained in their use by the methods devised by British strategists B. H. Liddell Hart and J. F. C. Fuller, came very close to losing us World War II in May–June 1940.

Terylene, discovered in England in 1941, was first marketed in 1950 as Dacron by an American firm.

Most of the contrary examples of British inventions successfully developed in Britain date from the eighteenth or early nineteenth century, such as the piston and condenser steam engines, the locomotive, the spinning jenny, frame and mule, the power loom, gas lighting and the ship's propeller. A partial exception appears to be the Hovercraft, sponsored by the National Research Development Corporation and now apparently on the threshold of wide-spread worldwide use. It is still, however, too early to judge results here. Technical men involved have expressed unhappiness publicly, and foreign concerns have in some respects outpaced British operators in starting international services from Britain.

It seems quite clear that while inventiveness has remained, despite all discouragement, a prominent feature of British life, inventions as a basis for new British industries underwent some crippling collapse soon after 1840, from which it has never properly recovered. It is a matter not of decadence but merely of chronic incapacity in British industry, or at least in too many parts of it, to discover quickly and apply promptly the fruits of new invention, which often cut across the grain of existing practice and arrangements.

CHAPTER 5
"The English Sickness"

The British economy today is such a varied and confusing mixture of the up-to-date and the obsolete that it almost defies summary analysis. Yet the Japanese economy shows even more extreme contrasts between great ultra-modern super-efficient groups and a welter of small almost medievally primitive industries and trades. In spite of this the competitive strength of Japan in such varied areas as the building of giant ships and the making of electron microscopes, the mass production of radio transistors or the development of automobiles able to stand up to Japanese driving appears uninhibited and virtually unhandicapped by this background.

Professor G. C. Allen in his recent searching analysis of *Japan's Economic Expansion* (OUP 1965) states that "contemporary Japan stands before the world as the classic model of a rapidly growing economy" and lists the following factors as mainly responsible for that country's rapid post-war growth:

1. The closing of the technical gap by the impact of new technology.
2. An exceptionally high rate of investment buttressed by a very high rate of saving, both institutional and personal.
3. The direction of investment into uses which yielded quick returns, and the absence of wasteful investment in armaments.
4. The large reserve army of workers and its successful transference from low-productivity to high-productivity occupations.
5. The reconstruction of the *zaibatsu* and the creation of other business groups capable of organizing developments.
6. A monetary system and policy which were successful both in accelerating expansion and in avoiding "overheated" economy.
7. A taxation system which kept clear of measures likely to curb industrial investment and damage personal incentives.

8. The effective use of official controls over foreign trade and payments.

In not a single one of these eight decisive points can it reasonably be claimed that the managers of the British economy have kept abreast of the Japanese. Yet the Japanese are far from being supermen; their own defects and mistakes have been many and gross, as they would be the first to admit. The speed with which they have overtaken Britain in so many fields so soon after their annihilating defeat in World War II is just one of the yardsticks which compel any honest and informed observer to reach harsh conclusions about the System.

One conspicuous feature of the British economy is the relatively slow growth of the labor force, which has expanded only by 50 percent since 1900, to a total of some twenty-four million. Owing to heavy emigration in previous decades and to the loss of 1·2 million killed in the two World Wars, the structure and balance of the working population has been weakened at a time when rapid technological change and the imperative need to overtake past arrears of modernization have been demanding massive retraining and redeployment. In certain respects the British record of mobility has been good, and this applies particularly to the field in which most countries lag—the movement of excessive manpower off the farms into manufacturing industry and services. British agriculture, while retaining only 3½ percent of the total working population, manages to supply the nation with some two-thirds of its temperate-zone grown foodstuffs. Many countries still have more than half their workers in agriculture, and while most advanced nations have greatly reduced the proportion during the past few decades Great Britain has consistently led the world in maintaining this trend. (It is fair however to emphasize that as vast food-exporting countries the United States and Canada are inherently much handicapped in achieving any such extreme reduction.) British agriculture has provided for British industry something of the labor reserve which has been furnished by immigration in some of the new countries overseas, but clearly this process must now be nearly at an end. Its cessation intensifies the need for greatly increased labor mobility, and higher levels of industrial training.

The comparative totals are as unfavorable to British industry as they are favorable to British agriculture. Somehow, whatever reasons or excuses may be put forward for it, British industry needs roughly two-thirds as many workers in total as United States industry to produce an aggregate value of some £26 billion ($72,800,000,000) * as against some $200 billion. As there are important elements in British industry which are as efficient as any in the world the level of the majority is even lower than these totals indicate.

Here, unmistakably, is a field of critical importance in which the British performance has lately been inferior to that of others. It probably out-ranks the break-up of the British Empire as a source of international doubts regarding the future of Britain, and so long as it persists no achievements or progress in other fields are likely to set such doubts at rest. Yet there is no simple or uncontroversial explanation of the causes, or recipe for the cure, of this poor performance. Learned expositions are apt to boil down to an expanded and complicated version of the Victorian porter's answer to the passenger asking why his train was late: "Well Sir, the train before was behind, and this train was behind before besides."

It is widely suggested that British workers "do less work" than their counterparts in other countries. In terms of hours worked, or at any rate spent at the workplace, this can be shown to be incorrect. Leading continental countries, and the USA, work shorter hours and take more paid holidays a year than British. The British average of weekly hours worked was 47·5 in April 1965, only marginally below the 1938 level of 47·7.

Three modifying factors have to be examined here—loss of time from labor disputes, unemployment and sickness absences. In none of these, however, is the British record bad.

Strikes and labor disputes are always ranked high in the scale of news values by the British press, and salutary as this is it may well give an exaggerated impression of the proportion of working time lost on that account, and of the international implications. In fact, as the figures show, the percentage of time lost was quite small, and it compared favorably with the record of other advanced countries such as the United States and France. It did not, however, compare at all favorably with the record of Switzerland where days lost on this account were nil, and until Britain can match Switzerland in this way no one need be surprised if the Swiss exercise their right of criticism when they are asked to support sterling.

Sickness also constitutes a disturbing toll on the national manpower. During 1963 the number of new claims for sickness benefit was

* Figures used for dollar equivalents are based on exchange rates before the devaluation of the pound.

about 9·3 million, and the number incapacitated by sickness at one time ranged from under 900,000 in August to 1,244,000 in February, or about 5 percent of the labor force. Excessive as these figures are they can hardly be reckoned a major factor in the performance of the economy in comparison with any reduced level which might practically be attainable, or is in fact attained by other countries.

The third great toll on manpower in statistical terms is unemployment, but here the British record is excellent, with a total of registered unemployed ranging from as low as 280,000—little over 1 percent —in July 1965 to peaks of 573,000 (1963 average) and 600,000 (Jan 1967). Unemployment in USA in 1965 (May) was estimated at 3,335,000 (4·4 percent). Such levels have been characteristic of the American economy in recent years, but as the United States working population in 1965 was almost exactly three times the British (75·7 million against 25·1 million) the consequences of such a ratio to the national output are not necessarily comparable. It should also be noted that as the ratio of total population of Great Britain to total population of the USA is only 1:3.5 the British proportion of workers is significantly higher. Moreover the British figures include a significant residue whose true reason for unemployment is that they are unemployable.

Whatever, therefore, may be the explanation of the comparative failings of the British economy, they cannot be attributed to an insufficient labor force, to working shorter hours, to an inadequate level of employment, or to excessive levels of working days lost through holidays, or through industrial disputes, or through sickness. Unemployment, moreover, has ranged during the past forty years from a peak of three and a quarter million in September 1932 to a level well below the number of unfilled vacancies without apparently much affecting the disappointing relative progress of the British economy—a significant indication of the deep-rooted and massive character of the underlying weaknesses. These, like a stubborn layer of hard-pan, underlie the fertile-seeming soil of British industry, and have stultified many honest and able efforts to transform its productivity.

In trying to narrow the range of possible causes and explanations one must turn next to the stock of modern equipment and of available amounts of power which are so vital to economic productivity. Here three factors are probably decisive—the investment and horse-power per worker, the quality and up-to-dateness of equipment and the much less readily measurable adequacy of equipment in relation to requirements. (Energy consumption per worker in the United Kingdom in terms of coal equivalent was in 1967 11,197 lbs. compared with 19,339 lbs. in USA and a world average of 3,400 lbs.)

Since L. Rostas in 1948 produced in his *Comparative Productivity in British and American Industry* the long-needed statistical analysis of the growing gulf in industrial performance which had been worrying the less purblind British observers for nearly a century, vast numbers of words and statistics have been published on this subject. Sometimes the object has been to advance knowledge and sometimes to hammer the facts home to those who simply will not begin to believe them until they have been repeated enough in words of one syllable to ensure that anyone who keeps more than half awake on these matters knows them by heart. The sheer time which it has taken to awaken British industry to these basic and elementary facts is a most eloquent indicator of the lack of economic competence and the somnolence and resistance to enlightenment of large sectors of it. A hundred years is really too long.

An excellent summary, already seven years old, is given in PEP's *Growth in the British Economy: A Study of Economic Problems and Policies in Contemporary Britain,* from which it is worth quoting the summary of Dr Rostas's findings as supplemented by Professor Frankel in 1957:

> Out of thirty-four industries chosen for their comparability and the availability of data, American labour productivity (output per man-hour) exceeded British labour productivity in thirty-three industries in 1948. The one exception, where British productivity exceeded American, was the manufactured ice industry. Among the other thirty-three industries, United States output per man-hour was over four times the British in seven industries; over three times the British in five; over twice the British in a further seven; and over one-and-a-half times in another nine industries . . . The rather reassuring things that can be said about economic growth in the rest of the world in peace time during the present century in relation to the United States cannot be said about the United Kingdom in the period since the second world war. A good deal of statistical information exists for this period, and however one interprets the figures or questions their accuracy, they cannot but show a lower rate of growth for the United Kingdom in comparison with most other industrialised countries.

A table comparing growth in real national productivity between a pre-war year and 1957 shows that "The United Kingdom has by far the lowest rate of growth, only 35 percent, against an average of 59 percent for the OEEC countries as a whole, 120 percent for Western Germany and 129 percent for the United States."

Even in the steel industry, which has one of the best labor relations records, an American management consultant has calculated that three workers are required to produce in Britain an amount which one would produce in America. In automobiles each American worker averages 11 vehicles produced in a year; the British average is just over 5.

It was commonly estimated in the early 'fifties that the American worker in manufacturing industry enjoyed between two and two-and-a-half times as much mechanical assistance as his British counterpart, this being also precisely the difference in their industrial productivity. Emphasis was therefore placed on the poor showing of Britain compared to other industrial countries in net investment rate. Although an expansion in this was achieved in the early 'fifties it was not enough to catch up with continental industrial countries such as Western Germany, France, Italy, Sweden and Belgium. Worse still, during the mid-'fifties the British percentage increase in output per man-hour remained the lowest in the "league", being hardly more than a third of Italy's, and lower even than that of Denmark, the only country with a lower investment per employee, and also sharing a low population growth.

While the lack of modern equipment appeared until recently to be a main factor in Britain's lagging industrial performance recent experience has shown that the true explanation cannot be so simple. During the later 'fifties and early 'sixties strenuous efforts were made to increase investment, with some success. In 1964 British gross domestic fixed capital formation rose to £5,800 million ($16,240 million) compared with £4,912 million ($13,754 million) in 1963—an increase of 18 percent. It formed a similar percentage of the Gross National Product, slightly higher than that for USA and still much lower than the ratios for Japan, Germany, the Netherlands, France and Italy. Yet this expanded investment somehow did not, as had confidently been expected, lead to a soaring level of production. For 1965 that level was only 2½ percent above 1964. Lord Cromer, Governor of the Bank of England, who shared the widespread mystification over this, said in February 1966, "I have constantly been surprised that the aggregate new investment in industry in this country, which has been very substantial over recent years, has not produced more output." As he pointed out, although British investment overseas has been large there is no recent evidence that British industry has thereby been deprived of capital. For some reason the investment which has belatedly been made in Britain has not brought the level of results which contemporary experience in a wide range of competing nations would lead us to anticipate. What are the reasons?

One undoubtedly is that Britain, the pioneer of selective and well-judged productive investment in the nineteenth century, has partly forgotten the importance of backing the most progressive managements in the most promising growth industries. There has been too much appetite for economically unjustified investments, either through lack of rigorous appraisal, or on grounds of "social" or "prestige" considerations, the true price of which has never been reckoned up and faced, particularly by politicians.

The general impact of prestige spending on the performance of the British economy must be outlined here. Part of that impact is indirect. The mistaken attempt to keep Britain equipped to act like a twentieth-century imitation of some imaginary and idealized nineteenth-century Great Power led to excessive and usually abortive expenditure on a disappearing series of vast overseas bases in Egypt, East Africa, Cyprus, Malta, Singapore, Aden and elsewhere. These bases called for large conventional military forces, ships and aircraft to lend them credibility, and also for the backing of greatly expanded diplomatic, technical aid and propaganda services. Not content with all this, shattered Britain after World War II insisted also on becoming an independent nuclear power, which involved a vast, and, as it proved, largely abortive investment, not only in nuclear research, development and production, but in extremely costly delivery vehicles such as rockets and V-bombers. So little was the disparity of these commitments to future British resources understood by the governments of the 'fifties that powerful lobbies were allowed to develop for additional prestige adventures, such as joining the space race and developing supersonic commercial aircraft. The idea gained currency that to keep up Britain's station as a "Great Power", she needed not only to maintain far more costly overseas forces than ever before, but also to dazzle the world by spell-binding new projects whose utility, if any, was far from commensurate with their cost.

The penalty of these vain and foolish policies was multiple. Not only did they divert huge sums from badly-needed productive investment in education, new highways, port and railway modernization, electronic equipment and health, libraries and other services, but they tended constantly to overstrain the balance of payments and thus create the notorious "Stop-Go" mismanagement of the economy for which the 'fifties and 'sixties will be remembered. The sense of frustration created by this chronic process in turn reduced the morale and damped down the enterprise of British management, while the accompanying high levels of personal taxation greatly reduced incentive among the most able and vigorous. Some of these joined the "brain drain" while others alleviated their frustration by "taking things easy" and refraining from initiating promising but personally unrewarding projects. The effect of "Stop-Go" was greatly to extend in many cases the period between the original planning of a project and its eventual full operation, thus raising costs, and prolonging uneconomic working of plant or premises due for replacement. Changing circumstances had meanwhile not infrequently partially outdated the new facility, or rendered it inappropriate to altered market or operating requirements. Where managements attempted to cope with such situations by revising plans or altering specifications, further wasteful expenditure or frictions were introduced. Thus the higher productivity on which any chance of a healthy balance of payments rested was partly inhibited by the recurrent dislocations of the economy imposed to deal at short notice with emergencies resulting from the disparity between commitments too lightly assumed and earnings over-estimated, on an assumption that British industrial managements would achieve a rate of progress which they failed to make. Part of the failure was traceable to the disruption of their work by the arbitrary and sometimes panic decisions of the managers of sterling, and so the vicious circle completed itself.

There were, however, other important factors working in the same direction. Lack of adequate economic analysis, the obstinate refusal seriously to study or learn about "planning", and the lack of training and full professional competence, both in the economic departments of government and elsewhere in the management of the economy, resulted in a large-scale misdirection and misapplication of investment.

The denial of much-needed investment resources for highways is described on pages 246–251.

Heavy investment was, however, allowed to proceed in the commercially profitable speculative building of office blocks in city centers. This usually added greatly to traffic congestion and passed on concealed extra costs to industry and the community. Here again the losses were aggravated by persistent denial of the necessary resources for effective long-term planning to adapt city redevelopment to modern needs. Congestion, loss of working time, and delays in production schedules and in delivery of exports were a few of the forms in which the omission of necessary investment, and the acceleration of investment much less essential at the time, had its impact on the sluggish economic growth of Britain during the 'fifties.

In addition, much of the investment for which in broad terms a good case existed was done in a way which much reduced its value. Sometimes the reasons were political. A good example was the government insistence in 1959 on proceeding simultaneously with no less than five vast nuclear power stations costing upwards of £60 million ($ 168 million) each. That decision was made in the course of a panic, based on a mistaken view of forward fuel shortages, with the result (which I forecast at a public inquiry in December of that year) that the country has been saddled with hundreds of millions of pounds' worth of nuclear plant already outdated by the time of coming into commission. This was not the fault of the Central Electricity Generating Board, which was bound by a Ministerial directive. In other cases bad misjudgments have been made on technological alternatives, such as the choice of diesel traction rather than electrification for railway modernization in the 'fifties. The government's advisers half a century ago recommended main line electrification, but they never lived to see their views at last proved correct in 1966–67.

It is clear from the disparity between investment and increases in production, compared to results achieved in other countries, that there must have been a serious and widespread failure to direct recent British investment to the points where it would best be reflected in gains to the national economy. Unfortunately, thanks to the tradition of deciding such matters in the dark, there is such a dearth of relevant information and analysis that it will not be possible for several years to reconstruct at all accurately in detail just where the investment effort of the 'fifties and early 'sixties most seriously went wrong. Like the survivors of the Charge of the Light Brigade we can only be sure, as we lick our wounds, that someone has blundered. Is it really ours not to reason why?

This, however, is still not the whole of the story. Much effective re-equipment has been achieved, and there is now room for argument how far British equipment actually is older and less efficient at the present day. A study by the McGraw-Hill organization, published in 1966 with the backing of the Ministry of Technology, the Board of

Trade and the Machine Tool Traders Association shows that 62 percent of machine tools in use in Britain are over ten years old, compared with 59 percent in 1961, but an American survey on identical lines made by McGraw-Hill in 1963 showed that, at least at that time, the percentage of over-age machines was even higher than in Britain now. The French situation generally was no better, although some British industries, such as ship-building and marine engineering, textile machinery makers and heavy industrial plant constructors made a particularly poor showing, with more than 75 percent of their machinery over age.

It is in the utilization of plants that comparisons become more strikingly adverse to Britain. Firms with works abroad as well as in Great Britain produce copious evidence that restrictive practices and rigid resistances to shift working deprive the British economy and the British worker of most of the potential cost advantages of labor-saving modern machinery.

In February 1966 the Chairman of English Sewing Cotton, Sir Cyril Harrison, stated that, working identical machines in the US and Lancashire, they obtained double the production per man-hour in America, where the machines were worked 144 hours weekly, 51 weeks a year with 100 percent staff attendance, while in Lancashire the machines were operated only for 100 hours a week with 10 percent absenteeism for a 49-week year.

An interesting cross-check is provided by Professor J. H. Dunning's recent survey of US-owned companies operating in Britain. In terms of output per unit of input employed compared with the average for British companies, the US-owned firms were ahead by nearly 60 percent in chemicals, nearly 40 percent in vehicles and over 20 percent in metals, and in food, drink and tobacco they showed higher labor productivity, lower ratio of administration to total costs and higher capital/labor intensity.

Such examples, which could be multiplied indefinitely, are no accident. The wasteful use of labor is one of the dominant objectives in the running of British industry, and is promoted and maintained by continuous effort on the part of union officials and shop stewards. It is acquiesced in, more or less gracefully, by a cowardly tradition of management, which has largely prevented the facts from becoming generally known until the recent economic crisis at last smoked them out. The number of man-hours devoted actually to preventing the economic use of man-hours in Britain must be substantial. Even in 1966, after all the interminable exhortations, lectures, appeals and Parliamentary and government interventions the great new automated colliery at Bevercotes in the East Midlands stood idle for months because the trade union side was unable to agree on a modern pay structure accepted by the workers concerned themselves. It took years of intense top-level effort to secure a green light from the trade unions for the new liner freight trains. Apart from the tremendous economic loss involved in this chronic stupidity the diversion of top management effort and thought from problems that really contribute to production is perhaps equally serious.

It needs to be borne in mind, in discussing what may be termed the gratuitous British-made inefficiencies, such as restrictive practices of many types and refusal to operate costly machines long enough to realize their potential, that these are far from representing the sum total of wealth lost through inefficiency in general. That sum also includes vast losses through such "normal" factors as staff standing idle waiting for the next job to be ready, or because their particular tasks have an intermittent or seasonal character, or through futile and unnecessary paper-work.

L. N. Norton, Finance and Administration Director of General Precision Systems Ltd. has given estimates based on consultants' observations of time not fully employed in *efficient* companies. They indicate that, even in such relatively advanced firms, time utilization can be as low as 25 percent in maintenance, around 30 percent in drawing offices, 40 percent in production control, and up to 65 percent in Accounts and Wages. A 35 percent waste of paid time is thus among the more favorable performances for indirect production workers, whose relative numbers are rapidly rising—in engineering their ratio to direct producers was 2:1 in 1966 against 1:2 in 1950. Mr. James Duncan, President of a specialist firm of consultants, is quoted as stating recently:

> The equivalent of approximately 4,000,000 additional workers would contribute to increased national output of industry and business if the United Kingdom were to adopt and foster an attitude for full labor utilization, and effect proper controls.

While the basis of this estimate is not clear the order of magnitude suggested appears quite conservative.

Poor performance therefore is a compound of several quite distinct elements—deliberate insistence on over-manning and under-use of modern equipment, deliberate and vigilant persecution of particular workers whose zeal leads them to exceed a pace dictated in the interests of the slower and less industrious brethren, unreadiness on the part of managements as well as workers to face change in such matters as working hours, even where it would increase output, pay and effective leisure, and failure on the part of managements to avoid time-consuming and frustrating holdups in the flow of work, even where these are chronic and readily preventable by known methods. Probably few of these factors are unique in Britain, but what is unique among advanced countries is the extraordinary stranglehold which they have been permitted to acquire over the economy at so many key points. In addition there are the factors among managers themselves, such as lack of training, scarcity of men able to make sound technical and economic judgments, and unwillingness to make great exertions for small and heavily taxed remuneration. According to a report by Associated Industrial Consultants the "take-home pay" of an executive earning £2,500 ($7,000) a year is only £1,977 in Britain against £2,320 in France, £2,174 in Canada and £2,143 in West Germany.

For perspective, however, certain other points should be borne in mind. Although it in no way excuses the conduct of those who have so badly let Britain down, it is somewhat remarkable that the nation has been able still to carry such a burden of parasitism and such excessive overseas commitments without sinking under them much more rapidly and completely than it actually has. None but a basically strong and tough nation could stagger on so nearly by its own efforts under such a load. Although Britain's crisis is "real" and grave its identification and its present repercussions are as much as anything a function of recent advances, still fragmentary and imprecise, in econometric techniques. The patient, in other words, has been as sick as this before, if not more so, in days when no doctor had the skill and instruments to point it out to him and to the world. During roughly the first third of this century the United Kingdom's national income per head was virtually at a standstill—in three decades it grew only by a miserable total of 1 per cent in real terms. During the second three decades, ending in 1959, the growth was 14 percent, notwithstanding that the level in 1946 had been set back by World War II to lower than it had been ten years earlier. Had we a Wellsian Time Machine we could send back into the London of 1906 a group of economists perfectly equipped to trigger off a British economic emergency fully as alarming as that of sixty years later. Edwardian complacency and mystique at that time shielded the nation from exposures which would have done it plenty of good, and saved untold national and international suffering.

The great Railway Age expansionist economy, which yielded increases in income per head of some 20 percent in each of the three decades between 1856 and 1886, had been allowed to run down to no more than one-eighth of this level of growth during the two decades preceding World War I. Although we are apt fondly to think that at least the golden sovereign of Edwardian Britain possessed a long-lost stability of purchasing power, in fact it depreciated by 10 percent in the five years 1905–10—a curve already pointing straight towards its present miserable level of three shillings in terms of the pound sterling of 1900. This great economic defeat, from which stem, at least in part, nearly all Britain's later defeats, was and is generally unrecognized outside specialist circles. How differently it would have been reported and enlarged upon if it had happened in the economically more sophisticated and literate conditions of today.

Finally, the climate of politico-economic opinions changes almost as rapidly as the feminine hemline. Although the severity of the recent shake-out is undoubtedly a salutary and welcome thing for Britain's future, those who have justly been saddled with responsibility for it may secretly console themselves that they might have escaped as lightly as their equally culpable predecessors if the storm had not happened to break after a probably temporary burst of economic growth in a number of countries whose capacity to maintain it is still problematical. Where now, for example, does the German economic miracle stand? The particular indices on which most stress is currently laid may well put a somewhat worse complexion on Britain's relative performance than fuller indices which will be available by the 'seventies, probably in a weighted and combined form doing less rough justice to the intricacies of international comparisons in this difficult field.

It would be wrong to use any or all of these considerations to minimize the economic emergency, or to discourage going right through with most drastic remedial measures. But they may at least give encouragement for applying, in reference to the longer term, the maxim that no bad news is actually so bad, just as no good news is really so good, as it seems under the shock of its first impact.

Perhaps one feature of the recent economic deadlock which will most astonish those who reflect on it after wiser counsels have prevailed may be the fact that the very groups in Britain which most complacently resisted any changes before they were too late—both on the Left and the Right politically—were those who were most vociferous in demanding to spend, either individually, or through the State, the expanding income which they were ensuring would not be earned. Another, closely related, was the childish and unreasonable resentment publicly and officially directed in the earlier stages of the crisis against those in Europe who quite properly and discreetly pointed out problems outstanding in Britain which the British government should itself have pointed out first, had it not chosen to leave to foreigners the odium of forcing it to face its duty to the nation.

There are many possible indices, simple or combined, of economic progress, and not all of them give the same comparative results. In any case, there cannot in the nature of things be any direct and comprehensive way of measuring the relative progress of widely differing national economies. The indices employed as indirect indicators are in each case open to technical criticisms regarding their content and method of calculation, and may also be interpreted in conflicting senses. Nevertheless they all have a certain significance, and when most or all point the same way it would be foolish to ignore their message.

One of the latest and most thorough specialist contributions to the subject is the paper on "International Comparisons of Income Levels —A Suggested New Measure", by two Oxford economists, W. Beckermann and R. Bacon, published in the *Economic Journal* for September 1966, pp. 519–36. Out of hundreds of possible bases they have concluded that the best for estimating "real" consumption per head is a combination of cement production, steel consumption, number of domestic letters sent, meat consumption and numbers of radio receivers, telephones and road vehicles, all calculated on a per head basis for 1960 in relation to the UK, which thus has an index of 100. Being based on consumption rather than on production these figures may unduly favor a country temporarily living beyond its means. Being based on 1960 they give a more favorable place to a country which is slipping back than would currently be justified. With these cautions they will serve as a useful guide. Of the eighty countries so listed, Ethiopia is at the bottom, with an index of only 1, and two of the world's six largest nations, Pakistan and Indonesia, come in seventy-fifth equal place with 4, narrowly surpassed by the second largest nation, India, with 5. China, the largest of all, comes fifty-first with 15 and the USSR twenty-sixth with 35.

For the top twenty nations, the indices and ranking are:

USA	140	1
Sweden	125	2
Canada	108	3
Australia	106	4
UK	100	5
Switzerland	96	6
New Zealand	95	7
Denmark	87	8
West Germany	86	9
Norway	83	10
France	75	11
Belgium	74	12
Netherlands	73	13
Finland	67	14
Austria	66	15
Italy	53	16
Iceland	48	17
Ireland	47	18
Japan	46	19
Czechoslovakia	45	20

This probably gives as fair and balanced a picture as is currently practicable of average standards of living in the various countries. Such a concept is however more meaningful for fairly homogeneous, egalitarian and smallish countries such as the Scandinavians than for large, diverse, socially stratified ones such as Japan and Italy. In these a large minority group is much better off, and the much larger majority much worse off, than the figures suggest.

Among the larger nations Great Britain and the United States are intermediate, having a relatively high general minimum standard but also a pretty wide spread of incomes. The low ranking of the USSR reflects the low priority given to consumer goods in Soviet planning.

A distinction must also be borne in mind between the socialist, or Welfare State, type of structure with high taxation and much redistribution of personal income in cash and in kind through collective channels, in contrast to the more individual pattern. There is a contrast, too, between both these and the state carrying heavy tax burdens for such remoter purposes as military commitments, economic aid or space research, which do not contribute so directly or simply to standards of living. Some countries such as Great Britain may fall in more than one of these classes; in our case the first and the last.

Another distinction is between the well-established rankings and those only recently attained by *arriviste* nations from lower down the scale. In such cases the significance of the figures is very different, partly because the income is related to very different backgrounds of family and social capital equipment. This is perhaps most conspicuous with the oldest established mass-consuming country the United States, but in Great Britain also the percentage of households equipped with many articles formerly considered luxuries is now fairly high. The following figures based on the AGB Home Audit refer mostly to June 1965:

Percentage of British households possessing:

Electric Irons	94	Electric Cookers	34
Television Sets	87	(do. and Gas together)	97
Water Heaters	85	Electric Hairdriers	32
Household Radios	85	Record Players	24
Vacuum Cleaners	78	Radiograms	23
Electric Fires	77	Clothes Driers	19
Gas Cookers	63	Electric Toasters	16
Washing Machines	56	Tape Recorders	14
Gas, Paraffin and Solid		Central Heating	13
Fuel Room Heaters	48	Electric Food and	
Electric Kettles	45	Drink Mixers	8
Refrigerators	42	Electric Floor	
Electric Blankets	40	Polishers	2
Dry Shavers	37	Electric Dishwashers	1

According to the class analysis of the British population used for listener research by the British Broadcasting Corporation the "upper middle class" accounts for 6 percent of the total, the "lower middle class" for 24 percent and the "working class" for the residual 70 percent. All the items ranking above record players in this list must therefore be more or less widely present in "working-class" homes.

In 1963 total consumers' expenditure in the United Kingdom worked out at about £366 (about $1019) per head of the population, the percentage breakdown being: household food 26·9; Housing, including taxes on it 9·9; Clothing, including footwear 9·3; Durable consumer goods, including private vehicles 8; Hotels, catering, laundries, dry cleaning etc. 7·7; Tobacco 6·6; Alcoholic drinks 6·0; Fuel and light 5·1, and a number of minor items. Some of the more significant of these were: Travel by Public Transport, 3·3; Private motoring running costs, 3·2; Consumers' expenditure abroad, 1·8, and entertainments

1·6. In terms of 1958 prices the annual increase of consumer expenditure over the previous seven years had ranged between about £300 million ($840 million) and £700 million ($1,960 million), or roughly £6–£14 ($16·80–$39·20) a head. Also on a per head basis, personal-savings averaged £33 and taxes £35.

In certain fields such as housing, hospitals and schools there are serious disadvantages in having attained a relatively high standard long ago, in the shape of excessive numbers of over-age but still serviceable structures which should but need not be demolished and replaced. In the case of housing the United Kingdom ranks sixth among countries for which figures are available, with an estimated 17·5 million dwelling units in 1965, or nearly one to every three persons. Of these in 1961 98·7 percent were equipped with inside piped water and 78·7 percent (England and Wales) with baths.

To round out the picture it is necessary to add a number of indicators of the use of services and of cultural and leisure activities. Among indoor occupations watching television programs is one of the most significant. There were 12·75 million TV licenses in Britain in June 1963, and it is estimated by BBC Listener Research that, taking all programs together, the hours of viewing weekly amount to about eleven for the "upper middle class" and about thirteen for the "working class". Of the competing networks Independent (commercial) Television has a markedly stronger hold on viewers under thirty and on "working class" viewers as a whole, while the BBC is stronger relatively in the higher age groups and the higher social groups. In 1964–65 the average British daily TV audience was nearly twenty-five million, or just under half the population. In 1964, Britain accounted for more than one in four of TV sets in Western Europe, and nearly one-twelfth of those in the world as a whole.

The British remain among the world's most avid newspaper readers. Circulations such as those of the *Daily Mirror* (five million), *Daily Express* (four million), *Daily Mail* (two and a half million), and of several Sunday newspapers are rarely matched elsewhere.

London as a center of international film production has advanced strikingly in relation to such rivals as Hollywood and Rome, although largely with the aid of American capital. There is even reason to believe that the series of internationally successful films originating from London is transferring here the doubtful privilege, so long held by Hollywood, of presenting the world first and foremost with an unforgettable picture of our national idiocies and weaknesses.

The revival of the live theater and of British acting, and more lately play-writing, has placed Britain in the forefront of the world stage. With some 200 professional theaters, thirty of them operating in London's West End, the British stage is quantitatively as well as qualitatively in a leading position. This is a recent development based largely on sound and thorough training and on intelligent and keen patronage.

In music, particularly since the Festival of Britain in 1951, progress has been spectacular, and if London is not already the musical capital of the world it is now very near becoming it, with an embarrassment of riches in simultaneous concerts often of the first order. Design and construction of modern concert halls has advanced much faster than that of the National Theatre, and of other cultural buildings such as libraries, where the record has been appalling. The Royal Ballet keeps Britain among the leading countries in that field.

In sculpture Great Britain has in Henry Moore the recognized world leader, with a number of others in the front rank. British painting has since the days of Constable and Turner failed to hold a place of pre-eminence, and despite the recent abdication of French painters from their long supremacy painting must be ranked with literature, both prose and poetry, as currently falling well short of its highest former flights in Britain. Nevertheless the work of Francis Bacon is perhaps now more influential internationally than that of other living painters except the ageless Picasso.

In sport, so largely a British invention, the record over recent years has often been disappointing. The Olympic Games, where international standards are set and measured, have not indicated so far any remarkable revival, such as was however registered by British footballers in winning the World Cup in 1966. The attitude towards amateurism in sport generally has been similar to that of the British Civil Service towards amateurism in administration, and has led to similar results. Even on the Turf, so long a pride of British sport, victories of foreign horses have become monotonous.

One of the more disturbing, although only roughly measurable, recent trends in Britain has been the great increase in betting and gambling. In 1961 turnover in its organized forms was estimated at between £750 and £1,000 million ($2,100 and $2,800 million) an apparent jump of some 50 percent since two years before. British football pools have spread their influence quite widely over the Continent, locking up man-hours and paid manpower on a significant scale.

While the British governments of the 'fifties had no great success in expanding national production generally, their legislation in favor of gambling certainly hit the jackpot. It stimulated a rate of expansion which would have been highly appreciated had they been able to achieve it in some more useful field. Licensed Betting Offices, an innovation introduced in 1960, had climbed to over 15,000 by June 1964, in addition to over 11,000 bookmakers and 113 Betting Agency permits. Gaming machines in use in January 1964 numbered 24,699, two-thirds of them being in social clubs; total annual net takings from this source alone were £10·3 million ($28·8 million).

In the Metropolitan Police area alone more than a quarter of a million indictable offenses were known to the police in 1964, an increase of 11 percent on the previous year, while the proportion of crimes cleared up fell from 24·2 to 21·6 percent. 1964 was the first year in which nationally more than a million indictable offenses were known to the police, cases of violence against the person having increased by 17 percent.

Law enforcement and respect for law must therefore be numbered among the important areas of civilization in which Britain has definitely fallen back under governments since World War II. One belated advance which at last removed Great Britain from the list of backward countries in a significant respect was the abolition of capital punishment from 1964.

Although so imperfectly capable of policing the United Kingdom itself, British governments still aspired to police much of the rest of the world on a unilateral or bilateral basis. In 1960 the total strength of the three armed services was 503,000, compared with 759,000 in 1900, when the Boer War was in progress. Defense expenditure then rose to £124 million ($347 million). At the peak of World War I it reached £2,400 million, falling again to a low point of £103 million in 1932 after the 1931 cuts, and rising to a World War II peak of £5,125 million in 1944. From this it was reduced to £741 million in 1949, only to climb again to £2,120 million in 1965–66. While the Army has been reduced since the outset of the century by more than 60 percent, the Navy's manpower stood at about the same level. In 1900, however, the Royal Navy was stronger in ships than any two other navies in the world while in 1966 it would no longer, even if augmented by all the world's other navies, equal that of the United States. The operational Fleet was reduced to only six vessels of cruiser size or larger. The only respect in which the relative importance of the armed forces of the 1960s matched that of 1900 was in the weight of its burden on the British taxpayer and the British balance of payments.

Summing up this condensed and inevitably selective review, the evidence regarding the relative progress or falling behind of a nation such as Britain is inherently a complex blend of subjective and objective, measurable and imponderable factors. Having discussed in the previous Part the broad long-term historical and geographical elements, it has remained for this one to seek to focus the recent and current form which the nation has shown over a fairly wide spectrum of developments and activities. These together illustrate trends and changes in relative ranking compared with other countries, in much the same way as changes in the current prices of items in an imaginary housewife's shopping basket are accepted by statisticians and by public opinion as defining trends in the cost of living. The method has its obvious limitations and faults, but at least it is more reliable than the purely descriptive and rhetorical alternatives.

Population changes are shown to have worked against the former successful pretensions of Britain as a world power. In addition to London's loss of control of subject populations running into hundreds of millions, the United Kingdom itself now makes up little more than 1½ percent of world population, as against 3 percent at the outset of this century. The emergence of much larger states, combining greater resources, more advanced technology and equally active worldwide political and economic interests would in itself have involved inescapable readjustments of status and priorities to the disadvantage of Britain, even if British performance generally had been improving faster than it has. On the other hand it is arguable that Britain's loss of first-class power status is not the most serious feature of recent trends. That status was in important respects an illusion, created during a long vacuum in power politics. In the nuclear and jet age the new so-called super-powers are themselves at the mercy of all kinds of curbs and limitations on their freedom of action. These now come very near to denying effective Great Power status to any state, however strong, and to placing in commission that historic role. It would only be a slight exaggeration therefore to say that on the level of Great Power politics Britain has lost something which she never had, beyond sharing a widespread illusion of possessing it, and which no one else has permanently taken from her, because such a role is passing beyond national reach. As any rejected lover knows, that is not to say that the anguish involved or the sense of being deprived of something to live for is any the less keen and real.

Quite equally important, although still little understood, is the value in the future world of having a well-balanced population freed from the awkward or even nightmarish effects of uncontrolled increase, and consistent with realizing the full potential of the nation in terms of education, health, housing, work and leisure. Although the British rate of population increase is still inconveniently rapid, there is reason to believe that the present birth control revolution will soon bring it more nearly into balance. While other countries, including all the largest, will for some time be still struggling with the increasing embarrassments of mounting over-population Britain will be the best placed for concentrating national resources on the systematic improvement of the quality of living. To indicate the likelihood of such an opportunity is not to predict that it will be seized. That is quite a different matter, in view of the old British custom of entrusting authority to those who can be best depended upon to throw any such opportunities away.

Perhaps the most critical area in this respect is education, and here the great question-mark hangs. Will the new-found and terribly belated awakening to the importance of education for Britain be matched by the necessary revelation of what education in the scientific age really means, and just how it differs from traditional scholasticism? At this moment it is probable that Britain is in educational terms more seriously at a disadvantage compared with several other advanced nations than at any time since the fifteenth century. The situation is fluid, and although at least another decade must be lost before it can be adequately corrected, the possibility of far-reaching correction has at least been won by recent efforts. Closely linked with education is the problem of vocational and professional training at all levels. Here the response to the challenge of new conditions is even less advanced in Britain, but again it has begun, and it may be sufficiently speeded up to provide the necessary leadership and expertise for a major British revival before too long.

Health in the widest sense is a second area of decisive importance, in which the organizing efforts of the 'forties over the National Health Service have fulfilled only a fraction of their promise. Nevertheless, in contrast to education, there is in existence now a first-class scientific base for the qualitative and comprehensive fulfillment of that promise by a second great effort during the early 'seventies. It seems that only a lack of resources aggravated by mistaken priority choices can now stand in the way. There is no substantial reason why Britain should not fairly quickly be able to establish a position of world leadership in this sphere of health and medical care, but it is undeniable that during the past few years the national position has been slipping. If the rot is to be stopped, it must be stopped without further delay.

In science, so far as brief generalization is possible, it appears that since World War II massive expenditure and a most-favored status have enabled Britain to maintain a leading position internationally. At this moment there are few fields in which comparisons prove more satisfactory to Britain. This achievement however, has been predominantly due to encouragement and support by the official Research Councils. It will remain brittle and precarious until the universities develop a greater capability for themselves fostering new growing points, and more adequately training post-graduate research workers.

British technology is still in the early stages of rehabilitation from the massive injury inflicted on it by university jealousies and academic snobbery. The damage was greatly aggravated by the absurdly small number of qualified and trained men in directing positions in most British industries. Few had even the flair and the perception for attracting and using first-class technologists in the interests of keeping Britain technologically abreast or ahead of countries such as the United States, Germany, and now Italy and Japan. The pace is heating up further, and the record in this unfortunately vital field is plainly and incontestably on balance highly discreditable and depressing for Britain. Whether the numerous recent reports, speeches, adjustments and handouts of public money will really turn the tide remains questionable. It is difficult at the moment to find hard evidence that the gap between Britain and the new front runners is narrowing. Narrow it must, if other major conditions of British recovery are to be fulfilled.

Consideration of the performance of the British economy as a whole brings out the great complexity of the problem and the neglect hitherto to study a number of its most significant elements. Even now we cannot feel sure that a balanced and dependable diagnosis has been achieved. We can, however, state with some confidence that most of the cruder and simpler explanations which have been proposed are either wrong or are at best half-truths. Not only economic and technological, but sociological and administrative elements are deeply involved. For this reason there is some hope that the crude therapy of the 1966 economic crisis may bite deeper and produce greater and more enduring results than previous efforts, which can now be seen to have been quite inadequate in relation to the scale and profundity of the trouble. The psychological resistances to adapting British industry to modern competitive requirements are both a cause and an effect of generations of mistaken attitudes and mistaken decisions. These are now often most conspicuous on the part of the organized workers, but are no less significant, if subtler and more cryptic, on the part of management, who in any case, simply because they *are* management, must bear primary responsibility. There is one important qualification here. It is quite clear that government interference, especially through the recent Stop-Go pattern of economic policy, has rendered good management impossible in many sectors, and difficult in all. To that extent management has an alibi, but it is at best a partial one. The occasion for most of the harmful government intervention should not have arisen if management had been doing its job in the first place up to the better American, Continental and Japanese standards.

Apart from the all-pervading psychological weaknesses it appears that the more crippling handicaps of British industry are to be found not in insufficient hours worked, too many days lost in disputes or even in too little investment so much as in a failure to deploy the available man-hours and to focus the main effort on the most worthwhile tasks. The neglected blind spot is the frittering away of time and money on inessentials or on badly thought-out, inadequately designed and supervised operations unrelated to actual market needs. The consistent and dazzling success achieved by the great chain store, Marks and Spencer, in following skilfully throughout the past third of a century methods of organization differing decisively from those favored by the majority in British industry and commerce is a clear indication that results which need fear no comparison anywhere in the world would have been attainable throughout the period of recent British economic difficulties, given efficient management guided by up-to-date principles and practice. It is significant that market and product research, good design, high standards of staff training and treatment, and a fast-moving flexible management structure with a minimum of bureaucracy and paperwork have ranked high among the factors involved in this success. These are the very points on which large parts of British industry and commerce had proved weakest.

A staggering sum has been lost, or sacrificed through misgovernment and mismanagement. These are twin evils affecting Britain most deeply in innumerable ways. Their respective influences and effects are almost impossible to disentangle. As a general principle, however, where faults are found at two different levels in a hierarchical organism the correct course is to fix the responsibility upon the higher of these two levels. That is why this book stresses "misgovernment" rather than "mismanagement", although there is plenty of that as well.

"Misgovernment" embraces the end-product in terms of wrong decisions and of costly blunders, as well as the operative mechanism composed of the wrong people with the wrong training doing the wrong job in the wrong way.

Prima facie this part shows that despite many remarkable achievements in very diverse fields there is substance in the worldwide suspicion that the British nation has been losing ground compared with others. Unfortunately this is not due to any temporary factors capable of easy and rapid correction but is the cumulative effect of wrong decisions of cumulative strategic importance over more than a century, aggravated by the psychological resistances and social attitudes to which they have lent strength and durability. Nevertheless there is no reason to suppose that anything beyond drastic structural adaptation to modern requirements is necessary in order to enable Britain to resume a leading role in the world in those terms which all nations sharing world leadership will in future be bound by, as the days of individual Great Power politics recede into history.

In conclusion it is necessary to repeat that such a review as this must necessarily confine itself to factors which are more or less measurable, and are therefore largely quantitative. There is ample evidence to indicate advances during recent years in Britain in the status and role of women, in the treatment of children and in various aspects of family life and what are called inter-personal relations. The emergence of an articulate and vigorous younger generation, even if some of its manifestations are disturbing, is basically an indication of vitality and of the shaking off of old attitudes, habits and beliefs, some of which at least were quite ripe for discarding.

Many of the highest mountain climbs, the longest singlehanded ocean voyages, the most popular modern songs, the fastest cars and drivers, the shortest skirts, the freest ways of living, the most significant scientific discoveries, the most advanced ways of caring for the natural environment, the most exciting actors, plays and films and the most challenging fashions in dress today come from Britain. Perhaps it is no coincidence that few of these are in any way under the influence of government, and most of them reflect entirely free individual or group effort.

When government lags, all who rely on it or are affected by its decisions must lag also. There is a strong presumption that this is the true diagnosis of the present "English sickness".

PART THREE

GOVERNMENT
AND GOVERNED

CHAPTER 6
The Governed

The relationships between government and the governed are often incorrectly viewed simply in terms of superior and inferior status, or of something approaching a chain of command from "top" to "bottom", in a thin democratic disguise. A more suitable model would be of a flow process of exchange of signals and of energy which works both ways but is often blocked or distorted. As the basic structure has never been coherently designed for such a purpose, and has been modified with little regard for it, that can only too easily occur. Moreover the scale of the load to be carried has far outgrown the original provision, rather like an Asian city with a current population of two million people depending on water-pipes and sewers designed for 300,000.

The scale and nature of these blockages have been aggravated by other factors, which call for more serious study than they have had. Although a two-way flow process is demanded for the management of a great modern state by inherent social-psychological principles, and is ostensibly conceded by the democratic set-up, there has been a deliberate attempt to operate the System behind the scenes as an essentially hierarchical, one-way mechanism. As this is fundamentally at variance with the alleged modern constitution, it naturally produces a nonsense situation in terms of social engineering, which was only tolerable so long as the electorate was largely unsophisticated and apathetic, and the System appeared to know what it was doing and be capable of achieving it. Now that both these preconditions are ceasing to be fulfilled an overt breakdown, followed by general loss of confidence, is the natural and inevitable outcome.

There is also an area of intellectual insolvency underlying the whole thing. Quite apart from the thinness of the social science foundations there has been an astonishing lack of thorough up-to-date analysis of the semantics and taxonomy of political processes relevant to the British situation. Contrary to the incessantly reiterated propaganda about their political maturity and practicality, the English are chiefly characterized in politics by an inordinate passion for endless half-baked theorizing on such matters as free trade, planning, Commonwealth development, and collective security, with a minimal effort to find the facts and try out by experiment what will actually work.

Political writing is richly represented in English literature, but the woolliness and slovenliness of so much of the centuries-old debate has left us with a most unsatisfactory legacy in terms of semantics. Despite the high claims made for classical education the British still lack a workmanlike vocabulary for getting to grips with what really goes on. The course is studded with loaded, colored, biased, baseless or merely muddled expressions, and with hallowed phrases serving as booby-traps for the investigator. To an English observer the domestic politics of the United States seem grotesquely cluttered up with such twisted fragments of traditional ritual, and with buckets of stale bromide, but there is no ground for complacency here—the reason why he does not observe the same features at home is because he has become so steeped in them that he has lost the necessary detachment even to recognize them when he sees them.

Who are the governed, *alias* the sovereign electorate, *alias* the tax-payers, *alias* the citizens, *alias* the gainfully occupied, the housewives and those "of independent means", *alias* the consumers and so forth? If we set up, at some suitable street corner, our mistnet or trapping station, and actually catch one of these elusive specimens, we may learn from his passport that he has the official status of a "British Subject: Citizen of the United Kingdom and Colonies", and that "Her Britannic Majesty's Principal Secretary of State for Foreign Affairs Requests and Requires in the Name of Her Majesty all those whom it may concern to allow the bearer to pass freely without let or hindrance, and to afford the bearer such assistance and protection as may be necessary." Hastily apologizing for the let (or hindrance) we therefore reluctantly release our specimen and pursue our further investigations by less direct means. Who really is he, as a political animal? Why is he a "subject" first and a "citizen" second? What is the significance of "and Colonies"? Just how is the subject/citizen from Wigan enlarged by holding citizenship also in Antigua, Gibraltar, Hong Kong and the British Antarctic Territory, not forgetting the condominium of

Canton and Enderbury Islands, where he finds among his fellow-citizens almost the entire adult population of the United States?

Among these various intriguing aspects it is unfortunately possible here to pursue only one, whose importance and relevance are outstanding for our study. For the diversity of guises in which the protean British citizen appears is due to the central fact, so often overlooked in textbooks, that the particular hierarchical relationships in which he is placed arise not within the context of some static structure, but are part of, and governed by, his role within a great living and evolving organism called Britain. Constitutionally it may seem anomalous that he should at once be in part the sovereign, in part the subject, but biologically it makes good sense. Once this is recognized, we are launched on an exploration of the actual and the desirable functioning relationships between the different roles in which this busy and misunderstood character is often simultaneously cast.

This, however, is still a gross over-simplification, since "he" is not a lay figure of standard type or dimensions, but may be a Scot—and then a Highlander, Lowlander or Shetlander and so forth —or Welsh, or Northern Irish, or a Northumbrian, a Cornishman, a Yorkshire-man, a Norfolkman or a Londoner, not forgetting too that he might be a Kentishman or on the other hand a man of Kent. But this is still to over-simplify, since we may be dealing with a Glaswegian or Liverpudlian of Irish origin, or a naturalized Londoner who originated in the North, or even in Germany, Poland or Italy, or a Jewish Zionist with one foot in Britain and one in Israel, or an ex-emigrant to the United States or the Commonwealth who has returned to British domicile, perhaps after more than one generation.

Not only is the variety of characters who currently comprise the British nation exceptionally wide, but this diversity has exceptional weight and importance in the culture and society, because many of those whose background is least typical of the majority are among the most lively and articulate. It might not be too wide of the mark to say that the more perfectly an individual conforms in pedigree, type and character to the "normal" Englishman, the less is likely to be seen and heard of him in social and public affairs. These are Chesterton's "secret people", who never have spoken yet. Of the fifteen British Prime Ministers so far this century one was a Scot born in Canada, two (Churchill and Macmillan) had American mothers, four more were Scots, one Welsh and one from a family of Welsh origin, and only six, at most, of basically English descent, three from the North, two from the Midlands and just one from London. Some such breakdown would probably recur in the upper levels of most national activities, but it would be rash to infer that the true English occupy any inferior or less influential role in general in England. Being, however, less articulate, and less apt to come forward and stick their necks out, they tend to become rather more a jury deciding what will and what will not do than the architects and leaders of innovation and formers of policy. Moreover, the legacy of the Norman conquest and serfdom has left a distinct element of "poor white" attitudes, both in the rural and the urban proletariat. It is this element which, as in other countries, tends to aggravate racial tensions with the latest immigrants, especially from the Caribbean and the Indian sub-continent. Such tensions were much less marked with the refugees from Hitler and other recent immigrants from Europe, probably less because they were European than because they mostly at once placed themselves in mobile social groups and occupations where centuries-old suspicions and resentments were less pronounced.

Although social and geographical mobility has greatly increased, its incidence has varied widely in different parts of the country, and at different social levels. Customary hours of local mealtimes, diet and eating habits, use of hats or caps, or hatlessness, numbers and membership of clubs and societies, religious beliefs and observance, leisure orientation towards horses, foxhounds, greyhounds, pigeons, budgerigars, poultry or trout, taste and preference in design, and differing standards of what people can be expected to tolerate in their surroundings, all subtly differentiate the communities and groups at varying stages of displacement from the traditions of pre-industrial Britain. The middle regions, between the Trent and the Clyde, have suffered most widely and drastically from the destruction of their finer cultural and social fabric by the industrial revolution, and from the agonizingly long delay in creating a new one of high quality—a task which has in general only just begun. To some extent regional differences in habits, tastes and attitudes simply reflect a long timelag in the advance of new ways of life from the lower Thames to the Outer Isles and the inner valleys of Wales, where the old ways die hardest. But, owing to the profound differences in race and history, the process is selective. For example the Puritan revolution, with its crassly anti-aesthetic obsession, never touched the Catholic Gaelic communities in such islands as South Uist or in parts of the West Highlands, where the lively survival of the enchanting native music and song attest the loyalty of the Celts to their traditions, and their stubborn and cunning resourcefulness in resisting all kinds of unacceptable alien encroachment. The more governable and accessible English, on the contrary, surrendered so far to this barbarism that they nearly lost, and are only just reviving, one of the most creative musical traditions in Europe.

The English, less tribal and clannish, less fixated on the past, less superstitious and more socially adaptable than the main Celtic groups in Britain, have had the centuries-old advantage of being easier to fuse into effective and close-knit communities independently of blood-ties. Indeed there is a marked tendency, far back in English history, to regard the family as rather a bore. Most successful Englishmen have readily been able to resist the temptation, to which the Welsh-born Richard Burton recently yielded, for assembling a hundred and fifty of their relatives in a family party at the Dorchester. Even before they acquired educational respectability for the practice by converting into boarding schools a number of the foundations originally endowed for the teaching of local boys, as at Harrow, the English aristocracy lost no time in dispatching their troublesome offspring to be trained as young pages in some lordly home at a suitable distance away from the parents. Such an attitude, besides opening the way to a keen love of animals, made it easier, for example, to replace primitive devotion to family vengeance by acceptance of royal justice. The evolution from tribesman to clubman was in train. Thus the Englishman's good citizenship and devotion to the rule of law is closely linked with his readiness to consign his young son to even the most unhappy of boarding schools, and his old mother to a dismal hostel for aged people.

But this English predisposition to accept the authority and to take part in the processes of government extends only thinly and precariously beyond the range of local government, and of accessible functional authorities. Here we are near to the heart of the riddle, why so politically adaptable and mature a people as the English should have been so naïve as to adopt, and so supine as to endure for a full century, such a manifestly unsuitable and unsuccessful pattern of central administration. Instinctively and traditionally they are at home in local, or at most in regional government. Any type of central executive government is distasteful and alien to their inner feelings. For centuries therefore they clung to a cherished type of highly incompetent amateur local government, largely through Justices of the Peace, and resisted all attempts to give them more efficient central government.

When this attitude could no longer be maintained the more influen-

tial leaders successfully devised an examination formula which made
it possible to constitute the new higher Civil Service from a social
group akin to the Justices of the Peace, with the same obsession for
amateurism. The fact that its yoke is increasingly irksome and disastrous is either evaded, partly for fear of the implications for politics of
any drastic reform in the administration, or is borne with masochistic
pleasure as demonstrating how well-based is the Englishman's mistrust and dislike of central government as such.

A point specially to be noted here is that central government, aided
by force of events, has now finally broken the power, destroyed the
local character and flavor, and removed the main initiating functions
from local government, without having been able to offer anything in
its place to provide new forms of participation and communication between government and governed. In such a situation it should be easier
to bridge the gulf at local and regional level by a thorough and efficient
overhaul of those parts of administration, than to break the communication block solely or mainly by efforts from the center. The curious
predominance, already noted, among recent Prime Ministers of Celts
and northerners over the traditionally southern English ruling classes,
may be related to the curiously limited capacity within these classes to
become really at home in central government without a good deal
more education and training for it than they have been willing to undergo. Biographies of English Prime Ministers and their senior colleagues reveal a surprising number as hopelessly miscast.

By contrast the courageous Welsh, although militarily the least
effective and historically the most readily subdued of the minority
Celtic nations of the British Isles, have been the most coherently and
enduringly successful in preserving the vitality of their language and
way of life. Wales has never experienced the triumph of a Bannockburn, but neither has it experienced the disaster of a Flodden. Scottish
propaganda for Scotland has been extrovert, uninhibited and brilliantly sustained, anticipating by generations some of the most prized
discoveries of modern advertising technique. Yet the much less obtru-
sive word-of-mouth propaganda for Welshness among Welshmen has
been domestically perhaps even more effective. The greater prestige
and better survival power of the Welsh tongue has helped greatly. "If
you talk to them in English here, you've had it," I was candidly and
correctly advised by a Welsh scientist in discussing some negotiations
about an area in Merioneth.

Unfortunately, although strong in producing teachers, clerics, agriculturalists and some others, Welsh education has been handicapped in fulfilling its full potential by being yoked to the narrower demands of national culture, and at the university level the conflict is acute and embarrassing. Personalities and provincialism also exercise a distorting influence. North Wales, secure around the Snowdonian mountains, tends to regard itself as Welsher than thou in relation to the much more populous but more English-tainted South. As the Princes of Gwynedd originated in what is now southeast Scotland this claim is questionable, although effective.

Taking the United Kingdom as excluding Southern Ireland throughout, Wales held the same 5 percent proportion to the whole in 1961 as in 1821, in contrast to Scotland, which fell back from 13·5 percent to below 10 percent, and Northern Ireland, which dropped even more dramatically from nearly 9 percent to 2·7 percent. The only comparable drop in England was in the southwest region, from 11·3 percent to 6·5 percent; the rest, between Dover and the Scottish border rose from 61 percent to nearly 76 percent.

A central problem for the British people today in relation to their government is the question of their identity. Who actually are they? What are they expected to do? Is this what they want to do, or are capable of doing, or are they being miscast by their rulers? What became of that Empire, and is the sense of awkwardness about its peculiar disappearance something to be felt as a defeat, as a natural event, as an injustice of fate, or as good riddance? And what about the rulers who have preached so fervently about holding on to things which have collapsed and then not been much missed after all? Can these same rulers be looked up to still as if nothing had happened? If not, how should they now be regarded? Have they a clear idea where they are trying to lead the nation, and have they learnt to be any more trustworthy about bringing it off? Are they aware of the System, and do they really want it to go on? What is it worthwhile to pursue in the future, and how can it be shown to be worthwhile and to be practically attainable? All these embarrassing questions, and many more, float unspoken through the summer air, but no Englishman wants to make a scene, and maybe beer is best. Another good idea is to go away and mow the garden lawn.

This deep muddle over national identity is by no means peculiar to

Britain. The Germans have torn up Europe twice within a century, try-ing clumsily to unearth the German soul somewhere. The Americans have devised endless rather pathetic rituals and folkways to reassure themselves from the cradle to the grave that they are not guilty of being un-American, or at any rate not in a way that anyone more truly American than themselves can find out. The French have gone so far as to interrupt their long anarchic political tradition in order to install a supreme guide and father-figure in the art of being nobly, superbly, and irresistibly French. The Irish have done a temporary deal to trade their distressful happy-go-lucky identity for plumbing which works and no beggars on the streets, but not to worry, the Irish identity prob-lem will return, and the entertainment industries of the future will profit by it. The Russian authorities have much more brutally inter-rupted the equally agonizing and even more artistically rewarding game of seeking the Russian identity, but this game also must soon revive, and indeed it has already begun again in the wake of *Dr. Zhi-vago*. Unfortunately, even the most self-confident and uninhibited governments of every complexion agree in classing this problem as unmentionable, and on looking away whenever they chance to set eyes on it. A short course for governments on how to understand and cope with their nations under stress of temporary or partial loss of national identity would be a real boon. They ought to begin to learn about it, and most of all HMG, which is partly responsible for the fact that it has on its hands a peculiarly embarrassing and difficult case.

As usual the problem has deep roots far in the past. People who lived on the island when the Romans came thought they were the Brit-ish, until gangs of English sailed in from across the North Sea and in-sisted that they were really Welsh—a word meaning alien. Just as the English themselves began to feel cosily settled the Normans took over the country and left the English in no doubt that they were only there on sufferance as second-class citizens. The Normans attempted to convince the Scots that this also applied to them, but were themselves finally convinced by good arguments that it did not. The Scots had al-ready learnt the game pretty well from their long maneuvers to take over the larger Pictish kingdom, and later the British kingdom of Strathclyde and the tough immigrant Anglians, whose King Edwin probably gave his name to Edinburgh. At various times also the Cath-olics, the nonconformists, the radicals, the politically articulate workers, the agnostics, the conscientious objectors to warfare and all kinds of other people have been told that they did not really belong in

Britain, or would be tolerated only provided they would give up or keep very quiet about what they most believed in. Britain is therefore full of people who have good reason to feel pretty sensitive on this score. From Hermaness to Dover and from Land's End or St. David's to Lowestoft, uneasy men and women struggle to come to terms with their alleged identity. Actual persecution in any form is now rare— almost certainly rarer than ever before in Britain, and probably rarer than in other advanced societies generally. The permissiveness of modern Britain is one of its most conspicuous features to visitors from overseas. Nevertheless certain groups in British society still feel some sense of persecution, especially, of course, the latest immigrants, who can find themselves locally a target of thinly disguised racial discrimination which adds to the normal difficulties of the unadjusted newcomer, living as a stranger in a strange land. A number, probably often exaggerated, of young people, and members of cultural minorities such as chapel going Welsh speakers may feel strongly the same way.

CHAPTER 7

The Alienated

Any tendencies towards positive persecution are very few, mild and insignificant, compared with the much greater and fast-growing problem of alienation, indifference and neglect. This is among the greatest, and in itself the most neglected, of the issues between government and governed. From the angle of government certain groups in society are actively or passively troublesome to handle. These are a mixed bunch, including conscientious objectors to military service or to vaccination, non-conscientious but artful objectors to paying customs duties or taxes, non-answerers of official communications, and non-fillers-in of forms, systematic evaders of regulations, homosexuals, addicts of anti-social practices such as drug-taking and gambling, followers of offbeat ways of life such as Seventh-day Adventists and what used to be called beatniks, and of course the entire delinquent and criminal brotherhood. The work of government and the practice of bureaucracy would be immensely simplified if such minorities did not exist. At best they complicate it; at worst they make it nearly impossible.

Regarded from the standpoint of the governed, however, the problem is much wider and more serious. The mere existence of government is from this angle at best a necessary evil, and as the functions and interventions of government multiply, the occasions when it appears to develop from this into an unnecessary evil and then into an intolerable imposition are liable to multiply also. This multiplication is however very uneven in its incidence on citizens. Never in history have so many been so much messed about by so few, but large bands among the many are either too passive to mind it, or are too keenly conscious of the benefits which they derive from the all-pervasive welfare state to do more than grumble mildly at its yoke. The paintings of

Lowry say all that need be said about the downtrodden herds of the governed, hemmed in between the hard walls and square blocks of industrial urbanism. The British people, with all their diversity, are almost invariably slow to formulate any fundamental grievances, and even slower to get round to complaining at all effectively about them. The virtual moratorium on such complaints during World War II, and the subsequent confusion and contradictions, have left a large part of the population seething with still inexpressible and undefinable frustrations and grievances. Some day these may emerge in full flood, but hitherto they have remained pent-up, or have been translated into hostile apathy.

In the anatomy of social and political frustration two elements are of critical importance—which social groups become conscious of which specific grievances, and what overt reactions they make to them. A grievance which, objectively regarded, looks fairly small may prove very dangerous indeed if it is passionately distressing some strategically-placed group, able and ready to proceed to extremes of anti-social action such as interference with essential services, or mass emigration. Conversely an undeniably grave grievance may cause little anxiety to the kind of government we have, so long as those affected are too public-spirited, too dispersed, or too leaderless to make a real nuisance of themselves about it.

This, however, is a superficial attitude. Many years ago, on a scientific expedition in the Amazonian rain-forest, I was admirably assisted and served by members of the Arawak tribe, among the gentlest and most dependable of the human race. They had, however, one well-known peculiarity. If they were badly treated they would never complain or give notice, since they hated argument: they would simply, without asking for their wages, pack up and steal silently away in the night leaving the party to fend for itself. Having established this reputation they hardly ever needed to act upon it; they were always well treated and always gave of their best. They were pioneers of secessionist protest, an art now widely practiced in various forms anywhere from Aldermaston to San Francisco and from Amsterdam to Saigon.

Secessionism is a course of action, or rather a series of alternative similar courses, brought about by profound lack of confidence in, or disagreement with, the basic ends sought and means adopted by authority on what are regarded as vital issues. The lack of confidence or disagreement takes shape first, and, after discussion and dissemination, begins to crystallize into an attitude. This then becomes shared by a broadly recognizable although possibly quite unorganized group of likeminded persons. Unless this dissident attitude is met in time by a suitable response from authority, or unless the issue itself dissolves or recedes into the background, some form of secessionism will tend to grow, either subtly and obscurely, or openly and aggressively as with the Dutch Provos.

It is now becoming evident that modern affluent societies are peculiarly susceptible to secessionist protest, not least because they are so blind to the entire process, until it goes to extreme lengths. Britain today is riddled with it, at various stages and in many forms. Its most obvious and extreme form is voting with one's feet to leave the country. An Englishman's right to quit England is one of the most essential of his historic liberties, fought out even before Magna Carta in the *Ne exeat regno* affair between Henry II and Becket. From the Pilgrim Fathers, who preferred to be excused from living here under the Stuarts, to the latest Rhodesians, in search of somewhere more like Bournemouth than Bournemouth has now become, such groups have repeatedly left Britain's shores, carrying in their baggage ambivalent attitudes to their motherland. The brain drain has an element of this too, and is proving an effective means of compelling weak politicians and purblind administrators to pay some attention to long-term interests.

Some of the impulsive expatriates find their new social environment even less attractive and return here. Conversely, Britain continues to attract a strong minority of often talented and active expatriates from the United States and other English-speaking lands, and also from continental Europe, while the band of temporary expatriates working away from their homeland goes on swelling in both directions. Such people are of peculiar significance in the process of keeping Britain abreast of overseas practice and trends, and of disseminating elsewhere British ways and methods. They overlap with secessionism, but often represent quite different attitudes.

Distinct from the outright expatriates are those who may be termed expatriates at heart, most of whom do participate and stick it out in Britain to the end, but tend to feel that at the drop of a hat they would clear out and start life again somewhere else. The size of this group can only be guessed at, but the indications are that it may be fairly substantial, and that qualitatively it is of much importance. Their allegiance is given to an ideal Britain, or at any rate to one much less remote from it than that which they are currently expected to serve.

The next and in some ways the most interesting and problematical group are the ethically and intellectually alienated. Some of these leave the country but many remain, continuing in it but not of it in their own exclusive circles, often in closer contact with like-minded beings even as far off as California, than with their nextdoor neighbors. While it is easy to show similar examples from the past, headed perhaps by Shelley and Byron and their circle, these contemporary secessionists are becoming much more numerous, and in some ways more separate, than anything with which they can be compared for a long time back. Perhaps the Albigensians, who caused so much trouble to the civil and ecclesiastical authorities in medieval Provence, might be the nearest to a parallel in their hedonist, pacifist, unorthodox and unco-operative role in the community. While the present intellectually complacent Affluent Society acts as if it had less to fear from such contamination than medieval Christendom this standpoint may not prove to be fully justified. At any rate their rejection of the creed of higher productivity, greater consumption and better hygiene could scarcely be more complete.

The impersonal and the artificial repels them, and to this extent they resemble the recurrent movement of reaction towards a simpler life, in which communication with people and contact with nature should play a greater role. They profess concern with deeper values and truths, and they mistrust and keep aloof from organization in every shape or form. Not only are they "agin the government", whatever it may be, but they are wary of, and quick to disown, any attempt to create a hierarchy among themselves or to bind them to any body or platform. They are, in effect, the *reductio ad absurdum,* or the logical and honest expression, whichever you prefer, of anarchism, in purer and more perfect form than would be practicable for a single day except within the protective ambit of an efficiently serviced affluent society, on which they are unashamedly parasitic.

The inchoate and dispersed character of this element, its relatively recent emergence and its cosmopolitan attitudes and responses probably render premature any attempt to evaluate its influence or to forecast its future development in Britain. As one of the most permissive and tolerant parts of the worldwide affluent society of advanced countries Britain is evidently sure to be very much involved. In so far as poetry is one of its most favored pursuits it might well prove a seedbed for a poetic revival in Western civilization, which is badly overdue. Pop art and pop culture generally might well be strongly influenced by it in a counter-materialist direction, which would be all to the good.

Internationally its firmly apolitical trend could be a valuable solvent of tensions, especially among the sort of young people who were so readily gulled into identifying themselves with Communism in the 'thirties. The Aldermaston marches and the Nuclear Disarmament movement, although at times somewhat marred by errors of judgment and excesses of emotionalism, did on the whole manage to bring into the open, as a warning to addicts of the power game, a deep and wide civilized feeling of the absolute necessity of thinking again about The Bomb. Its international influence, although hard to assess, was widespread, and it showed Britain in her historic liberal role, inspired to action from the grassroots, outside the bounds of any pre-existing organization or movement and in successful defiance of much heavy discouragement from the authorities, from political party leaders, and even initially from the press. No civilized nation now would tolerate the irresponsible and carefree attitudes to the possibility of using The Bomb which were common, in British government circles as well as overseas, before the long shaggy columns of Aldermaston marchers trooped up Whitehall each Easter. Although these protests concerned a matter of some public interest, namely, the survival of the human race, and were conducted with exemplary restraint and freedom from violence, the British system of misgovernment revealed here a disturbing capacity to deprive the citizen by chicanery of his constitutional rights. By the use of a fourteenth-century statute, passed to restrain armed vagrant soldiers returning destitute from the French wars, and not free from suspicion of subsequent amendment by forgery, one of the greatest living Englishmen, Bertrand Russell, was sent to prison at the age of ninety. His secretary, sentenced to nine months' imprisonment for inciting persons to obstruct the highway by sitting down in it, was told by the magistrate that "we all have to live in the world as it is today, and from what you have said your efforts have done nothing to improve it. You are a nuisance to the police, who are overworked and understaffed."

In a city whose streets are frequently made almost impenetrable by avoidable obstructions, which the police and the magistrates do nothing effective to check, such a sentence raises grave doubts regarding the reality of British freedom and the nature of the will of those in authority to maintain it. That the sentence was later upset on appeal, through a technicality, is irrelevant to that issue.

A dissident, detached, contemplative element in society can thus contribute to its progress and balance precisely through being itself uninvolved, even if its contribution to the national productivity figures is negative and its consumption of soap is inadequate. But there must be a rather low limit to the desirable size of such an element, and its recent growth seems rather to reflect a widening and deepening sense of alienation than a desire or capacity to find a satisfying way of life which is fruitful in anything beyond a strictly reproductive sense of the word. Much further growth would probably give rise to friction, in view of the distinctly parasitic way of life involved, and would do no credit to the authorities in whom the movement essentially represents a vote of no confidence. While the problem may solve itself, it might equally give rise to real trouble. A first precautionary step would be to study how young people so often drift into such ways of life today, and what is lacking, in society as well as in them, to put them off more normal career choices. Society needs the participation and energies of all its young people, especially the more gifted ones. Any failure to convince them of this and to win their good opinion and support cannot wisely be shrugged off as arising from some supposed fault only in the young people themselves. This book, although covering only a segment of British national life, shows that there is justification for a sceptical and unforthcoming attitude on the part of new recruits to citizenship, until much that is now wrong has been conceded and has begun to be righted.

There are many more unhappy, frustrated people in Britain who might become overt secessionists if they found it economically or socially practicable. This clearly applies to large numbers of young people who are readily attracted by high earnings to enter jobs in which, rightly or wrongly, they have little interest. Their imaginations and energies are often devoted to leisure activities prominently catering for a desire to find some quite fanciful identity, and to separate themselves as far as possible from activities approved or understood by their elders. The latter, therefore, can be faulted in their threefold role as parents, as educators, and as managers and rulers when the child crosses the threshold of adult life. The extent and depth of this manifest failure is frightening.

Perhaps the largest army of the frustrated and alienated is among the manual workers. Taught too little, in overcrowded classes in squalid and old-fashioned schools, eked out with plenty of self-pity disguised as a demand for social justice, they are dumped on a still fairly primitive "labor market" in which their true earning capacity may never in their lifetime much surpass the level which they can expect to reach automatically as they first reach manhood. Using their massed bargaining power, which is all they have, to extract a larger share by industrial or semi-political pressure, or to "spread the work" over larger numbers of what are known as "workers", are among the few opportunities left open to them for wringing more interest or more reward out of what they do. Here, as so often in British life, there has been an entire failure to realize the importance of sharing enough drama at all levels, and of not making it virtually impossible to enjoy drama and to release aggression without injury to the main common effort. While conditions in education and in personnel management have evidently improved, still greater improvements will be needed even to begin to overtake the immense arrears in the practice of human relations in industrial Britain, and to clear the way for anything worthy of the twentieth century, let alone the twenty-first.

The seriousness of the problem was brought vividly to national notice in 1966, partly by revelations of the long-concealed, scandalous stranglehold of certain groups of workers on the newspaper industry, which had proved impotent to keep its house in order, and partly by the events which paradoxically compelled a Labour Government to assume almost dictatorial powers over wage-claims, sponsored in many cases by its own party's affiliated trade unions. In form, the national trade unions were run by democratically elected officers according to a constitution and rules. In fact, the rank and file, led by shop stewards or other on-the-spot ringleaders, had in many cases come to take for granted that they could repudiate or disregard any agreement entered into in their name as often as it suited them to do so, and that they had a right to a pay increase every year or two as a matter of course, irrespective of whether productivity had increased. In effect, both trade union leaders and managements had largely lost control of the situation, and although both strongly resented and objected to the government intervening, the seriousness of the balance of payments position and the maintenance of foreign credits left no alternative.

Inflation and the adverse foreign balance merely reflected the virtual breakdown in communication and control which had finally occurred over large sectors of British industry, having its origins back in the period of the General Strike (see p. 209) and even earlier. Ignorant and complacent managements at that time, having lost markets to competitors and failed to develop new lines, had fallen back on sacking men, cutting wages and other expedients which had widely undermined confidence in their keenness or ability to take due care of men whose lives were invested in the industry. Today's generation of managements, themselves still often only partly abreast of world standards, and lacking adequate authority and confidence, were in too many cases failing to cope with their task, aggravated as it was by successive governmental blunders in the general management of the British economy. Indeed, until an end to these systematic blunders of the Stop-Go period could be counted upon, the task of many managements was virtually impossible. Even on that assumption, a vast healing and recreative campaign would be necessary to reconstruct a tolerable pattern of management–labor relations in Britain. Palliative efforts to settle particular disputes and to eliminate certain restrictive practices largely failed to touch the deep and broad underlying problems, and the intensely difficult and delicate process of re-establishing genuine two-way communication.

In their use of the strike weapon, and in other specific acts of industrial aggression, the workers, through their unions or shop stewards, are functioning as intermittent secessionists. Essentially, as regular non-joiners in any movement outside their own narrow interests and those of their immediate political bosses, they are secessionists all the time and all the way, except when it comes to war or catastrophe.

Next in the spectrum of alienation come a series of important occupational groups which have gone sour, and whose desire to avoid creating serious trouble can no longer be counted on—the medical doctors, the schoolteachers, the farmers, even the civil servants and the police. In a free-for-all world, with inflation almost unchecked, such traditionally respectable groups find that nothing short of a credible and imminent threat to raise hell for the administration will win them consideration or fair play under the System. That such people have been compelled to act in such ways is in itself a devastating indictment of the System which allowed it to happen. It is unnecessary to do more at this point than to put in a reminder of the similar dissatisfactions and discontents of such racial or regional minorities as the Scottish Highlanders, the Welsh-speakers, the Cornish and the Tynesiders, and more scattered groups such as communities of fishermen and coal miners. Railwaymen facing redundancy in remote areas, and even very prosperous groups such as workers on automobile assembly, are among the latest recruits.

A distinct class of discontented persons consists of those who have recently had to give up a privileged or more advantageous situation for one which they find inferior. To some extent nearly all the upper sections of the established middle class are in this position, although some of their former status symbols such as large houses with servants are now receding so far into the past that the ache is becoming fainter. Similarly the landed gentry and their relatives and associates have swallowed with stoicism drastic cuts in their former standards, and by their tenacity and continuing contribution to the vigor of rural society have confuted the old-time radicals who regarded them as little better than parasites. Devotion to the land and resolution to maintain family traditions impel them to work longer hours and to suffer worse conditions than many of their traditional social inferiors would dream of tolerating.

The old school of company directors, the City leaders, Anglo-Indian and other overseas-oriented families and groups, and senior professional men of every kind have lost absolutely in various ways, and have suffered some relative decline in status and in social self-confidence. It is perhaps here that a certain running-down of impetus and wavering of leadership in terms of direction and of principle can most nearly be pinpointed. Eroded and discouraged by decades of inadequate success and reward in their conscientious, if at times misguided, efforts at public-spirited leadership, the British middle classes have to some extent given up the struggle and withdrawn more into their own immediate professional and family preoccupations. The gap thus created has not been otherwise filled, and has led to political and social pressures for all kinds of unsuitable and maladroit government interventions, both centrally and locally, which on balance have probably made the situation worse, and have further alienated those still ready for voluntary service and possessed of public spirit. That the middle classes themselves have largely created the problem by their passionate loyalty to out-of-date educational patterns and their vocational inadaptability does nothing to mitigate the national dilemma.

Here we are touching the mainspring of modern British progress. Its lack of tautness and its inability to rewind are among the factors most clearly indicative of the inroads of the System into the sources of national renewal and of national capacity to adapt. Misguided and unbalanced applications of social justice, and levelling down, reinforced by high taxation, reduced personal and office service, and ever-extending bureaucratic encroachment have enfeebled, divided and to a considerable extent neutralized the ability of the British middle classes to go on functioning as the social dynamo in British civilization. Some substantial reform and adjustment was undoubtedly needed, but the shape it has taken is very much awry. The accelerating shift of middle class energies from participation in leadership to alliance with the alienated should be among the worst nightmares and most pressing preoccupations of any British government which purports to know what it is at.

Another less open and challenging but equally significant form of alienation is the switch into escapist activities, sometimes of merely trivial but often of a clearly anti-social nature. The increase here has been spectacular. It would need too much space to list all the growing activities in this field of substitution for or evasion of life's more serious challenges, but you name it, we have it. Among the most baffling aspects of the policy of Conservative administrations in the 1950s was the accompaniment of a refusal to embark seriously on economic planning, and to set a course for the Common Market until much too late, with the large-scale release and encouragement of commercial interests in gambling, greatly expanded consumer credit, gross speculation in land, property and company promotion, and mass propaganda through commercial television for counter-productive and inflationary patterns of development. The natural and inevitable result was a more and more uncontrollable economy moving farther and farther from the line of sound development, a population fortified by official encouragement in pursuing every form of self-indulgence, and an alarming expansion in the professional criminal class and its financial and structural base as a state within the state—something which it had taken generations of struggle to eliminate under the early Georges and Queen Victoria.

The confidence of citizens in law and order, the protection of property and of personal safety, and the morale of the police were thus reduced by the 'sixties to a level which generations of British people had fondly assumed could not happen here. The precautions which a normally prudent citizen is now expected, as a matter of course, to take for protecting his home and property would have been regarded as the hallmark of a neurotic forty years ago, and yet the resulting security is not more, but a good deal less. There are few more reliable signs of misgovernment than a rising number of precautions which the citizen has to take in order to sleep soundly at night. The power and influence of the new criminal class, and its capacity to deal on equal terms with the police, was shown by a series of spectacular escapes from allegedly secure prisons, by the Great Train Robbery, by the prolonged criminal control over a multi-story car park in the middle of London Airport, and by many other episodes. This trend culminated in the Home Office's admission of inability to safeguard juries from being tampered with by criminal influences, and the proposal to counter this by abandoning the immemorial rule of unanimity for verdicts.

In some ways paradoxically, yet in practical terms explicably, the dwindling authority of hitherto accepted social standards and of official agencies concerned with enforcing law and conducting administration has led to a growth of pressures for "reasons of state" to discipline the ordinary citizen more strictly, and to undermine the safeguards of his liberty of person and property. The grudging admission, extracted after years of intense public agitation and pressure, that Timothy Evans had been wrongly convicted and hanged for the Rillington Place murders opened many eyes belatedly to the peril in which the citizen now stands. A review of what was said at his trial, in the light of what we now know about the ex-policeman-criminal Christie, exposes a built-in tendency to attach undue weight to police evidence. In view of the modern dilution of police standards, the overburdening and inadequate supervision of many officers and the sheer weight of numbers of police witnesses, such evidence ought to be treated more critically. From personal experience as foreman of a jury at the Old Bailey I am impressed with the risk that, however fair the trial itself, a stupid but innocent citizen may end up by being wrongly convicted.

The net effect of these recent trends has undoubtedly been a setback to that universal confidence in the rule of law and in the fair and efficient administration of justice which has long been regarded as the cornerstone of British liberty. An interesting and well-informed, although sometimes controversial review of the subject, which merits more notice than it has received, is Raymond Blackburn's *The Erosion of Liberty,* published in 1964 in the Isle of Man. In view of its apparent scarcity the following summary from the author's Introduction seems worth quoting here:

> To-day, in Britain, the State, the trade unions, and even the employers interfere with a man's freedom to work. No man can work without cards issued by the State, and most men must also have cards issued by a trade union.
>
> We cannot take more than a small amount of money abroad.

Moreover, the State frequently prevents people from borrowing money from their banks although the banks would normally be pleased to lend them the money.

We are not free 'to stand and stare' on the footpath. The law only gives us the right of passage.

Over an enormous area of industry there is no such thing as free enterprise. Monopolies and restrictive practices abound . . .

The powers of the police and of a host of officials have been immeasurably increased. The ordinary man must accept that they have whatever powers they claim. He is virtually at their mercy. It is only because most uniformed policemen and officials are unwilling to use their powers tyrannically that we are not citizens of a far more servile State than at present.

Then there is the destruction of freedom by lawyers. For instance, not one prisoner in a hundred who appeals to the Court of Criminal Appeal is permitted by that Court to attend Court and see his judges. Not one in twenty is provided with anyone to represent him on the hearing, which therefore, in practice, never takes place at all in the vast majority of cases . . .

Lord Atkin's famous speech deprecating the attitude of judges who are 'more executive-minded than the executive' could be the text for the detailed charges made in this book that the modern Bench has failed in its duty to protect the liberty of the subject . . .

Lawyers indeed bear an immense share of the guilt for the decline of liberty. They draft the legislation and steer it through Parliament, where they wield great power. They interpret it. Theirs is the major blame for the multiplication of offences as a result of which magistrates hear over one million cases a year . . .

If we believed passionately in freedom and carried our beliefs into practice by a sweeping review of all the powers of law and Government, of industry and trade unions which now cause the erosion of freedom, we could set our feet on a new revolutionary path. Athens gave its citizens the greatest freedom in the days of Pericles. The result in thought and the arts was prodigious. If Britain could emulate the Athenians in the complicated sphere of modern life, it would find that it had lost its empire only to achieve a greater glory in the more lasting world of the mind of man.

In view of the undisputed benefits of the modern economics of scale and of national and international planning, one cannot help feeling that Pericles and his friends had a somewhat easier problem. But the trends in management towards greater devolution and decentralization are amongst several factors leading me to agree with Raymond

Blackburn's main contention that a great deal of the current interference with British liberties is not only highly objectionable, but could be eliminated with practical advantage. This, however, could only be successfully accomplished on the basis of a much more modern and more responsible approach by the great majority of citizens to the nation's social and economic needs. This dilemma is best illustrated by the drastic but most reluctant intervention by the government in the regulation of prices and incomes. It is undoubtedly a gross interference with liberty, but it is the inevitable outcome of chronic irresponsibility over the essential needs of the national economy by both managements and labor, aided and encouraged by all political parties in the past.

Planning and freedom are entirely reconcilable, but reassertion of responsibility must accompany reassertion of liberty. The problem of reviving British liberty is the problem of finding a new approach and way of life which will safeguard the total long-term interests of the British peoples and, at the same time, make possible a general disarmament of laws and regulations mistakenly seeking to make people good and co-operative by Act of Parliament. If laws and statutory orders are clumsy, objectionable, excessive and ineffectual, as they clearly are, our task must be to achieve the same objects, in so far as they are largely sound and necessary objects, by alternative means, through sweet reason and sweeter incentives. Meanwhile, let us not be misled by nostalgic yearnings that Britannia should at least continue to rule the waves of the Indian Ocean into forgetting to attend watchfully to that other line which asserts that "Britons never, never, never shall be slaves." And that means slaves of THEM, just as much as slaves of the Nazis or of Napoleon.

In moving farther into escapism and alienation the British are making the wrong type of protest against their misgovernment in the wrong way. It would be much better for all in the long run if they grew angrier for a change, and had a real direct argument about the whole trouble, which would clear the air. That was how British liberties were won, and it is the only real means of reasserting them and reinstating them in terms of tomorrow. The national habit of leaving the other fellow to stand up publicly for our rights, and looking down our noses while he does so, is one of the meanest and least creditable facets of the British character.

While alienation from government is to some extent an inherited feature, it is remarkable and disturbing that the more government becomes viewed as an instrument for satisfying social needs, the more the alienation from it seems to grow. There is something sadly wrong here. If the young, the old, the workers, the middle-class intellectuals and managers, the Scots, the Welsh, the landowners, the doctors, the teachers, the Navy, the police and quite a number of other groups feel their sympathies so strained that they prefer to detach themselves more or less from full participation and involvement in the national life, and to brood over their particular wrongs in growing isolation, it is plain that the System is getting near the point of no return in creating the kind of understanding which ought to exist between government and nation.

What is the penalty for further delay in tackling this problem effectively? First it must be anticipated that the rate of deterioration, as indicated by resistance to measures for increasing productivity, by the brain drain, by renewed sectional pressures implying inflation, and so forth, will quicken, and the already alarming "drag" in the economy will increase. The climate will then exist for some form of activist movement, probably quite different from the Provos in Holland, but no less unpleasant and discomfiting for authority. It is remarkably fortunate, in view of the extent of frustration and disillusionment, that nothing resembling the fascist, communist and other threatening movements of the 'thirties has yet emerged. But the hour is late, and it would be rash to assume that this will not happen unless government finds some more sensible and effective way of actually communicating with the groups in which discontent is most pronounced. As has been seen with Poujadism and the OAS in France, with the neo-Nazi movement in Germany, and with McCarthyism and the Goldwater and John Birch movements in the United States, it is now possible, if conditions become sufficiently strained, for a major threat to the established order to blow up at much shorter notice now than even in the days of the advent of Italian fascism and German Nazism between the two wars. With the added tensions of racialism, and the utter failure of any of the established political parties to enlist in a big way the loyalties and enthusiasm of the young, we are moving across thin ice, and can only hope that it holds until we get to the other side, assuming that we do not continue to wander round in circles until it gives way. The performance to be expected of the Home Office and of the other civil Departments in coping with any future major civil emergency does not bear thinking of. Let us then hope for the best, while bestirring ourselves not to tempt providence further by supposing that another little dose of misgovernment will not do us any harm. Many of us would strongly prefer *not* to wait until smoke bombs start being thrown at the Queen.

What is the converse of alienation, at which we must aim to put us on the road to national recovery? Some think in terms of a Cause, a New Inspiration, an Ideal, which will burst upon the nation with overwhelming impact, and generate vast new energies to overcome all evils and make good the errors and omissions of the past. Sometimes this is pictured in secular, perhaps Utopian terms; sometimes as a return to some favored brand of religion. History, and above all English history, gives little ground for supposing that anything of this sort would be at all likely to happen. Perhaps the four nearest approaches to it were in the reign of Edward the Confessor, in the Crusades, in Cromwell's Commonwealth and under the Tractarians and other evangelists of the mid-nineteenth century. The first of these episodes led to the conquest of England by the Normans; the second to such misgovernment that it evoked Magna Carta; the third created an overwhelming demand for the restoration of the Stuarts and the fourth is strongly to be suspected of playing a large part in making the ethos which has moulded the last century of misgovernment in Britain.

There is in any case little evidence that any kind of strong and sustained religious feeling has ever directly influenced more than a very small minority in Britain at any time. Where that minority has already possessed or has later captured power, its efforts to convert or coerce the majority have merely resulted in a greatly increased output of hypocrisy, and a grave build-up of psychological tensions, with on the whole unhappy results. The contention that the undoubtedly large falling-off in public manifestations of religious feeling must be correlated with a loss of the social dynamic which is presumed to have arisen from it is not proven. A more demonstrable feature of organized religion has been its effectiveness in holding together large numbers of permanent, localized, social groups possessing and conferring on their members a definite, acceptable, and respectable status, so that for them much of the problem of uncertainty of identity has been automatically solved. One paradoxical result of this is that the churches, which in Christian theory should be most alienated from and in conflict with modern materialist society, appear in fact to be among the best-adjusted and least uncomfortable groups within it. Various conclusions might be drawn from this; what concerns us here is that it appears to offer a control instance tending to support the hypothesis that unsatisfied hunger for fulfillment, in terms of identity and status, is at least among the main elements in the current disintegration of British social fabric, and in the consequential loss of coherent relationship between government and governed. A nation including too many identity-starved citizens can readily degenerate into an identity-starved nation. Remedying that deficiency, and bringing about satisfying relationships not only between citizens personally but between them and the State and local community, appears a more practical approach to future progress than the preaching of crusades, with however much revivalist fervor.

Indeed it is arguable that mid-Victorian religiosity, which played so conspicuous a role in the creation of Gladstonian liberalism, had such unfortunate results because it went far enough to impose itself fairly strongly on British society at its more superficial levels, but did not go deep enough seriously to mitigate the selfishness, the callousness and the vulgar superficiality to which that society was so prone. While the struggle to convert the nation engaged a number of very high-minded persons, and left its stamp on British education and public service as well as on the churches, it ended by making the worst of both worlds. It found the British an inventive, inquisitive, exploring, forward-looking, romantic, bawdy and earthy, country-loving nation, with strong sceptical and poetic streaks. It assured them that they ought to be a tightly inhibited, stuffy, strait-laced, respectable, imperialist nation of urbanized, conventional, materialist Christian gentlemen and their admirers, addicted to healthy sports and contemptuous of artistic creation, thinking or planning ahead. The change thus vigorously imposed from above fitted in well with the British tendency to justify mental laziness and moral torpor by seizing upon any handy offering of patriotic or sentimental cant. With its instinctive, slow British wisdom the emerging generation is now busily engaged in reversing it. Tom Jones is back IN and *Eric (or Little by Little)* is finally OUT. Unhappily, while the mid-Victorian miasma is at last being blown away from everyday life, the governmental institutions and practices which were constructed under cover of it are still in full and almost unchanged operation. This is one of the main reasons for the growing estrangement of the governed in Britain from its preposterous system of government.

British governments in the eighteenth century were wildly inefficient and unrepresentative, but they did to some extent understand what sort of people the British are, and by minimizing the incidence of government they left opportunity wide open, and also minimized at least some types of friction. In the nineteenth century, when the issue of providing more and better representative government could no longer be postponed, those who had to organize it made an utter hash of the job, but the jerry-built structure which they improvised has been merely added to and shored up here and there ever since. The basic pattern is too unfitting, and the accumulated distortion too vast, to permit the confidence of the governed to be restored without pretty substantial changes. The extent of these changes will depend partly on how much longer they are delayed. This aspect is discussed and a number of suggestions are put forward in Part Seven.

Meanwhile, impelled by deep frustration and a bankruptcy of alternative ideas, government and governed reluctantly and almost instinctively agree to seek refuge in the womb of Mother Europe. On the plane of policy there is a strong case for such action, but General de Gaulle may be forgiven for suspecting that thorough working-out of the policy and of all that it eventually involves is not the route by which either the British government or the British nation have come to that conclusion.

It remains to be fully faced that there is not now, and there never should be again, any superior or mystic sanction entitling THEM, who claim to know better or have a direct line from God, to try to drive the nation along any other road than the one it wants to take. The process of government starts and ends in the mind of the citizen. Government should study, educate and in due time be guided by that mind, should learn and determine how best to fulfil its broad intent, and should initiate and handle all the resulting legislative and executive business by the simplest and most economical channels and methods. Its work should be kept always as close as possible to the citizen rather than withdrawn unnecessarily to some bureaucratic stratosphere, and should be handled in ways which are as near as possible to those of commonsense everyday life, and as far as possible from the mystiques and pretensions so beloved in Whitehall.

Government is, or should be, a big citizen's aid bureau. It should use to the full modern methods of opinion testing, consumer investigation and market research to ensure that what it does and the way it does it is in the greatest practical harmony with the needs and wants of the nation. These methods should, with rare exceptions, guide the government in its actions; they should not be used merely to try to bamboozle the public over something quite distinct which THEY have resolved to do already. In government, as in education, many methods of pressurizing or instructing people are now known to be self-defeating, and to add to the build-up of frustration, alienation and non-absorption of the message. The mechanisms and objectives of government must be harmonized with the stimuli and the approaches which arouse co-operative social behavior. It follows that not only politicians but administrators must be well versed in these matters, selected for their insight and perception and then trained to use them to best advantage, so as to enable the fullest devolution to be practiced, and the most effective co-operation and teamwork maintained, at all levels, and at all distances from the center.

Much of the work of government is a process of indirect management, trying to cause things to happen or prevent them from happening by laws and regulations, by taxes and subsidies, by preferences and licenses and so forth. In this process the vital spot is the interface between government and governed. If government does not know and understand and take full account of the capacity of the governed to digest and accept their dose of government, trouble will arise. Yet government retains the outlook and methods of an old-fashioned producer-minded industry in whose eyes the customer can be taken for granted. It could learn a lot from Marks and Spencer.

It must be recognized that the social energy on which national progress depends is not a fixed quantum, but can expand or dwindle according to the degree of satisfying participation on the one hand or of sullen frustration and bewilderment on the other. A share in the choice and working out of goals, fulfillment of reasonable expectations and hopes, assurance against traumas and reversals and participation in some of the drama of life are among the essentials denied to the citizen by the current System. Without them it is optimistic to expect high morale, or indeed to expect the nation to wake up from its torpor.

In the emerging electronic world of multiple parallel systems of communications, the linear logic of the one-track traditional schools is being displaced by new, subtle, and compact forms of social apprehension. What we see in a television discussion, or on the cinema screen, or by projected color transparencies, or maps, or aerial or ground photographs or diagrams, or in books or periodicals and so forth are not merely different media for expressing the same things, but methods of conveying a variety of distinct experiences which could not be fully conveyed in any other way. Against this background the standard Whitehall minute is more than half-way back to the Dead Sea

Scrolls as a tool of effective communication. It is not just primitive; it distorts, it clogs, it strangles. On the other hand the British talent for forming patterns of ideas, idea-systems, social stereotypes and so forth is perfectly fitted to the emerging wealth of media of communication. In contemplating electronic devices for communication it is too often assumed that the difficult thing is to design and make them. That is a misconception; making them is dead easy compared with learning to use them, and adjusting entire patterns of life accordingly. As recent activities of the younger generation indicate, Britain has immense reserves of adaptability to such challenges. These are among the grounds for supposing that big advances can be looked for here, if the system of misgovernment can be effectively and quickly dealt with.

PART FOUR
HOW BRITAIN IS GOVERNED

CHAPTER 8

The Sovereign Electorate

Having no written constitution, and being both a limited monarchy and a Parliamentary democracy undergoing rapid changes, the United Kingdom is an unusually complex and difficult subject for students of government. It is still more difficult for those who are merely interested as laymen, or are affected by its acts or omissions. Yet before seeking to explain or criticize its performance some kind of grasp is needed of what it is, and how it purports to function. Many excellent statements exist on the historical evolution of the British System, and on its legal basis and division of powers. What is needed for our purpose, and what this Part seeks to supply, is something different. The concern here is with the main recent changes and trends in the organization and conduct of the System. It needs to be viewed as a flexible but definable structure meant to express a set of values, principles and ideas, and forming the framework of an everyday flow process for determining its own agenda of problems, and dealing with them in an acceptable and efficient way. Whether they know it or not, and whether they like it or not, everyone from the Prime Minister to the most obscure "don't know" among the citizens must carry round with him some kind of mental picture of what this creature called government is. In so far as that picture is unduly vague and fuzzy, or is grossly at variance with the truth, or consists only of a confusing set of unrelated fragments, or is merely one of a chaotic series of differing and quite irreconcilable pictures seen by different individuals or groups, there will be so much more unnecessary grit falling into the working parts of government, and so much less likelihood that it can function acceptably and efficiently. In order to produce a picture which will be reasonably adequate for practical purposes, and can readily be grasped, it will be necessary to be highly selective, and to simplify or omit many important points which are inessential in this context.

Government is about the exercise of authority, and of the power which should accompany it. In many countries, where revolution or military overthrow has brought an abrupt discontinuity, the present government can point to a clear moment in time and a more or less clear written specification of the origin, nature and scope of its mandate. Written constitutions are by no means always as plain and comprehensive, or as prescient about future situations, as their authors would have wished, but at least they form a definite basis from which any argument about sovereignty must start, and on which proposals for constitutional reform must rest. Where, as in the United Kingdom, the constitution is largely unwritten, and is derived from a mixed series of events and enactments over many centuries, the problem is different. It is therefore not surprising to find that in Britain no single, generally accepted definition of sovereignty exists.

A century ago John Stuart Mill, in his *Representative Government,* defined his subject as being "that in which sovereignty, or supreme controlling power in the last resort, is vested in the entire aggregate of the community". Popularly attractive as such a simple formulation is, it is of no more practical use in law than such a mere slogan as "the dictatorship of the proletariat".

A. V. Dicey, in his *Introduction to the Law of the Constitution,* stated in 1885 that "The principle of Parliamentary Sovereignty means neither more nor less than this, namely, that Parliament thus defined" (as Queen-in-Parliament) "has, under the English constitution, the right to make or unmake any law whatever; and further, that no person or body is recognised by the law of England as having a right to override or set aside the legislation of Parliament". (It is interesting to note, as an instance of the looseness and subjectivity of even the highest authorities, that Dicey was writing of the Parliament of the United Kingdom, in the very year in which Gladstone convulsed it by deciding in favor of Home Rule for Ireland, which, like Scotland and Wales, was strongly represented in it. Yet Dicey thinks and speaks of it as if the partners other than England simply did not exist. Walter Bagehot actually entitled his great essay *The English Constitution,* and used "English" and "British" as synonyms from the outset.) With such eminent authority behind them the many foreigners who still say "England" when they mean "Great Britain" or "The United Kingdom" may claim to be in good company, deeply as they distress the

Scots, Welsh and Northern Irish compatriots who do not appreciate being wrongly lumped together as sections, or worse still as satellites, of the English majority in the politically unified state.

In his definition Dicey rejects any claim that the nation at large is the origin of, or even possesses a share of, its sovereignty. He wrote:

> The sole legal right of the electors under the English constitution is to elect members of Parliament. Electors have no legal means of initiating, or sanctioning, or of rejecting the legislation of Parliament. No court will consider for a moment the argument that a law is invalid as being opposed to the opinion of the electorate; their opinion can be legally expressed through Parliament, and through Parliament alone.

But Dicey added an illuminating comment:

> This is not a necessary incident of representative government. In Switzerland no change can be introduced in the constitution which has not been submitted for approval or disapproval to all male citizens who have attained their majority; and even an ordinary law which does not involve a change in the constitution may, after it has been passed by the Federal Assembly, be submitted on the demand of a certain number of citizens to a popular vote, and is annulled if a vote is not obtained in its favour . . . The plain truth is that as a matter of law Parliament is the sovereign power of the State . . . It is however, equally true that in a political sense the electors are the most important part of, we may even say are actually, the sovereign power, since their will is, under the present constitution, sure to obtain ultimate obedience.

In other words proximate sovereignty rests with the Queen-in-Parliament, but ultimate sovereignty rests with the electorate.

Dicey only clarified an ancient, evolutionary legal tradition. The classic definition of the sovereignty of Parliament was that of the eighteenth-century judge Blackstone:

> The power and jurisdiction of Parliament is so transcendent and absolute that it cannot be confined, either for causes or persons within any bounds . . . It hath sovereignty and uncontrollable authority in the making, confirming, enlarging, restraining, and providing of laws, concerning matters of all possible denominations, ecclesiastical or temporal, civil, military, maritime, or criminal; this being the place where that absolute despotic power which must in all governments reside somewhere, is entrusted by the constitution of these kingdoms . . .

It may be recalled that Blackstone's work was a best-seller in what were in his time the British colonies in eastern North America. But law evolves, and in the *Oxford Essays in Jurisprudence* for 1961 is found an enlightening statement by R. F. V. Heuson:

> If then we take our stand at about the year 1930 we survey a confusing scene. It is generally agreed that Parliament is a sovereign body which can repeal or amend by way of a simple majority in both houses even the most time-honoured principle of the constitution. This principle is, however, established merely by a series of *obiter dicta* by eminent persons, whether sitting on the bench or in the professorial study, rather than by any judicial decision of binding authority. Indeed, if we confined ourselves to the law reports, it has never been decided either that Parliament is a sovereign body or that one of its acts cannot be challenged . . . But by 1940 a new doctrine has begun to make considerable headway—a doctrine which has the advantage of being couched in the calm, hard, tightly-knit style of the common lawyer, rather than in the vague and emotional language of the political scientist. The concept of sovereignty, as a result of a conscious and subtle re-examination from within its own four corners, so to speak, has been shown to be at once less terrifying and more complex than had been thought. It appears that the lawyer can, without reservation or evasion, subscribe not only to the unlimited powers of Parliament, but also to the possibility of legal restraints upon (at least) the mode of use of that power.

Heuson comes to the following helpful and concise conclusion:

(1) Sovereignty is a legal concept; the rules which identify the sovereign and prescribe its composition and functions are logically prior to it.

(2) There is a distinction between rules which govern, on the one hand (a) the composition and (b) the procedure, and, on the other hand (c) the areas of power of a sovereign legislature.

(3) The courts have jurisdiction to question the validity of an alleged act of Parliament on grounds 2 (a) and (b), but not on ground 2 (c).

(4) This jurisdiction is exercisable either before or after the royal assent has been signified—in the former case by way of injunction, in the latter by way of declaratory judgment.

It thus appears that behind the popular and Parliamentary use of the term "sovereignty" has been hidden a good deal of uncertainty and even confusion, which is gradually being resolved on the plane of law, but is perhaps no nearer to solution than ever on the plane of political philosophy.

Reference to Part Four shows that from the General Strike in 1926 through the Suez episode in 1956 to the economic crisis of 1966 questions of sovereignty arose in British politics in a practical and acute form, and they are of course deeply involved in the question of joining the Common Market. It is interesting therefore to note that suggestions implying that some "surrender of sovereignty" or other is a clear-cut matter, like the loss by a municipality of county borough status, are much too simplified. We have to think very hard in each case just what we are asked to "give up" and in whose possession it now is, and what practical use it is as it stands, with regard to political and economic realities.

There is a further aspect which should be borne in mind. In the debates about sovereignty one is constantly led back to the electorate. Ministers appear in a secondary role, as being members of one or other house of Parliament, and as having been formally entrusted with their seals of office by the Queen. Government Departments, and the civil servants who staff them, have no share at all in sovereignty; they are simply servants of the servants of the sovereign trinity. This is a fact which no one should forget.

The British Parliamentary electorate, now some thirty-six million strong, has grown sevenfold since 1900, partly through increase of population, but largely through great extensions of the franchise in time for the elections of 1918 and 1929. This most massive part of the sovereign body has exercised its powers at a general election only seventeen times since 1900. The percentage turnout has fluctuated somewhat arbitrarily within a fairly narrow range between 70 percent and 87 percent. During the first two decades of the century it elected Parliaments of between 670 and 707 members, but the size has since been reduced to between 615 and 640, being now 630. During the two World Wars there were intervals of nearly eight and nine and a half years between General Elections, but with those exceptions the longest has been Queen Victoria's last Parliament, which outlived her and lasted for slightly over five years. It had a Unionist majority, but was followed by three Liberal Houses in succession, a coalition, a Conservative, a short-lived stalemate in 1923–24, another Conservative and another stalemate in 1929 and then two National coalitions, two Labour, three Conservative and two Labour. While Labour has never been granted more than six years of rule in succession, and has twice had to manage with majorities under ten, the National coalition of 1931–45 enjoyed an average majority of 336 and the latest trio of Conservative Parliaments covered thirteen consecutive years with a majority ranging between sixteen and a hundred.

The traditional two-party system has thus proved fairly successful in producing governments with a workable majority, except during the 'twenties, when there was an interregnum on the left between the Liberal and Labour parties. But the swing of the pendulum is hesitant. Since 1950 the electorate has three times elected governments with derisory majorities.

Yet the electorate has refrained from bestowing Parliamentary seats on any sizeable number of candidates independent of the two main parties. It is the electorate, rather than the party machines, which has destroyed the back-bench MP's independence. It appears that the voter resents independence in his MP, and prefers one who is tied by the two-party system to what he, perhaps optimistically, regards as predictable policies and stable leaders. No doubt, also, many voters feel that representation by an Independent excludes their constituency from any participation in real power, whichever party may be in office. Since 1950, despite repeated enthusiastic attempts to promote a Liberal revival, the combined number of Conservative and Labour MPs has always been well over 600 in a house of 630.

The pattern of behavior of the British electorate at General Elections is thus reasonably clear and consistent, and satisfies the elementary needs for providing a workable Government. If the Government does not actually work it cannot be blamed upon the electorate. The electorate from time to time does exercise the privilege of behaving freakishly at by-elections, but this is all within the rules of the game, and can be a very salutary lesson for its partners in sovereignty, the politicians.

The electorate is not a straightforward national constituency, as in many other countries, including Federal ones, but is composed of distinct nationalities with their particular rights. Thus Northern Ireland, which has its own provincial Parliament at Stormont, sends a guaranteed twelve members to what is still somewhat quaintly called there the Imperial Parliament in Westminster. Scotland is assured of not less than seventy-one seats, or one-ninth, although the Scots form less than one-tenth of the United Kingdom's population. Wales with 5 percent of the population has a guaranteed thirty-five seats, or about three to four more than it is proportionately entitled to. Although England is thus relatively under-represented the massed constituencies of Greater London, followed by Lancashire and Yorkshire, dominate the British political scene, making even Glasgow, Glamorgan and Birmingham look small in comparison. More than four members out of five are returned to the House of Commons by English voters, although a number of these are Scots or Welsh by origin. On the whole the reluctance to change party allegiances appears greater in Scotland and Wales than in England, and is greatest of all in Northern Ireland, where anyone but an Ulster Unionist stands a very indifferent chance of election.

Until very recently the feelings and beliefs of the electorate have been *terra incognita* to social science, and have been described only in the travelers' tales and folk-lore of politicians. Recently, in the face of much criticism and abuse from many politicians and a large section of the press, the validity and usefulness of opinion polls and similar sample investigations have been demonstrated so frequently and so conclusively that even the crassest of the critics have given up displaying their ignorance and prejudice against research. (It still emerges occasionally in the *schadenfreude* with which they greet any apparent slip or contradiction among the pollsters.)

Unfortunately, although the relatively straightforward social-statistical aspect of this work has been well developed recently in universities, and has indeed blossomed out as the new science of psephology, the motivations and processes behind the voter's performance in the electoral ritual remain virtually unexplored in Britain. No study exists of the British voter, of his perception of parties, politicians and policies, of the formation, nature and consequences of his partisan loyalties, which can compare with the work done in America by Angus Campbell, Philip E. Converse, Warren E. Miller and Donald E. Stokes. Pending the expected filling of this gap it is necessary to rely on the highly-articulated theories of voter-perception and loyalty-formation which they and other American sociologists have recently developed, and which appear equally valid in the British context, although this must be subject to verification through full study.

The authors define four levels of voter-perception. At the top comes a small fraction of the electorate—in America about 10 percent—which thinks of politics primarily in terms of abstract interrelated concepts derived from the protagonists and the specialist spectators of the political game. This level is characterized by a capacity to relate

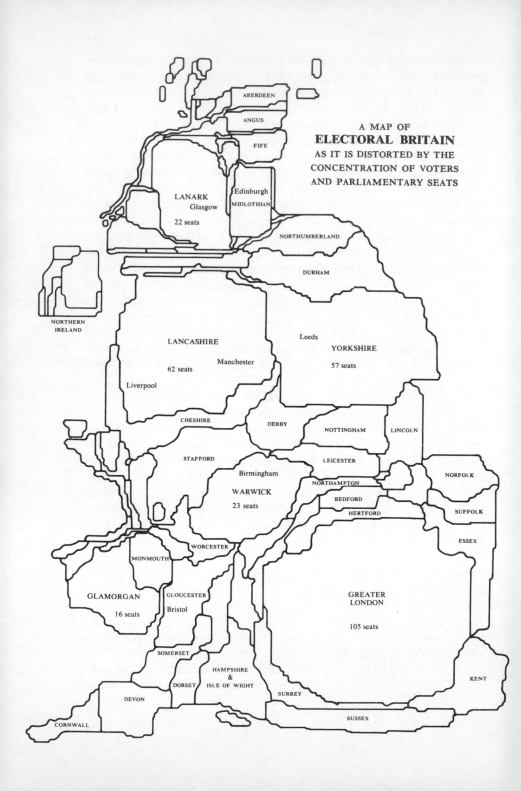

A MAP OF
ELECTORAL BRITAIN
AS IT IS DISTORTED BY THE
CONCENTRATION OF VOTERS
AND PARLIAMENTARY SEATS

ABERDEEN

ANGUS

FIFE

LANARK
Glasgow
22 seats

Edinburgh
MIDLOTHIAN

NORTHUMBERLAND

DURHAM

NORTHERN
IRELAND

LANCASHIRE
Manchester
62 seats

Liverpool

Leeds

YORKSHIRE
57 seats

CHESHIRE

DERBY

NOTTINGHAM

LINCOLN

STAFFORD

LEICESTER

Birmingham

WARWICK
23 seats

NORTHAMPTON

NORFOLK

BEDFORD

HERTFORD

SUFFOLK

ESSEX

WORCESTER

MONMOUTH

GLAMORGAN
16 seats

GLOUCESTER
Bristol

GREATER
LONDON
105 seats

SOMERSET

HAMPSHIRE
&
ISLE OF WIGHT

DORSET

SURREY

KENT

DEVON

CORNWALL

SUSSEX

remote and seemingly unconnected trends and incidents to such concepts, and thus to follow the course of the game and understand what the score is at any given moment.

At a second level are many more voters—in America an estimated 45 percent—who are so guided only at second-hand, for example through interest groups, more or less organized and articulate, such as bodies of employers, workers, outdoorsmen, Protestants, Irish or animal-lovers. These groups tend to develop settled views concerning which political parties or elements are most friendly or like-minded, and to influence their adherents accordingly. The extent and effectiveness of this influence depends upon the degree to which the individual identifies himself with the group, on his lack of alternative approaches to politics, on the group's political identification or otherwise with particular policies, politicians and parties, and on the centralization and caliber of the group's leadership. Voters in this class may be said to make their crucial political choices at second-hand. Once they have committed themselves to their chosen special interest group, their voting is determined by their loyalty to its preference.

At a third level there are what are termed "goodness-and-badness-of-the-times" voters. These were the ones whom Prime Minister Macmillan was aiming at in his notorious assurance that "you never had it so good". They are guided almost entirely by the fortunes of themselves and their families in the recent past and present, and it is a healthy fear of their dreaded "thumbs-down" gesture which leads governments expecting to face the electorate shortly to dress the shop-window, often regardless of the capacity of the national economy to realize their promises. This type of "floating voter" is characterized, in America, and probably here also, by a taste for simple condemnatory moral judgments, a special sensitivity to corruption, an intense dislike of "mudslinging" and a tendency to become easily confused and distressed by cross-party polemics which expose their unusual ignorance and lack of understanding of political events, issues and personalities. Politically they are hardly admirable elements, but in a world so apt to be fooled by slogans, prejudices and appearances they exercise a salutary influence in applying, however selfishly and partially, the much-needed test of results. Like predators in the animal realm they unerringly identify and strike down the weaklings.

The fourth and final level is that of the "personality voters". These are the most detached from, and the least interested in, the political issues themselves, and are therefore the most likely to abstain. Their

UNITED KINGDOM STRUCTURE OF GOVERNMENT (existing)

LEGISLATURE

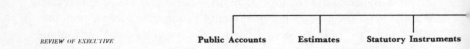

REVIEW OF EXECUTIVE

Public Accounts   Estimates   Statutory Instruments

Comptroller and Auditor-General

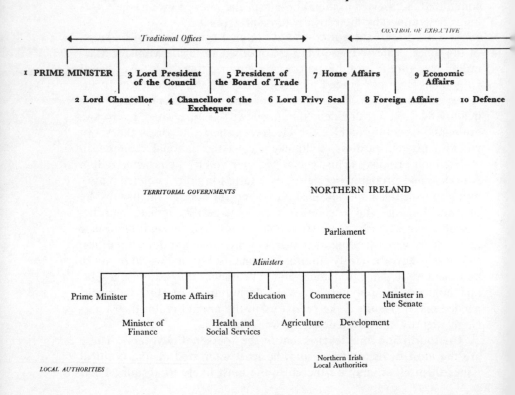

CONTROL OF EXECUTIVE

◄──────── Traditional Offices ────────►   ◄──────

1 PRIME MINISTER   3 Lord President   5 President of   7 Home Affairs   9 Economic
                          of the Council   the Board of Trade   Affairs

    2 Lord Chancellor   4 Chancellor of the   6 Lord Privy Seal   8 Foreign Affairs   10 Defence
                            Exchequer

TERRITORIAL GOVERNMENTS   NORTHERN IRELAND

                                              Parliament

                                    Ministers

    Prime Minister   Home Affairs   Education   Commerce   Minister in
                                                                               the Senate

          Minister of   Health and   Agriculture   Development
           Finance   Social Services

                                          Northern Irish
                                          Local Authorities

LOCAL AUTHORITIES

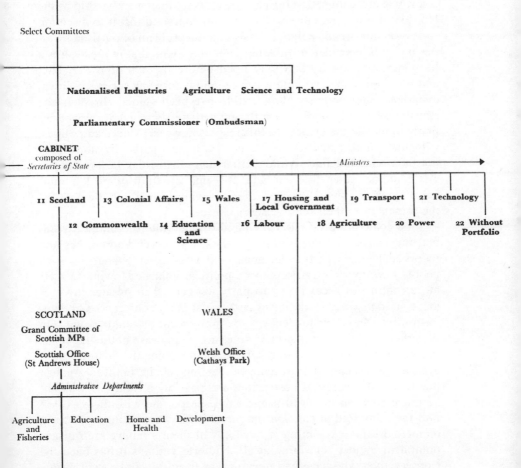

PARLIAMENT

Select Committees

Nationalised Industries   Agriculture   Science and Technology

Parliamentary Commissioner (Ombudsman)

CABINET
composed of
Secretaries of State ———→   ←——— *Ministers* ———→

11 Scotland   13 Colonial Affairs   15 Wales   17 Housing and   19 Transport   21 Technology
                                                   Local Government

12 Commonwealth   14 Education   16 Labour   18 Agriculture   20 Power   22 Without
                      and   Portfolio
                      Science

SCOTLAND   WALES

Grand Committee of
Scottish MPs

Scottish Office   Welsh Office
(St Andrews House)   (Cathays Park)

Administrative Departments

Agriculture   Education   Home and   Development
and   Health
Fisheries

Scottish   Welsh   English
Local Authorities   Local Authorities Local Authorities

motive for voting is interest in the personal characteristics of candidates, and perhaps a mild excitement about the gladiatorial aspects of a contest. The interest and support of this type of voter is clearly more susceptible to being stimulated through successful television appearances than by any other medium, and recognition of this is a factor in the intense and growing concern of political parties with the capacity of their leaders and spokesmen to make a good impression on television. We may have reached the point where a poor television manner is a worse disqualification for party leadership than membership of the House of Lords, and moreover is one much more difficult to disclaim.

It is on this broad analytical basis that the problem of partisan loyalties has to be considered. In America it was found that in most cases a life-long party loyalty had developed before the age of twenty-one, and thus before the first vote was cast, and before any serious political experience and understanding could have been gained. In such circumstances family tradition or the immediate social environment are likely to dictate the choice. In this respect however American politics, with their more ritualized and even less logical party divisions, may not be a reliable guide. While similar ingredients may be present the mix could be rather different here. It seems safe to distinguish a number of types of voters, however, even if we must remain in the dark for the present as to their relative significance.

First come the good party men and women, the true-blues, the unblushing singers of "The Red Flag", those who never doubt or hesitate to proclaim their party allegiance, and who never change it. Such people have in some respects more political influence, owing to their more continuous accessibility to party workers, their greater involvement, in some cases including attendance at party conferences or demonstrations, and their tendency to be more vocal on major issues. On the other hand the fact that their votes are in any case in the bag tends to lead party managers to worry more about wooing the floating voter, even at the expense of outraging the feelings of the faithful. Against this their only redress is abstention, and possibly a subdivision might be made between the dyed-in-the-wool sheep, who will always troop into the party fold at election time, and those who, while never for a moment dreaming of voting otherwise, will silently relieve their disappointment by just not voting at all. Hitherto perhaps it has been the Conservatives who have had most to fear from this, but recent events may well have created a counterpart in the Labour camp. One further specific feature of this group is its proneness to hyphenate its party loyalty in some more or less awkward and more or less permanent sect. Thus there were in the inter-war period Simonite National Liberals, Lloyd George Liberals and Liberals without prefix or suffix who became divided into separate splinter parties. Similar tendencies have emerged with Bevanite and ILP socialists and with Bow Group and Suez Group conservatives, to mention only a few examples. Sometimes such groups have their main significance within the Parliamentary party, sometimes in the constituencies, but always their existence complicates the task of party leaders and makes for a more sophisticated and delicately balanced formulation of policies in which two-way communication, if only with a limited small fraction of the electorate, becomes a vital factor.

The other types of elector need not be discussed in detail, as their role is more self-evident. First in logical order come the party converts —those who own a definite party allegiance, but change it once or more during their lifetime. These possess an importance out of proportion to their numbers because they take politics, and usually also themselves, very seriously, and are often vocal in justifying their standpoint, whatever it may be at the time. They are valuable in personifying and acting out tensions and contradictions in the body politic, and thus contributing to the process of change.

Next come the more or less constant fellow-travelers—those who do not participate in or subscribe to a party—except perhaps through not contracting out of the political levy in their trade union—but who almost invariably support the same party at election time, and who, if too disgusted with its current policy to do so, would generally prefer abstention to voting otherwise.

A distinct group, particularly unpalatable to the politically active, are the mugwumps—people who take a genuine and sometimes intense interest in public affairs but prefer always to form their own conclusions, and whose vote is determined on each occasion by their degree of satisfaction with the record and explanations and program of each party, rather than by any liking or commitment towards any of them. This book is, of course, written from the standpoint of a lifelong mugwump, and its perusal will no doubt sufficiently explain the acute irritation with which such people are regarded.

A much larger group, whose size and composition is one of the most critical mysteries of British politics, are content to ignore public affairs, until the approach of election time, when they make up their minds more or less freshly on each occasion and vote accordingly.

These are the dreaded floating voters, no doubt overlapping largely with the last two levels of the American voter analysis mentioned earlier, and also with the "Don't knows" of the opinion polls. Among the many mysterious features of this group is their capacity in many cases to make up their minds and then stick to them not during a General Election campaign but some little time before it begins.

Finally there is the residue of civic illiterates, lacking either motivation or information for exercising their little share of sovereignty, who will vote only if more or less compelled to do so by some form of browbeating, exhortation or press-ganging into the polling booth. These are a very mixed group, ranging from the numerous mental defectives, psychiatric cases, half-wits and clots, who for some reason are never quantified in ordinary statistical analyses of the British population, to gifted artists, fashion designers, pop musicians and others who simply do not join.

What do the people want? A hundred and fifty years ago when the franchise was sharply restricted, it would have seemed very odd that voters should be much interested in electing a government to provide them with a wide range of services and even goods for their personal use. The privileged minority, who then monopolized the votes, were far from being more altruistic than their successors today, but they knew very well that any such system of handouts would be conducted at their own expense as taxpayers, and that they would be poor value for money. This must be so because they had consistently blocked the creation of an efficient public service, such as had been developed a century earlier in Germany. Matters would be made worse by the pickings which some of their number would surely take from the kitty first, in the form of bribes, irregular payments and improper appointments to salaried offices. If they felt, as they often did at election times, a craving for pecuniary reward for doing their sovereign duties, they had no inhibitions about collecting it in cash on the nail from the candidate to whom they promised their non-secret vote.

The masses of new voters, added especially during the present century, viewed things very differently. Most of them felt themselves not among the "haves" but among the "have-nots" of society. They looked on the machinery of government, now purged of corruption and nepotism if not, unhappily, of inefficiency, as a heaven-sent instrument for taking from the wealthy as much as possible of the lavish resources with which historical accident or social injustice had endowed them, and redistributing it among their poorer fellow-voters. The British

Liberal movement, with its uncanny capacity for invoking the loftiest ideals and ending with the most squalid results, spent much of the Victorian era in blocking public expenditure on higher education, research, and technology which could have enabled the nation to keep abreast economically of the United States, and on the growth of welfare services, which could have kept it abreast of Germany. In clinging to the creed of free trade as a means to cheap labor they crippled the development of national productivity to this day. They thus forced the new electorate into an increasingly cynical and political approach towards obtaining the share of national wealth of which they not unjustifiably felt themselves cheated. This, in turn, led to a process of unedifying bargaining between parties to outbid each other for the support of the new voters. The Liberal Party was eventually outbid and virtually wiped off the Parliamentary map, while remaining quite a substantial minority scattered throughout the nation.

Unfortunately, after this just retribution overtook the Liberal Party some forty years ago, it was succeeded by an electorally narrower and intellectually weaker Labour Party. This, partly through doctrinaire tenets, partly through a chronic inability to tell what time it is, and partly through the continuing feeble but troublesome competition for votes from the surviving Liberals, persisted on the same path of neglecting or obstructing economic adaptation and expansion, and sought to substitute political means of redistributing an increasingly unsatisfying sum of national wealth. It was only as a result of the 1966 economic crisis that the leadership of the Labour Party found itself compelled at last to tell its supporters the facts of economic life, and to insist on the subordination of political pressures to economic effort as the basis of raising standards of living.

Here ringing out clear and loud is the melancholy theme of British misgovernment, on which variations have been performed over the whole of the past century. Those who could and should have studied and interpreted the facts failed to do so adequately, and gave no warning, or incorrect and belated warning, of what to expect and to provide against. Those who should have led failed to lead, or led in the wrong direction, partly because they were so poorly briefed and advised, partly through sheer bias and wrongheadedness. Those who should have followed and performed largely failed to do so, partly because they justly mistrusted the wisdom and *bona fides* of their leaders, and partly on account of ignorance, inertia and irresponsibility. Thus the nation drifted into its present state. The disease lends itself neither to simple diagnosis nor to easy remedy, but until the true diagnosis is established further efforts at remedy must meet just as little success as the slipshod and unworthy efforts of the past.

In assessing systems of government four points must be discussed. Who participates in government, on what terms and within what limits? What are their qualifications to participate, whether abstract and ethical or practical, in terms of education and training, assumption of responsibilities, payment of taxes and so forth? Is the system designed, and does it in fact work, to maintain an acceptable relationship and a positive, constructive social dynamic throughout the nation? And finally, is the system fully efficient, in the sense that it makes the best use of the latest knowledge and technology to perform the tasks which it sets itself? The answers to these questions will do most to enable us to ascertain whether the system under scrutiny is rightly to be described as one of government or of misgovernment.

Participation in the form of a right to vote at Parliamentary and local elections is open to all who could reasonably claim it, except for those aged between eighteen and twenty-one, and a small minority who are in practice disfranchised by administrative limitations which may or may not be inevitable. Participation for the majority is, however, limited in practice to voting for one or other of two or more candidates. These, if elected, will only be free to carry out their election pledges if it suits their political party leaders at the time to permit it. Having performed this ritual the sovereign electors are at all other times expected to, and largely do, function as more or less passive members of a governed race, subject to a somewhat dwindling number of safeguards for personal liberty luckily inherited from a more robust past, and more or less effectively sustained by the courts of law. Citizen participation in British government over the past forty years has been meager, intermittent, and only occasionally effective, although when effective it has sometimes been dramatically so.

The question how far citizens are denied by the present system a fair chance of playing a role as partners in sovereignty rather than as units among the governed will be discussed later. The issue here is their capacity to play such a role, given the opportunity. Reformers in starry-eyed pursuit of social justice have tended to neglect the question how the sovereign people, once endowed with the long-sought privilege of the vote, would acquire the somewhat exacting capacity to make full and wise use of it. Social justice is admirable, but there is also a need for social efficiency and the cultivation of a social dynamic.

It is now horribly clear that, in preening ourselves on our great strides towards the first, we have fallen down badly over the second and third. Let us face the fact that the current British elector is for the most part not qualified by keenness of commitment, by political flair or training, by basic education and information, by a clear personal stake in the prosperity of the nation, or by any regular or continuing responsibilities towards it, to exercise what, say, an Ancient Greek would have regarded as the full and serious role of a citizen in an advanced civilized state. To say this is not to criticize or to dissent from the recent policy decisions to go so far towards universalizing the adult franchise, but merely to emphasize the amount of unfinished business which these decisions involve, and the great urgency of getting on with it. It is just a century since a Victorian statesman was understood to say, "We must educate our masters", but the task has hardly seriously begun. This illustrates one more chronic and recurrent theme of the British system—the appalling timelag between the emergence of a need and the action to meet it.

CHAPTER 9

Parliament and the Crown

It is no doubt widely assumed that the very imperfect capacity of the ultimate sovereign body, the electorate, should be and is compensated by the performance of the proximate sovereign body, Parliament. The record, particularly of the past forty years, gives little support for such a proposition, even if it could be admitted as in principle legitimate. Although forcibly reminded at intervals that the electorate are its masters, Parliament is fully aware of the impotence of the electorate to do anything to assert that status in between elections, while even at election time there are many ways for the politician to immunize himself.

One of the main reasons why Parliament has been unable to fill the sovereign role is that the real power, which it wrested so late in history from the Crown, has already passed to the executive. Indeed, much that has been said above about the incapacity of the electorate applies, *mutatis mutandis,* to Parliament itself.

The House of Commons also includes its different levels of political perception, ranging from the highly sophisticated, well-educated professional élite through the bands of members whose association with interest groups has done much to shape their attitudes to those trying to keep up with their constituents (who are trying to keep up with the Joneses) and to the more quixotic who follow a chosen leader or cause. Here again there are the sworn party men, whose ostentatious loyalty is sometimes split by their allegiance to splinter groups or to some Old Guard within the Parliamentary Party itself, and the various bands of sheep whom the Whips need normally never worry about, and goats who can worry them a great deal. Two changes must, however, be specially noted here. During the inter-war period quite a number of MPs were under pledges, treated with great solemnity regarding particular features of policy, such as tariffs, free trade, Sunday observance, nationalization, or the means test. Perhaps as a result of such rigidities adaptation of law and policy on such matters was painfully slow. Possibly owing to the number of MPs who finally had to eat their words on such issues, possibly owing to the fashion for "a doctor's mandate" so outrageously but triumphantly set by the National Government of the 'thirties, or perhaps owing to the decay of concern with principles, it appears that present-day members have been less rash in nailing their colors to the mast and more are free to go where their good judgment or a three-line whip sends them. A melting of political dogmatism and a strengthening of political flexibility are evident trends during the period. This has apparently reduced pressures to change party allegiance, and, perhaps for the first time in more than a century, the higher ranks of politics no longer include anyone who began a political career in one party and has continued it in another. A cynical interpretation would be that principles now count for so little and pragmatism for so much that entire parties can now be drilled to perform such a volte-face as in earlier times would have demanded crossing the floor.

A second change, in which the record of both Houses of Parliament diverges from that of the greatly enlarged modern electorate, is a distinct improvement in the quality of members. The reasons differ in the two cases. The House of Lords, whose deprivation of its financial and veto powers under the Parliament Act of 1911 has been cumulatively influencing its modern development, sought with some success a fresh role as a Second Chamber of a less partisan character, devoting itself increasingly to the informed and dispassionate discussion of long-range issues, minority problems and the assessment of progress in broad fields. Divesting itself in large measure of its hoary oligarchic and semi-feudal image, and minimizing its traditional role, it has emerged as a much-needed organ of review and of non-partisan initiative and adjustment. It has thus attracted recruits of high caliber, especially since the Life Peerages Act of 1958, which has revolutionized its composition and is further converting it into a uniquely qualified Second Chamber of the meritocracy, with a small and dwindling hereditary element still taking an active part. The Peerage Act 1963 has enabled inheritors of peerages to disclaim them.

In the case of the House of Commons there has been no such dramatic change, but the progressive raising of MPs' pay from the initial £400 in 1911, adjusted to £600 in 1937, £1,000 in 1947, £1,750 in 1957 and £3,250 in 1964, together with the institution of pensions for ex-members of at least ten years' service, has radically changed the terms and conditions of Parliamentary life, and has enabled many more able and younger men, even with young families, to afford to serve. One consequence is a marked increase in the proportion of graduate MPs, from 42 percent in 1924 to 58 percent in 1966. Although universities other than Oxford or Cambridge now claim 21 percent, against 13 percent in 1924, Oxford graduates outnumber all of them with 22 percent; there are 15 percent from Cambridge.

Lawyers have long been a prominent element in the House, but have declined from an inter-war average of 23 percent to between 15 percent and 20 percent since 1945. Before World War II lawyers, company directors and trade union officials comprised over half the House; now they make only one-third. Journalists, teachers, lecturers and executives have taken their vacated places. Trade unionists have fallen strikingly on the Labour benches from about 50 percent pre-war to only 11 percent in 1966, while on the Conservative benches there has been a parallel but less marked fall of company directors from 39 percent in 1945 to 26 percent in 1966. Perhaps the most striking divergence of the House from the electorate has been the fall in "working-class" MPs from perhaps 45 percent inter-war to only 20 percent in 1966. (As already mentioned the proportion of British population currently classified as "working-class" is 70 percent.) Probably never in its long history has the House been so largely composed of members so different in social origins, training and occupation from the majority of their constituents.

The traditional basis of sending to Westminster men regarded as largely typical of those who sent them has been superseded by the emergence, still very incomplete, of a new class of middlemen, of professional politicians whose expertise must lie not in being bred to utter what their constituents feel, but in being trained to interpret national policy to their voters, and to try to see that it is tempered to the broad and long-term needs of their constituencies. It is important to note here that the transition is still in its early stages. Even in the absence of other change, the MP of the 'seventies will be a different person from the MP of the 'fifties, and still more of the 'thirties, when such anachronistic worthies as the aptly named Sir Waldron Smithers were still able to be returned time after time to pursue their comical travesty of the role of a British legislator. One beneficial result of the growing power of party central offices has been their successful pressure on constituency associations to cease selecting for safe seats candidates whose permanence at Westminster spoils the image of the Party before the general electorate, and often gravely embarrasses the party leadership in Parliament. The screening out of freaks, bores and eccentrics may take some of the color out of Parliamentary life, but it also removes a good deal of grit from the works.

Unfortunately this definite improvement in the quality of the House of Commons has coincided with a threefold decline in its scope and liberty of action. The liquidation of the dependent Empire, and related changes in the British international role, have much reduced the worldwide authority and prestige of the House, especially in view of the accompanying failure to enter the European Common Market. The cumulatively more severe crises in the United Kingdom economy have forced the House, even more than has recently been usual, to abdicate much of its authority in favor of the Government, which alone can handle such a complex and fast-changing situation. This governmental near-dictatorship has in any case been superimposed on a tighter and tighter control over individual MPs by the Whips and the Party. Constitutional specialists may lay down that sovereignty is in the hands of Parliament, but the member of Parliament soon finds out that it is not he as part-sovereign who sends for a Minister and points out to him the error of his ways, but quite the opposite. Not since George III was beaten under doctors' advice during the treatment of his alleged madness has such rough medicine been dealt out to the heirs of British sovereignty as to present-day MPs by their parties.

While the quality of MPs, unlike that of their constituents and of the Civil Service, has recently been improved rather than diluted, their status and independence has been reduced. To a considerable extent this seems due to the fact that the present-day MP falls between several stools. He usually lacks the prestige and weight of a man important in his own right in his own community, and sent to Westminster as such to speak for it. He may be a full-time politician, but is likely still to be a part-timer, inhibited by other ties and functions. The local sources of information which are peculiarly his own have been shown to be highly unreliable, for example by opinion polls which are equally available to others. He thus tends to be a merchant of services which can more readily and efficiently be drawn upon from other sources. His constituents largely regard him as a potential local ombudsman and helper in time of trouble rather than as a shaper of policies which may affect local fortunes. He is expected to keep abreast of an impossibly wide range of problems, on which independent and comprehensive information is difficult to come by, except through the assistance of interest groups. It is a harassing, undignified and often frustrating existence, from which many able men have opted out in disgust. Popular interest in debates has declined, and even the sales of *Hansard* fell from 8,889 in 1945 to 2,170 in 1963.

The recent history of the Crown, this third, once first, partner in the sovereign trinity has been curiously different from that of the other two. The main and decisive struggle of the groups then controlling Parliament to wrest effective sovereignty from the Crown took place during the seventeenth century. Under the usual British timelag, however, it was about another two hundred years, in late Victorian times, before the Glorious Revolution of 1688 could be said to have been totally accepted in the Palace. By that time the anxieties of the social groups who had hitherto been almost exclusively concerned in the struggle were fixed on the growing threat from lower orders in society to take over as much as possible of the winnings. Thus the ranks of Society with a capital S closed round the monarchy, which, whatever might have been going on in private, was henceforth accorded a public deference and invested with a mystique that would have seemed strange to the Whigs and even the Tories of the eighteenth and early nineteenth centuries, when disrespect for it was the rule.

The prolonged withdrawal from public view of Queen Victoria during her widowhood, and the empty pomp and circumstance favored by Edward VII got the monarchy off to a poor start for the twentieth century. Shortly before 1914 it had been confronted with a series of agonizing dilemmas regarding the curbing of the House of Lords, the threatened civil war in Ireland and the shadow of the coming World War I. These at once tore up the long ties of German kinship and influence, shook to its foundations the traditional British hierarchy, and unloosed powerful new forces unused and unsympathetic to the idea of monarchy, and eager for drastic change.

Despite the intense hatred of Germany, which among other things compelled in July 1917 a change of name of the Royal House from Saxe-Coburg and Gotha to Windsor, the effect of the tragic drama of the war and of the simple sense of duty of King George V and Queen Mary was to give the monarchy a new hold on the feelings of the nation, and to make the Royal Family the first family in a deeply symbolic sense. Continuous intense publicity, aided by the glamor of the Crown and by many well-judged personal appearances and broadcasts, brought the King and his family close to many millions, and freed them to some extent from their dependence on and association with court circles. Intimate and continuous knowledge of the inside story of public affairs gave the King an advantage in handling the successive crises of the 'twenties and early 'thirties. In 1923, when Bonar Law as outgoing Prime Minister declined to advise on the choice of his successor, King George V passed over Curzon, who had the greatest experience of high office, and chose instead Stanley Baldwin, on the ground that under a recently evolved constitutional convention the Prime Minister must be in the Commons, not the Lords. The man whom he thus, no doubt rightly, selected was to have, thirteen years later, the even more delicate assignment, unique in British history, of arranging for his eldest son Edward VIII to abdicate the throne in favor of his younger brother Albert, who ascended it under the now reassuring name of George VI. The situation of a Prime Minister suddenly departing, leaving the succession to him in doubt, recurred in 1957 on the resignation of Sir Anthony Eden, and although the action of Queen Elizabeth II in choosing Harold Macmillan was subsequently fully endorsed by Parliament and the electorate it was felt that the monarch ought not to be exposed to such a delicate situation in future. The maneuvers technically known as "soundings" in the Conservative Party on the resignation of Harold Macmillan through illness were accordingly handled by the outgoing Prime Minister, by means which call for no comment here, as they did not involve the monarch in a decision.

A decision of comparable delicacy and magnitude arose in 1931 when the Labour cabinet, in a minority in the Commons, found itself unable to agree upon measures necessary to meet the economic crisis. King George V thereupon suggested to the Prime Minister, Ramsay MacDonald, that he form a coalition National Government, and this advice, when taken, was overwhelmingly confirmed at a General Election in the following month. But the monarch is not always right, nor always deferred to. In 1940 King George VI made clear to Chamberlain his preference for the Earl of Halifax as next Prime Minister, in contradiction to the principle which his father had followed in choosing Baldwin. Nevertheless the mind of the House of Commons was clear, and it was Churchill who was appointed.

These few instances from recent history must suffice to show how wrong it is to regard the monarch as even now a constitutional cipher.

Like the electorate, but unlike Parliament, the monarch has only rare opportunities to exercise a significant share of sovereignty, but they can be nevertheless decisive on the grand scale.

The monarch has the constitutional right, as Bagehot put it, to be consulted, to advise and to warn. When Anthony Eden resigned as Foreign Secretary in 1938 King George VI protested to Neville Chamberlain, the Prime Minister, that he had not been kept properly informed. It is clearly a valuable safeguard that Prime Ministers should be under such an obligation, and should have to bear it in mind when they may be tempted to arbitrary action. Cabinet papers, Foreign Office dispatches from overseas posts and major departmental memoranda are sent to the monarch. The Palace takes more newspapers and periodicals than a public library, and runs a press-cutting service to match. Every week while Parliament is in session, the Prime Minister calls on the monarch for a discussion of the political situation, usually lasting about an hour. Distinguished political visitors are often met by the monarch when they come to Britain, and similar contacts are frequent on state visits abroad.

When a reign has run some years the monarch has thus acquired a knowledge of affairs of state greater than that of any single politician. Potentially, therefore, the monarch's opinion can be of unique value. Whether it is so in fact depends on a number of circumstances, varying from one occasion to another. If it is unmistakably well founded on a wealth of relevant experience and on strict political impartiality its weight will be impressive to all concerned. If it falls short of such standards it need not be followed. In any event it strengthens and enriches the constitution that an opinion based on such a conception of duty, and such a wealth of confidential information, can be sought in time of special stress or uncertainty. The evidence strongly suggests that the Crown as it has recently acted within the sovereign trinity has contributed much to the wise solution of some of the most critical national emergencies. Unlike the other parties in sovereignty the monarch has been carefully trained for the job since youth, and rarely if ever has to reach a conclusion without having adequate information, knowledge and time to do it properly. There could be better and more stable ways of discharging such functions, but in contrast to many other things in Britain the monarchy as it is appears to stand the test of results in comparison with any alternative patterns of discharging the function of Head of State which present themselves in other countries. The happenings in Dallas on the afternoon of November 22, 1963, underline this point.

If this is true in relation to sovereignty it is quite equally so in the monarchy's other publicly symbolic and personifying function, at times of national grief and rejoicing, in knitting together different regions and territories within the ambit of a shared personal relationship, and in encouraging those who are doing well to do better, and those who are inert to stir themselves. The sheer organization and timing of royal journeys and visits constantly throws up problems which would trouble a film or television producer on a generous budget, yet the commentators and reporters who are so alert for the slightest hitch or mishap are usually disappointed. Even in bad weather, and among people soured by previous neglect or political ineptitude, the Crown can still sparkle.

The only two significant grounds for criticism which have persisted as a live issue in recent years have been the supposed built-in tendency of the crown to favor continuance of outmoded class divisions, and the issue of expense. As regards the first it has been plainly demonstrated that the modern monarchy does not need and indeed may be rather bored by the survivals of a traditional court and its numerous hangers-on, social and commercial. Expense is hardly to be taken seriously as a criticism on its own account; it simply emerges as a useful stick to pick up in furtherance of some other campaign. Perhaps the chief liability of the monarchy coincides with one of its chief assets—its historic antiquity. Largely unaware of the extent to which it has functionally adapted itself to the present, many assume that the monarchy must be as out of date as it is ancient. In fact it is among the least cobwebbed working parts of the British governmental mechanism.

History shows many examples where some division of sovereign powers, such as now exists in Britain, gives rise to continuous or intermittent friction, and even to fierce internecine struggles. The otherwise troubled and scarred history of the past forty years here shows little trace of such problems. Why is this? There seem to be two reasons for it, one good and one bad. The good one is that Parliament and the electorate have successively concluded to their full satisfaction their protracted struggles for a share of sovereignty. They have all they want, and they are satisfied that the full limitations and protocol of limited constitutional monarchy will in future be punctiliously observed by the Crown with which, therefore, they have no quarrel.

If the relations between the sovereign trinity of electorate, Parliament and monarchy are amicable and work well, and if no one of the partners seriously wants to disturb them, we appear to be confronted with something too good to be true, and this is where the bad reason emerges. In fact, sovereignty has degenerated into something which would be a wonderful thing to have if only it were possible to do something with it. The exercise of sovereignty, and most of the activities which carry power and may seem fun, have been surreptitiously removed from the control of all three partners in the sovereign trinity, and transferred to others through whose clutches they must now be followed in order that we may have the answer to the question which every ecologist must ask about every ecosystem—"What's going on here?"

CHAPTER 10

Parliament and the Nation's Business

Theoretically the electorate might present each new Parliament with a kind of shopping list or outline program of those matters which it wished Parliament to deal with, but, of course, the British electorate does not go in for that kind of initiative. At most, the electors may vaguely convey that they are concerned about some long-standing defects, some scandal or some unfilled need, and that they will favor some suitable action being taken. There may be some individual or some voluntary body which has put forward a project or program evidently congenial to the voters, and therefore meriting at least lip-service from politicians. There may have been some disaster, some public blunder or some dispute which has sufficiently impressed itself on the public to render suggestions for remedial or preventive action politically expedient. In all such cases there will have been public discussion and some opportunity to gauge public opinion, both on the intensity of the demand for action and on the general form which action should take. Ministers will thus have a fairly concrete basis for instructing Departments to prepare a scheme, which can then be discussed in detail with interested parties before being put into final shape. In such cases the constitutional flow process is nearly complete, involving all parties from the electorate to the final executants.

A frequent variant is where the process of initiation begins overseas. There may be a clash with some other state or its nationals, as over the Icelandic fishery limits, or the tenure of Gibraltar. There may be some grouping to which Britain belongs, such as NATO, the North Atlantic Treaty Organization, or desires to belong, such as the Euro-

pean Common Market, which gives rise to negotiation and to prepara-
tions for adjustments at home. Police action or open hostilities may be
involved, as in Aden or Borneo, and it may be thought necessary to
send out reinforcements of men and materials. The common element
in all such business is that it is triggered off in the first place not by one
of the sovereign partners at home but by some party beyond the realm.
That party may be hostile, rival, neutral, friendly or in some way allied, or it may be an international organization of which Britain forms
part. The closer it falls to the latter categories the more it tends to raise
the problem of limitations or of shared sovereignty. There is a timelag
between theory and practice almost as great as the lag between need
and action, owing to the national habit of doing something fresh gradually, and often belatedly, in response to a convincing need, and then
leaving some academic later on to try to rationalize and integrate it in
political thought. A realistic theory of sovereignty would already have
to take cognizance of the fact that, in addition to the sovereign trinity
within Britain, an effective and legal share in the exercise of sovereignty is also allowed to other parties such as the United Nations, and
to alliances such as NATO, and of course prospectively the signatories
of the Treaty of Rome. The nation bows, too, at least sometimes, to the
quasi-sovereign decisions of a Commonwealth Conference. In theory
the Statute of Westminster, 1931, was designed to free the six then
existing dominions, all peopled by Europeans, of the remnants of subject status and of liability to constitutional interference from the Parliament of the United Kingdom, sometimes loosely and irregularly
termed the Imperial Parliament. In fact, and inevitably, having let
loose these "autonomous communities within the British Empire,
equal in status, in no way subordinate one to another in any aspect of
their domestic or external affairs, though united by a common allegiance to the Crown, and freely associated as members of the British
Commonwealth of Nations" (to quote the report of Lord Balfour's
Committee of the 1926 Imperial Conference), Britain was soon to find
that the boot had been put on the other foot. It was now the turn of the
Commonwealth to exercise something like a veto over British policies
unacceptable to other members—a trend which culminated in the extreme pressure laid on Britain by other Commonwealth countries over
Rhodesia.

No doubt in another few decades some other solemn conclave will
discover and explain in lofty prose that since time immemorial it has
been the practice to share British sovereignty with the Canadians, the
Indians, the Ghanaians, the Americans, the Dutch, and all members of

the United Nations, NATO, the International Monetary Fund and so forth. Present-day official doctrine however expects us to close our eyes to this *de facto* situation, and thus no constitutional distinction is made between those parties who possess something very like a share in British sovereignty as of right, and those who merely compel us to reverse firmly held policies by *force majeure,* like the Icelanders in the dispute over territorial limits at sea, and President Makarios over Cyprus. This approaches, but is not identical with, a distinction which has been drawn between "political sovereignty" and "legal sovereignty".

Since such problems originate beyond Britain's shores, they are almost invariably taken up and handled throughout by the government, subject to the fitful scrutiny of Parliament and of private groups of citizens. Often these matters become very urgent and delicate. The messy way in which they arise and develop lays a disturbingly heavy strain on senior Ministers and officials, who are thus often precluded from giving the attention to long-term United Kingdom affairs which they should, in order to avert the build-up of crises at home. The period of colonial liquidation has been particularly difficult in this respect, and its distractions have played some part in the neglect of Britain's internal problems of adaptation. A further difficulty is well illustrated by the imports surcharge of 1965 which, when adopted as the best solution of an internal problem, was stated to violate no less than nine international treaties or agreements to which Britain was bound.

Another large group of items on the agenda is originated within the executive mechanism, sometimes by Ministers wishing to translate some electoral promise or cherished policy into action, sometimes by Departments eager to proceed with further steps in their secular expansion, or in the correction of anomalies and weaknesses, and sometimes in pursuance of general policies or plans for national development, or for participation in worldwide advances. The special feature of this category is that they represent a positive initiative rather than a response enforced by some initiative or event which has happened on some other account. It is possible to assess the caliber of governments by checking how much of their effort is directed to developing their own plans and policies, and how much is diverted to coping with whatever happens to be hitting them from outside. The more muddled and incompetent the administration, the more its agenda will be dictated by others, rather than decided and carried through by itself.

In these and other ways fresh subjects are continually proposing themselves, in the choice of agenda. Failure to define their nature and seriousness, and to accord the right priority to each, will be penalized by a formidable accumulation of unfinished business, a harassed and overburdened administration, and the emergence of a chronic condition of congestion and inability to secure the orderly and conclusive dispatch of official business. One of the most vital managerial functions of government is to police the gate through which fresh problems enter, and to prevent them from diverting resources needed elsewhere. In Britain this has been one of the most neglected of government functions. Being in essence policy-framing and regulatory rather than managerial, the administrative hierarchy is incapable of continuously adjusting resources to priorities. The varying shares of manpower and money assigned to different tasks can be explained in many cases only by assuming, often correctly, that no one in authority gave the matter a thought. As we conduct our survey we should bear in mind these questions; How and whence did this or that item get on the agenda of government? Has its nature, and have the implications of trying to deal with it, been correctly appraised? Is it being tackled at the right level in the right office in the right way? What resources does it call for, and is it getting more or less than necessary? Where does responsibility lie for assessing results, and securing adjustments or new decisions in the light of them? and finally; What role does it play in the strategy of the government's program, and in the satisfaction of the requirements of the governed? So many people, not only outside but within government, adopt a naïve and undiscriminating view towards its agenda, and tacitly assume that there must be some objective validity in whatever Departments or offices happen to be doing at the moment. This is an illusion. Even the distinction between problem-defining and problem-solving functions is largely blurred, and we are confronted in all directions with costly staffs listlessly working on bits and pieces of problems which have never been thought out and correctly framed, or even selected as worthwhile tasks in the first place. It is rather like a building program in which almost anyone can start new works and no one minds how many ever get finished. No wonder, therefore, that the Civil Service continues to grow.

Parliament, as the first and foremost of the active agents in the constitution, has a role which takes several forms. As the supreme legislature, Parliament must contemplate, enact, amend, codify and repeal laws, and must confirm or review many of the statutory orders and regulations promulgated under these by Ministers. The substance of these laws ranges from provisions affecting individual conduct, and even morals, to complex and highly technical frameworks for the activities of professionals and specialists, and to many matters which are at least partly administrative. Lacking the basis, widely adopted on the Continent, of Roman Law, England and Wales have a legal structure radically distinct from that of Scotland. Parliament thus has to legislate in terms of two different legal systems. Moreover, the existence of the Common Law in England and Wales creates an area of considerable uncertainty and fluidity, which can result in the legislature overlooking important consequences destined to emerge at the interface between the provisions of a new enactment and the Common Law. During the past forty years great strides have been made in improving the flow process from the initiators of legislation to Parliamentary draftsmen, and through the various processes of Departmental consultation, reference to interested bodies and groups, policy consideration by Ministers, and fitting the completed Bill within the exacting timetable of Parliament. Much more stress is laid nowadays on the closest possible approximation to plain English in legal drafting. This good progress towards modernization has only partly been matched in the attempts to codify many separate and sometimes inconsistent laws, often originating from widely differing periods and conditions. The law still remains too copious, too diverse and too obscure. Nevertheless it is perhaps as a legislature that Parliament in its recent performance emerges at its most professional.

There has been a lack of recent comparative study of the relative effectiveness of different national legislatures as mechanisms for processing new or amended legislation and producing workmanlike and understandable measures which achieve their objects with the minimum of confusion or uncertainty. It appears, however, that between 1946 and 1964 the record of the United Kingdom Parliament overall could compare quite favorably with any other. There is unhappily reason to fear that some of the latest measures, especially in the economic and fiscal field, have badly blotted this good record, the fault of course being that of the government rather than primarily of Parliament itself.

Vast as is the task of a legislature it is only one facet of the activities of Parliament, which is indeed one of the most complex social organisms in the world. Underlying all else it is the theater of numberless

individual and group ambitions and struggles, all demanding a stage
on which to act themselves out, and few averse to claiming the largest
spotlight for their particular act. It is a place steeped in tradition, lav-
ishly clothed in ritual, yet continuously exposed to every wind of
change that blows. Here the sovereign representatives of the sovereign
electorate speak for the nation in times of crisis, and here also they
cringe like apprehensive schoolboys under the open, if blandly toned
down, tyranny of the party managers and Whips. But here too Ministers flinch under the searching ordeal of Question Time, a uniquely
British device, which for practical purposes may fairly be regarded as
a development of the past century, and is still finding its full potential
as a means of maintaining discipline within the Executive, and inspiring the fear of exposure. Here again, from time to time, is improvised a
kind of uninhibited court of rough and summary justice, before which
a wide range of power-wielders from individual Ministers downwards
may suddenly find themselves arraigned on account of some alleged
injustice, inequity, negligence or error of judgment, and, if unable to
clear themselves, may be punished by loss of office or reputation. Here
too is a standing clearing-house for suggestions and ideas in relation to
government, and a perpetual general meeting of the nation's proxies in
their capacity as taxpayers and consumers, with all the faults and inep-
titudes to which such general meetings are notoriously prone. And besides all this the House is expected to keep under wise and informed
review the state and progress of the nation in all its aspects, and to be
continuously considering the lines of future advance, while not forgetting to tackle the task of modernizing and reforming itself.

After recalling these many-faceted functions in the barest outline it
is small wonder that inside Britain Parliament is one of the most criticized of British institutions. Such a complex almost defies measured
objective assessment in relation to performance, which is the approach
attempted, however imperfectly, in this book.

Parliament is above all a means of two-way communication between government and governed. However efficiently it may be conducted its success or failure will mainly be determined by the degree of
confidence and empathy which it can hold among the electorate. The
voters unashamedly count on it to do magic for them, and in disappointing them, as it needs must, it cannot afford to lose its *mystique*
and to let itself be exposed, like a clumsy conjurer who fails to produce
the expected but inexplicable rabbit out of the hat. If businessmen fail
to sell their goods abroad, or to service them satisfactorily, if Olympic

Gold Medals go too exclusively to other nations, if parents let loose too many delinquent offspring on the citizens, then Parliament is expected to do something about it, and that something is rarely plain, agreed or simple to achieve.

Confronted with such expectations it would seem sensible to develop, using every available modern technique, a carefully designed network of communications on three levels. First, to ensure that Members of Parliament jointly and severally have better access, by opinion sampling, social studies and otherwise, to more reliable knowledge of the thoughts, feelings, anxieties, aspirations and co-operative potential of their constituents. Given constituencies as large as around 40,000 persons it is totally unrealistic to hope to keep adequate contact with them on the traditional person-to-person basis, and any efforts to do so merely fritter away time and energy which might be better used elsewhere. This is not to say that MPs could or should become less accessible to constituents who have genuine personal need to see them. The MP, however, should no longer be expected to spend so much time, unless he personally desires it, as a kind of general welfare officer mediating on detailed and more or less routine affairs with all kinds of agencies. Looking back over the past forty years before the appointment of the first Parliamentary Commissioner or ombudsman, there is a clear trend in this direction. A number of agencies have organized their public relations and consumer affairs so effectively that cases concerning them are rarely referred to an MP. Many others, however, have not, and many voters are too ignorant or too idle to go to their local Citizens' Advice Bureau or to the right office of the agency concerned if it is made easier to enlist their MP in sorting it all out for them. The line of progress is to provide good modern public relations and consumer services wherever such problems occur, and to see that the public know about them, with Citizens' Advice Bureaus, and local ombudsmen where required on the spot, and the Parliamentary commissioner available to take over or share in clearing up appropriate cases at the center. On no account should the delicate ground between the MP and his constituent, with the right of access to him, be encroached upon. It is a question of siphoning off, by attractive and efficient public relations and consumer services, matters which can best be resolved by the agency direct in the first instance. There will always be some which cannot.

Secondly, MPs need much fuller, better and more independent information to be available to them over the whole range of Parliament's work, and they need it promptly provided in a form suitably condensed for such busy users. The main sources at present are Civil Service products, often rather poorly adapted to Parliamentary needs, and the offerings of numerous lobbies, interests or pressure groups, to be discussed later in this chapter. During the past forty years there has grown up quite a wealth of institutes and other learned and objective sources, both within and outside universities, which could contribute much to the sound and fair long-term appraisal of national problems, and in some cases are already enlisted, by individual Members or otherwise, to do so. Most of this potential, however, at present runs to waste through lack of contact and organized communication, and often through lack of funds to put something resulting from a study into a form suitable for Parliamentary purposes. Parliament is still asked to handle matters referred to it from government or other interested sources in the light of such limited or fragmentary information as these sources think fit, or can find the time, to disclose to it. Full information tends to come too late, when Bills or projects have crystallized into final and often unalterable form, or through the pertinacity of Select Committees, which tend only to get to grips with something at the inquest or *post mortem* stage.

Thirdly, valuable as Question Time is within its limits, there are grossly insufficient opportunities for constructive direct contact between MPs and many public Departments or other agencies. How to enable the representatives of the electors to achieve such contact without infringing the responsibilities of Ministers, or of top administrators and managers, is a problem which remains to be fully solved, although a good deal of thought has been given to it recently. The most significant example is the case of the Select Committee on Nationalised Industries. Such a specialized investigatory committee, with the power to summon witnesses and documents and the right to report, was an answer to the dilemma, created after the extensive nationalization program of the Attlee administration of 1945–51, under which Parliament was responsible for the nationalized industries, but in order not to undermine the morale and authority of their managements had to make a self-denying ordinance restraining Members from asking questions about these concerns, except on broad matters of policy. The Select Committee keeps up a running inquiry into the work of a public corporation without deterring innovation or handicapping it in its role as a competitive commercial enterprise. It affords back-benchers a valuable function, and has improved Parliamentary scrutiny of the Executive.

One critical problem, successfully solved here but not easy to deal with on a wider scale, was the finding of suitably qualified Members to serve. Of thirty-four members of the Select Committee on Nationalised Industries, twenty-two had direct industrial experience, as officers in nationalized industries, or in responsible managerial posts in private industry, or as applied scientists. Five other members had been or later became junior Ministers in Departments concerned with nationalized industries.

The House of Commons, as recently constituted, has only gradually been gaining reinforcements in such much-needed types of expertise, and would currently have much difficulty in manning a number of such Committees of adequate caliber. This, however, need not be a permanent obstacle. There is reason to believe that a number of suitable members have actually left the House from boredom and through lack of just such interesting opportunities for specialist service, while others would no doubt come forward if the need arose. Indeed one of the main advantages of such developments might be in helping to redress the balance between the minority who know their way about this technological age and the majority who are largely clueless over it. At all events this example must suffice to show that the possibilities of devising new contacts and means of constructive communication between the House and the executive mechanism have not been entirely missed. In this way Parliament might achieve a commanding status as the effective strategic link between the swollen electorate and the ever more ramifying executive mechanism at all levels: a role which belongs to no other body, but which Parliament itself has only somewhat feebly and intermittently sought to fill.

Public opinion, however, does not use such abstract criteria, and tends to judge the performance of Parliament by an odd mixture of highlights which impress themselves as illustrating its merits or its follies, and perhaps most often the latter. Ministers indulge in some angry exchange with the Opposition, the House is kept sitting all night over a contested measure, some personal scandal blows up, or someone's words have to be eaten again more quickly and embarrassingly than usual. The news travels far and wide, losing nothing in the writing of the press reports or in the telling over the radio or TV, to be fed into the rather fuzzy substitute for a computer which is known as the Mind of the Voter. That respect for the House is not thereby enhanced is not necessarily bad; in showing itself human Parliament may both attract more notice from the average voter and be less readily dismissed as a remote and Olympian body. A decision to televize some Parliamentary proceedings live would no doubt result in some corrections to the current image, not inevitably for the better, but welcome as reinforcing communications between Parliament and the electorate.

It is difficult to know what weight to attribute at any given time to criticism of Parliament, but two interesting indications are available. In the earlier part of the past forty years criticism increasingly took the form of a denial of the fundamental arguments for having a Parliament. There were influential and growing political parties, both Communist and Fascist, which made little secret of their ambition to do away with it if they ever had the chance, as in other countries they did. It was not at that time impossible to persuade a constituency to send to Parliament a member holding such views.

Now the situation is very different. No British political figure of any consequence, and no Party in a position to nominate a candidate who would not lose his deposit in an election, has denounced Parliament, or would be open to any suspicion of harboring an aim to go beyond reforming it. If this does not mean that Parliament is fundamentally approved and its future assured, it at least must mean that any threat to it is certainly not within sight during the next few years. Nor do turnouts at elections reflect any massive increase in apathy and abstention.

Why Parliament should apparently be so strongly entrenched at this moment is not entirely clear. Positive satisfaction with it is much less often expressed than grave misgivings and calls for drastic reform. It is possible that more radical dissatisfactions exist below the surface, lacking as yet a suitable leader. Recent electoral successes by Scottish and Welsh Nationalists are significant. Perhaps the most plausible interpretation is that the pre-war anti-Parliamentary parties, Fascist and Communist, were not home-grown organisms, but were so blatantly subservient to foreign parties that they committed political suicide, and made it politically suicidal to follow in their footsteps. If this is correct the current absence of anti-Parliamentary manifestations could be misleadingly reassuring. In so far as the British Parliamentary model has been exported to newer countries equipping themselves with constitutions for the first time, recent experience has not been altogether happy. More or less benign military governments have taken over in Pakistan, Nigeria, Ghana and elsewhere, while surviving civilian administrations have shown little enthusiasm to encourage loyal Opposition. On the other hand the export of Parliament has not proved by any means a flop, and, even where insuperable difficulties are held to exist locally, the Westminster Parliament retains considerable prestige and admiration. While many nations might conclude that it is not for them, few would be likely to claim that they possess or are likely to develop anything superior. At worst, therefore, Parliament has another chance to reform itself before any threat exists of having to reform under intense pressure from outside.

The other interesting indication is in the supply of candidates. Quantitatively, despite the somewhat severe deterrent of having to find a deposit of £150 ($420) which is forfeited by all those who fail to poll more than one-eighth of the total votes cast, there is no shortage of champions who are ready to have a go. Though recent totals have been considerably lower, 443 deposits were lost in 1950. Impossible to measure, but pretty clearly established, is the improvement in quality, which is reflected in the increased proportion of graduates and professional men mentioned earlier. This is in sharp contrast to the depressing experience of the Civil Service Commissioners, now regularly failing to find enough qualified candidates coming forward to fill their vacancies. At the 1966 election the *Economist* even stated that in one contest both the candidates were so excellent that it was unfortunate that both of them could not be elected. Good men in a national legislature of this size and scope are necessarily in a minority, but the minority is encouragingly strong and buoyant.

Is Parliament in decline? There is no reliable means of telling, but it appears fairly plain that those whose loss of confidence in Parliament would immediately and seriously affect it do not currently behave as if they thought it was. Nevertheless we can state with confidence that Parliament is daily and gravely disappointing many who believe in and support it, and that a continuance of this situation would be bound to lead to most unfortunate results. If it is not worse than it was, it may still be failing more seriously to measure up to what it should be.

Evidence regarding the nature and extent of recent changes in the business of the House of Commons is unfortunately not readily interpreted without many qualifications. It is clear that pressure of other business has much lessened the intensity of detailed financial control by the whole House, during a period when the great increase of the Budget and the proliferation of Departments would in any case have required much more Parliamentary time if control was to be maintained at anywhere near its nineteenth-century intensity. Time given to estimates, or supply as such, was halved between 1908 and 1964, much of the saving being taken up by debates held on motions on a wide range of topics. The old method was cumbersome and time-consuming, and not necessarily efficient; had a more efficient substitute been found the change would have been welcome, but unfortunately it was not, as shall be seen later.

Greater, more varied, and more urgent claims on Parliamentary time have diversified the business of the House and have curtailed the time available for every item of it. Sessions have lengthened and much more business has been sent to standing committees. Between 1900 and 1913 the average session lasted 142 days; during the 1920s 130; during the Attlee administration 190, and between 1951 and 1964 160. According to Sir Gilbert Campion, sessions between 1906 and 1913 averaged 72.6 legislative days; between 1929–30 and 1937–38 they were much the same at 73.4 but the number of Acts passed rose from under fifty to fifty-seven and they averaged two and a half times as long. Unfortunately, while Parliament is one of the oldest national activities, Parliament's study of itself is one of the newest. Until it has made further headway there would be little point in attempting to analyze such changes in fuller detail.

It would be incomplete and misleading to consider the role of Parliament in the making and dispatch of its agenda without reference to two of its constant partners in these processes, both unofficial and unknown to the constitution, but both of great and apparently growing influence. These are the political parties and the organized interests, often known as pressure groups or lobbies. (A third informal partner, the press and broadcasting, is of course also very important, but as its workings are overt and are focused within fairly well defined and generally understood limits it seems unnecessary to extend this account by more than a bare mention of them.)

While it is generally accepted that there has been considerable change in the working of Parliament over the past couple of centuries, since the days of Burke, Fox and Pitt, few citizens fully recognize how far-reaching and fundamental this change has been, and how strongly it is still occurring. Every living organism possesses a structure which has a settled continuity, subject to certain processes of growth and of renewal, and is fueled and enabled to function by an input of energy, of information and so forth. This is processed within the structure and gives rise to an output in terms of activity, of maintenance and of voided waste products which form the potential input of other organisms in the ecosystem. In certain animal organisms, such as a giant tortoise, the input is small and occasional and the activity slow and limited, forming a low-turnover system. In others, such as a wren, the input is large relative to its size, and goes on during most of its waking hours, and the output in food-seeking, singing and defense of territory, nest-building and reproductive activities is remarkable, forming a high-turnover system. Such high-turnover systems are favorable to accelerated evolution, and the analogy is suggestive for such a social organism as Parliament, which is continually in receipt of an input much larger and more diverse than it can properly digest. In the struggle to do so each new Parliament—for, though we speak loosely of Parliament as if it were everlasting, each newly elected Parliament is of course a fresh and autonomous organism which will expire after its five-year maximum life—adapts itself and even may exhibit some mutation which proves favorable to survival. Each successive Parliament has a habit of trying so far as possible to *look* like its predecessors, but in fact it is a different organism, in a different political environment, tackling more or less altered functions by modified methods. There was a time when MPs were still regarded as individuals exercising their own judgment, and when the feeling of the House was an effective element quite distinct from the various party lines. One of the continuous underlying trends can be expressed statistically. In 1800 the population of Great Britain was some ten and a half million, and the number of Members of Parliament was 558. By 1900 the population of Great Britain was some thirty-seven million, the electorate had risen to 6,730,935, and the number of MPs for constituencies in Great Britain was 555. Now the population is fifty-three million, the electorate is thirty-six million and the number of MPs is 618 (all figures excluding all Ireland). It will be seen that the number of inhabitants has risen five times, the number of voters has risen six times and the number of MPs has increased by only just over 10 per cent. Since a House of anything like 3000 Members is far beyond practical possibilities the only way out has been to make each Member purport to represent more and more constituents. As the House is also required to perform more functions in respect of many more subjects and problems its contact with the individual voter must necessarily be less direct and must involve more supplementary mechanisms. This is where the political parties and the organized interests come in.

Political parties are in many ways protean bodies. Their principles, programs, personnel, methods and supporters undergo frequent transformations, even if many of these are more a matter of window-dressing and reshuffling than of any basic change. One clear tendency is for the full-time salaried staff to become more numerous and more influential, and to play a larger part not only in organizing political effort but in policy-making and in selecting, or even themselves becoming, candidates for Parliament. A corollary of this is the decline of the country house and the political London club as places where key decisions are talked over and taken. The Labour Party in any event never had many country houses available, and their leaders were largely unaccustomed to that sort of life. Even in London Labour Ministers, except a few of the intelligentsia, have normally not been much given to meeting one another away from their regular places of political business. Partly on this account the House of Commons Committee of Privileges under the Attlee administration reported in 1947:

> In modern times the practice of holding private meetings in the precincts of the Palace of Westminster of different parties has become well established and . . . must now be taken to form a normal and everyday incident of parliamentary procedure, without which the business of the House could not conveniently be conducted . . . Your Committee therefore conclude on this matter that attendance of Members at a private party meeting held in the precincts of the Palace of Westminster during the parliamentary session to discuss parliamentary matters connected with the current or future proceedings of Parliament, is attendance in their capacity of Members of Parliament.

Observe the careful wording, which was accompanied by a hint that the more such meetings were restricted to MPs and not opened to outsiders the better. Nothing could more precisely illustrate the grudging, love-hate relationship existing between Parliament, as such, and political parties, as such. For, while Parliament must always strive and pretend to be a fully autonomous self-contained organism, it is in fact committed to a degree of commensalism, and of mutual relationships with parasites, far surpassing anything known in biology. For generations unskilled observers have predicted that the parasites will kill or take over their host, yet decade by decade the host finds ways of carrying more and heavier parasites without apparently being much the worse for it. The secret lies in imperative mutual need, and in mutual tacit consent not to allow the process to assume a form threatening the survival of either.

One of the most conspicuous and baffling of these conventions is that which insists on there always being a two-party system. The formidable strength and endurance of this convention has been demonstrated by the prolonged efforts to break it on the part of the Liberal Party. Evidently there is a deep built-in self-righting mechanism which corrects any tendency for the British ship of state to deviate from a two-party rhythm of motion, even though others manage not too badly with more complex combinations.

The fact that only two parties really count in terms of capability for forming a government makes it possible to run fairly substantial and expensive national party organizations. This in turn eliminates the type of powerful local party bosses long familiar in the United States, and foreshadowed as a possibility here by the Chamberlain regime in Birmingham earlier this century. The drive for the building of party machines has come from busy politicians who felt unable any longer to lick their own stamps and to answer the telephone. Once created, however, the salaried helpers did not stop there. Agents resident in a constituency or region saw themselves as called upon to keep their party MP or candidate in the picture about local feeling and local issues. They were often invited by headquarters to contribute to assessments and appreciations of the political situation which, it is now clear, must have been very misleading. They have however several invaluable functions, and form the backbone of the Party's continuing activities up and down the country. They are the servants of the local party association in the constituency, which has its own committee and may at times not see eye to eye either with its candidate or sitting member, or with the Central Office. Admirable as local autonomy is in theory, bitter experience has taught the unwisdom of leaving too much to the constituency committees. Their choice of a candidate for a safe seat may be tantamount to his election, subject to the formality of going to the polls, even if he is a nonentity, or is quite unfitted for national party politics by some personal characteristic or by the oddness and stiffness of his views. Central Office intervention can often ensure that chance or fashion does not entirely exclude, or grossly underuse, certain types whose value in Parliament may be disproportionate to their glamor or convenience in the eyes of an average local selection committee. At times intervention is carried to the extent of virtually obliging a local committee to nominate a particular unseated or seatless Minister or ex-Minister.

The brutal fact remains that the sovereign electorate are supposed to choose between two or three semi-finalists already selected out of a much larger number by a local party committee, which may well have eliminated, before they are consulted, the very man the voters would have preferred. Moreover, the fact that parties, centrally and locally, have this patronage within their gift, and that without it a would-be MP is politically a dead duck, gives the party machine great power to ensure that the electorate return only Members with safe or acceptable opinions from the standpoint of the party. The electorate, however, seem content with this arrangement. The regular massacre of independents and dissidents at the polls suggests that the weeding-out which occurs cannot be much at variance with what they would do themselves if they had the job.

Opinion testing by professional polls has now largely replaced the older amateurish soundings, but, apart from keeping abreast of public opinion, party Central Offices find themselves increasingly involved in the much more delicate task of helping to devise programs and appeals.

The triumph of Herbert Morrison's "Let's face the future" in 1945 and of R. A. Butler's deliberate matching performance with the new conservatism in 1951, have been held to show that the electorate prefer well-developed constructive concrete programs to vague generalities, and, above all, to negative and backward-looking disputation and abuse. But history has yet to provide an instance when such architects of victory reaped their eventual reward by becoming Prime Minister. In British politics the framer of a well-devised winning program seems—can it be mere coincidence?—to be destined to be always a bridesmaid, never a bride.

Linked with this is the uncertain and ambiguous role of the so-called party research centers. It appears that the degree of party interest and support for such activities rises when the party is most plainly getting nowhere with public opinion, and subsides when the tide is running its way. As politicians who have served in such centers seem to make better than average progress in their Parliamentary careers it does not seem that the results of their labors can often be irrelevant or unsatisfactory. The impression given is that research, here as elsewhere, is looked upon as an unpalatable and indeed un-English intrusion into the political game. Medieval magnates no doubt took a similar view of being forced to associate with clerks, on the ground that the fellows could actually read and write. Be that as it may, the inadequacy and fitfulness of research sponsored by political parties aggravates the weakness resulting from the gross incapacity in this respect of the Civil Service.

Once more there is evidence of a chronic and fundamental source of misgovernment. No adequate and enduring provision has been made for studying existing or for anticipating future problems in public affairs, and for taking timely and sound dispositions to deal with them. Where important issues, such as the need for technological education or the need for planning, are raised by others they have habitually been ignored or tackled on a too-little-and-too-late basis by both politicians and administrators. The System robustly provides that the blind shall lead the blind. Where such issues are not raised by others they are normally not raised at all, since neither the political parties nor the Civil Service has proved willing to sustain, or even to tolerate, units or groups which might have the capability of raising them. Such men are dangerous.

CHAPTER 11

The Cabinet, Civil Service and Justice

While some have seen Parliament's authority being undermined by interest groups and other sectional bodies tending to face it with *faits accomplis,* others have viewed the enhanced power of the Cabinet, and of the Prime Minister over it, as the main threat. Here again, there is a similar accelerated trend to institutionalism, from the days, two centuries ago, when the advent of a foreign dynasty and the enterprise of Walpole had first created a solid Cabinet under a Prime Minister (both for long afterwards remaining unknown to the Constitution) until the modern emergence of an increasingly dominant and "Presidential" Prime Minister and of an increasingly formalized and far less mysterious Cabinet, to whose unanimous decisions Parliament must bow.

It is a rule in politics that the faster the business must move and the more there is of it, the more fully a large assembly must renounce any pretense of detailed consideration and decision in favor of some more businesslike smaller group. No doubt this was sensed by the staunch conservatives who long sought to limit, so far as possible, any extension of the scope of Parliamentary business. If such a limitation could have been achieved it would have diminished the pressure to develop Cabinet rule. Under King George III, during the last years of any serious attempts by the Crown to rule as well as reign, and to that end to manage Parliament, it was the Crown which dragged its feet in keeping the sphere of government as narrow and traditional as possible, and in turning a blind eye to the industrial and agricultural revolutions, to new social and political movements, and, until the eleventh hour, to the maturing communities in the colonies. Indeed, the defeat of George III and his protégé Lord North, through the successful Declaration of Independence by the United States, finally precipitated the full transfer of power over British governments to the House of Commons, and created the particular constitutional balance, actually to survive for less than a century, which has been imprinted on students and practitioners of British politics as the classical normal equilibrium. But politics march on, and power flows where it listeth.

How does the Cabinet handle the concentration of power which has gradually passed in its direction, and to what extent can it be regarded as exercising, and as likely to hold on to, the power which it is reputed to possess? This abstract and partially fictitious mechanism, which is referred to for convenience as "the Cabinet", consists of the following distinct components:

> The Prime Minister, the man whose own office desk is the Cabinet table, and whose conversations, often highly informal, with his colleagues and others, often do much more to shape Cabinet decisions than anything which happens at actual Cabinet meetings.
>
> The group of, normally in these days, somewhat over twenty senior Ministers who officially constitute the Cabinet, but whose formal meetings will often be attended by non-Cabinet Ministers and senior professional advisers when matters much affecting them are discussed.
>
> The various unpublicized Cabinet Committees, which are carbon copies of the Cabinet, generally with one of the Prime Minister's senior lieutenants in the chair, covering some broad range of subjects such as home affairs, and hammering out in the first instance agreed policies and programs between all the Ministers (not necessarily of Cabinet rank) whose Departments are primarily concerned with each issue, their agreements being, in important and controversial matters, sent on for confirmation or review by the Cabinet itself.
>
> The Cabinet Secretariat of civil servants, now closely allied to and dependent on the Treasury, who prepare, record and ensure Departmental knowledge and follow-up of the decisions, working on some matters closely in touch with the Prime Minister's personal staff of secretaries and advisers at No. 10 Downing Street.

It is impossible in administrative terms to disentangle the respective roles of these four components, although politically their functions are quite distinct. In so far as it is profitable, and this is somewhat doubtful, to probe into where power lies, we could find a spectrum of instances, from decisions which the Prime Minister takes in communion with himself in his bath, and promptly has executed through his Private Secretary, to those on which he may informally, perhaps by telephone, consult two or three of his senior colleagues most concerned, to those which may be the subject of an informal *ad hoc* meeting, perhaps hurriedly convened, and on to those which come to Cabinet as oral items, those which come as papers or bevies of papers direct from Ministers, and those which have been sieved first through some Cabinet Committee, ending up with those which (as the Profumo Inquiry first made public) may be settled with a Minister or Ministers by the Head of the Civil Service without the Cabinet even being told.

The Cabinet, therefore, is not some fixed, monolithic, all-seeing, all-powerful group which sits saying "Yea" or "Nay" on all the principal business of government. Like everything else in the British system it is more like a set of Chinese boxes, any one of which when picked up and scrutinized is likely to be found half empty. As the body which is listed officially on paper the Cabinet may perform as little as forty man hours of work in session during a week, and even at its most busy it cannot possibly cover more than a fraction of the major activities of government, and that only in a hurried and often superficial way. The Cabinet is however not only the mystical but to a large extent the practical point of focus and authority. Although it never sees a great deal of what is done in its name most of those who receive the instructions are none the wiser about that, and the instructions themselves are none the worse. Thanks largely to the highly professional and remarkably rapid paper work and telephonic follow-up service of the Cabinet Secretariat the flow of instructions into the executive mechanism and the feedback of progress reports and checks works with great efficiency. We have come far from the days of the first War Cabinet in World War I, when a non-Cabinet Minister observed that it was his practice to read the directions of the War Cabinet with care and to carry them out when he could attach any meaning to them, but otherwise to do as he thought best.

The concentration of power in the Cabinet stems from the fact that its leading members combine a number of distinct key roles. *Vis-à-vis* the ultimate sovereign electorate they are, while in power, the best-known national politicians, and in troubled times the best-known figures of any kind—familiar faces on TV and newsreels, familiar for their caricatures and their quoted remarks in the press, and even familiar as names occurring in arguments in pubs. Increasingly during the past thirty years the Prime Minister, unless of an Attlee capacity for unobtrusiveness, has come to dominate in this way. Aided by the vast government and party publicity machine he receives an over-whelming build-up which makes him, as a person, real and immediate to each citizen, in a way perhaps unknown hitherto since the Athenian city-states. No mayor of any major city is nearly as familiar to his citizens.

In relation to Parliament, all Cabinet members must be MPs, save for a few, not including the Prime Minister, who may have their seats in the House of Lords instead. They are not only all drawn from the majority party but customarily from each of its main wings or distinctive opinion groupings, so that if there are any personal loyalties to particular potentially rebel chieftains within the party these are so far as possible swept up by the Prime Minister in the course of his Cabinet-making. Perhaps the greatest recent *tour de force* in this respect, which may or may not have served its purpose, was the press-ganging into Parliament and the Cabinet of Frank Cousins, the dissident boss of the powerful Transport and General Workers Union, during the early part of the Wilson regime in 1964–66, after which he broke away. Under an ineffective or passive Prime Minister this practice can have the result of permitting small but dangerous "inside" pressure groups to form around particularly strong Ministerial personalities, as happened, with eventually disruptive effects, during the Attlee administration.

Once again, we are reminded, with Cabinets as with Parliaments, that although students of politics like to write of them as a single continuing body, in fact each new one is quite distinct, and may function very differently from its predecessor or its successor. Some of these differences soon lapse, others are like mutations which prove their usefulness and persist, and in doing so change the course of Cabinet evolution.

Prime Ministers in the inter-war period were often criticized for reluctance to remove obvious failures, and for maintaining "the old gang". Some more recently have lived up to the maxim that the first qualification for the post is to be a good butcher. There are a number of distinct reasons why an administration may be re-formed. It may have been started with a number of elderly and loyal old stalwarts to whom the Party owes a debt, but who are tacitly or otherwise informed that their days of Ministerial glory cannot last long, and that they must be prepared to make way for younger men, who must be trained and given fresh incentive. Changed conditions may indicate that a particular man (or men) has the potential to tackle some trouble spot which is proving too much for the present incumbent of the office concerned, and is embarrassing the government. Some Ministers are just unlucky, others come in conflict with colleagues or with powerful interest groups on whose co-operation their Departments may depend, and they have accordingly to be shifted or dropped. Sometimes it looks to even the most charitable observer as if the need for better window-dressing has been uppermost in the Prime Minister's mind, especially as the time for a General Election is approaching and the record of some Ministers is such that it might be dangerous to rely on the short-ness of memory of the sovereign electorate.

One of the most important of the factors on which the national authority, and therefore the power, of a Cabinet rests is at least a plaus-ible appearance of cohesion, unity, and common purpose. Nothing is more ominous to a Prime Minister than the appearance, however speculative, in newspaper headlines of the dreaded words "Cabinet Split". It is of the essence of the Cabinet's power, and one of the main reasons for its successful take-over of this from the Commons, that it needs, and passionately desires, to hang together rather than to risk hanging separately. In this imperfect world the appearance will often be courteously if not naïvely accepted as a substitute for the substance, but some credible appearance of solidarity there must be, or authority melts away.

Most immediately, of course, the authority of the Cabinet jointly and severally rests on the fact that its members are the heads of impor-tant Departments of government, while some of them in addition may hold office or wield great power behind the scenes in their party orga-nization, as Herbert Morrison did in the post-war Attlee administra-tion, and Lord Woolton in the post-war Churchill administration, both occupying the post of Lord President of the Council, with its freedom from Departmental burdens. Ministers in this way wield not only im-mense executive power, but a vast patronage influence over the career prospects and the aspirations of many thousands of the nation's key men, who look towards positions which it may be in the power of a Minister to confer on or withhold from them, either now or later. The removal from their control of Civil Service recruitment and promo-tions a century back has been handsomely compensated by the devel-opment of so many quasi-public or grant-aided bodies, and by the flowering in its full lushness of the modern Honours List.

But all such power is only potential unless it can be exercised effec-tively, and this is where the snag comes. The record shows only too plainly that British Governments during the past forty years have constantly been expecting something to happen quite other than what did happen, and have constantly been trying to contrive or to prevent something happening with total lack of success. This is what government is all about, however, and a system which so chronically falls short by these two all-important tests is a system not of government but of misgovernment.

In the simplest terms a Prime Minister and his Cabinet have the choice between:

(a) a passive approach, waiting for problems to "emerge" and then seeking to deal with each on merits in the light of party attitudes, or

(b) an active or positive approach, seeking to review the state of the nation and to initiate a series, separate or integrated, of measures, projects, policies or programs which will to some extent deliberately transform the future situation.

In the Gladstonian period, when the existing Civil Service was established, the general sense of the electorate and of Cabinets of either party approximated to (a). Now, but only since 1957, it approximates to (b), yet Cabinets are still stuck with a Civil Service which only makes sense in terms of (a).

The outcome over the past decade is abundantly clear. In practice (b) is not open to governments because they lack the mechanism to implement it, and above all, to save them from being shipwrecked by every economic wind that blows while they are laboriously preparing for it. Thus the practical choice for a Cabinet seeking some variant of (b) in existing circumstances is either:

(c) to disregard the incapacity of the machine to implement it, and express suitable astonishment every time they are made fools of by events and are forced to eat their words, or

(d) to set about recasting the executive mechanism by progressive stages of decentralization and reallocation of functions between Whitehall Departments and alternative agencies, reinforced by infusions of new men, new techniques and new flows of information, and meanwhile to face the fact that current programs must be restrained within the current capacity of the machine to handle them, as well as within the limits of national resources that can be released from less productive use, or can be newly created. While the fact of Britain's financial insolvency, and the hard limits which it dictates, has at last begun to sink in, the lesson still has to be learnt that there is a parallel and equal problem of administrative insolvency to be dealt with before the scale of advances recently envisaged can be attained.

The executive machine is headed by, and is supposed to fulfill the demands of, the Ministers in the Cabinet, but also includes such indirect elements as the Nationalised Boards, the Regional Councils and local government.

The structure and flow of public business in Britain cannot be understood without some prior consideration of the nature of the British public service. Until the twentieth century British affairs were in the hands of a minority electorate which traditionally and vigorously disliked and distrusted government *as such,* and did not wish to see it strong or professional. Professor H. Finer in *The Theory and Practice of Modern Government* summed up the situation in England from the mid-sixteenth to the end of the eighteenth century:

> It is impossible to estimate in quantities the financial loss and the physical and spiritual misery suffered by the people of the parishes and towns of England because there was no central officer to watch and control the behaviour of the local authorities. It was enormous and terrible . . .
>
> In the late years of the eighteenth century, then, England possessed an administrative system which could be described as decentralized, non-professional—save for the Whitehall officials—non-bureaucratic, liberal, with a dispersed and incoherent arbitrariness.

No doubt because of the philosophy thus prescribed for the reformed Civil Service about a century ago, and the public school training of its recruits, no attempt was made, nor has any yet been carried through, to modernize the whole layout of governmental functions in a coherent series of Departments. The core of the administration, apart from the Admiralty and the War Office on the defense side and the Foreign and Colonial Offices for external political relations, was and is formed by the Treasury, flanked by the Home Office for general internal affairs and the Board of Trade for commercial and industrial aspects. In 1889, after the prolonged agricultural depression, suffered in the cause of cheap imported food and low wages, a Ministry of Agriculture had to be created, although not yet under that title, the term "Ministry" not being adopted in Britain until World War I. In 1899 the shambles entrusted with responsibility for education was rearranged in a Board of Education under the aegis of the Lord President of the Council. In 1911, a nucleus was formed of what was to become the Ministry of Labour. This was a first attempt to cope with the plight of the host of poorly paid and insecurely employed workers, and to make good some of the long arrears which had been permitted to develop in social welfare provisions.

In 1871 the confusion and backwardness in following up the mid-century reforms in local sanitation, hygiene and provision of community services necessitated the formation of a Local Government Board.

World War I was a period of forced expansion and innovation in the Civil Service, but of the Departments then created only the Air Ministry and the Ministry of Pensions survived as separate Ministerial offices into peacetime. During the inter-war years, however, a Ministry of Transport was budded off from the Board of Trade, and a Dominions Office (later Commonwealth Relations Office) from the Colonial Office. Of the older specifically territorial offices, the Irish Office disappeared (to be followed after World War II by the old India Office) and the Scottish Office alone throve and won its own Secretary of State in 1926. Owing to the political ineffectiveness of the peculiar voting pattern in Wales the Welsh had to wait for theirs nearly forty years longer. Two ancient common service Departments, the Post Office and the Office of Works, carried on throughout, but their Ministerial heads have ceased to be included in modern Cabinets, and the Office of Works has been made to change its name for the worse, having now sunk to becoming the Ministry of Public Building and Works.

The only serious independent consideration given to the distribution of central government functions as a whole during the past century was by the Haldane Committee on Machinery of Government, reporting in 1918. It proposed, in the light of vivid experience of the defects of the inherited structure, a radically different regrouping into ten divisions. With the ending of World War I, however, it became possible to put the whole subject back in its appropriate Whitehall pigeonhole, and this was of course done. Following World War II certain limited measures of rationalization became practicable. Inter-Service working had been called for so often and so generally during and after the war, and the example and pressure of the American Pentagon was so close and so strong, that after nearly twenty years of half-measures, with a Ministry of Defence superimposed on the three Service Departments, the plunge was at last taken in 1964 by unifying the lot. Contrary, however, to unqualified Ministerial assurances given at the time the law of Professor Parkinson was strictly observed. The combined staff soon totalled rather more than the sum of the staffs of the previously separate and overlapping branches of the three Service Departments, and it was the Minister who was made a monkey of.

It is difficult to trace with any precision the growth of the Civil Service, owing to its long tradition of producing bits and pieces of statistics which are neither comparable for different Departments at any one time, or even for the same Department over a period of time. The total number of non-industrial civil servants (immediately before World War I) at the beginning of August 1914 was 282,420. In April 1930 it was 306,154 and in 1960, also at the beginning of April, it was 637,374, an increase of about 125 percent.

Such crude figures, however, can support no valid inference beyond the obvious fact that the Civil Service has grown greatly, and (as more up-to-date returns show) is still growing fast. The relevant issue here is the role of the Civil Service *vis-à-vis* Ministers in the exercise of the sovereign powers which belong to neither of them, but which for practical reasons come their way. The intense difficulty of probing this subject is aggravated by the protean and indefinite character of the Civil Service, especially in past days. Until World War I the theory and practice of the constitution had been so Parliament-centered that Members of either House who became Ministers had been visualized as acquiring with their seals of office a kind of quiver-full of statutory or other responsibilities in discharging which they called upon some miscellaneous band of officials from within the new magic circle of those holding certificates from the Civil Service Commission. They did not so much (in theory) go in to head a Department as to gather their own posse of henchmen around themselves.

As had been recognized a great deal earlier on the Continent, modern administration cannot actually be conducted in this way, and following its favorite maxim of "softly, softly, catchee monkey" the Civil Service gradually managed to coalesce into recognized permanent offices. It was, however, not until as recently as 1920 that the Civil Service National Whitley Council's *Report of Joint Committee on the Organisation of the Civil Service* ventured to put into currency the term "Departments of the Public Service" as a label for what had long existed unobtrusively. This situation, of course, played into the hands of the practitioners of internecine power politics in government offices, and of the worshipers of traditions, some of which had been virtually invented by themselves. One of the most extraordinary of these was that of "Treasury Chambers", the letter-heading under which the gentlemen practicing in these imaginary "Chambers" wrote to their client Departments in terms appropriate to the ruling of Lord Welby in a minute, dated 21 November, 1879, that:

The Treasury itself is rather an office of superintendence and appeal than an office of administration.

Yet as far back as 1903 a well-informed authority could already write of "the permanent Civil Service whose chiefs have been, at least since the days of Bagehot, recognized as the real rulers of the country." The context of British administration has thus very gradually changed from that of a picked band of permanent officials operating under the aegis of a succession of individual Ministers to that of a succession of Ministers being grafted more or less temporarily on to the permanent and firmly structured organism of a Department of State, presided over by a Permanent Secretary to whom the staff look as their boss, subject to the superior jurisdiction of the official Treasury.

How far does this mean that the true authority to exercise sovereignty, which long since passed from the Crown to Parliament, and thence to the Cabinet and thence largely to the Prime Minister, has in practice passed once more from the Ministerial level as a whole to the permanent heads of the Civil Service?

This is a question to which there is no simple answer. A correct answer would vary from Department to Department, from administration to administration, from Minister to Minister, from Permanent Secretary to Permanent Secretary, and from situation to situation. In principle, beyond question, the Minister is the boss, just as in principle a man is master in his own household. There are various situations in which practice may approximate fairly closely to this principle. If the issue is one on which the Minister's party has a definite and well-thought-out view, backed by something like an election pledge, an announced Cabinet decision or inclusion in some wider action program, the Minister's word is likely to be law, unless he behaves very stupidly. Or if the issue is one dear to the Minister personally, over which his wishes can be met without exposing the Department to significant embarrassment or inconvenience, or affecting its long-term staffing and commitments, his will is likely to prevail. Conversely, where the issue is one over which the Department has already taken a stand, and is likely to be involved in internally embarrassing adjustments or in losing face before other Departments through changing it, the Minister will be up against a stiffer situation, in which he may be called upon to show a good deal of strength, firmness and persistence to get what he wants. Here he courts a setback if there is any substantial weakness in his position which can be exploited in resisting his arguments, especially if these are viewed by his officials as either theoretical or partisan.

Apart from such definable issues the general relation of the Minister to his Department will be influenced by his standing in the country, in Parliament and with his Ministerial colleagues, his training and experience, his capabilities for mastering papers and for seeing that he gets those which he needs and is not bogged down in the other sort, his industry and pace and method of working, and of course by what manner of man he is, and how good he is at getting his own way. Ministers who work unusually late, or arrive unusually early in the morning, or insist on plunging into much detail, or who have special gray eminences or protégés, outside the Service and Parliament, whom they insist on bringing into the act, are almost sure to be unpopular, but can sometimes by such means partially wear down the ordinary defense mechanisms of the Service, and get their own way oftener. Seasoned Ministers, with successful experience in other Departments, or even new Ministers whose other previous experience enables them to speak the same language as the administrators and to understand the background factors to which the Department attaches importance, have, naturally, an advantage over those whose experience has been wholly in politics, business or a dissimilar profession such as law or medicine. Even able men coming late to office may never sufficiently learn the ropes to be able to deviate far from the path set for them by their Departments. Such Ministers tend to become spokesmen of their Departments' views rather than operators capable of using their Departments as instruments for the government's own ends. Eminent lawyers on becoming Ministers are especially prone to this fault. Owing to the unwieldiness of the long Departmental hierarchies, the slowness of two-way communication, the inevitably heavy work-load at the top, and the drag in imparting new attitudes and approaches, any Minister, however dynamic and clear-headed, is compelled simply to rubber-stamp almost unseen or unconsidered a great deal that the Department chooses to submit for his authorization. He can only hope that it will not too often contain some blunder for which he has to answer, or some choice too plainly inconsistent with that which he would himself have made, and which his Party expects of him. In a well-run Department this will normally be the case, but there are exceptions, and they can be bitter.

Permanent Secretaries, like Ministers, are quite capable of forming their own views, which may be strongly held, but unlike Ministers they may not voice them too publicly. The convention is that they may reason most frankly with the Minister in case they think he is wrong or unwise, but at the end of the day, as my first Lord President used to say, it is the Minister who must decide. Once he has decided it is the duty of the Permanent Secretary to see that the decision is fully and promptly carried out, whatever misgivings he may personally feel about it. In general this seems a sound practice, and with a strong and intelligent Minister and an able and open-minded Permanent Secretary it works well. In other circumstances, however, it can lead to the Permanent Secretary brain-washing or over-persuading his Minister to adopt or to decline a particular course, sometimes with unsatisfactory results. It is clear, if Ministerial statements emanating from a particular Department are compared with those made under previous administrations, and with personal utterances of the Minister before taking office, that this sort of thing does happen. An apparent example was the unexpected refusal of Sir Frank Soskice, as Home Secretary, to grant a fresh judicial inquiry into the conviction for murder of Timothy Evans of Rillington Place, Notting Hill. Sir Frank had strongly favored this before taking office, and was afterwards compelled by Parliamentary pressure to agree to it, with the result that his successor as Home Secretary found it necessary to advise a posthumous free pardon, thus confirming how very wrong and unjust had been the official advice on which Sir Frank was first persuaded to act.

The manning of the London end of the administration of the overseas dependencies, and of relations with self-governing Dominions, together with the general diplomatic and economic relations involved, formed an important part of the work of Whitehall during the past century. This work included recruitment for the large Indian and Colonial Civil Services, as well as the Sudan and other more specialized corps. From the standpoint of professional employment the loss of these outlets has been very roughly offset by the expansion of the Home Civil Service, whose Administrative Class had risen from about 1,100 in 1930 to 2,261 at the beginning of 1964. The grading within the Class has become preponderantly more senior, the lowest grade (Assistant Principal) having actually diminished from 290 to 218, while Principals have approximately tripled, Assistant Secretaries have multiplied themselves four times and the highest posts have more than tripled. These figures exclude Commonwealth Relations, Trade Commissioner and of course Foreign Office posts, all of which have since 1965 been combined within HM Diplomatic Service. This is administered by a new Diplomatic Service Administration Office, although as Departments the Foreign Office and Commonwealth Relations Office remain distinct. There is now some slight interchange between the Home Civil and Diplomatic Services. The outcome of these reforms is further to emphasize the contrast between the unified public service pool of personnel and the archaic and largely unreformed layout of functions as between Departments, or between the Civil Service as a whole and other types of public body. Most of the recent changes in these functions have been thought up and executed, with reckless haste, to meet transient political conditions, like the egregious Department of Land and Natural Resources, which was killed within a couple of years by the same Prime Minister who so rashly conceived it.

From quite early times the importance of certain essential services such as naval defense, carrying mails, looking after public buildings and the printing and publication of official reports, has been found to call for State operation of supply arrangements. As these operations cost, and in some cases also earned, money they became amenable to the management of the public finances, which fell in due course under the control of the House of Commons in succession to the Crown. It followed naturally that responsibility to the House for each of them was assumed by a Minister, and that they accordingly passed through the stages of being a field of jobbery and patronage to being staffed and controlled by the reformed, competitively recruited Civil Service. Being merely essential services, lacking in glamor and in policy issues, they proved, with the exception of the Admiralty, unattractive to the bright young men from Oxbridge who now formed the Administrative class. Yet the arbitrary whims of politicians, the demands of reformist campaigns and the reluctance of Departments to become saddled with strange and intractable or merely boring additional functions had the result that however many *ad hoc* independent bodies might be swept up in regular Departments there were always more springing up to maintain their population and importance. From their very nature such bodies are highly miscellaneous and difficult to classify. Sir Arthur Street, who as much as any man contributed to their recent revival and success, divided them into Regulatory Bodies (Non-Industrial), Regulatory Bodies (Industrial) and Managerial Bodies, but as he himself remarked this classification is imperfect and artificial. It seems best to carry the breakdown somewhat further on the following lines:

1. Tribunals, and other bodies mainly concerned with administrative justice (subdivided into those tied to a single profession, service or industry, and others).
2. Supervisory, licensing, grant-aiding and decentralized administrative bodies.
3. Upper-tier managerial bodies, undertaking a defined share of management the rest of which falls to subordinate bodies or to individuals.
4. Entire self-contained management bodies—national.
5. Entire self-contained management bodies—local or regional.
6. Other public bodies, not integrated in central or local government (an inevitable but small residual category).

Reviewing these categories briefly in order:

1. Examples of such bodies (apart from the special cases of the Ecclesiastical Courts and of Tribunals created *ad hoc* to inquire into particular current issues such as the Aberfan coal-tip disaster) are the Industrial Court for the settlement of trade disputes, the Office of the Umpire to decide appeals under Acts concerned with employment, the National Board for Prices and Incomes, the Monopolies Commission, reconstituted under the Restrictive Trade Practices Act 1956, the National Assistance, National Insurance and National Health Appeal Tribunals, the Mental Health Review Tribunals, the Pensions Appeal Tribunals, the Lands Tribunal and many more. Owing to recurrent public anxiety over the implications of such tribunals for the liberty of the subject Parliament in 1958 enacted the Tribunals and Inquiries Act, which constituted the Council on Tribunals to keep the field under review, and to submit annual reports to Parliament.

Much excellent and necessary work has been quietly and efficiently done by many of these bodies, but the manner in which they have been permitted to proliferate without any adequate comprehensive thought and supervision by Parliament or rational relation to the courts of justice is disturbing. Far more disturbing, however, has been the growing assumption, directly by Departments, of so-called quasi-judicial powers, which forms one of the most disturbing of all modern inroads into British liberties, and constitutes a rich field for studies in misgovernment.

2. Examples of this category are the Water Resources Board, the National Insurance Advisory Committee, the National Ports Council,

the National Parks Commission, the Arts Council of Great Britain, the Air Registration Board, the Air Transport Licensing Board, the Traffic Commissioners, the Independent Television Authority, the Horse Race Totalisator Board and many others, shading into the previous category.

Their main distinction from it is that, rather than arriving at judgments on points of equity, awards in accordance with defined rights, or recommendations on particular cases, they are primarily concerned with broad and long-term development within some defined area of responsibility, in pursuance of which they either offer financial incentives such as grants, or exercise powers of persuasion, sometimes backed by mandatory directives to bodies which have specifically been rendered amenable to these by Parliament, such as the commercial television undertakings and the road service operators. Other bodies such as the official Research Councils, although predominantly relying upon grant-aid, fall broadly within this class.

One significant aspect of these bodies is that their work tends in its nature to overlap the types of work done by conventional government Departments; thus the way it is done and the results obtained can form a useful yardstick for measuring the performance of these Departments.

3. Two-tier statutory divisions of function occur both in local government (with which we are not here immediately concerned) and in nationalized industries. Perhaps the best and one of the most successful current instances is the Gas Council, which has gone so far to "assist the Area Boards in the discharge of their functions" that through its initiative over new methods of gas production, and over exploration for natural gas in the North Sea, it looks like bringing about a fundamental improvement in the national fuel resource base, and therefore in the national economy. The former Electricity and British Transport Commissions were other instances. If a satisfactory division of functions can be found, and if the top management is good enough to win the confidence of the areas or other units immediately below it, and to render real service to them, this approach forms a possible solution to the awkward problem of gearing local or specialist initiative and responsibility to the requirements of national policy. It also enables the economies of scale to be secured in providing certain functions through the largest possible unit. Although current examples are rather few, this could prove an important growing point, provided the level of managerial competence and of teamwork can be kept high enough to justify it.

4. Unitary organization and management of entire industries or services, under public ownership but not through government departments, is a relatively new development in Britain. After World War I early examples were the Forestry Commission, the British Broadcasting Corporation and the London Passenger Transport Board. After World War II came the National Coal Board, the British Overseas Airways Corporation, British Railways and Waterways Boards (formerly British Transport Commission), and others, including some important reconstitutions such as the nationalized Bank of England and the Central Electricity Generating Board.

Concerns in this group vary in important particulars—one of them at least, Cable and Wireless Ltd., is disguised as an ordinary company, but is wholly state-owned. Some are national monopolies, others have more limited geographic or functional scope. They include, however, a substantial part of British economic activity and of the British labor force, and the chief of them rank among the largest concerns of any kind in Europe. Neither Parliament nor the Civil Service possess the training, outlook or managerial experience to provide supervision of the necessary caliber for great enterprises of this nature. After protracted friction they have on the whole been persuaded to give up trying to interfere with their normal operations. The situation, however, remains precarious and unsatisfactory, and seems bound to continue so until there are at the head of affairs in Whitehall more men who speak the same language as the managers of the great public concerns.

5. A leading example of this somewhat smaller and more localized type would be the North of Scotland Hydro-Electric Board: the Port of London Authority, dating from 1909, is a particular example of some historical interest. If such localized public concerns are dependent heavily on national funds, as was the case with the first-named, they are inevitably caught up in politics. Some, although in principle national, like the new British Airports Authority, operate only in a few limited areas.

6. Perhaps the most important group in this miscellaneous category have been the producer-elected agricultural Marketing Boards set up under the Agricultural Marketing Acts during the 1930s. Initially these played an important role in the organization and modernization of British farming, but changing conditions after World War II removed much of their significance. The Crown Estate Commissioners are a special case of some interest, in that they administer the land revenues surrendered by the Crown to Parliament two hundred years ago, in return for the fixed annual payment

known as the Civil List. They are, among other things, responsible for much of the foreshore round the coasts of Britain, and they pay in to the Exchequer annually surplus revenue amounting to some 60 percent of their receipts.

As this brief outline has shown, the non-Departmental public bodies of Great Britain constitute a large, expanding and highly important sector of the public service, charged with a wide range of duties and tasks whose satisfactory fulfillment is essential to the satisfactory functioning of the nation. Owing to the grossly inadequate provision for study of such institutions, and to their heterogeneous nature, the significance of their existence is imperfectly known and grasped, even by many holders of important posts in British public life. The modernity of the origins of most of these bodies means that they have not yet had long to drift far out of touch with current thinking and requirements. The adaptations and new models which have recently been developed in a number of them indicate, however, that there is no time to be lost in making provision against this. Above all, some clear basis must be worked out for determining the appropriate relations between the public bodies, Government Departments, Parliament and the consumer, and for deciding whether a particular matter should be handled by a public body or by a government Department.

Bare mention must be made of the role played by a number of unofficial bodies such as the Trades Unions Congress, the recently amalgamated Confederation of British Industries, the Clearing Banks, the Stock Exchange, the Law Society, and others working with the machinery of government more or less closely through hybrid consultative or supervisory bodies or through fulfilling quasi-administrative functions. There are indications that this field of relationships is expanding, and there is certainly room for it to expand greatly in future, thus forming many more bridges between public and private sectors, and between government and governed. Perhaps it is not too fanciful to suggest that through such channels a few tiny particles of sovereignty have already flowed back, through Parliament, the Cabinet, and Whitehall, to the sovereign electors, or at least to some of them.

Besides the critical interface where the processes of central government touch those of private groupings and citizens, there is also a great interface between central and local government. History still plays a large part here. While even from Anglo-Saxon times and onwards townspeople were active in winning charters and establishing institutions which we would now call local government, in the countryside the somewhat Swiss-style local democracy of the hundred and the folk-moot could not survive the impact of Norman feudalism. Thus, apart from such picturesque relics of the most ancient institutions of government as the ritualized local managements of certain common lands, the countryside of England and Wales became the domain of the squires and magnates, who governed it until within living memory with an incompetence which still leaves its mark, and which proved the despair of generations of central administrators. The boroughs, on the other hand, were overtaken from the seventeenth to nearly the mid-nineteenth century by the somnolence and corruption which became endemic throughout other corporations, such as the universities and the Church of England, at the same period. Nearly all the vital forces of the nation bypassed them through other channels. The problems and scandals of the population explosion resulting from the industrial revolution led Parliament and Whitehall first to set up or develop a network of *ad hoc* institutions. The eventual overlapping and confusion among these compelled the establishment around 1888 of what was virtually a brand-new two-tier structure of local government throughout Great Britain, composed of County Councils with subordinate more localized bodies, from among which the County Boroughs were allowed to contract out as autonomous island areas.

Needless to say, Britain being Britain, by the time this elaborate new pattern was launched it was already obsolescent. The great conurbations of the Midlands and North of England, and of Central Scotland and South Wales, were already reaching across local authority boundaries and sprouting hybrid, suburban communities whose most important common interest might be that all their drains ran down to the same main sewer. Recalcitrant or isolationist *ad hoc* bodies stood out for decades against becoming embodied in the new all-purpose authorities. The last of them —the Boards of Guardians— disappeared as lately as 1929. The financial basis of local authorities had already been undermined by the long stagnation which began in Britain at about the same time as they did, accompanied by agricultural depression and later by wartime inflation and the depression in export industries. The state, having thus failed to provide conditions in which local government could be viable, proceeded during the 'thirties both to bring it financially into subservience to Whitehall, and progressively to remove from it a number of its most cherished and important functions, including in the end hospitals, relief of the needy, gas and electricity and others. A single city, Hull, managed to retain its own telephone service, as a token of municipal independence.

At the same time the State began, with slow but gradually increasing resolution, to decentralize itself for certain purposes. The chief example so far has been the development of St. Andrew's House in Edinburgh as a Scottish Whitehall, where the great majority of governmental functions specifically affecting Scotland were grouped under integrated Scottish Departments solely answerable to their Secretary of State. In the peculiar case of Northern Ireland the process went even further, with the establishment under the Government of Ireland Act 1920 of a separate Parliament and a governor, as well as an executive with absolute delegation of powers within wide limits.

While Northern Ireland thus received an equivalent of self-governing colony status, fiscal and external relations matters being reserved, Wales continued as a nominally equal partner, but in practice a non-self-governing colony, of England. Very recently some steps to correct this have been taken by appointing a Secretary of State for Wales with a Welsh Office and a Minister of State to assist him, and by designating Cardiff as the capital of Wales.

Within England, although limited palatine jurisdictions have survived from the Middle Ages in the Duchies of Lancaster and Cornwall, serious steps towards decentralization of the modern government structure have only just begun, with the development of "regional Whitehalls", serving appointed regional councils and regional economic planning boards in Newcastle-upon-Tyne, Leeds, Nottingham, Bristol, Birmingham and Manchester.

Converging with this movement towards decentralization is a movement to merge local authorities in much larger and stronger two-tier authorities. The first of these, the Greater London Council, has replaced the former administrative counties of London and Middlesex, and taken in also parts of Essex, Kent and Surrey, since 1964–65. Its second tier is formed by thirty-two new London Borough Councils, with populations ranging from approximately 150,000 to 350,000 each. There is also a partial reversion to the previous *ad hoc* authorities in the shape of the Inner London Education Authority. How far, if at all, this is to be regarded as a prototype for local government reform generally will presumably emerge from discussions now being held by Sir John Maud's Royal Commission. The reconciliation of modern economies of scale, and the more coherent and integrated policies open to larger units with the representative and neighborhood principles basic to local government is an intractable difficulty.

Always bearing in mind that historic and flourishing city corporations constitute an exception of great significance, it is broadly true to say that in the countryside, and in most of the smaller towns, the new regime of 1888 represented not so much a reform of long-established local government as a new start on often bare and even barren ground. It was hoped, rather than calculated with assurance, that after so many years of being virtually denied a voice in local affairs all kinds of new men would come forward and prove able by means of an unwieldy committee system to launch and manage all kinds of new services for the public. This was optimistic, and although it nowhere proved absolutely impossible to man and run some local authority, such situations were averted only by accepting in a minority of cases undesirably low standards. People interested in such activities as construction, and in dealing in land and property, were often notably more willing to sacrifice their time in committees where they always stood a chance of hearing something to their or their friends' advantage, than ordinary, and especially well-educated citizens. The alternative common pattern was of excessive reliance on the *noblesse oblige* element among the local gentry, eked out by injections of active yet retired people. Local government officers, who had to wait half a century for a comprehensive superannuation scheme, were normally regarded as a lower form of life than civil servants. They also had to suffer much frustration from elementary failures among the elected members to distinguish between matters of policy and matters of administration.

A main force originally compelling local government reform had been the scandals over cholera epidemics, which required provision of sewers and means of sewage disposal and treatment, collection and disposal of household refuse, public cleansing and sanitation, provision of public baths and wash-houses, and also maintenance of streets, parks and open spaces and burial grounds. Such communal services, financed by local taxation, and mostly used by all local residents, were added to the more ancient protective services such as police, fire brigade and ambulance, together with the policing of honest weights and measures, building safety, and protection of consumers from adulteration of food-stuffs. The successive Town and Country Planning Acts of the nineteen-thirties, 'forties and 'fifties gave geographic form and physical framework to these environmental community and protective services.

Other social services, notably education, poor relief and housing were important local government functions, but in recent years these have tended increasingly, like Trunk Roads, to be dealt with if at all on something near an agency basis for central government. The large group of Trading Services, although dear to the hearts of many in local government, can now be seen to be largely more appropriate to more management-minded bodies, often operating over wider areas. Thus the 1888 attempt to launch a new structure of local government able to balance and complement the expanding central machine, although by no means a fiasco, fell far short of real success. It is pretty commonly recognized now that what amounts to another fresh start must soon be made. It is to be hoped that this time the demands of efficiency and of acceptability can be more successfully reconciled, and that a type of local government will emerge capable of attracting much more local interest and participation, and thus able to form a genuine counter-weight to central administration, if only within limited fields.

Nowhere was the need for such a counter-weight, and for avoiding central control, more keenly felt than over the police. A national police force would, it has always been felt in England, be highly dangerous to civic liberty. Unfortunately local control has not proved in practice a reliable safeguard against abuses, while the expanding and increasingly sophisticated, well-equipped, and amply financed fraternity of criminals has profited from the lack of co-ordination between local forces, and their slowness to avail themselves of technical aid, even when this is readily obtainable through Scotland Yard. An awkward and embarrassing situation has thus arisen between the Home Secretary, the citizen, and the police, which helps and pleases none but the wrongdoers. Confidence in and public readiness to help the police are probably lower than for a long period, while the police themselves suffer from low morale, high wastage and difficulties in recruitment. Until recently the British tradition of unarmed police whom criminals seek to outwit but not to kill has worked fairly well. The recent outbreak of breaches of this tacit rule has aggravated the bad feeling in the police force, coinciding as it has with the long overdue abolition of the death penalty and with a series of disturbingly easy and frequent escapes by convicted prisoners. It is impossible to avoid the impression that the Home Office and the Treasury have been singularly ham-handed since World War II in their handling of relations with the police, which must accordingly be noted among the more serious aspects of misgovernment.

The dwindling effectiveness of the police and the increasing number of unsolved crimes is an embarrassment in turn to the courts of justice, which must here be considered in relation to the processes of government. One of the earliest developments in the English machinery of government was the remarkable initiative by Henry II in developing a new school of law, only distantly related to the civil law then being revived in his continental possessions. He reached out to attract to the King's Court and to his traveling justices many actions which would otherwise have been tried by varying and old-fashioned standards locally in the shire courts. The excellence and popularity of this system, coming so soon after the lawlessness under Stephen, gave stability and general acceptance to what came to be called the Common Law, and led to its rapid dissemination through the new system of trial by jury. It was reinforced by the subsequent enlistment of Knights of the Shire, as Coroners to vindicate the King's rights in judicial and other matters. This bold departure led not only to the development of Justices of the Peace as local voluntary dispensers of justice, and even as amateur all-round administrators, but also to the broad and effective composition of the English Parliament and its capacity to speak for the whole nation. But more and more the executive and legislative functions became separated from the judicial, although the judges still go on circuit three times yearly to this day round the seven traditional parts into which England and Wales fall, and the combination of the offices of the Clerk of the Peace and Clerk of the County Council often serves as a reminder that justice and administration were once inseparable.

As the liberty of the subject and his immunity from arbitrary interference or punishment have been the mainspring of political evolution in England, the upholding of the rule of law as superior to the will of any aspiring tyrant, from a monarch to a bureaucrat, has often been the crux of constitutional conflicts from Magna Carta onwards, throughout the ensuing three-quarters of a millennium. It follows that the judiciary have occupied a key role, and but for their tenacity, skill and personal courage on many occasions all that was gained earlier could easily have been lost or whittled away. The occasions when critical issues of principle have arisen have however become less and less frequent, while the gradual transfer to Parliament of control over nearly all the executive functions of the Crown enabled the House of Commons to take care of the situation without difficulty.

Recently, however, the problem of personal liberty and of property rights has become transmuted into a new and dangerous form. No longer is it a case of all public-spirited citizens watching for and ready to resist encroachments by some ambitious monarch, with the aid of the courts and the House of Commons. A New Despotism, dramatized by Lord Hewart in his polemic work under that title in 1929, has been discerned in the operations of bodies, nominally under Parliamentary control, which Parliament has appeared unable or unwilling to discipline. The citizen has become liable to fines, imprisonment, or confiscations such as compulsory purchase, in hundreds of thousands of situations, any one of which if created by a Stuart king would have had the whole country up in arms against him. The scope of administrative courts and administrative regulations has been so immensely expanded as to make the Star Chamber look like a mere pin-prick.

One of the most serious aspects of this trend is the extent to which Parliament has acquiesced in seeing the judiciary deprived of any effective power of review or intervention which could help in safeguarding the constitutional rights of the citizen. It is often implicit that Parliament itself will undertake the review and supervision, but this it has not proved able to do on any adequate scale, as the recent decision to appoint a Parliamentary Commissioner or Ombudsman recognized. It can now be said without serious exaggeration that the courts remain only as a protection for those segments of the Englishman's constitutional liberties of which he has not been already at least potentially deprived by collusion between Parliament and the Executive. Here again is an area of misgovernment. There are many possible excuses, some quite reasonable, for many limitations on personal liberty, but the slipshod, chaotic and underhand manner in which so much of it has been accomplished, and the failure of Parliament to set clear limits and clear principles for the process are less excusable. No personal tyrant would have dared, or could have hoped, to get away with using "reasons of state" as they are used today to deprive citizens of their historic liberties and rights. Limited as their opportunities have become for playing their historic constitutional role, the judges have not neglected those which have arisen, but they have only recently begun seriously to think and act together on the contributions to legal and judicial reform which are within their power. In principle, with free legal aid available to needy and serious litigants, the courts today are for the first time in centuries free of the reproach of being open to all like the Ritz Hotel. They should be popular, but they are hardly that. Although compared with those of the United States, France and other leading countries their handling of even the most difficult cases is remarkably expeditious and conclusive, their prestige has been shaken by a number of recent events. The worst was the reactionary image presented by the criminal judges regarding the abolition of the death penalty and of corporal punishment, coinciding, as it unhappily did, with the long-denied but finally admitted fatal miscarriage of justice over the Rillington Place murders. Weaknesses in the police have deprived the courts of one of their main props, while faults in the prison service and the monotonous frequency of escapes by key prisoners also, however unfairly, shake the ordinary man's confidence in British justice. Another disturbing weakness has been increasingly revealed in relation to juries. Only those who have had to serve on them can fully appreciate the risks inherent in according such decisive authority over the processes of justice to its most stupid element. Public opinion has been disturbed by the evidence of jurors being summoned despite a criminal record, and of interference with members of juries and the terrorizing of witnesses. While these matters compromise the good name of the courts it is the Home Office, with its responsibilities for maintaining an efficient and reliable police and prison service, which has been primarily to blame.

While immense importance has historically been attached to the independence of courts of justice in England it is only quite recently that they have been nearly as effectively separated from politics as the Civil Service. Out of 139 appointments to judicial office between 1832 and 1906, eighty were of Members of Parliament, and only seventeen of these were members of the opposition at the time. Now that such appointments are made, irrespective of politics, to barristers of the right seniority who have achieved the professional esteem of their colleagues, there is no longer any point in winning a seat in Parliament as a step on the way to the bench. This may have a bearing on the decline in the number of lawyers in the House of Commons noted earlier. In its level of professionalism and of training the law is fairly sharply distinguished still from both politics and public administration, except at the lower levels. Here the process of weeding out Justices of the Peace who try cases without having taken any legal training, and often as an honor which comes to them *ex officio* as Mayors or other dignitaries, is only just belatedly getting under way. The errors of unpaid magistrates, and the harm done by detailed hearings, reported *in extenso* by the press, before committal to a higher court on charges of some grave offense, are among the sore points of a system of justice which in general is efficient and humane, and is much more up-to-date in outlook and working than its favorite traditional trappings and ceremonies might lead the casual observer to suppose.

One of the greatest differences within the polity of Great Britain is the maintenance in Scotland of a totally distinct system of law, closely based upon Roman Civil Law, and of quite different arrangements for the administration of justice. The obvious opportunities for comparative study and evaluation of the merits and workings of the two systems might well be more fully exploited, especially since both systems appear unusually efficient compared with those of a number of other countries. There is much more to it than the widely advertised change of marriage laws which begins at Gretna Green. Unfortunately, as so generally happens in Britain, serious research into the administration of justice and in criminology and related sciences has begun very belatedly, largely under the influence of scholars from the Continent, and much of the field has still to be investigated.

An interesting fringe problem here is the increasing practice of appointing judges to head not only judicial but administrative and political investigations which the government has been persuaded to set up. While the trend appears popular and seems to give acceptable results it could, if it continues to grow, have repercussions on the independence of the judiciary and upon judicial manpower. It is noticeable that the holding of public inquiries under civil servants responsible to Ministers has not proved publicly acceptable beyond the realm of hearings about proposed projects or plans of development, and more or less straight-forward investigations into such matters as causes of accidents.

On the whole the courts of law and the administration of justice may be regarded as one of the areas of public affairs into which the most and the best efforts of many previous generations in Britain have been put, and as one where the sheer quality and the intellectual basis thus provided have stood the test of time pretty well. As a popular British institution the courts have been almost unique in frowning upon mental indolence and on the sloppy preparation and presentation of material. While they have often fallen short of their own high standards, the standards themselves have not been let down. The fact that the legal profession is becoming less central and dominant in the body politic, although inevitable and in some respects welcome, places all the more responsibility on professions which are superseding it in this respect, notably public administration, to pull up their socks and seek to attain comparable professional standards.

As one of the producers and distributors the private citizen plays a part in sustaining the national economy, from which he draws an income within the limits of its capacity to pay, part of which as a taxpayer he hands over to the State. As a consumer he spends his earnings, or has a wife and family who help him to spend them, and here also he draws his modern dividends in increased leisure, and enjoys or contributes to the contemporary culture as his desires suggest to him. He becomes at this point in the sequence less a means to an end, and more of an end in himself. Beyond this point, as a functioning citizen, he is uplifted from the ranks of the downtrodden producers and consumers—the governed—to the more exalted plane of the electorate, as one of whom he shares in a modest way in the sovereignty of the United Kingdom with Her Majesty the Queen and the Lords and Commons in Parliament assembled. Thus he demonstrates that one man in his time acts many parts. But are the parts satisfying? Are they meaningfully related? Is the actor competent and does he find his creative powers and yearnings fulfilled by them? Do they give him enough feeling of status and authority in relation to his servants who populate the desks in the great public buildings and bombard him with pieces of paper? When he is not engaged in the rare and fleeting privilege of governing, is he being governed or misgoverned? Do his governors themselves really know what they are doing and why they are doing it? Who are they, anyway, and by what right or process did they get there? Do they know and understand about the governed, and his rights, needs, and sensibilities? Do they try to keep him happy and to make him feel he is participating with them in their common task, or do they antagonize and alienate him? These are constitutional issues no less important than the privileges of the House of Commons, but no Committee of Citizen's Privileges stands ready to hail before it those who presume to treat with disdain and to traverse the sacred rights of the Englishman, the Scotsman and the Welshman. Theoretically they may be sovereign, but practically they are expendable. Why is this? Must it ever remain so?

Much of the British constitution is fluid, and little of it is hard set. The rule of law remains a fairly firm basic principle, in so far as it has not been eroded by administrative processes. The sovereignty originally vested in the Crown alone has come to be shared with Parliament and the electorate on terms and in ways that all find acceptable, partly because it is all so vague and partly because real power, which is the business end of sovereignty, has been conveniently and completely separated from it and carried away elsewhere. We may therefore happily forget about sovereignty, but the question of power remains, as discussed in Part Three, a troublesome one.

Where does the misgovernment lie? Perhaps seven distinct areas can be discerned in which misgovernment may be said to be prominent.

First the elector. He is supposed to have a share of sovereignty but so far he has simply been sold a gold brick. The right to mark a ballot paper at long intervals for one of two or more persons who have been pre-selected for him by organized parties which have got him into the mess where he now is can only be termed sovereignty in a very special sense. He requires much greater opportunities for effective and frequent or continuous participation in the guidance of his destinies. He in turn needs much more education, training and information in order to use part of his growing leisure as a useful and fulfilled citizen.

Secondly the citizen as one of the governed, with his constitutional rights. Here again, he has simply been swindled. He sees the High Court Judges and the Lord Chancellor in majestic procession in their full-bottomed wigs and assumes that he enjoys the same protection for his person and property as his forefathers. In fact he has been quietly done out of much of his historic free status, and the Judges themselves have been as quietly shouldered into a situation where they are often unable any longer to offer him effective protection against the Executive.

Thirdly, Parliament, which has permitted itself to become swamped in detail and irrelevances and, like the Trades Unions Congress, has spent so long being adamant when it ought to have been adaptable that it now finds its views brushed aside and itself impotent on issues where it would be entitled to be adamant. Past Parliaments have had a shocking record of failing to insist on necessary modernization, and of failing to veto usurpations and encroachments which they should have resisted. An entire regrouping and rethinking of the true role of an effective Parliament in modern terms is overdue.

Fourthly, the Civil Service. This archaic non-profession, constituted on mistaken lines to fulfil a role which has long since ceased to exist, needs to be promptly and completely replaced by something reasonably related to the world in which Britain now has to function, and to the kind of people that the British are.

Fifthly, the general layout and organization of government, which centers still on offices dating from the eighteenth century or earlier, to which have accreted far too many fresh Departments and Ministers, chaotically organized, and flanked by a vast number of public concerns, tribunals and other paragovernmental agencies.

Sixthly, the now admittedly impossible mess in local and regional government, the existing pattern of which no longer has defenders, and which is hopelessly out of relation to central government.

Finally the entire failure to find facts, analyze problems and trends, forecast probable developments and to provide for devising and revising acceptable and professionally competent plans of many kinds for the guidance and co-ordination of all concerned.

PART FIVE

BRITAIN'S PERFORMANCE
1926–1966

CHAPTER 12

Return to the Gold Standard and the Strike

In this fifth part an inevitably selective review is attempted of a number of the apparent turning-points in the British record over the forty years immediately past. This record of what the British did, and how and why they did it, is perhaps the most nearly objective and reliable guide to who the British now are, which way they are going, and where they have got to so far. It must, however, never be overlooked that what stands on the record as having been "done" by "Britain" largely consists of something done to or on behalf of Britain by a small ruling group. Only rarely is it possible to get through the upper crust of the state and make contact with the nation underneath.

The choice of this particular period, spanning four decades, must be somewhat arbitrary, but it has clear advantages. It covers events from the aftermath of World War I to what seems to be the fluid and formative stage following the rigid aftermath of World War II. It falls within the span of life of many now living, yet what happened before it is of rapidly dwindling recollection and relevance in public affairs. Certainly no other four decades in all British history would show such deep and widespread change, yet even so there is a strong impression abroad that the change has been inadequate, and a disturbing doubt whether it has been in the right direction.

Selection implies a standpoint. Here it has been guided mainly by two criteria. The first has been the items which seem to throw most light on the choices made and decisions taken upon those issues apparently of greatest strategic significance to British progress or decline. The second has been the extent to which events have deeply and urgently engaged the thoughts and emotions of the nation, such as the General Strike of 1926, and the slump and devaluation of 1931, and the balance of payments and prices and incomes crises of 1965–66.

At such moments, when men become angry or emotional, and their feelings burst unbidden into words which the record catches, we see vividly reflected the tensions and undercurrents which usually flow more or less hidden from our view. But these, too, are often moments of truth, when, as was remarked in one of them, the skies are darkened with the broken promises and neglected opportunities of past years coming home to roost. Rarely, despite appearances, do such crises arise without warning or wholly from external sources. It is the cumulative divergence between national needs or expectations and national provision for effectively satisfying them which becomes transformed into an intolerable dilemma by some event.

In picking out issues of strategic importance special attention will be paid to the four critical weaknesses pointed out in Part 1—the misconceived Victorian measures for reconstructing British administration, the legacy of chronic weakness through mistaken economic policy, the failure to develop education, science and technology as a dominant element in national life, and the false steps down the path of imperialism.

Following the belated and costly avoidance of defeat in World War I, the challenge to successive British governments was to cope with these four perhaps decisive problems, among many others only less formidable and acute, and thus to restore Britain to a position of inherent strength and leadership, rather than of growing feebleness and backwardness. That British governments, despite their various achievements, on the whole failed in this, their main task, is now an indisputable matter of record.

Winston Churchill's decision to return to the Gold Standard in 1925 was at the time widely supported, and was regarded as a successful culmination of British post-war monetary policy. Although the decision antedates the period to be discussed, the effects of this major change strongly color the events to follow. Most representative trade associations agreed that its restoration was necessary, although there was some disagreement on the desirability of the actual date chosen. Prestige reasons were uppermost in many minds, as were the advantages of being able to receive the interest payments, from the considerable overseas investments, in a non-depreciated currency.

The restoration of the Gold Standard had been anticipated for as much as eighteen months. One important step forward was made in July 1923 when the Bank rate was raised from 3 percent to 4 percent. Keynes called this move "one of the most misguided movements of that indicator that has ever occurred . . . The Bank of England, acting under the influence of a narrow and obsolete doctrine, has made a great mistake." The same economist made the desirability of the Gold Standard a live issue for the first time in his *Tract on Monetary Reform,* which boldly proposed the alternatives of devaluation or deflation.

After Churchill's decision, the force of Keynes' contention that sterling was over-valued became increasingly clear. His contention was that the return to the Gold Standard over-valued sterling by about 10 percent and over-priced British goods in the export market by the same amount. Hence industries would have to cut prices and wages. "Thus Mr. Churchill's policy of improving the exchange rate by 10 percent was, sooner or later, a policy of reducing everyone's wages by two shillings in the pound." The government, however, made no plans to deal with this necessity—perhaps they failed to realize that it *was* a necessity. Ultimately they would have to face the fact that the only way to force down money wages is to create unemployment and, although this might soon appear in the exporting industries, it would not spread to the "sheltered" industries, without measures of credit restriction.

Keynes gave two reasons for the mistake. First, by comparing wholesale index numbers in Great Britain and the US (which were made up largely of raw materials of international commerce which necessarily adjusted themselves to international rates of exchange) the experts concluded that the gap to be bridged was only 2 percent to 3 percent. If they had looked at the cost-of-living, wage and export price figures, they would have seen that it was more like 10 percent to 12 percent. The second reason was that:

> . . . Mr. Churchill's experts . . . misunderstood and underrated the technical difficulty of bringing about a general reduction of internal money values. When we raise the value of sterling by 10 percent we transfer about £1,000,000,000 into the pockets of the rentiers out of the pockets of the rest of us, and we increase the real burden of the National Debt by some £750 million (thus wiping out all our laborious contributions to the Sinking Fund since the war)

. . . I think that the minds of his advisers still dwelt in the imaginary academic world, peopled by city editors, members of Cunliffe and Currency Committees 'et hoc genus omne' where the necessary adjustments follow 'automatically' from a 'sound' policy by the Bank of England.

Even before 1925 there was some imbalance between costs and prices, which the government had made some attempt to tackle. Yet, at the same time, British currency policy tended towards over-valuation. In 1924 the purchasing power of the pound sterling in US dollars was estimated at $4.40. After a steady rise throughout the year the rate of the exchange improved to US $4.80 early in 1925. The rise was undoubtedly in anticipation of a restoration of the Gold Standard, which, since it was restored at the pre-war parity, meant that £1 could buy US $4.86. This process was matched in Britain by a rise in the price of gold, the cost of living and wages. An index, taking the pre-war level as 100, shows that the cost of living, expressed in terms of gold, rose from 157 in March 1924 to 176 in March 1925, and wages from 155 to 177. In sterling terms, the cost of living rose from 178 to 179 (after considerable fluctuations), and wages from 176 to 181. In the United States, however, the cost of living, in terms of gold, remained constant at between 156 and 158.

The over-valuation of British exports subsequently became glaring. Between 1927 and 1929 the average of British export prices (1913 = 100) was 162, compared with 101 in France and 123 in Italy. The average volume of exports was 85 for the United Kingdom, compared with 147 for France and 136 for Italy. In 1925 there was a sharp rise in the relative price level of exports to imports. The failure to reduce costs was equally clear by 1931. From 1924 to April 1931 the cost of living index fell by 18 percent, the wholesale price index by 38 percent, and real wages rose by about 20 percent. The Macmillan Committee on Finance and Industry (1931) concluded that "the very existence of the unemployment problem demonstrates that there is a disparity between prices and costs of production, which has the result of diminishing or eliminating profits and damping down all incentive to the expansion of output." The Committee observed that, not only had Britain failed to reduce her costs, but her competitors in France, Belgium and Germany had benfited from currency adjustments which decreased their gold-costs of production.

The "unsheltered" (staple export) industries were already at a considerable disadvantage compared with the "sheltered" industries. The process of economic adjustment was made more difficult. New industries could not expand sufficiently quickly because cheap imports invaded their home markets and expensive exports harmed their prospects of establishing a foothold in new, overseas markets.

Recognition of the error made in 1925 was slow. The Committee on Industry and Trade admitted, in 1929, that the restoration of the Gold Standard put some "strain on the economic organism" and that exports and employment were depressed but considered it "unquestionably necessary and ultimately beneficial". The Macmillan Committee was appointed in an atmosphere of general dissatisfaction with the monetary policy of the nation, based on "an impression that the return of this country to the Gold Standard in April 1925 . . . had impeded instead of promoting our economic recovery from the consequences of the war . . ." Its final Report recognized the country's "competitive handicap" and, in his evidence to the Committee, even the Bank of England governor Montagu Norman admitted that the post-war policy might have been mistaken.

Few recommended the abolition of the Gold Standard. A distinction was drawn between its restoration at the pre-war parity and the inherent value of the standard itself. But the system which the Gold Standard represented had a number of weaknesses which contributed to its adverse effect. There was a gap between theory and practice.

Compared with the nineteenth century there were now two differences. First, the expansion of the output of gold was no longer equal to a desirable expansion of production. Secondly, the value of gold was no longer determined by independent forces—the United States had largely absorbed the world's gold reserves. In its new role as a creditor country, that nation had employed its surplus receipts for actual gold or short-term liquid claims rather than for additional imports or additional long-term foreign loans. In normal circumstances, with or without the Gold Standard, such a surplus of money would inflate costs and prices in the creditor country and thereby price it out of the export market. The Federal Reserve Board, however, had not been automatically increasing the volume of currency or credit in the USA on the receipt of gold; it had sterilized the inflow. In other words, the US operated a "managed currency". Thus, said Keynes, was "gold . . . demonetized by almost the last country which continued to do it lip-service, and a dollar-standard set up on the pedestal of the Golden

Calf." In Great Britain and other countries, on the other hand, a loss of gold did not, for social reasons, transmit its full effect to wages and costs.

Further, the money market was no longer dominated by purely commercial considerations. The burden of war debts and loans raised for political rather than productive purposes tended to influence the market rate of interest so that it bore little relation to the actual yield of new capital investment. In Britain, the Treasury's annual remittance of £29·5 million ($82.6 million) in debt interest to the United States was a case in point.

Despite all this, British attitudes to a "managed" currency remained curiously backward. The detailed proposals of Keynes and other economists were rejected, not only on the grounds that the "composite standard of value" which would be involved would be insufficiently flexible and sensitive, but also because the critics doubted the "capacity, integrity, firmness and . . . independence" of the Treasury and the Bank.

The issue in 1925 was thus in part a choice between the stabilization of internal or external prices. Keynes' views on this matter were not generally accepted by the Macmillan Committee in 1931, which, considering "the question whether adherence to an international standard may involve the payment of too heavy a price in the shape of domestic instability," concluded that "such continued adherence" would involve intolerable strain only in the case of debtor countries operating in a narrow range of primary products. These words had an ironic ring a few months after the publication of the Committee's Report.

The return to the Gold Standard in such circumstances threw a vivid light on four of the grosser faults in the mechanisms of decision-making. First, the points at which decisions were to be reached were fixed not by considerations of trained technical competence but by the fortuitous results of the power game. It so happened that Britain possessed at this moment one of the most brilliant of all economists in J. M. Keynes who, although uniquely fitted to advise on this problem, and remarkably correct in his judgment on it, was not asked and not listened to. The responsible minister, the Chancellor of the Exchequer, was Winston Churchill, perhaps the least interested and least gifted with economic understanding of all who have held that office in this century. His chief advisers were the Governor of the Bank of England, Montagu Norman, and the all-powerful Permanent Secretary of the Treasury, Sir Warren Fisher. Churchill, accustomed in the Services to high professional advice, felt dissatisfied and, according to his then private secretary P. J. Grigg:

> he accused the Treasury officials of not consulting enough with R. G. Hawtrey, who occupied the somewhat weak position of Director of Financial Enquiries. I remember his demanding from time to time that the learned man should be released from the dungeon in which we were said to have immured him, have his chains struck off and the straw brushed from his hair and clothes, and be admitted to the light and warmth of an argument in the Treasury Boardroom . . .

Churchill's conviction that he had been let down by the Treasury "professionals" led him to take unparalleled steps towards demoting it at the outset of each of his Premierships. Of all the major chapters in his life this was the only one which he never returned to write up and defend in his characteristic retrospective reviews of his career. He had been persuaded to do the wrong thing by the wrong advisers with the wrong qualifications, who had used their offices to deny the really qualified advisers access to him. The only unusual feature here is that the discreet curtain which usually hides such maneuvers has been pulled aside just enough to let the world see through a narrow chink what was going on.

Coupled with technical incompetence to evaluate the economic situation was a paralyzing lack of data, later exposed by the Macmillan Committee, in relation to the balance of payments, in its Report of 1931:

> the figures for recent years . . . have doubtless been the best obtainable without elaborate special enquiries, for making which the necessary resources have not existed. But they have been based on pioneer private enquiries, made by *The Economist*, Sir Robert Kindersley and others: they have been subject . . . to frequent (and large) revisions after publication: and it is evident that there is so much guesswork in them as to render them liable to an unduly wide margin of inevitable error.
>
> Exact quantitative knowledge concerning the chief elements of the monetary and financial system is, we consider, of the utmost importance, both to provide the necessary data on which to base the management of the system and also for the purpose of making gradually possible a more definitely scientific treatment of these problems than the existing state of our knowledge of the facts allows. There are, moreover, many matters of importance which are now the subject of controversy, yet need not be so if they could be put to a

statistical test. We should aim, therefore, at obtaining a complete inventory of the economic life of the community under its several aspects, in such a form that we could crosscheck the accuracy of our information by being able to work up the final totals in more than one direction.

So far was the machinery of government from being able to comply with this very reasonable requirement that by 1931 only two volumes had yet been published of the *Census of Production for 1924.*

Yet Haldane's Machinery of Government Committee in 1918 had laid great stress on the proposition:

that in the sphere of civil government the duty of investigation and thought, as preliminary to action, might with great advantage be more definitely recognized.

Haldane himself, returning briefly to power as Lord Chancellor in the first Labour Government in 1924, had initiated a Committee of Economic Inquiry "To ensure that national problems were actually being faced and thought out in advance on a basis of fact." That government fell before it could be launched, but the Conservative Lord Balfour in 1925 adopted the proposal under the name of the "Committee on Civil Research" to give "connected forethought from a central standpoint to the development of economic, scientific, and statistical research in relation to civil policy and administration." Although Ministers of both main parties so decided, the Treasury thought otherwise, and virtually nothing was done.

The two other faults which the Gold Standard decision revealed both arose from the undue advantage of the City, and its mouthpiece, the Bank of England, in dictating economic and financial policy. Both were at fault in being out of touch with and ignorant about the fundamental problems and requirements of British industry—a defect which it took many years to rectify. Partly for that reason, both yielded to the further fault of overrating the contribution of "invisibles" and the role of the City in keeping a healthy balance of payments, and underrating the extent to which the vital interests of the City and of industry might be diverging.

Formulated by advisers whose lack of technical expertise could not be fully compensated by their abundant arrogance, based on a culpable lack of factual data, and swayed by an exaggerated assessment of the importance of the City, the return to gold failed. It was, nonetheless, a richly instructive episode. The disparity between export prices and internal costs created by the return to the Gold Standard naturally made their first and greatest impact on the staple exporting industries, and above all on coal. This impact was soon to lead, in May 1926, to the gravest civil disturbance in modern British history—the General Strike.

The origins of the General Strike lie in the general unprofitability of the coalmining industry after 1918, which was temporarily hidden in the early 1920s, first by a coal strike in the United States and then by the French occupation of the Ruhr. The renewed prosperity of the industry facilitated a fresh wage settlement in May 1924, which super- seded that of 1921. This settlement raised the minimum addition to the standard wage from 20 percent to 33½ percent and lowered the owners' standard profit from 17 percent to 15 percent of the sum pay- able as standard wages. But the basic situation was highly unhealthy.

From 1909 to 1913, British coal exports had averaged 65½ million tons a year; by 1923, the figure was 79½ million tons; by 1925 it had dropped to 50·8 million tons. There was a further decline after the 1926 stoppage. During 1926 itself, German exports increased from 22½ million to over 38 million metric tons and Polish from 8¼ mil- lion to 14¾ million tons. At the same time, the British increase in technical efficiency was slow. In 1914, output per man-shift was 20·32 cwt.; by 1927, it had only increased to 20·61 cwt. Between 1924 and 1934, Great Britain increased her output per man-shift by only 5·3 cwt., compared with an increase of 18·6 cwt. in Holland and of 24·2 cwt. in Polish Upper Silesia. The increase in mechanization was simi- larly sluggish. In 1913, 8 percent of the total British output was pro- duced by coal-cutting machines; in 1921, 14 percent; in 1925, 20 per- cent.

After the occupation of the Ruhr had ended, the owners' profits be- gan to decrease. On June 30, 1925, the owners, wishing to abandon the national minimum percentage, served notice to end the 1924 agree- ment. In response, the miners' leaders called a strike for midnight on July 31, in which the TUC was to effect an embargo on the movement of coal. Baldwin's efforts to settle the dispute were abortive and he refused the industry's request for a government subsidy to avert a de- crease in wages.

A few hours before the strike was due to begin, however, Baldwin saw the miners' leaders and, in return for assurances of co-operation in an inquiry into the productive efficiency of the industry, the government promised a subsidy which would allow wages and hours to remain unchanged. The government envisaged that the subsidy would last for nine months. It cost over £23 million ($64.4 million).

The resulting Royal Commission, appointed on September 5, comprised Sir Herbert Samuel, formerly Liberal Home Secretary and British High Commissioner in Palestine, General Sir Herbert Lawrence, a banker, Sir William Beveridge, an ex-civil servant and a prominent economist, and Kenneth Lee, a Manchester cotton manufacturer.

While the Commission was sitting, the government took precautionary measures against a possible General Strike. Some of these were criticized as being unnecessarily provocative.

The Commission reported on March 6, 1926. It recommended the state purchase of mineral royalties and, complementary to this, the amalgamation of existing mines where units were too small; the closer integration of mining with allied industries and in particular the establishment of a National Fuel and Power Committee; the provision of sufficient funds and facilities for effective research, with state aid if necessary; the formation of co-operative selling agencies and a standardized system for the sampling and analysis of coal. For the promotion of better labor relations it urged joint pit committees, a redistribution of working hours, pithead baths and revised methods of pay to give the men not employed at the coal face a "direct interest in output". It recognized, however, that the industry must make an immediate saving in costs and that, although the men's subsistence allowances must continue, the bulk of that saving would have to come from their pay packets. In return, the Report presented the miners with three inducements: there should be no lengthening of the working day; national wages agreements should be continued, and prior undertakings should be given about improvements in the organization and efficiency of the industry. This Report, which was to become a key document in the history of the coal industry for the next thirteen years, was sold at a price of threepence for its near 300 pages.

The Commission's Report brought the two sides no nearer to an agreement. The miners refused a reduction of their wages; the owners held out for an increase in hours and insisted on district agreements. Despite the realism of the Report neither the miners, the mine owners, nor even the government were yet capable of shedding the deep-rooted preconceptions which prevented them from getting the message. The myths were too strong. As J. M. Keynes remarked in an article in *New*

Republic (May 19, 1926): "If all the miners worked eight hours, we could not sell the coal produced, even if we were to capture the entire export trade of Germany and the US."

Baldwin remarked that: "You can never get an agreed amount of what a miner is earning. Neither owner nor miner will ever agree upon a figure. At that moment a Cabinet Minister, not necessarily a mathematician or a chartered accountant by profession, is called in and expected to understand these matters, and expected, with a divine impartiality to make these two sides agree . . ." This showed a naïve assumption that the basic economic situation was not amenable to governmental remedies, and that anything other than deadlock between the parties was possible as long as it remained unremedied. The Prime Minister was placing all his essential powers in the hands of the idol of laissez-faire.

As a result of the deadlock, the Industrial Committee of the Trades Unions General Council asked Baldwin to intervene on April 14. After the Prime Minister had met both the owners and the miners separately, there was still deadlock. By April 30, two-thirds of the miners were already "locked out" having refused the owners' new offers. At Baldwin's request, the owners produced their current proposals, which amounted to an insistence on a return to the eight-hour day for at least three and a half years and to the wages standards of 1921. Baldwin offered the miners an "authoritative inquiry" into the best method of following up the Commission's recommendations regarding selling organizations and amalgamations. The miners' response was skeptical: they would consider no agreements until the government presented the plans for reorganization. "I want to see the horse I am going to mount," said Herbert Smith.

The General Council, however, had a clearer idea of the range of horses which could be mounted than the government. But, at the same time, it made it abundantly clear that only the Government had the necessary facilities to produce a clear, well-defined plan for reorganization. In this sense, there was a fundamental divergence of aims between those concerned in the negotiations. The General Council complained that: "attention has been concentrated almost exclusively upon questions relating to the wages, hours and working conditions . . . Far more consideration needs to be given to the drastic reorganization which both the Commission and the mine workers consider is required." It pointed out that the diverse nature of the industry "makes it essential that an analysis of the economic and geological conditions of the industry" be made and that "the Government should obtain and produce figures relating to the actual individual collieries. The miners have no direct access to such statistics and the Government alone has the facilities for collecting them."

Meanwhile, both sides were preparing for a showdown. The government proclaimed a state of emergency and circulated to the local authorities a list of the civil commissioners and their staff who would be responsible for the implementation of the government's emergency powers. The General Council proposed its plans for co-ordinated action in support of the miners, which were approved by the trade union executives on May 1. Individual unions were left to call their men out on strike at midnight on Monday, May 3. "Conduct of the dispute", however, was handed over to the General Council.

Baldwin met the Industrial Committee of the TUC that night. The negotiations were successful, and most of Sunday was spent awaiting the return of the miners' executive to London to approve a draft agreement. On the evening of Sunday, May 2, the negotiations were under way again. While the interested parties were hammering out details of the agreement, the printing operatives at the *Daily Mail,* on their own initiative, refused to set the newspaper's leading article. This article spoke of "a great political struggle, which the nation has no choice but to face with the utmost coolness and the utmost firmness," implied that the miners' leaders were under Communist influence; described the proposed General Strike as a "revolutionary movement intended . . . to put forcible constraint upon the Government"; and called upon "all law-abiding men and women to hold themselves at the service of king and country."

The government, on receiving word of this incident, reiterated its proposals that negotiations be resumed on the condition that the miners would be prepared to accept "such interim adjustment of wages or hours of work as will make it economically possible to carry on the industry" while a reorganization was proceeding. But it now added another condition. The TUC must make "an immediate and unconditional withdrawal" of its circulated instructions for co-ordinated action and must repudiate certain "overt acts". The latter, as the General Council commented in its reply, were not specified: it was simply stated that they included "gross interference with the freedom of the Press".

The government considered that the circulation of the instructions for the General Strike was an act of provocative character. It made it quite clear to the TUC that negotiations would not be continued with such a threat hanging over it. It considered that the TUC was prejudicing the success of the negotiations by taking action to cover an unsuccessful outcome. Later, Baldwin criticized the machinery by which the General Council had arrived at its decisions, claiming that "they did not consult their members by ballot before taking this momentous step, when their rules required such consultation." He spoke of "this despotic power" of the Trade Unions' Executive which "is a gross travesty of any democratic principle".

The General Council, in what was claimed as a "conciliatory reply", pointed out that the negotiations had been subjected to the atmosphere of strike only because they had already been subjected to the atmosphere of lock-out. They denied all knowledge of the "overt acts" and continued:

> It [the General Council] cannot accept any responsibility for them, and is taking prompt measures to prevent any acts of indiscipline. The Council regrets that it was not given an opportunity to investigate and deal with the alleged incidents before the Government made them an excuse for breaking off the peace discussions which were proceeding.

It concluded by describing the government's decision to issue the ultimatum as "precipitous and calamitous". The government never actually rejected this reply because the Cabinet had gone home by the time it was brought to the Cabinet room. The militants, headed by Churchill, Chamberlain and Joynson-Hicks, had triumphed over the peace party led by Baldwin, and supported by Steel-Maitland and Birkenhead. Baldwin himself is believed to have been showing signs of exhaustion after the long days of negotiations and was, therefore, unequal to a fight with his own colleagues.

Thus the immediate cause of the General Strike was a negotiating technicality rather than a fundamental deadlock on the mining situation. The TUC instructions for co-ordinated action, of which the government made such an issue, were not, according to Ernest Bevin, "ready to hand to the General Secretaries . . . until after we had received in our room the news that the Emergency Powers Act had been signed". The course of the strike made it abundantly clear that the government was much more prepared than the TUC.

Under the Emergency Powers Act, according to C. L. Mowat in *Britain between the Wars:*

The Government took power to seize land and buildings, food and other essentials, to commandeer vehicles, issue special drivers' licences, take over docks, railways, shipping, coal stocks, petrol, to control the supply of electricity, gas and water. Public meetings might be prohibited where there was apprehension of disorder, acts calculated to cause sedition or disaffection among the armed forces, police, firemen or 'among the civilian population' were offences under the Act, and the mere possession of papers which might contribute to disaffection was an offence. A sweeping right of search of premises where such documents might be found was given to the police under the direction of the Home Secretary.

The government's emergency machinery was, however, more important than its powers under the Act. Indeed, the effectiveness of the former rendered the emergency powers largely unobtrusive. Few lands and buildings were seized—Hyde Park was among the exceptions. Milk was the only food directly distributed by the government. The Road Commissioners' directional powers of commandeering vehicles were rarely necessary. Only when the Port of London came to a standstill did the government appoint a civil commissioner for the docks and organize a special convoy to move flour. The Home Secretary directed that the supply of electricity, the transport of motor spirit and the maintenance of the railway service were vital necessities. Naval ratings were used for the docks, electricity, and petrol, but volunteers also filled many of the gaps.

The government aimed at a "decentralized organization" based on the local authorities. It divided England and Wales into ten divisions, each with a Minister acting as civil commissioner who was detailed to be the link between the government and the local authorities. The divisions were divided "into suitable areas for administering essential national services", each with a government-selected Chairman who was responsible for recruitment of volunteers, a local Food Officer, a local Road Officer and Haulage Committee and a local coal Emergency Officer. Their task was to organize the existing channels of distribution sufficiently to maintain essential supplies. It was essential to the smoothness of the operation that the "existing channels" be used and that they be used without undue coercion.

The General Strike established a new historical fact. Transport by road was enough. The railways were no longer an indispensable service.

Although it is a myth that there was no violence during the General

Strike, it is true that there was no loss of life. Most of the rioting centered round food lorries and the small amount of friction between police and strikers was usually ascribed to police imported from outside. The most serious outbreaks of violence were in Glasgow.

The government, however, took considerable precautions against trouble. Speaking in London, on May 5, the Home Secretary appealed for recruits between the ages of twenty and forty-five for the Special Constabulary and specifically mentioned the need to protect those who desired to remain at work. On May 10, he asked for 50,000 special constables in London "to enable me to allot two to every vehicle". The object was to release the regular police "for perhaps sterner work". By the end of the Strike, the membership of the Special Constabulary had risen from 98,000 to 226,000. In response to another government appeal on May 5, a further 18,000 enlisted in a Civil Constabulary Reserve. Most of the specials were used only on traffic duty, but they were armed with batons, tin helmets and, in some cases, rifles in case of trouble. The private Organisation for the Maintenance of Supplies (OMS) issued instructions to volunteers (before the Strike) telling them to hit hard, even hit to kill. Special constables and their families were promised allowances and pensions in the event of injuries or death. In the *British Gazette* on May 8, the government made an announcement:

> All ranks of the Armed Forces of the Crown are hereby notified that any action which they may find it necessary to take in an honest endeavour to aid the Civil Power will receive . . . the full support of HMG

which provoked the King to instruct his Private Secretary to protest to the government. The King intervened again on May 11, when he learned of the government's decision to introduce immediately a bill to define illegal strikes and make the use of trade union funds in such a strike an indictable offense. On this occasion he warned the Home Secretary and the Attorney-General that "anything done to touch the pockets of those who are now only existing on strike pay might cause exasperation and serious reprisals on the part of the sufferers," and counseled the Prime Minister not to provoke the strikers "who until now had been remarkably quiet". Private members, employers, the party whips gave similar advice, and the proposal was abandoned.

The TUC confined itself almost entirely to exhortations to "stand firm" and the like. It instructed trade unionists "to be exemplary in

. . . conduct and not to give any opportunity for police interference". It instructed local strike organizations to meet employers "and offer to supply light and power for such services as house, street and shop lighting, social services, power for food, bakeries, laundries and domestic purposes." Its lists of messages of support from abroad conspicuously excluded any messages from Moscow. Indeed, it returned a large cheque from the Russian trade unions. The Communist International itself recognized that the leaders of the TUC were scarcely likely to provoke a revolution. It instructed "the British Communist Party to form committees of action and wrest the leadership of the strike from the hands of the moderate leaders . . ."

The TUC decision to call out the printers may have had a considerable effect on public opinion of the General Strike. The absence of newspapers made the break from ordinary routine sharper and gave the public mind a more vivid conception of anarchy and chaos. Furthermore, several commentators suggested that, considering the circumstances in which the Strike began, the TUC would have had a fairly favorable press and, therefore, damaged their chances of a sympathetic public response by calling out the printers.

The disappearance of the newspapers made these nine days a landmark in the history of broadcasting. Suddenly, the importance of radio increased tenfold. Many people placed considerable faith in its accuracy and listened to the crystal set to find out "what was really happening". No labor or trade unionist speaker was allowed on the air during the Strike, and the news of the Archbishop of Canterbury's peace appeal was delayed. In the latter case, however, Reith was under the threat of a government takeover, and once the government had formally decided not to proceed with such action, he allowed Davidson's appeal to be broadcast. Reith strongly resisted an attempt by the editor of the *British Gazette* to turn the BBC into a subsidiary propaganda organ: ". . . I was not going to have that at all," he wrote in his diary.

The government's insistence on far-reaching emergency powers and its precautions against violence were the natural corollary of its image of the situation. It began by criticizing the TUC because its power and authority were inadequate to prevent the printers' strike; as the Strike progressed, it accused the TUC of being a despotic tyrannical power which aimed at an overthrow of the constitution. Baldwin recounting the events of the night before the Strike said:

> Stripped of all accessories, what was the position in which the Government found itself? It found itself challenged with an alternative Government, and that Government ignorant of the way in which its commands were being carried out, and incapable of arresting disobedience to them.

The TUC was accused of putting political pressure on the government. Their action, it was said, was an attempt to force the government to maintain the mining industry "at a loss". Some asked where this kind of pressure would end. "I see no difference whatever between a general strike to force Parliament to pass some Bill, which the country does not wish for, and a general strike to force Parliament to pay a subsidy," asserted Winston Churchill.

Hence, the government saw the Strike as a struggle for the constitution. Baldwin announced that "the freedom of our very Constitution" was imperiled. He spoke of the country being nearer to civil war than for centuries—a remark that made a particularly strong impression in the US.

The *British Gazette* attacked the very existence of the TUC: "Up to two or three years ago, there was no such thing as the General Council of the TUC. There was a Parliamentary committee, and the action of the trade unions through their annual congress was always constitutional": a "GHQ for Labour" was the result of persistent agitation by "younger and wilder spirits". The newspaper characterized Ernest Bevin, who was one of these "spirits", as an unscrupulous manipulator behind the Strike.

This view of the TUC had little enough reality in practice. During the months preceding the Strike, resolutions demanding Workers' Defense Corps, Factory Committees and similar organizations were defeated both in the TUC and in local Labour organizations. J. H. Thomas put the TUC's attitude in a nutshell when he remarked:

> I have never disguised that in a challenge to the Constitution, God help us unless the Government won . . .

Some trade unionists, however, took up the government's tune and indeed regarded the Strike as a challenge to the constitution. One Trades Council reported that the Strike "was regarded as a straight fight between the TUC and the Government" and was "a fine political weapon for Labour".

The government's attitude to the TUC was illustrated in the contro-

versy over food permits. On May 1, the General Council informed
Baldwin that in the event of a strike it was "prepared to enter into arrangements for the distribution of essential foodstuffs". The government withheld even an acknowledgment. The General Council's offer
of assistance was later described as "an act of constitutional presumption" and "an attempt to usurp the duties of Government and Parliament."

The widespread belief that the General Strike was illegal was based
on two eminent legal opinions. The first was delivered on Tuesday,
May 4, by Mr. Justice Astbury, when granting an injunction restraining
the branch secretary and six delegates of the Tower Hill National Sailors' and Firemen's Union from calling on their members to strike
without the authority of the Executive Council of the Union. The
second was made by Sir John Simon on Thursday, May 6, in a famous
speech to the House of Commons.

These two assessments are crucial to an understanding not only of
the constitutional implications of the General Strike, but also of the
circumstances of its settlement. Astbury maintained that:

> The so-called general strike . . . is illegal . . . and those persons
> inciting or taking part in it are not protected by the Trades Disputes
> Act of 1906.

Since there was neither a trade dispute between the individual unions
and their respective employers (excepting, of course, the miners) nor a
trade dispute between the TUC and the government, or the nation, the
General Strike was unlawful. Therefore, noted Astbury, the unions
were not entitled to withhold benefits from those who refused to strike,
nor indeed were they entitled to use their funds to pay strike pay "to
any member who illegally ceases to work and breaks his contract in
pursuance of orders which are unlawful . . ."

Simon's speech emphasized that workmen were obliged "to give due
notice to their employers to terminate their engagements." Not until
such notices expired were they entitled to withhold their labor. Such
notices had not been given; hence, every single workman who was on
strike had broken the law and was liable to be sued for damages, as
were his trade union leaders who had "advised and promoted that
course of action."

Some critics claimed that the generality of the strike made it, in
some way, illegal. A. L. Goodhart refuted this opinion in these words:

The generality of a strike would make it more probable that the strike would succeed, but probability of success is not a ground for liability. Having once granted that a sympathetic strike is legal we cannot draw a line between the number . . . which are legal and those which are not!

The validity of Astbury's judgment depended upon the definition of a "trade dispute". The 1906 Act made such a definition:

. . . the expression 'trade dispute' means any dispute between employers and workmen, or between workmen and workmen, which is connected with the employment or non-employment or the terms of the employment, or with the conditions of labour, or any person, and the expression 'workmen' means all persons employed in trade or industry whether or not in the employment of the employer with whom a trade dispute rises.

The concluding words seem to make it clear that the Act is meant to cover sympathetic strikes, and this was the opinion of the House of Lords in the case of Conway v Wade (1909) and of the Court of Appeal in the case of Dallimore v Williams and Jesson (1912). Hence, the issue was whether the General Strike was genuinely in furtherance of a trade dispute. The TUC assured everyone that it was, and talk of revolution was confined to its opponents.

The chain of events which were to culminate in the conclusion of the General Strike began on Thursday May 6 when Sir Herbert Samuel returned from Italy. He contacted J. H. Thomas and conducted secret negotiations with the Industrial Committee of the General Council. Samuel was to draw up a memorandum, based on the Royal Commission's Report, which would propose the terms of a settlement of the coal strike, and was to "strongly recommend" its acceptance by the government. The latter, however, distrusted Samuel's intervention, and Steel-Maitland informed Samuel that it could not negotiate with either the TUC or the miners before it had received an unconditional withdrawal of the strike notices. His letter contained an ominous sign of things to come:

They [the government] hold that the General Strike is unconstitutional and illegal. They are bound to take steps to make its repetition impossible. It is therefore plain that they cannot enter upon any negotiations unless the Strike is so unreservedly concluded that there is not even an implication of such a bargain upon their side as would embarrass them in any legislation which they may conceive to be proper in the light of recent events.

Although the government would be prepared to give due weight to Samuel's advice, his negotiations were "not clothed in even a vestige of official character". Samuel replied that he had made this quite clear to the trade unionists and that "there has been no possibility of misunderstanding on that point."

The Samuel Memorandum proposed the resumption of negotiations, the subsidy to the coal industry being temporarily renewed for that purpose; the establishment of a National Wages Board for the industry with an independent Chairman; the establishment of a Committee, on which the men would be represented, to oversee the reorganization of the industry; the fixing of a minimum wage; the prevention of the recruitment of new miners, when unemployed miners were available; and the provision of relief and redeployment facilities for "workers who are displaced as a consequence of the closing of uneconomic collieries." One of the crucial points of the memorandum was that there "should be no revision of the previous wage rates unless there are sufficient assurances that the measures of re-organisation proposed by the Commission will be effectively adopted" and that, in any case, the wages of the lowest-paid workers should not be reduced.

The TUC was unable to persuade the miners to accept the memorandum. The latter felt that it implied some reduction of wages and felt that there were no guarantees that the government would accept it and the lock-out notices be withdrawn. In exasperation, the TUC decided to go ahead without the miners and call off the Strike, feeling that they would not be "tied to a mere slogan". At 12.30 pm on May 12, the TUC personally informed Baldwin of the "unconditional surrender" (a personal visit was not allowed until Baldwin's Private Secretary, Sir Horace Wilson, had ascertained that this was their intention). The Prime Minister felt impelled to "thank God for your decision."

The public reaction was one of surprise, since no news of the negotiations had leaked out. In working-class homes, it was often one of dismay and anger.

Why did the General Council surrender so suddenly and so tamely? The Samuel Memorandum had its advantages, as had the Royal Commission's Report, but there was no guarantee that either the government or the mine owners would take any more notice of one than they had of the other. Indeed the following year Baldwin piloted through a Trades Disputes Act which made any repetition of the Strike virtually impossible. The abortive efforts of the Coal Mines Reorganisation Commission in the 1930s confirmed the inability of the government to fulfill the basis of the settlement.

The Labour Correspondent of the *Manchester Guardian* listed a number of reasons for the TUC's decision. First was the fear of the consequences of extending the Strike to the "second line" and cutting off gas, electricity and postal services. This would be a grave challenge to the government and the resulting breakdown in communications would allow each strike committee a dangerous freedom of action. Secondly, "Government action seemed to be intensifying." In the last few days of the Strike, the government had placed an embargo on foreign aid for the strikers, had limited the paper supplies and raided the office of the *British Worker* and had hinted legal action against trade unionists. The Astbury judgment and Simon's speech were other ominous signs. Thirdly, the General Council resented the "miners' obstinate reluctance to compromise". Finally, the General Council was exhausted:

> The General Council was the very opposite of a revolutionary committee of action. It was a body of tired trade union officials living in an unhealthy smoke-laden atmosphere, suffering from lack of sleep, wearied of wrangling with miners and Cabinet Ministers and insistent deputations of strikers, worried by fears of disorder, subject (in the absence of a public press) to panic rumors, in remote touch with the great industrial centers and, anxious above all things that the situation should not pass out of control. On the one side, there was the Parliamentary Labour Party, naturally timid for its future, on the other was the left wing and the Communists, happily so far prevented (by the Press embargo) from the dissemination of a conscious strike philosophy but pressing to go ahead.

Hence, the correspondent concluded ". . . the Council determined to cut its losses at all costs . . ."

What impression did Britain make abroad at this time? Many foreigners saw it as a triumphant vindication of the British constitution, and a monument to the British temperament. *The Evening News* of Sydney, Australia, was reassured "that no class or section . . . however strong . . . can overturn the foundation stones of British freedom." The *Echo de Paris* reported that "at one stroke from one end of Europe to another all subversive elements have received a severe setback." *Ere Nouvelle* believed that the government's performance had saved "the whole course of law and order in Europe". On the previous Sunday afternoon, a minor royalist demonstration in Paris had resulted in more bloodshed and more deaths than in the entire British General Strike.

The American reactions were mixed. On the one hand, the idea of a General Strike was abhorrent to them; on the other, they sympathized with the plight of the miners and accused the British government of an inadequate handling of the situation. One American journal compared the General Strike unfavorably with the revolution in Italy, the latter being "constructive" and "bringing a wonderful new spirit of unity and co-operation" while the Strike was "destructive . . . like civil war". But the same journal spoke strongly in favor of reorganization and even "national ownership of coal resources and mines", on the grounds that a more efficient industry would, far from encouraging socialism, provide a safeguard against it.

Some American newspapers saw England approaching dictatorship and martial law. The Board of Trade's order regulating the use of coal was described as Britain's "first taste of dictatorship". The civil commissioners were seen as "District dictators" who had "the support of the military".

A friendly French commentator remarked that as the English were so good at knowing how to behave in terrible crises it was only natural that from time to time they should have to create terrible crises in order to show how well they could behave in them. He had some excuse for saying so, since such a reason would have been no more asinine than the multiple blundering which caused the General Strike, despite nobody wanting it and nobody profiting by it. Almost all the leading faults and errors predominating in British history over the past century contributed to it. And it was a purely home-made affair, in no way necessitated or triggered from abroad. As a demonstration it did more credit to the nation's heart than to its head.

Its delayed consequences were perhaps no less serious than its immediate impact. It confirmed and deepened the alienation of the politically-conscious working masses from the employers, and made the task of every British management more difficult throughout the ensuing forty years. It broke the will and capability of the Trades Unions Congress to play a more positive co-ordinating and guiding role over the separate unions, the lack of which was so bitterly felt in the 'fifties and 'sixties. On the other hand, it left widespread feelings of guilt among the middle classes towards the workers which led, during and after World War II, to an excessive swing of the pendulum in the direction of leveling down incomes, thus contributing to the later brain drain. Paradoxically also Ernest Bevin, himself so vilified in the General Strike when at the height of his powers, was to experience as a sick old man the conferment on himself and the Trades Unions Congress of an almost embarrassing status and responsibility in national affairs, which far outran their capacity to fulfill it.

Like Dunkirk, the General Strike caught the nation by surprise in a vast traumatic experience. Like Dunkirk, too, without being a battle it was a resounding defeat, threatening the very existence of the United Kingdom. And, again like Dunkirk, its massive dose of drama so thrilled and intoxicated the nation that many recalled it psychologically almost as if it had been some inverted kind of victory. That impression was mistaken, both times.

After the General Strike the bubbling tunes of the 'twenties continued more tunefully than ever; records in aviation, sport and athletics were pursued by a few, and enjoyed by many, as a means of reassurance of British virility; and changes took place rapidly in standards and ways of life for the middle and upper classes. Yet, as in Edwardian times, the economy was making only the slowest progress. At 1900 prices, *per capita* income in the United Kingdom, which had been nearly £42 in 1905, was still below £46 in 1925 and just below £50 in 1930. Having risen by only some £8 in a quarter century, it was to rise by half as much again during the following decade. But before that the next grim national emergency had to be encountered in 1931, this time an imported one of worldwide dimensions.

CHAPTER 13

The Great Depression

The origins of the Wall Street crash which triggered off the Great Depression lay in the United States construction boom of 1925–28. In these four years $38 billions were spent, which was approximately double the value of the construction in the four years 1919–22. The result was a huge growth in business profits, as a result of the circulation of purchasing power which had no relation to any corresponding increase in the production of immediately consumable goods. Learning of many cases of getting rich quick, Americans succumbed to an orgy of speculation, financed largely on borrowed funds and entirely unrelated to any realistic appraisal of future earnings. To counteract this galloping inflation, the Reserve authorities persuaded the New York banks to cut off the Stock Exchange's supply of call-loan money. This simply had the effect of raising call rates and making them an attractive proposition. Thus, European money flowed to the US. Both US and European bank rates rose, as a defensive measure.

The result was a universal policy of hard money, when economic conditions required cheap money. For the index of industrial production ceased to expand in the United States after June 1929, and the construction boom had passed its peak. The speculative bubble burst in the Wall Street crash on October 29, 1929. American money, on which the world's primary producers depended, and on which German reconstruction had been based, ceased to flow.

These factors, coupled with a demand for gold in France, put considerable pressure on the London money market. In 1928 and 1929, half of the bullion sold in London was bought by the Bank of England. In 1930, of £43·91 million sold the Bank was able to buy only £1·41 million. The average gold stock fell from a maximum of £173 million for the month of September 1928 to £150·2 million in February 1929. In that month, the Bank rate was raised from 4½ percent to 5½ percent. After July, the Bank steadily lost more gold, and, by October, the average monthly figure for the gold stock stood at only £130·9 million. On September 26, therefore, Bank rate was raised a further 1 percent. It was later reduced.

It was some time before the full effects of the crisis were felt in Central Europe. But when the lack of American money became clear, industrial share prices began to fall. Most of the banks had invested heavily in industry, often using short-term credits for fixed capital and speculation. On May 11, 1931, the Credit Anstalt, the main bank in Vienna, collapsed. In June, however, the Bank of England still felt strong enough to lend £4·3 million to the Austrian National Bank, which was guaranteeing the Credit Anstalt's foreign liabilities. The Austrian collapse reacted upon Germany. In the last two weeks of June, the Reichsbank lost 690 million marks and then another 150 million in two days. New York, Paris, the Bank of England (again) and the Bank of International Settlements provided credits. President Hoover on June 20 proposed a year's moratorium on war debts and reparations. France, financially strong, held out for favorable terms.

On July 6, the Hoover Moratorium was finally accepted by all the powers. At the same time, the German Nordwolle (a wool industry concern) failed. The flight from the mark began. On July 14, the German banking system broke down. The result was a demand for liquid money in Europe.

On July 15, the run on sterling began. From then, until the end of the month, the Bank lost £2½ million ($7 million) of gold a day. Bank rate was raised in two stages from 2½ percent to 4½ percent. By the end of the month, the Bank's gold holdings had been reduced by £32 million to £133 million ($372 million) on July 30. Two-thirds of these withdrawals went to Paris; the rest to Amsterdam and Zurich.

On July 20, 1931, the London Conference of Ministers, which had been called to discuss Germany's financial crisis, failed to achieve anything positive. Meanwhile a government-appointed committee on National Expenditure—the May Committee—had been considering economies on public spending. The May Report, published at the end of July, found that the main existing services were likely to require a net increase in expenditure of £12,150,000 in 1932 and £17,500,000 ($34.1 million) in 1933, and that the "trend of long-term commitments . . . is most disquieting". When it came to consider the Depression, the Committee concluded:

> We are at last awaking to the fact that the cure is not to be found in the temporary and limited stimulus afforded by relief works, but in a resolute grappling with the fundamental problems of each industry, in a frank recognition of world changes that are irreversible and in a realignment of our economic life to meet them.

Amongst its proposed economies for Unemployment Insurance was a 20 percent cut in benefit payment, which the Committee claimed would not be "excessive". A "typical" case would be reduced from 30s to 24s a week. "On this basis the benefit would be worth more than the benefit deemed suitable in 1925 and only 10d a week less than that paid as recently as 1928."

The Committee recommended total savings of £96,578,000. These included £66 ½ million on unemployment insurance and £9 ½ million on development schemes. The gap of £20–30 million between the recommended and the necessary economies must be found either by negotiating an all-round reduction in incomes or by additional taxation. The causes of the nation's difficulties were traced to inadequacies of the machinery for financial control. The Report recommended "a standing Finance Committee of the Cabinet".

Some distinguished public men poured scorn upon the May Report. Keynes was quoted by the *Daily Herald* as calling it "the most foolish document I have ever . . . read". He later described the Labour Chancellor Snowden's reductions in road-building and housing programs as "a triumph of the Treasury view in its narrowest form."

On July 30 Parliament adjourned as usual for the summer recess. The crisis month of August opened with the beleaguered Bank of England obtaining credits of £50 million ($140 million) from Paris and New York. At the same time, the fiduciary note issue was raised by £15 million ($42 million).

For the next few days, there was little hint of the upheaval to come. The credits temporarily halted the outflow of gold. On August 5, Snowden still assumed that the Cabinet Committee, now appointed to advise on the May Report, would not have reached tentative decisions until September. The next day, however, the bankers addressed a memorandum to the Prime Minister and the Chancellor of the Exchequer. According to Samuel, it gave realistic advice on "certain matters which, while vitally affecting banking interests, lay entirely outside their control." It warned that the economic position of the country was "threatening the depreciation of the currency, with all its consequent evils." Great economies were necessary to prevent "complete budgetary disequilibrium"; the consumption of the general public must be reduced. The recently-obtained credits would prove useless without such measures. "What we have urged other nations to do," the memorandum concluded, "we must now do ourselves, namely restrict our expenditure, balance our budget and improve our balance of trade."

On his return from Scotland on August 11, Ramsay MacDonald, the Prime Minister, was informed by the Bank of England that the basis of the crisis was political, rather than financial, and that the necessary confidence could be attained only by balancing the Budget. The Bank warned that the Government itself might have to borrow £80 million ($228 million) to avert a moratorium.

On August 12 the Cabinet Economy Committee held its first meeting. Snowden estimated a deficit for 1932–33 of £170 million— this was £50 million above the May Committee's estimate. The Treasury's suggestions to the Cabinet included a 10 percent cut in unemployment rates, not the May Committee's 20 percent.

By August 13, the Opposition leaders—Chamberlain, Baldwin, Samuel and Maclean—were in London. On the Bank's suggestion, MacDonald and Snowden consulted them. Throughout the ensuing week, the Cabinet Economy Committee deliberated. On August 19, the Cabinet considered its proposals for economies totaling £78½ million; it provisionally agreed upon £56¼ million, of which £22 million were to come from the unemployment insurance scheme. The agreement was subject to discussions on the possibilities of conversion of the national debt and on further reductions in unemployment payments. An additional possibility was a revenue tariff.

With the Cabinet's permission, MacDonald and Snowden met Opposition leaders on August 20. They were informed that the Budget deficit might be £50 million higher than the committee's estimate and that economies of £78½ million had been proposed.

That evening, a deputation from the General Council of the TUC met the Economy Committee again and told them that the TUC would not accept the government's policy. Four alternative proposals were presented. First, unemployment insurance contributions from worker, employer and state should be replaced by a graduated levy upon profits, incomes and earnings; secondly, there should be new taxation on fixed interest securities and unearned increment; thirdly, the Sinking Fund should be suspended. The fourth proposal took the form of a hint that a revenue tariff might be desirable, although "a matter of such fundamental importance could not be decided by the General Council." In reply, Snowden made it clear that he considered the TUC's appreciation of the seriousness of the position to be deficient.

On August 21, there was another long Cabinet meeting which settled for the £56 million already agreed upon. MacDonald and Snowden informed the Opposition leaders, who had intended to propose economies additional to the Economy Committee's £78 million. They now insisted that £56 million was quite inadequate and assured MacDonald of their support if he increased the figure.

On August 22, Cabinet members were surprised to be summoned to another meeting, and told that, if the Opposition was to be satisfied, further economies of £25–30 ($70–84) million must be made, the bulk of them by reducing unemployment pay. Moreover, unless credits of £80 million could be negotiated, a moratorium would be inevitable by August 26. The Cabinet wrangled all day. Suspension of the Sinking Fund, re-examination of the Gold Standard, increased taxes on the wealthy, a revenue tariff: all were proposed, all were rejected by Snowden, all were adopted by the Chancellor after the formation of the National Government.

Eventually, MacDonald and Snowden were authorized to submit tentatively to the Opposition economies of £76 million. These included a 10 percent reduction in unemployment allowances which was to save £12¼ million ($34.3 million). The Opposition and the Bank supported these proposals, without enthusiasm. The latter told the government that such economies would probably be sufficient to get further credits from New York.

On Sunday, August 23, MacDonald met the King and spoke of the possibility of a split in the Cabinet precipitating the government's resignation. George V consulted Baldwin and Samuel. The latter advised him that "the saving of British credit was the predominant consideration". Both expressed willingness to serve under MacDonald in a National Government, although both felt that the economies could best be put through by a Labour Government.

At 7 pm the Cabinet gathered for a meeting, but they were kept waiting for New York's advice on the credits. At 8:45 pm a telegram arrived from J. P. Morgan and Co. giving it as their opinion that the proposed economy legislation would be both necessary and sufficient to raise the loan required. But the communication ended with an important question:

> Are we right in assuming that the program under consideration will have the sincere approval and support of the Bank of England and the City generally and thus go a long way toward restoring internal confidence in Great Britain. Of course our ability to do anything depends on the response of public opinion, particularly in Great Britain, to the Government's announcement of the program.

MacDonald appealed to his Cabinet to approve the economies of £76 million. Ten Ministers, however, held out against the inclusion of a £12 ¼ million saving on unemployment benefit. At MacDonald's request, the Cabinet placed its resignation in his hands. He conveyed it to the King that evening but his own resignation was, in effect, refused and he was urged to reconsider the situation.

A meeting with Baldwin and Samuel was arranged for the following morning. Although MacDonald informed his Cabinet of this meeting, he did not mention the possibility of a National Government. The Cabinet was doubtless prepared for that possibility, but it probably considered a Conservative–Liberal coalition to be the most likely outcome. It might indeed have been the outcome had the King not taken the initiative and made a decisive appeal for a National Government. At noon on August 24, the ex-Cabinet was informed that a National Government of individuals was to be formed, including MacDonald, Baldwin and Samuel. On August 28, New York and Paris granted credits of £80 million to the British Government.

On September 10, 1931, Snowden presented his Budget to the House of Commons. He estimated deficits of £74 million in the current year and £170 million in the next full year. Even these estimates assumed that borrowing for the Unemployment and Road Funds would cease. Snowden announced that the appropriation for the Sinking Fund would be reduced by £17 ½ million (an economy he had rejected when it was proposed by the Labour Cabinet); that income tax would go up 6d and exemptions and children's allowances be reduced — with an increase in surtax as well, the total yield would be £51 ½ million; and that indirect taxes on beer, petrol and tobacco would bring in an extra £24 million. Further economies were to be embodied in a subsequent Economy Bill. These were to include salary reductions for teachers (of 15 percent), ministers, MPs, judges, the police and the armed forces; and reductions in unemployment expenses. The latter comprised a 10 percent cut in benefit rates, increased contributions, the limitation of the benefit period to six months in the year and a means test for transitional payments. The total savings from the Economy Bill would be £22 million in the current year and £70 million in 1932–33. Snowden ended the speech with a quotation from Swinburne.

The International Gold Standard, which these sacrifices were meant to save, was already in decline. The US boom of 1928 had increased domestic demand for capital, and thereby reduced her earlier capacity for exporting capital. The US, taking her balance of payments surplus in gold, and France between them accumulated gold reserves of 2,232 million dollars between 1925 and 1931. This was roughly equivalent to the world's total gold production in this period. Since other countries (for example, Holland, Belgium, Switzerland) increased their gold reserves as well, the reserves of the rest of the world suffered a drop.

Neither France nor the US used their newly-acquired gold for credit expansion. Indeed, their price-levels fell. Thus, the primary producers (usually debtor countries already) had to produce more and sell more to offset deflation. Many of them failed, and abandoned the Gold Standard.

This worldwide decline of gold stemmed from the cessation of London's central control, which caused disunity and conflict in the operation of the standard. There was also the decline of price flexibility, and the new concern for internal stability rather than external equilibrium. Three added factors aggravated Britain's Gold Standard crisis. One was the domestic strain, which culminated in the Invergordon "Mutiny" on September 14, making foreign depositors particularly nervous; another was the unstable Continental situation, especially in Germany, which was a considerable short-term creditor to Great Britain. A third cause was London's position as a holder of deposits for reserve, as distinct from commercial, purposes. If London failed to meet demands in gold, the security behind, for example, the Dutch currency would be reduced in value.

The Bank had appeared, for a time, to be weathering the storm. August had eventually shown a net gain in gold. In September, however, the deluge began again. On September 16 £5 million worth of gold was withdrawn from London; on September 17, £10 million; on September 18, £18 million.

On September 19, the Bank of England recommended departing from the Gold Standard. The government immediately informed the

American and French governments and asked about the possibilities of obtaining further credits: their replies were discouraging.

On the evening of September 20, the government issued a statement saying that foreigners, not British citizens, had been withdrawing money. It concluded:

> His Majesty's Government are securing a balanced Budget, and the internal position of the country is sound. This position must be maintained. It is one thing to go off the Gold Standard with an unbalanced Budget and uncontrolled inflation; it is quite another thing to take this measure, not because of internal financial difficulties, but because of excessive withdrawals of borrowed capital. The ultimate resources of this country are enormous, and there is no doubt that the present exchange difficulties will prove only temporary.

Snowden spoke in similar vein to the House of Commons the next day. In his autobiography, he recalled: "We had balanced our Budget, and there remained no danger of having to print paper, which leads to uncontrolled inflation."

On September 21, Britain went off the Gold Standard, by a Bill rushed through Parliament. Introducing the Bill, Snowden remarked:

> Our action, no doubt, will have wide repercussions and increase the dislocation and instability for the time being of international trade and finance, but at the same time there is no need to exaggerate the difficulty. Apart from temporary panic sales . . . I see no reason why sterling should depreciate to any substantial extent or for any length of time, provided, and this is vital, that the finances of our country are administered with proper care.

The Opposition front bench did not oppose the Bill. The Labour backbenchers, however, were less conciliatory, and 112 of them voted against the second reading.

On the same day, Bank rate was raised from 4½ percent to 6 percent and the government, in response to the naval "mutiny" and the teachers' campaign, announced that no pay cuts would exceed 10 percent. As C. L. Mowat has pointed out in *Britain Between the Wars:* "The proposed reductions in navy pay and pensions would, at best, have produced little over £1½ million ($4.2 million) in savings and over this trifle Britain had its 'mutiny' and lost the gold standard." It is arguable that the triggering off of Japanese aggression against Manchuria was a further byproduct of this "saving".

The government's suspension of the Gold Standard raised scarcely any interest, let alone panic. But foreign opinion was shocked. The pound dropped from $4.80 to $3.72 by November. At one point, in December, it dropped to $3.23, but by the New Year it had settled at around $3.40.

A post-war economic historian (E. Nevin, *The Mechanism of Cheap Money*) was to write:

> . . . 21 September 1931 is as clear a dividing line as is possible in a context of this kind. The fundamental nature of British monetary policy was quite different after that date from the policy which preceded it. In September of 1931 there was withdrawn from British monetary policy the foundation which had underlain it for 200 years—adherence to the Gold Standard, which can be said to have begun in 1717 and certainly ended with the Gold Standard (Amendment) Act which became law on 21 September 1931. The essence of the problem of monetary policy during the years that followed can be said to be the creation of a substitute for that foundation . . .

The Gold Standard, which had been held to be of such paramount importance that its restoration justified hazarding the whole future of the national economy, was accordingly abandoned for ever after only a half a dozen years by the very authorities who had so stubbornly insisted upon it. No contingency plan for a managed economy had been drawn up before the nation was plunged into it, but so thoroughly unfounded did the arguments against it prove that, even when thus hastily and amateurishly improvised, it at once began to work surprisingly satisfactorily. At this heavy price the nation at least gained one lasting benefit: the blind veto and undue influence of the City over the national economy lay in ruins, and the pompous and stupid men who had wielded them were cut down to size. Their equally culpable but more resilient and better entrenched fellows in the Treasury were, however, readily able to pick themselves out of the ditch and soldier on to fresh heights of power.

CHAPTER 14
Neglect of British Industry

Just before the first world war, London's new overseas capital issues in 1911–13 had totaled £162 million (about two-fifths in the Empire), against only £38 million at home, or less than one-fifth of the combined sum. In the later 'twenties criticism of the City became so fierce that a grudging redeployment was made, and between 1925–29 home borrowers got £165 million out of £280 million. City spokesmen pointed out that funds for foreign investment were derived from the country's active trade balance and were thus limited, while funds for domestic investment were of a different order, irrespective of the trade balance. It seemed, however, not to be appreciated in the City that, having during the mid-nineteenth century been given an effective monopoly in British financial affairs at the expense of the rest of Britain (except Scotland), there was an obligation on them to study and cater for domestic investment needs, and particularly those of the small growth industries which, simply by reason of their small size and different institutional requirements, were starved of development capital.

In 1926, after the Treasury had refused to come to the rescue of the great engineering firm of Armstrong, Whitworth and Co., the Bank of England undertook a successful salvage operation. This was simply due to the accident that the firm happened to be a commercial customer of the Bank in its ordinary banking capacity, and could not be allowed to founder. The following year the Governor would have nothing to do with a suggestion to establish a financial institution to facilitate necessary amalgamations in iron and steel.

Only in 1930, when the red light was showing bright, did the Bank at last recognize the desperate needs of British industry for financial guidance and support. J. H. Thomas, as the Minister concerned, then announced:

> As a result of consultations which I have had, I am now in a position to state that the City is deeply interested in placing industry on a broad and sound basis, and ready to support any plans that in its opinion lead to this end. Those in the City who have been studying this matter are convinced that a number of our important industries must be fundamentally reorganised and modernised in order to be able to produce at prices which will enable them to compete with the world. Industries which propose schemes that, in the opinion of those advising the City, conform to this requirement will receive the most sympathetic consideration and co-operation of the City in working out plans and finding the necessary finance. In the case of individual undertakings the City will be similarly ready to help, provided that the scheme under discussion fits in as part of the *general plans for the industry* in question as a whole and gives reasonable promise that the changes will enable the undertaking to become an effective unit in combination and co-operation with other similar undertakings.

This considered statement, drafted for the Minister by the Bank, is notable—apart from its forgetfulness of the text "Physician, heal thyself"—in two ways. It implicitly confirms that the City had not up to 1930 been concerning itself with what would appear to be an elementary and vital aspect of its duty to the nation, and had only begun to do so then under intense outside pressure. It also, especially in the words which I have italicized above, makes one of the most revealing and earliest official endorsements of planning—an expression which remained a dirty word in the City for many years after this, but was evidently not too visionary to be insisted upon as a prudent condition before hazarding City funds in industry. There was, incidentally, at this time no industry, with the dubious exception of coal-mining, which could be said to have any "general plans".

The City's long-continued neglect of the investment needs of British industry, however, only hurt certain industries at certain times. A much more widely pervasive and continuing disservice was in the management of credit from London. Throughout the late 1920s, with British industry stagnant and unemployment rising, the Bank's volume of credit lagged behind increases in fixed deposits and the potentialities of industrial growth. In the last six years of the decade, while industrial output per head increased by 10 percent and job-seekers by

7 percent, the Bank's active assets expanded by only £70 million, against a rise of £132 million in fixed deposits.

Condemning this policy, the authoritative Macmillan Report pointed out that if, while the potential output of "the country may have increased by somewhere between 15 and 20 per cent, it is found that the active deposits are substantially unchanged or slightly reduced, it is evident that deflationary forces have been at work . . ." It was not good enough for the bankers to argue that all "sound" demands for credit had been met, when their management of the economy had reduced business profits below normal and had nipped in the bud growth projects which would otherwise have come forward.

In such circumstances superficially glamorous offers were favored at the expense of more solid ones. Out of £117 million subscribed for new capital issues in 284 companies in 1928 nearly half had already been lost in terms of market valuation by May 1931, when the quoted worth was £66 million. No less than 106 companies had either been wound up or had no capital of ascertainable value. The failure to provide any kind of financial vetting facilities for domestic investments resulted in a sad waste of the scarce capital which could at this time have mitigated the tragedy of the unemployed millions. It was not until 1930 that the Bankers' Industrial Development Company was formed, with Bank of England backing, "to examine, assist and finance the amalgamation, reconstruction and reorganisation on an economic and rationalised basis of groups of British companies engaged in important industries", in fulfillment of the promise already quoted. This was, however, a reluctant concession, and the Bank told the Macmillan Committee that it "did not consider such institutions to be necessary in normal times". It still argued that the City catered adequately for British industry, and shrugged off suggestions that it might usefully acquire "statistical information and knowledge of the situation" with the Governor's words. "I do not attach importance to great elaboration of statistical information."

Much more thorough homework was done in the City regarding overseas investment, and it was strongly contended that this indirectly provided finance for British exports. Consideration of the actual recipients indicates that although this claim might be true in certain cases it was much exaggerated, and, given the conventional and stereotyped nature of the main types of borrowing agency, any such result would be fortuitous. The more the modernization of British industry lagged behind, under its economic and other handicaps at home, the more such activities of the City would tend to benefit its competitors, and further weight the scales against it. The Alternative types of investment, such as developing overseas subsidiaries of British industries to carry stocks and provide service, would have been a different matter, but these were also neglected.

It is thus impossible to avoid the conclusion that, while preaching sound finance, the City in the 'twenties, under Bank of England leadership, pursued policies and practices which, even had the world depression never happened, were bound to undermine the national economy, to throw more and more productive assets out of full employment, to damp down new growth and in short to lead to national bankruptcy.

How did it come about that this vast power for mischief was left, unchallenged and unregulated, in the hands of a set of purely private sectional interests at a period so vital to the survival of Britain after the disasters of World War I? The organ of government bearing virtually undivided responsibility for this catastrophe was, of course, the Treasury. Reading the excellent analysis and discussion in the Macmillan Report, and its accompanying and most revealing Minutes of Evidence, a modern observer must feel growing astonishment that the great Department of State bearing this responsibility should so utterly have failed to fulfil it that as late as 1930 such questions still had to be asked, and such suggestions independently advanced.

Reflecting on the fundamentally parochial and wrong-headed attitude to the welfare of the British economy in the City, one might expect to find the Treasury confuting these fallacies, robustly insisting on the interests of national economic reconstruction, and lucidly briefing Chancellors of the Exchequer on the measures which the leaders of the City should be pressed to adopt. But while the record shows frequent successes by the Permanent Secretary of the Treasury in encroaching upon the management autonomy of all other Departments, in instructing them on the hiring and firing of staff, in vetoing or overriding their considered views on the highest promotions and, by a crowning triumph of intrigue, in having himself declared Head of the Civil Service, the record of Treasury measures to repel usurpation by the City of its own essential functions of economic and financial management is almost a blank. The Permanent Secretary of the Treasury was too busily occupied elsewhere to spend much time on homework on his primary job. The historical result itself is enough of a condemnation of the Treasury's waste of opportunities and failure in understanding national economic requirements in the 'twenties. Meanwhile, every Chancellor of the Exchequer was badly let down by his officials, who grossly neglected to keep each in turn properly informed of the true situation, and pressed wrong advice on successive political chiefs, most of whom, unlike Churchill, were too gentlemanly to let their feelings be seen even long afterwards.

It cannot be claimed that no one could have given correct advice or used more advanced techniques and analyses. Even Lloyd George's somewhat general proposals published in *The Nation* as early as 1924, and in more detail in 1929 in the Liberal pamphlet *We can conquer unemployment,* can clearly be seen to have been much nearer the mark. Development of roads, electrification, the telephone network, the London Passenger Transport System and other basic requirements for a modern economic structure, were proposed. It was pointed out that, since World War I, the ratio of unutilized or "time" deposits to utilized or "demand" deposits had risen from 28·6 per cent to 44·7 per cent, and that merely reverting to the 1920 ratio would at once release for investment £210 million ($588 million) from the dozen leading banks, apart from savings to the Unemployment Fund and other possibilities such as using the Road Fund to finance a loan.

Coming just before a General Election these proposals put the Baldwin administration sufficiently on the defensive to call for a reply in the uncommon form of a White Paper entitled *Memoranda on Certain Proposals relating to Unemployment* (Cmd 3331). This included (rather oddly as a piece of election literature) a Treasury Memorandum claiming that:

> We have always pursued the policy of providing the finance required for the economic development of the public services, and there is no justification for the charge that these services have been stinted. The proposals . . . that this programme should be greatly extended are open to very serious objection on financial grounds. The large loans involved, if they are not to involve inflation, must draw on existing capital resources. These resources are on the whole utilised at present in varying degrees of active employment . . . Finally, on the long view, the undertaking of a large programme of Government expenditure, if it were successful in increasing employment temporarily, would tend to prejudice our export trades by

encouraging our industries to struggle along on an uneconomic basis, instead of reorganising themselves to meet present-day conditions.

The sovereign electorate responded at once by turning out the government which had sponsored these specious arguments, but of course they could not turn out the Treasury, which continued to stonewall on exactly the same lines, but more discreetly behind the scenes. Unemployment, which at that time was a mere 1,144,000, rose by December 1930 to about 2 ½ million, by July 1931 to 2·8 million and by January 1933, at its peak, exceeded 2·9 million, or 22·8 per cent of the insured working population.

Perhaps the best means of testing the Treasury's contention is to consider the national record on highways. The historian Hilaire Belloc had, among others, argued in 1923 that "We need . . . immediately . . . a large number of great arterial roads very broad and straight with a special surface confined to motor traffic alone," and had commented that "the material rise and decline of a state are better measured by the condition of its roads than by any other criterion."

Although the subsequent Royal Commission on Transport disagreed with such contentions, Belloc was not far wrong. The pioneer work in highway improvement of Telford and Macadam in the early nineteenth century coincided with and sustained the most vital growing period of the industrial revolution. While long-distance improvements were curtailed as the railway network took over during the middle years of the nineteenth century urban highway innovations continued with the first flyovers at Holborn Viaduct and Highgate Archway, a century ago, and the first traffic signals in Parliament Square in 1868, together with such an anticipation of the urban motorway as the Thames Embankment. Then everything stopped, as the modern Treasury evolved sufficiently to take advantage of the Local Government Act of 1888 for terminating road grants from the Exchequer.

Already, by 1902, when the speed limit stood at fourteen miles per hour, Sir Arthur Stanley had put a motion to the House of Commons:

> To call attention to the entire suspension of road building activity . . . since the abolition of the Turnpike Acts: to the congestion of traffic and of population in the large towns by reason of the fact that no new trunk roads through and out of them have been constructed for several generations: to the growing difficulty and increasing cost of transporting goods by road and their serious effect upon the industrial efficiency of the nation: and to move that in the opinion of

this House immediate steps should be taken to facilitate the construction of new trunk roads . . .

Although it won some backing in the press Sir Arthur's well-conceived
initiative met only a dusty answer; indeed he could have repeated it
with only slight amendment every year for the next half-century. Even
the race of road engineers had practically been allowed to die out in
Britain. In 1909 the Road Board was created as the first national highway authority since the Romans withdrew from Britain, with a remit
for "constructing . . . absolutely new highways", but the Treasury,
which secured the power of appointment to the Board, soon took care
of that. As its Secretary, Rees Jeffreys, later recorded, a railwayman
was chosen as Chairman, and no alternative proposals to his were ever
submitted to the Board, which dealt piecemeal with local authorities,
forming no national view of its own and gathering little in the way of
data. Before its abolition during the post-war economies of 1919 it had
merely set up a testing laboratory for road materials, and had initiated
no new road of any consequence except the so-called Great West Road
out of London. First proposed in 1837, this received official approval
in 1910 and was partly finished in 1925: the remainder was held over
until after World War II, by which time the earlier section was so obsolete that it had to be replaced by M4 in 1964.

During the ten years of the Road Board's existence motorists paid in
to the Road Fund, through earmarked taxation much disliked by the
Treasury as an infringement of its control over public finance, a total
of nearly £40 million ($112 million). Of this, thanks to the Treasury's
efficient precautions, no more than £7 million including administrative expenses, was allowed to be spent on roads. After 1919 central
responsibilities were transferred to the Ministry of Transport, then
one of the lowest forms of administrative life, under a railwayman
Minister committed to the most savage economies, backed by an ex-
railwayman Secretary. There was a Director-General of Roads enjoying the dubious pleasure of direct responsibility for getting money released by the Treasury from the Road Fund. The most important re-
leases from this Fund were, however, from the Treasury to itself
through the successive "raids" of 1926 (£7 million) and 1927 (£12 million) in order to make "provision for the huge rent in the Sinking Fund
made by the disasters of last year"—namely the General Strike, the
inevitable outcome of the previous year's Treasury blunder in going
back to the Gold Standard.

The penalization of road traffic development was aggravated after

1920 by the extraordinary and protracted Treasury aberration of the horsepower tax, which forced upon British motor manufacturers intense specialization in producing a strange type of private car favored in no other country on earth, and thus contributed much to the retardation of the development not only of vehicle manufacturing but of iron and steel and other key industries. From a Treasury standpoint these peculiar machines had the immense advantage of implicitly demanding antiquated winding roads, since they were incapable of performing on modern straight roads, as those British motorists soon learned who ventured on to the inter-war German autobahns and Italian autostrada.

For, again thanks to the Treasury, who misappropriated the funds subscribed by motorists for this very purpose, it was the Italians and the Germans who were left a clear field to lead Europe in designing and constructing modern motor highways between the two wars, and who won immense prestige, and commercial as well as military advantage, from so doing. At the same time, private promoters who had sought powers in 1924 to build a toll motorway from London to Birmingham, Manchester and Liverpool were frustrated, and this project had to wait another forty years before its fulfillment, even in part. The economic loss resulting from this deferment is incalculable, not the least element in it being the much increased cost per mile and the added inflationary strain of doing the work when it eventually had to be done, instead of when costs were low and unlimited unemployed labor was available. (The 1,500 autobahn miles constructed in Germany up to 1937 cost on average only about £34,000 [$95,200] per mile—well under one-tenth of British post-war levels.)

British performance during the same period was pitiable, beginning with such notorious deathtraps as the Kingston By-pass and concluding with the London Western Avenue, whose story is worth a few lines. Originally envisaged as part of an arterial highway across the country from Swansea to Southend, it was submitted to the Royal Commission on London Traffic in 1903 and officially approved in 1920. Accelerated progress then occurred, with the actual construction of 6·21 miles in the next eight years. In 1926 tenders for the construction of another 4·55 miles were invited, but, on Treasury insistence, the contract was not awarded. After the 1931 crisis, while millions stood idle, it took until 1934 to get the work restarted. The Middlesex section was completed just before World War II, while the Buckinghamshire section continued through the wartime manpower shortage until it was finished in 1943, by which time the number of cars on the road was minimal. Forty-two years of discussion and twenty-five years of work had produced eleven and a half miles of highway, much of which had meanwhile become overloaded with suburban and local industrial traffic: the next instalment, towards inner London, began in 1966.

Yet authoritative voices had throughout been pointing the right route and warning against just such amateur interference and delays. In 1927 Frank Pick stated that the London General Omnibus Company alone was losing £1 million ($2.8 million) annually through actual out-of-pocket expenses attributable to delay and congestion on the roads. Sir Charles Bressey, commissioned by the Minister of Transport to report in 1937, summarized the position on the 525 miles of principal radial outlets from London as consisting of 32 percent single carriageway with only two lanes, 47·5 percent single carriageway with three lanes and only 3·5 percent dual carriageway. Blind corners or summits occurred every 1·2 miles, and abrupt bottlenecks every 3 miles. The cost was to be counted not only in money but in lives. Already by 1930 road deaths had risen to over 7,300 a year, a much higher level than any year in the 'fifties, although there were at that time only about 2¼ million vehicles of all types on the roads (compared with nearly 13 million in 1965 when, despite much increased speeds, road deaths were only some 700 higher). The cost of parsimony in lives could thus be approximately calculated. In 1939 the Alness Committee summed up their conclusions about the Ministry of Transport: they "were not impressed by the evidence which they heard from its representatives regarding the organisation and working of the Department" . . . They "formed an impression that there is . . . a lack of vision, of initiative and of driving force in the Department."

Thus, while HM Treasury had throughout thirty years completely frustrated Parliament's decision of 1909 for "constructing . . . absolutely new highways", it was the unhappy Ministry of Transport, denied the funds raised from taxpayers by Parliament for this purpose, and systematically enfeebled in its staffing by the Treasury's use of its new powers over higher administrative appointments, which had to take the rebuke and carry the can.

No wonder that, finding the highways such an easy victim, the Treasury was encouraged to go even further, as recounted in the PEP *Report on Growth in the British Economy* (1960):

In the period 1924–39 investment in roads and public lighting averaged about £30 million per annum at 1948 prices. In 1948–53 it averaged only £7 million per annum. Further, Redfern's calculations suggested that after allowing for depreciation, *real net fixed capital formation in roads in the post-war period to 1953 was negative, ranging from £7 million in 1949 to £11 million in 1953 at 1948 prices.* These calculations indicate that road investment in the post-war period to 1953 was not even keeping pace with the deterioration of existing roads, let alone catering for the rapid increase in the number of vehicles. The chief reason for the neglect of road investment seems to be that *Governments have considered road development low on the list of national priorities and long-term investment has been sacrificed to more immediate demands on the national product.*

The two passages, here italicized, as indeed the whole highway story, are of the utmost significance for connoisseurs of the System. The first shows that the Treasury has not stopped short at reducing, to even less than nothing, the share of essential elements in the national economy, when it can get away with that. The second is another way of saying that, having successfully reduced the status within central government of the custodians of national highway development to less than the dust, the Treasury then managed with little difficulty to bamboozle governments, drawn in these years from the Labour as well as from the Conservative party, to forget their duties to road-users and to the support of the national economy.

A special advantage of roads for purposes of study is that they are entirely internal; arguments about them involve little in the way of value judgments; they are automatically well documented, owing to the stages through which such projects must pass and the maps, designs, descriptions and costings entailed; and the pace, scale and nature of the results are exceptionally suitable for measurement and for comparison, not only domestically but internationally. The one major element still partly lacking, owing to the dilatoriness of the Treasury in asking for it and the universities in providing the necessary training, is an adequate technical basis of benefit/cost assessment of the economic consequences of the policy actually followed, in relation to alternative choices. A scholarly analysis in these terms is badly needed, and it would be an eye-opener in showing just what the Treasury has cost Britain over the past few decades.

For the roads are not merely a first-class element in the economy;

they are also an almost ideal tool for auditing its management, on account of the features just mentioned. The Treasury has placed immense difficulties in the way of those who may wish in the public interest to probe what it has done and with what results, and to distinguish it from the contributions and decisions of others. The open road, however, carries with it a built-in factor of historical and economic honesty which cannot be wholly evaded. To change the metaphor, we emerge at this point into a small, light clearing in the System's jungle, in which we can for a moment rub our eyes and catch a glimpse of what is going on, not merely here but in the many darker patches under the shelter of great banks of gloomy vegetation. There we can only hear the occasional scuffle and the quickly stifled cry of pain, without being able to observe, although we may well suspect, who is strangling whom.

In the case of highways, then, there is a sad example of what Parliament meant to be one of the first and most far-seeing of the great public concerns emasculated and absorbed in one of the most oppressed and ineffective sections of the Departmental Civil Service.

There was, however, one great service which was quite lucky— radio broadcasting or, as it was originally and characteristically christened by the technologically illiterate nation, "wireless". Radio transmission of messages, first accomplished by Rutherford at Cambridge in 1895, and extended to transatlantic range from Cornwall to Newfoundland by the Italian Marconi in 1901, represented a reversal of the stock pattern of British discoveries being left for others to develop, since radio waves had been discovered by the German, Heinrich Hertz, in 1887. The political climate over the next quarter of a century led to heavy emphasis on the imperial and strategic aspects of the new invention. After World War I ended, the government machine was mainly concerned to prevent interference with military communications. The first British broadcasting transmitter was sited at Daventry in the Midlands and its power restricted to 25 kilowatts with these considerations in mind.

By the enterprise of some radio manufacturers in 1922, after discussion with the Postmaster-General, and, after some pressure from him, it was agreed to pool commercial interests in one British Broadcasting Company, the BBC. This was originally a private company, owned by manufacturers of equipment and licensed by the Post Office, to broadcast from eight stations until January 1925. The Company took the wise step of appointing as its General Manager a young Scot named J. C. W. Reith, whose devoted labors, far-seeing concepts and rugged toughness in their defense were to mold the whole future development in this field. In particular his early espousal of the cause of public service broadcasting, and the confidence which he was able to inspire in his determination and ability to enforce the highest standards of impartiality and good taste, resulted in the successful repulse of repeated attempts at political, bureaucratic and commercial encroachment on this vital national service. The story, which is copiously documented, is too long to tell here, but certain especially relevant aspects must be noted. The financing of the BBC, as a service used by a large number of personally identifiable individuals within the nation, raised once more the issue of general taxation versus a special fee. Thanks partly to special circumstances, partly to the fact that the revenue becoming available was always fully spent and not allowed to accumulate in some tempting hoard, and partly to the character of Reith, the Treasury reluctantly had to accept that, in this particular case, earmarked taxation is not earmarked taxation but an acceptable service charge, tolerated as an exception to the cherished rule. The Road Fund could have supported a similar national service, matching the success story of the BBC, but its custodians were weak enough and foolish enough to allow its funds to pile up until they were first raided and later annexed entirely by the Treasury.

The BBC story is also important as a guiding example in the evolution of the British public concern, especially as regards the appointment and terms of service of its board of governors and their relations with the Director-General and with Ministers. On the whole, the composition of the governors and the choice of their Chairman has been predominantly conservative, as was the responsibility for their constitution, and this, paradoxically, has enabled the professional staff to get away with a more experimental and free-spoken critical line than might have been the case if the Corporation itself had been invested with a less austerely respectable image. The Corporation's senior administrators, although not as a group very obviously differentiated from the administrative class of the Civil Service, have found themselves compelled by the nature of broadcasting to support and tolerate and take responsibility for a very different kind of product, and to attend much more keenly to public opinion. In this way, the structure and practice of the BBC contains much that might be relevant to the modernization of central government, provided that the need for modernizing the BBC itself is not overlooked.

The other main relevant lesson from BBC experience concerns the origins and development of television. Contrary to widespread belief in Britain, this was not "invented" by J. L. Baird, but had its origins in Germany and Russia in the nineteenth century. These were used by Baird in giving the earliest public demonstration of TV in London in 1926, shortly after a transmission had also been achieved by Jenkins in the USA. As so often happens with pioneers, Baird's personality proved a handicap as well as an asset, and his techniques, as he developed them, failed to match the performance of the alternative system developed in Britain by Electrical and Musical Industries Ltd., which was adopted.

A certain coolness towards television in BBC circles was apparent from the outset, and Baird's firm, Television Ltd., formed in 1925, received little help or encouragement. The policy was described by the Assistant Controller as being "to resist television while it is still premature and to welcome it and give it every encouragement once it has reached a stage where it may fairly be regarded as being available for general service as an adjunct to broadcasting." Such a patronizing and negative attitude represented little advance on that to be expected of a Department, and its lack of vision over the future role of TV contrasted sadly with the far-sighted planning and development of the national radio broadcasting services. Fortunately, however, under pressure from the Postmaster-General, the BBC somewhat relented. From September 1932 public experimental transmissions were provided, using the BBC program material and staff, but expenditure on TV during 1933 and 1934 was only about £7,000 ($19,600) each year.

In May 1934 the government appointed a committee under an ex-Postmaster-General, Lord Selsdon, to consider the development of television. They advised that it should be entrusted to the BBC, which had now given an assurance that it was prepared to enter into it "wholeheartedly"—a point of some significance. The Report was speedily followed up, and the world's first public television broadcasting service began from Alexandra Palace, London on November 2, 1936, the number of sets then in use being about 100, rising by August 1939 to between 20,000 and 25,000. A decision in 1938 to build four provincial stations was overtaken by the war, during which television closed down. That a government-supervised public concern should have arrived at this stage so much in advance of the private enterprise television interests in the United States, where much of the technical development had been done, is a surprising testimony to the capabilities of the public concern model.

While the subsequent history of the BBC has shown even more caution in technical development, the Corporation's integrity and its enterprise in stimulating the broadest cultural use of both the sound and visual media have enabled it easily to hold its place as a leading British asset, which need not fear adverse comparisons elsewhere. Even when exposed to intense commercial competition in the television field it has not done badly. It has accepted risks and persevered with success in setting standards far beyond the capacity either of commercial or of Departmental organizations.

CHAPTER 15

Reconstruction and the War

One of the unhappy consequences of the botched and improvised origins of the Liberal Party in the mid-nineteenth century had been the conversion of the difficult and complex issues of national economic policy from questions to be settled on merits after due study to matters of fierce quasi-religious dogma. Any adaptation of that dogma would be fought to the bitter end by redoubtable groups within the electorate who had been misled by Liberal politicians into supposing that they were fully competent to decide such issues. Economists themselves were often more notable for their apostolic fervor than for their grasp of basic data or their command of analytical technique. Indeed, the more blatantly unscientific they were, the better they tended to succeed in the world. Almost total economic illiteracy in Whitehall was thus reinforced by an almost total veto on intelligent political discussions of the economic morass into which Britain was sinking more and more deeply from late Victorian times onwards.

As something had to give, the nation had made itself dependent on some big enough disaster, coming early enough from some external source, to break the deadlock. World War I appeared for a time to meet this requirement. Its exposure of the immense national deficiencies and technical backwardness in industries vital to national defense, such as dyestuffs and other chemicals, watchmaking and optical equipment, shook public opinion sufficiently to make possible the enactment of the McKenna Duties of 1915, as a first breach in the Free Trade dogma. These were followed up by the Key Industries Act of 1921 and its "Safeguarding Duties", intended to develop or revive specific industries under temporary protection. Inability to discriminate in favor of leading Empire commodities led to the device in the late 'twenties of the Empire Marketing Board. This Board was entrusted with the expenditure of more than half a million pounds annually, and by attracting a talented staff of refugees from ordinary Departments it became, during its brief and glorious existence, an outstanding pioneer of public patronage for market research, documentary films, public relations campaigns, and other significant growing points of modern government.

After the 1931 crisis, however, all pretense that protective measures were no more than a regretted temporary exception to the Free Trade rule went overboard. What remained of the nonconformist conscience on the matter proved of some value in inducing industries hoping to profit by the sin of protection to do penance for it by suitable measures of modernization. One of the many unfortunate features of this moralistic approach to economic policy had been a view of competition which regarded co-operation, integration or mere bigness as wicked, and which preferred countless small businesses, however weak, backward and inefficient, to mergers or rationalization. As American and German businessmen tended to take an opposite view, this factor aggravated the competitive weakness, retarded the growth and perpetuated the obsolescent attitudes of British industry.

During the nineteen-twenties two important steps were taken towards a more modern scale and pattern of industrial structure in leading industries. The first was in chemicals, where in 1914 a loose agglomeration of weak British firms had faced a comprehensive and well-organized German industry, with results for the war effort too damaging to be shrugged off. Britain at that time imported 90 percent of her dyestuffs, and manufactured only 3 percent of world production against Germany's 83 percent. The British government was compelled, as a result of this neglect, to subscribe capital for the reorganization of the industry. The explosives and alkali sections of the industry were also taken in hand, and in 1926 the largest firms—British Dyestuffs, Brunner Mond, United Alkali and Nobels—merged to form the £65 million ($182 million) combine named Imperial Chemical Industries. The merger gave the new firm the power "to deal with similar large groups in other countries on terms of equality . . ."

In the United States Du Pont had already moved from explosives to chemicals in 1920, and in 1925 Germany had established the giant IG Farbenindustrie. In combining, therefore, the British industry was not giving a lead, but following the lead of others. Nevertheless, viewed in domestic terms, the merger was, at the time, of breathtaking scale and audacity. It provided a yardstick against which the extent of the accumulated obsolescence of British industry could begin to be measured. It introduced a new managerial type, with new standards of recruitment, training and promotion, and with a new attitude towards research and the place of scientists and technologists in industry. Under the inspiration of Alfred Mond, the first Lord Melchett, it sought to set new and more human standards of labor relations, and to play a role in undoing some of the damage caused to these, at its inception, by the General Strike. After a brief period of centralization it also awakened to the need of decentralization in order to obtain the best results—a lesson to which no more than lip-service is paid in Whitehall to this day. On the whole ICI proved a success, and as the largest unit in British industry it exerted a progressive influence in many directions.

The second leap into large-scale organization was based on the already substantial business created by the first Lord Leverhulme. During the 'twenties, its Dutch competitors merged into the Margarine Union, which grew by further amalgamations. Discussions followed between Lever Brothers and the Dutch for some form of rationalization. After negotiations for partial arrangements had fallen through, the eventual conclusion was in favor of complete amalgamation, which was completed in September 1929, just before the Wall Street crash. The new concern employed nearly a quarter of a million workers, and traded in more places and in more products than any other in the world. Like the other great Anglo-Dutch firm, the Shell group, it stood in the first rank of world business units. Its international character foreshadowed the direction in which all Europe would eventually have to move if the competition of American business and the inevitable takeover bids from it were to be successfully resisted.

Where the pace was not so urgently dictated from overseas, progress in the rationalization of British industry was much less rapid, especially in the case of the traditional basic industries—coal-mining, steel, shipbuilding and cotton textiles. All these needed government intervention to secure even gradual advances towards a modern scale and structure. After the interesting and encouraging examples of the late 'twenties it came as a disappointment to find, during the middle and later 'thirties, such a falling-off in major new initiatives for modernization. After the bad scare of the General Strike and the 1931 crisis, the usual British tendency to slacken off and go to sleep again became evident. It was at this period too that the heaviest price had to be paid for the reckless slaughter during World War I in Flanders of so much of the flower of the younger generation, whose barely remembered absence made this probably the most favorable decade in British history for the attainment of the highest posts in the land by second- and third-raters.

One problem which could not be forgotten or entirely shirked during the 'thirties was the existence of chronic mass unemployment in the depressed or, as they came to be euphemistically called, the Special Areas. The southern and eastern regions of England came off much more lightly during the worst period of the slump, and recovered much more quickly and completely, than those in the north and west. In 1932, 36·5 percent of the insured population in Wales, 27·7 percent in Scotland and 27·1 percent in the North were unemployed. The situation in the worst "pockets of unemployment" was appalling. In the sunny May of 1934 Merthyr Tydfil had nearly 70 percent of its insured male workers out of work, while in Brynmawr the level exceeded 74 percent. In Durham, 80 percent unemployment was recorded in 1935 at Tow Law, and at Shildon it was virtually 100 percent. These were not just temporary setbacks, but symptoms of a chronic state. In Crook, Co. Durham, 71 percent of the unemployed in 1936 had been *out of work for more than five years,* and in the Rhondda, South Wales, 45 percent.

The dictatorship over the economy exercised by the remote and ignorant authorities in Whitehall and in the City, coupled with the backwardness and inadaptability of local managements and authorities in such areas, and their pathetic reliance on the patterns of production and selling bequeathed to them by their more enterprising early Victorian forefathers, made it inevitable that the relative decline of the British economy would be felt, not evenly and generally throughout the land, but with concentrated and savage impact in those areas in which the traditional staple industries had become localized. All these, it so chanced, were far enough from London to be literally outside the ken of the great majority of the decision-makers, whose intelligence sources were so scanty and slow, and whose imagination was so feeble, that if the trouble had been in Tibet it could scarcely have taken longer to shape itself within their consciousness.

In view of the gross misjudgments of factors vitally concerning the external balance of payments, the growth of road traffic and the expanding demand for electricity, which were immediately before the eyes of Whitehall, it is scarcely surprising that, even when the plight of South Wales, of Scotland and of the Northeast became known, action was inhibited. Such action was bound to conflict with cherished traditional policies and attitudes. Preferential and specific measures, directed to certain regions only, cut across the grain of the British governmental mechanism.

Public opinion was, however, so aroused after a series of articles in *The Times* during the six years 1928–34 that the government was finally compelled to act. Action took three stages. *The Times* had found that "Lack of concerted effort, of planned determination . . . can be charged upon the separate Government services that are coping with the situation . . ." (the word "coping" was highly flattering to them), and had recommended, instead of the usual committee, a one-man on-the-spot survey. Four influential men were picked to follow up this suggestion in the four main depressed areas. Captain Euan Wallace, in the Northeast, found unemployment up to nearly 57 percent in Jarrow on the Tyne, where coal-mining had had a heavy setback and the shipping, shipbuilding and marine engineering industries "will not for many years absorb more than a small proportion of those attached to the industry". He commented that "the industrial depression and the heavy unemployment in this area are due to causes outside the control of those who reside in it . . . there is no likelihood that the same forces which have created the present situation *will automatically readjust it, except after a lapse of time and at a cost of human suffering and economic waste which no modern Government would care to contemplate.*" (My italics.) The only way out was "some positive external assistance".

At last a chosen envoy from the heart of the System had clearly, though very tactfully, pointed to its three great faults in this respect —its groundless faith in "automatic" recuperation, its callous inhumanity towards the unmerited sufferings of these faraway people, and its refusal hitherto to face "positive external assistance" and to give up confining itself to all aid short of aid.

The others reported similar situations—in Scotland production had actually been allowed to fall by 10 percent between 1907 and 1930—and their findings led to the introduction in November 1934 of the Depressed Areas (Development and Improvement) Bill which soon became an Act, with the first word in its title changed to "Special". One of the unusual features of the new policy thus launched was the extent of its reliance not on committees, departments or civil servants, but on single non-Whitehall Commissioners, generally of high caliber, who were personally responsible for action, and had the experience and public status to direct it. Oliver Stanley, as the Minister, stressed the experimental nature of the approach, and somewhat prematurely announced to the House of Commons "We are all planners now."

The first Commissioner for England and Wales was the industrialist P. Malcolm Stewart who, in laying down his office after two years, had to report that attempts to increase industrial activity in the Special Areas by persuasion had, generally speaking, failed. In 1935, 213 new factories were established in Greater London, but only two, plus six extensions, in the Special Areas of England and Wales. In 1936, 551 new factories were established in Great Britain; only eight of these were in the Special Areas, where six factories closed in the same year. Of 201 factory extensions in Great Britain only three were in Special Areas.

The Commissioner drew attention to such nonsense as the embargo on his providing a grant for any feature of a scheme already within the grant jurisdiction of some Department, even if the rules and practice of that Department ruled out their making a grant in such a case. All road works, for example, thus fell between two stools. This remains a regular feature of the System, insisted upon by the Treasury in preference to decentralizing even such a minor element in financial control. The Commissioner expressed sympathy for the Ministries' "difficulty in departing from their general standards in specific cases" but declared himself convinced that such problems "must be tackled by the Government as a whole, and there is hardly a Government Department which cannot and should not help". The existing Departments already possessed the necessary machinery and experience, but because they were inhibited from applying these to such a problem a small, weak new Department, operating under their feet, had to be created for the purpose, however uneconomical and inefficient it might be.

In May 1937, nearly ten years after the urgency of this tragic problem had first been brought by *The Times* to governmental attention, a further step to facilitate some useful action was made in the Special Areas (Amendment) Act, which at last enabled financial aid to be given to the establishment of new industry. Thanks largely to the co-operation of Hitler, who simultaneously drove out of central Europe without capital a number of talented managers and inventors having, as refugees, little option but to avail themselves of the new facilities, some improvement was effected. But even the new Industrial Estates together employed by 1939 only some 12,000 workers, leaving well over 90 percent of the surplus workers in the Special Areas untouched. Efforts at resettlement on the land met even more limited success, and it was, in the end, only the arrival of rearmament and World War II which swept up the Special Areas problem in an immensely larger complex of hastily planned re-employment.

The Minister's fond hopes for the experimental potentialities of the Special Areas approach proved hardly less illusory than his well-meant suggestion of a conversion to belief in planning. The System neither favors nor understands experiment in anything resembling its scientific sense.

The Special Areas experiment, in so far as it proved anything, proved the total inability and unwillingness of the Whitehall machine either to attend to the problems of the various regions or to permit anyone else to do so. Its lessons, if learned, were not followed up at the time owing to the coming of World War II.

Preserving law and order at home, and peace or effective defense against external attack, are the most essential of all functions of government. After British policy for several decades had been shaped towards making a military attack upon Britain more tempting, the Liberal Government, by 1914, had drifted into a situation in which the imminent threat of European War almost precisely coincided with the quite independent and equally imminent threat of civil war over Ulster. Since both these threats had been plainly foreseeable for many years, to permit both of them to burst at once upon a still unprepared nation must be reckoned among the most spectacular achievements of the British system of misgovernment.

The 1914–18 war, although legitimately termed World War I, was almost entirely fought out on land over a very limited block of the earth's surface between the eastern end of the English Channel and the south-eastern corner of the Mediterranean, and between the Gulf of Finland and the Black Sea. Luckily for Britain, almost the whole of the farflung and indefensible territories of the British Empire remained immune from hostilities, except for what would now be regarded as little more than token air raids. In contrast, therefore, to World War II Britain got away very cheaply indeed with the vast strategic liabilities which she had assumed in taking possession of such an overseas Empire, and was even successfully tempted to add to it further after victory. While, as we have seen, the relative stagnation of British technological development in industry created grave munitions deficiencies, the degree of superiority of German technology was hardly reflected in the German war machine, which was largely on nineteenth-century lines. The U-boat and gunnery improvements at sea came fairly close to neutralizing British naval superiority, but the early concentration on the airship rather than the bomber for air warfare and on poison gases rather than a tank for land attack got the German forces off to a bad start technologically, in relation to what they would have been capable of. Appalling as was the slaughter of British infantry in trench warfare on the Western front, it was also fortunately mitigated by the maintenance of a second front against Germany by the Russians in the east until 1917, and by the arrival of American troops in the west later.

Having thus fortunately emerged intact, although much battered and exhausted, in 1918 the British Empire should have conducted a searching and realistic study of the future conditions for its survival in a world unrecognizably changed by the vanishing of the four other great Empires of Germany, Russia, Austria-Hungary and Turkey, the exhaustion of France, the vast expansion of United States power, the spread of Communism and the impact of science and technology. Unfortunately the necessary fact-finding and thinking was neglected, and provision for it within the Service Departments and the Foreign Office was notably meager. There was a fair amount of valuable effort towards modernizing the political relationships within the Empire and the Commonwealth, as it now became, but even this was largely vitiated by false and distorted economic theories of imperial trade, and by clinging to outdated concepts of domination over lesser breeds without the law. Although both Winston Churchill and Haldane held high political office during the 'twenties, and Hankey, its distinguished Secretary, was in his prime, the potentialities of the Committee of Imperial Defence, for devising a sound long-term strategy and the outlines of a program for fulfilling it, were missed.

This omission was all the more culpable because the climate of public opinion during the 'twenties and 'thirties was probably more widely and deeply concerned over the future development and security of the Empire than at any other period in history. The renewed movement of opinion away from "Continental entanglements" and towards something more like "splendid isolation" clearly called for a deep study of the realistic long-term prospects of a policy so founded, both as a guide for government decisions and as a basis for political education of the electorate. During the negotiations of the Treaty of Versailles a good deal of hurried thought was, as a matter of necessity, given to these problems, but amid distractions prejudicial to sound conclusions. These matters called for a thorough and objective later follow-up which was never carried through. Not only the populace but the government itself were largely content with frothy and vulgar "prestige" gestures, of which the British Empire Exhibition at Wembley in 1924 and 1925 was the most revealing and, to thoughtful citizens, the most profoundly disturbing. It demonstrated a resolution to look for inspiration backwards rather than forwards, to prefer bromides to self-critical reflection, to use science and invention as cheap gimmicks wherever they lent themselves to such use, and otherwise to neglect them, and to endorse a taste in design and the arts which stank of decadence.

The course and fruits of this non-policy-making in its strategic aspects are amply documented, perhaps most enlighteningly in Volume I of Liddell Hart's *Memoirs,* which relate the official events to what was going on behind the scenes. Even as late as 1936, "the Cabinet put off a decision about Britain's strategic policy and the purpose of an expeditionary force—Baldwin, characteristically, using the appointment of a Minister for Coordination of Defence, to which he had reluctantly agreed, as a convenient excuse for further postponement . . . After another year had passed, no decision had been reached on any of these important issues, and that nebulous situation persisted until the autumn of 1937."

Shortly before this, after a long discussion with Duff Cooper (then Secretary of State for War), Churchill, Trenchard (former Chief of Air Staff) and General J. F. C. Fuller he had recorded "a rather depressing effect. For here one had several of the outstanding men in the realm of defence . . . yet much of the discussion was chaotic, sometimes rhetorical rather than reasoned, and often marked by an obvious failure to grasp the point. Much of the talk showed clearly the *want of a scientific habit of thought in past study, and a lack of precision of thought in treating the points now. Until we can organise discussion of a problem properly, what hope can there be of a balanced solution, based on facts and not on fancies."* (My italics.)

These pregnant words, scribbled by Britain's foremost strategist in the small hours of February 15, 1936, remain a valid comment on the

British system of misgovernment to this day. That System flourishes through men who do not like or believe in finding the facts, who positively loathe ideas and long-term planning, who regard it as waste of time to review and draw considered inferences from past failures, and who prefer struggling along in a chronic state of muddle and overwork to accepting any modernization which might require them to do their jobs coherently, and to associate as equals with specialists or planners of different habits of mind. So firmly do these men cling to these views, and to the power to enforce them, that the defeat of armies, the sinking of great ships, the bombing of their country, the loss of lives, of territories and of wealth and the decline of Britain weigh as nothing in the scale against their conviction that they should continue to rule the state in this same way, as indeed they still do.

The same backward-looking stubbornness, and intolerance of new men and new ideas, had a crippling effect on British foreign policy.

As Liddell Hart comments over Abyssinia:

> while faint-heartedness was the main factor in producing the failure to curb Mussolini at this crucial junction, a number of members of the Government were instinctively hostile to the League idea, and their scornful attitude was shared by most of the service chiefs and officials in Whitehall. The cumulative effect resulted in Britain's policy falling between two stools—effective support of the League or a clear-cut return to nineteenth-century isolation. That wobbling course was bound to bring the maximum risk with the minimum insurance. Never again would there be so good a chance to check an aggressor so early, and the failure to do so in this case was the most fateful turning point in the period between the two wars.

Later, Neville Chamberlain brought to British foreign policy an unfortunate combination; a passionate interest and a narrow mind. Lord Strang, head of the Central Department of the Foreign Office after 1937, has written of Chamberlain and of his belief that he could bring peace to Europe:

> it is unlikely that any Minister who had the whole world within his purview and all the main problems of foreign affairs upon his shoulders daily would so long have persisted in such an opinion; but Mr Chamberlain was dealing with only one part of foreign affairs, which must by their very nature be regarded as one whole. If he had had to explain from day to day the progressive development and execution of his purposes to the French, United States, Soviet and other Ambassadors and to the Czechoslovak Minister and had been

obliged to watch and respond to the impact of his actions upon governments and peoples throughout the world, as a Foreign Secretary must do, he might not indeed have modified his policy, but he might have seized its implications better than perhaps he did.

This is the key to Chamberlain's mistakes; he ignored, even despised, professional advice on foreign policy. He did not, it is true, initiate the trend towards personal diplomacy. Lloyd George himself had dealt the first blows at the Foreign Office and the professionals. In the cases of both men, there were, as D. C. Watt has suggested, three main reasons for neglecting the ordinary machinery of diplomacy. In the first place, both could be described as radical, nonconformist businessmen who disliked the allegedly over-narrow social strata from which the professional diplomats were recruited. Secondly, both Lloyd George and Chamberlain were faced with divided counsel in country and Cabinet. Thirdly, their usurpation of the Foreign Secretary's role developed from the increasingly "Presidential" nature of the Prime Minister's office, reflected in the increasing appeal of "summit" conferences.

Chamberlain, contrary to custom, had no member of the Foreign Service amongst his private secretaries. When it came to the public service, he relied heavily on the advice of Sir Horace Wilson, who was, in fact, the Government's Chief Industrial Adviser. Eden, for one, regarded Wilson as an excellent industrial adviser but a disastrous foreign adviser. Wilson was supported by Fisher, the head of the Treasury, who, although aware of the need to rearm, was not keen to spend great sums of money and was, therefore, sympathetic to appeasement. The Treasury, since 1920, had had the power of controlling appointments in all Government Departments (see p. 244). Mr. Frank Ashton Gwatkin, a Foreign Office official in this period, has attributed the weakness of Foreign Office authority to this Treasury power. When Wilson was reprimanded by Eden for interfering in foreign affairs, the former warned Eden's friends that Civil Service advancement would not come easily to them if they supported the Foreign Secretary in this quarrel. On another occasion, Fisher attempted to transfer Sir Findlater Stewart from the India Office to the Permanent Under-Secretaryship of the Foreign Office. The move was balked by Eden because "it made no sense to bring someone who was inexperienced in international diplomacy into the most responsible advisory position in the Foreign Office."

Chamberlain also used unofficial contacts in his dealings with the Dictators—Lady Chamberlain, his sister-in-law, and Sir Joseph

Ball, an official of the Conservative Central Office. Neither, it is true, acted at his express behest and, indeed, the latter even informed the Foreign Office of his activities, but Chamberlain made use of, and did not disown, their initiatives. As Lord Avon has remarked:

> To have any specialist knowledge of foreign affairs was to be quite out of fashion; it was the day of the uninhibited amateur.

One of those with specialist knowledge was Sir Robert Vansittart, Permanent Under-Secretary at the Foreign Office until 1938. He was certainly out of fashion. In the summer of 1937, Dr. Karl Goerdeler, ex-Chief Burgomaster of Leipzig, visited London and communicated to Vansittart details of Germany's economic strains and of Hitler's intentions. Goerdeler's conclusions were that British policy should be "firm and clear". The government should obtain the correct facts about Germany and base policy "on a clear realization of them". Goerdeler was an informant of great authority: he had been considered as a possible Chancellor in 1932, he had recently resigned his position in Leipzig, after recognizing the nature of the Nazi regime, and he was to be a leading figure in the July 20 putsch. Yet Vansittart's draft of a memorandum incorporating these views, which he intended to present to the Cabinet, was suppressed by Eden. This was only one instance of Vansittart's inability to confront the Cabinet with valuable information and advice. In 1939 he believed that the Cabinet was not even reading the intelligence reports he sent them.

At the end of 1937, Vansittart was "promoted" to Chief Diplomatic Adviser, rather as MPs are "promoted" to the House of Lords. Ironically the new post was supposed to be parallel to that officially attributed to Sir Horace Wilson. Sir Alexander Cadogan took over as Permanent Under-Secretary. Under the new system, all papers were to be submitted by Under-Secretaries to Cadogan and by him to the Secretary of State. The latter would decide whether or not Vansittart's advice was required. Only papers relating to defense and propaganda would be sent directly to Vansittart. Thus, writes Ian Colvin (in *Vansittart in Office*, 1965, p. 174):

> a shadowy role of advice, political warfare and propaganda was allotted to him; but on matters of policy, in dealing with dispatches from abroad and receiving the Foreign Ambassadors, it was Cadogan who took over.

Meanwhile, in Berlin, Sir Eric Phipps, a veteran diplomat with no illusions about Nazi Germany, was replaced by the almost Germanophile Sir Nevile Henderson. Oddly enough, Vansittart himself recommended Henderson, in preference to two others, because:

> Sir Nevile has done his stint in South America. He shall have his reward.

Yet Henderson had never, in his thirty-two years' service abroad, been in a post where German was the spoken language.

Still less qualified for the task allotted to him was Edward Wood, Earl of Halifax, who succeeded Eden as Foreign Secretary. He had spent most of his public life outside Europe and had given little thought or interest to that continent's problems. While Foreign Secretary he confessed that he had never read *Mein Kampf*. He accepted the appointment with reluctance and was to allow Chamberlain an even greater freedom of action in foreign affairs.

These and other "uninhibited amateurs" were to dominate British foreign policy until 1940. No member of the Runciman Mission, sent to mediate between the Czechoslovak Government and the Sudeten Germans in 1938, had background knowledge or experience of either Central European politics or minority problems. The Mission repeatedly showed its ignorance about German political parties in the Sudetenland. When Chamberlain flew to Berchtesgaden he was accompanied only by Wilson and Strang. None of the three men spoke German. They took no British interpreter nor, so far as we know, any brief surveying the Czechoslovak question. The lack of an interpreter meant that Britain had no subsequent record of the meeting, since Ribbentrop curtly refused to furnish a German record. Halifax offered no protest against Chamberlain's decision to fly to Germany alone, either on this or subsequent occasions. The idea seems to have been adopted without the advice of any competent adviser, other than Henderson. Vansittart, who spoke fluent German, was certainly not consulted.

Throughout the early months of 1939, Britain remained incredibly optimistic about the international situation. The Berlin Embassy's dispatches contained no clear indication of when or how Britain might have to fulfill her pledges to Poland. Henderson continued to send optimistic reports, although none of his staff, least of all the service attachés, agreed with his views on Hitler's intentions. Hitler, wrote Henderson, "does not contemplate any adventures at the moment";

"he would like in his heart to return to the fold of . . . respectability"; "relative calm" could be expected. As late as August 25 he reported that, once the Polish question was settled, there would be peace in Europe; Hitler was "by nature an artist, not a politician".

Thus, in 1939, British foreign policy was as muddled as it had always been in this period. No effort was made even to help Poland to help herself. A Polish request for £60 million financial assistance in cash was met by a British offer of £8 million in credits which had to be spent in Great Britain, whose armament factories were working to full capacity. Hence, there was not a single armaments transaction between Britain and Poland before September 1939. As usual, the System was uninterested in action. Strang has summed up British foreign policy between the wars in these words (in *Home and Abroad,* 1956, p. 154):

> no clear policy was framed. The new problems of a changed and changing world tended to be interpreted in terms of old conceptions. Our position in the world had altered for the worse and we did not seem to recognise this in our actions . . . We behaved as though we could play an effective part in international affairs as a kind of mediator or umpire without providing ourselves with the necessary arms and without entering into firm commitments whereas the truth was that, for the lack of international solidarity, in face of the common menace, we were in mortal peril.

In a sense, such a disastrous foreign policy was inevitable, in view of the military deficiencies. The tank was a British invention which had proved resoundingly successful. The writings and ideas of the two leading British specialists on the potentialities of tank warfare were mainly responsible for shaping the German panzer arm and its use in World War II. Yet both these men—Captain Liddell Hart and Major General J. F. C. Fuller—were driven to resign from the Army, solely on account of being out of step in understanding how the next war would in fact be fought. Intervention by Churchill, then Chancellor of the Exchequer, failed to induce the War Office to agree to dispense with a cavalry division, and the utmost pressure was needed to secure the conversion into armored car regiments of even two of the twenty-two cavalry regiments. In 1928, after two seasons' trials of a half-hearted substitute for an Amoured Force, the experiment of having one was abandoned. In 1930, devious methods were needed to get even three fast medium tanks built, after which nearly a decade elapsed before a small batch was delivered to the Army, only just before the outbreak of World War II "by which time the Germans had produced hundreds, and of better tested types".

It is in the nature of misgovernment that proof of its systematic and consistent working is often incomplete or inadequate. The Liddell Hart *Memoirs* are of exceptional value in this connection because they deal with a tangible invention, of the utmost significance, and with a clearly formulated concept for exploiting it, and they show, in beautifully-documented details over some quarter of a century, precisely how this world-shaking British discovery was converted into an asset of less than nil effective value to Britain at the moment of her direst need in 1940. This was brought about by a series of neglects, errors of judgment, jealousies, professional incapacities, prejudices and what-have-you on the part of an extended succession of traceable political, administrative and military office-holders who personify and elegantly demonstrate the workings of the System. Liddell Hart proved not only a prophet of rare accuracy in his predictions, but also an observer of uncommon skill and penetration throughout the long process by which the entire benefit of his foresight was denied to Britain and presented to Britain's enemies. He happened to be on such intimate terms with key people as to be able to follow the ball wherever it was in play in the deepest and darkest recesses of the governmental machine. He recorded promptly and faithfully what they told him at each stage. He lived long enough to see it through to the bitter end, and to tell us what happened with a commendable suavity and charity. That is why, in addition to all his other services, he is a classic witness to the facts of the System. Readers of his story, who learn these facts with horror, should bear in mind that this is what goes on in many other branches of the civil as well as the military machine, where, unhappily, there has been no Liddell Hart to come back alive with the story.

It is illuminating to compare the history of the discovery and development of the tank, and the treatment of the battle-winning concepts of J. F. C. Fuller and Liddell Hart, with that of the other decisive invention—radar harnessed to the interception of air attacks, and the treatment of Sir Henry Tizard and his collaborators. How it came about in this second case that it was the British who developed the invention, applied the concept and won the battle themselves—the

Battle of Britain—is worth examining. Is this really a case where the System worked, or did someone have to triumph over it?

The Baldwin government was embarrassed by one of the Prime Minister's occasional bursts of candor to the effect that "The bomber will always get through." Early in 1935 the Air Ministry constituted an official committee "to consider how far advances in scientific and technical knowledge can be used to strengthen the present methods of defence against hostile aircraft." The Ministry's scientific adviser, H. E. Wimperis, was a friend and adviser of the Rector of Imperial College, Tizard, and had him appointed as Chairman. Previously, Tizard had been Secretary of the Department of Scientific and Industrial Research, which included a Radio Research Laboratory where Watson-Watt was doing pioneer work on radar. Tizard chose as his colleagues on the committee two future Nobel prizewinners, A. V. Hill the physiologist and P. M. S. Blackett the physicist.

The task now set in hand was to review the scientific devices which might have a decisive potential against bombers; to find and secure top priority for one which had that potential—namely radar, as it later came to be called; to ensure its rapid development in the most practical form for operational use; to arrange for full-scale testing by RAF personnel in service conditions; to work out and demonstrate the appropriate techniques for fighter pilots to follow radar guidance; to work out also the channeling of the flow of information about approaching hostile aircraft and the co-ordination, interpretation, and immediate use of this information for initiating interception by orders from ground control; to persuade all concerned at all levels to adopt these methods with confidence and efficiency; to assess correctly the eventual enemy reaction to successful use of these methods, in terms of a forced switch from day to night bombing; to prepare to fill the prospective gap thus opened in the defense system by developing a quite distinct equipment and technique in the form of a practical lightweight airborne radar for individual night interceptions; to study and resolve the resulting production, supply and maintenance difficulties; and once more to keep all concerned happy and confident about the eventual solution of a problem the mere nature of which was still obscure.

Tizard not only correctly conceived and analyzed the task but carried it right through, within six years, in a manner which even today's hindsight could not greatly improve upon. Tizard, unlike nearly all civil servants and most scientists, had trained himself to think throughout in terms of a continuous flow process from the abstract principle to the design and production of the means for a solution, and to the realization of this solution in working practice. In other words, he knew what he was at.

Tizard, as he himself was aware, was not a great research scientist, and his contributions to resolving the detailed, strictly scientific problems were probably minor. It was in his powers of higher scientific judgment about selection and priorities, and in his scientific leadership and powers of inspiring and holding together a team that he excelled. But the most remarkable and original part of the story is his successful initiative in designing and executing the full-scale operational trials and the consequential techniques and systems of fighter interception and of ground control, which on paper, as was sourly pointed out in some quarters, were none of his business. Unlike Sir Nevile Henderson's appointment to the Berlin embassy, it was indeed the antithesis of Admiral Fisher's famous comment; "some day the Empire will go down because it's Buggins's turn next!" Some day the Empire didn't go down because Tizard knew what to do and had the skill to persuade Buggins to stand clear and let him do it.

The story of Tizard's work has been told so well and so fully already that there would be no point in retelling it here: C. P. Snow made it an important part of the theme of his Godkin Lectures at Harvard in 1960, published as *Science and Government,* with an important *Postscript* in which he wrote:

> There is fortunately no doubt about his value. It is on the record, and cannot be argued with. To him, as much as to any single man, we owed the fact that there was an adequate fighter defence in 1940 —only just adequate but still it dragged us through . . . He was at one throughout with the serving officers. This mutual trust enabled him and his committee to introduce the operational use of radar just in time . . .
>
> The introduction of radar into Fighter Command between 1937 and 1940 is a textbook example of the successful application of science to war . . .
>
> By 1940 German radar was technically somewhat more sophisticated than the British: but the combination of Tizard and the officers of Fighter Command had ensured that the British knew better how to use it as a weapon of war.

From our present standpoint the one criticism to be made of Snow's excellent analysis is its insistence on the war angle; *mutatis mutandis* the lessons are equally applicable to harnessing scientific results for all kinds of civil use.

Here we have a record of two inventions, both, as we have seen, decisively applied in World War II, one by Britain and the other by her adversary, although both had British origins, not only physically, but, even more importantly, in their potential for use in battle. How did it come that the one which was only developed at the eleventh hour was ready, and justified all the hopes built on it, while the other, which had already been proved in battle more than twenty years earlier, was not ready, and was employed in the early years of World War II only against us?

The record shows plainly that it was of the essence of Tizard's achievement to have seen, and himself followed through, the essential requirement in all its aspects from beginning to end. To do this is to violate the inmost and most cherished convictions and feelings of those who guide and conserve the System. Such reactions were not wanting, but they did not prevail.

How, in this almost unique case, did Tizard get away with it? The answer, as usual in such cases, is largely luck. By the time of the Biggin Hill exercise, World War II was so clearly impending that it had become much more difficult to squash it in the way that the corresponding Mechanised Force trials had been stultified by the War Office ten years earlier, when there was supposed to be no war in sight. Also, coming ten years later, and in the younger, more technologically-minded Air Ministry and RAF Tizard's proposals were not faced with the strength and diversity of traditional resistances which stood in the way of British adoption of armored warfare strategy. More leading figures, better placed throughout the hierarchy, were working as Tizard's allies. Treasury resistance to defense expenditure had also been softened up by this time, and Tizard had better contacts there. The Air Ministry, moreover, had suffered much from being low in the Whitehall peck-order, and to have Tizard with them was an asset which they valued more highly, and were much more loth to lose, than the War Office probably would have been at that time. His bargaining position and status within the Department were thus more secure. Tizard also was fortunate that his requirement, although so important, was not classed as a new weapon in its own right but as an ancillary to one which had already been accepted at the highest level as of the highest priority—the fighter aircraft. And within this ancillary area he was filling a gap, not superseding some earlier four-footed model. Yet with all these and other assets he only just won, and having saved his country he was treated in the accustomed way by being sacked just when he could have been most useful. How that happened is another story which can only be briefly mentioned.

As a young man, Tizard, as Snow recounts, "specialised in chemistry, which was at that time the only adequate scientific school in Oxford . . . it is a bit startling to be reminded that the young Tizard in 1908, bursting with both academic honours and promise, could find no one in Oxford to work under . . . he decided that Germany was the place to find the masters of research. He went off to Berlin to work under Nernst." Thus driven abroad by the neglect of science in Britain, which we have already encountered, he met another young student, F. A. Lindemann, who, first as a friend and later as an implacable foe, was to dog his footsteps throughout his life. On May 22, 1935, Prime Minister Baldwin caused a shock by making an abject apology to Parliament for having denied, in February, Churchill's claim that the German Air Force was already equal to Britain's and would be twice as large by 1937. "There I was completely wrong. We were completely misled on that subject . . . it is the responsibility of the Government as a whole, and we are all responsible, and we are all to blame." At that time it seemed that, once more, responsibility was having to be accepted politically for an administrative failure. We know now, however, that it was rather a case of failure by politicians to use and credit quite reliable information from their staffs, and to prefer to rely on misleading amateur substitutes. Having thus erroneously conceded that Churchill was better informed than themselves, and being unwilling to have him in the Cabinet, Ministers were politically obliged to create a new high-level "Committee on Air Defense Research" and invite Churchill to join it. His condition for doing so was that his adviser, Lindemann, should join Tizard's Committee of scientists, which Lindemann promptly proceeded to pull to pieces. After a series of resignations in July 1936 the Committee had to be reconstituted without Lindemann, who however remained the close personal adviser of Churchill and moved with him to 10 Downing Street in May 1940, whereupon Tizard was crudely forced out of Whitehall.

The most serious consequence of this was leaving the field open for Lindemann to secure adoption of his concept of strategic bombing as a means of knocking Germany out. Early in 1942, he proposed a British bombing offensive to destroy 50 percent of all working-class houses in Germany within eighteen months. Tizard concluded that Lindemann's estimate of effectiveness was five times too high: in fact, as the outturn showed, he should have said ten times too high. Nevertheless Churchill adopted Lindemann's advice; Tizard was in disgrace and the resulting damage is best summed up in the words of P. M. S. Blackett:

> immediately after the war the US Strategic Bombing Survey was sent to Germany to find out what had been achieved . . . Without any doubt the area-bombing offensive was an expensive failure. About 500,000 German men, women and children were killed, but in the whole bombing offensive 160,000 US and British airmen, the best young men of both countries, were lost. German war production went on rising steadily . . . If the Allied air effort had been used more intelligently, if more aircraft had been supplied for the Battle of the Atlantic and to support the land fighting in Africa and later in France, if the bombing of Germany had been carried out with the attrition of the enemy defenses in mind rather than the razing of cities to the ground, I believe the war could have been won half a year or even a year earlier.

Blackett concluded that the campaign was "a disastrous flop".

Captain Roskill, the naval war historian (also quoted in Snow) adds:

> this writer's view is that in the early spring of 1943 we had a very narrow escape from defeat in the Atlantic; and that, had we suffered such a defeat . . . the main cause would have been the lack of two more squadrons of very long range aircraft for convoy escort duties.

It is no part of our task here to discuss Lindemann as a human being, on which the literature is in any case rapidly building up. As an administrative phenomenon, however, we can only conclude that he was a disaster. It is wrong in principle for a single scientist, of no outstanding achievement or repute among his peers, to be brought in by a backstairs route to be the chief adviser of a Prime Minister of whom he is a personal friend. It was much worse, as Snow has well stressed, that any single scientist should have been represented to gullible non-scientists as being competent to pronounce "an authoritative opinion" as a conclusive guide for action. "Whatever we do," Snow concludes, "it must not happen again." But for the treasured amateurism of the System it could never have happened at all.

Where Lindemann's advice on other projects was taken, in circumstances permitting a check on the outturn, the results, with one or two exceptions, fall in a range between unsatisfactory and calamitous.

While the proximate responsibility attaches to Winston Churchill, it is important not to overlook the fact that the original occasion for Lindemann's introduction to the center of power was the mistaken admission by Baldwin in 1935. This could not have occurred if the administrative heads in Whitehall had adequately supported intelligence, research and appraisal in the Whitehall machine. Part of this must be ascribed to a characteristic and almost invariable Whitehall deformity in relation to research, thinking and planning, but part also was due to the equally marked Whitehall vice of power-hogging, and of excluding as long as possible the inconvenient and uncongenial types who like to know, to think, and to foresee. It is a sad thing that those who begin by regarding professionals as if they were quacks are those most liable to finish by swallowing the advice of quacks as if they were professionals, or something more. The room in Whitehall where scientists should have had an honored place was kept swept and garnished and empty too long. History now threatens to repeat itself in the demand for a return to court politics in Whitehall, by introducing into departments political nominees to furnish Ministers with facts and appraisals which the Civil Service has failed to provide. If such a misfortune recurs, Whitehall will largely have itself to blame.

Much the same may well be true on an infinitely larger scale. Regarding the nature and workings of the Churchill wartime administration, with all its oddities, abuses, blunders and wastefulness, but with its intense awareness of national purpose, its genuine efforts at communication, its emphasis upon historic value, its vitality and energy, its generosity towards allied nations and its contempt for materialism, it is possible to wonder whether the British nation did not, for the duration of the war from the Fall of France, swap its customary pattern of misgovernment for an equal and opposite one. This was for some time not unwelcome, despite its grave shortcomings. Putting up with things had become a virtue, and for many people many of the earlier frustrations of life had been suspended, even if fresh and heavier ones had replaced them. Above all the nation, so long starved of that vital element in good government, drama, was now given its fill of it, under the guidance of a master impresario. That at least was a change from the yoke of Whitehall, which reacts to a touch of drama as it would react to a smell of drains.

The course of government in wartime has been studied and documented, far more carefully and fully than in peace, in a series of official histories, and in many other publications. Fascinating and illuminating as the story is, its relevance to our main theme is tangential, and to seek to do justice to it here would take more space than can be found. Only one main point for further reflection can be raised. Given that the regular Civil Service is based on the concepts that a good administrator learns by experience rather than by formal training, and that knowledge of the accumulated expertise and ways of Whitehall is a decisive asset for him, why was it that so many of the senior career civil servants showed up so indifferently, and that so many of the hastily inducted temporary Principals had to be promoted so high so quickly to fill the key posts in so many of the Departments on whom it mainly rested whether the war was won or lost? There seems to be something here which does not quite add up.

CHAPTER 16

Post-war Reconstruction

Britain irritably awakened again, at the end of yet another world war which British intelligence and British strength might have prevented, to find herself more nearly bankrupt and powerless than at any time for nearly three centuries. The sovereign electorate, having pondered these matters in its air raid shelters, in the queues and the black-out, and in the farflung canteens of the armed forces, dramatically ousted the final Churchillian instar of the Conservative-dominated National Government which had held office since 1931 and presented Labour with a majority in the House of Commons of no less than 146. The new administration, headed (after some slight discussion) by Clement Attlee, started less as a new management than as a receivership, virtually bankrupt after the early ending of American Lease-Lend, following victory in World War II in August 1945. Exhausted and sorry for itself, plunged into anti-climax, stripped of financial reserves and resources, industrially deployed in a posture irrelevant to post-war needs, the nation found itself fettered and depressed by the necessity for continued rationing and restrictions of many kinds. The irresponsible behavior of a small minority of influential ostriches, who could see no problem that could not be readily solved by an immediate return to the free-and-easy ways of the Edwardian period, did nothing to ease the immense difficulties of the first stages of reconstruction and recovery. On the whole, considering how crippling these were, they were ably and effectively handled, although at the cost of immense strain on individuals. The bitterest loss of these times was the collapse and death, aged sixty, of J. M. Keynes, one of those great Englishmen who, except in the war, had never been allowed to render the full service which he could and should have given to his countrymen in guiding Britain into the modern world.

While the excellence of the manpower policy in World War II, and the restraint of generals, had ensured that men of key importance for reconstruction were not slaughtered indiscriminately as in World War I, most of the senior men were stale and tired, and most of the younger men lacked training, experience, status and personal incentive to pitch in vigorously to the tasks ahead. The widespread recognition of the need to overtake the countless arrears and neglects of the locust years before 1939 was neutralized by lack of knowledge and understanding about the goal to be aimed at or how to attain it, and by the shortage of resources, and hampering restrictions which discouraged personal initiative. It was noticeable that much more and better preparation had been made for such social objectives as the National Health Service, unemployment insurance, housing and, at last, education, than for most of the urgent tasks of economic reconstruction and redeployment, to pay for these expensive improvements. As immediate transitional jobs were accomplished, the national sense of frustration, and the lack of adequate thought and preparation, gave rise to a brisk and senseless outburst of the less creditable expressions of party politics, both inter-party and intra-party.

It was probably inevitable that political clashes should have built up after the prolonged artificial truce of wartime. The regrettable feature was that the motivation and terms of these clashes so largely focused not on Britain's future but on the dead past. The more thoughtful conservatives, who joined with R. A. Butler in working out plans for a more worthy future, were mistrusted and hampered by hard-line true-blues who saw no reason for thinking themselves, or for permitting others to do so. Their counterparts on the left, unable to forget or forgive 1926 and 1931, sought to use the power of the state as a political instrument to uplift and reward their own supporters and to level down to the average anyone who had risen above it, in preference to working for the advancement of the nation as a whole. The Liberals as a Parliamentary party had now outlived nearly all their champions of high national standing but, profiting from the substantial scattered host of former adherents, and of recruits disgusted by other parties, they continued to claim their historic role in national politics, despite the suspicion that they were dead but would not lie down. Thus in an attenuated and debased form, the muddle and distortion imposed on British politics by Gladstone and Disraeli was revived to play out its last act during the two decades following World War II. The unimpressiveness as a national formative leader of Attlee, coupled with the romantically anachronistic last fling of Winston Churchill, ensured that, once again, the eyes of the British nation would be distracted from the contemporary ball and that others would dominate the game.

Thus countenanced, the Treasury and its acolytes, which had been in almost total eclipse during the war, re-emerged and set to work to rebuild a neo-Gladstonian administrative mechanism of government according to its heart's desire, and it was not prevented. As Professor Pollard well summarizes the defeat of the government's intention to develop economic planning:

> The Treasury found it easy to assert its former authority by concentrating all power in the financial and fiscal weapons of control. The cheap money policy was maintained with less force, and doubt about its future was by itself likely to send up long-term rates. The budget became increasingly the main instrument of control and 'the Economic Surveys became annually less ambitious. The "targets" of 1947 and 1948 became the "estimates" of 1949; in 1950 and 1951 the estimates became less detailed and more cautious; by 1952 they had almost disappeared.' [The quotation he makes is from A. J. Youngson, *The British Economy 1920–1957*.]
>
> With weak co-ordination, divided counsel and uncertain aim, the Government's post-war economic policy could not be said to have been a successful demonstration of the benefits of economic planning. But the picture drawn by some critics of a bureaucracy-ridden, atrophied planned economy, waiting with bated breath for a dash to economic freedom, bore little semblance to reality. In fact, the period 1945–1950 was essentially one in which, despite the colour of the Government, wartime controls were dismantled as fast as the highly vulnerable external position of the country and the need to preserve full employment would permit.

The fact was, as has abundantly been confirmed since, that it is idle to speak of economic planning in Britain so long as the Treasury remains with the kind of authority which it insists upon exercising, and with the kind of minds which it attracts, and believes in entrusting with power.

Between the upper millstone of partisan politics and the nether millstone of backward-looking departmental ambitions, many of the promising ideas and reconstruction plans which had blossomed under the encouragement given in wartime were crushed out of existence. A conspicuous casualty was the imaginative and far-seeing structure for town and country planning, developed under the inspiration of Patrick

Abercrombie and others, and with the forceful backing of Lord Reith. Political resistance proved too strong. It was aided by the unfailing instinct of Whitehall to co-operate wholeheartedly, at least when it is a question of making life unbearable for a new Department. After a brief and not particularly glorious struggle the Ministry of Town and Country Planning was swallowed up in that protean monster which currently goes under the name of Ministry of Housing and Local Government. The same fate befell the National Parks Commission, which has enjoyed the curious experience of being compulsorily regurgitated by the Department, at the behest of the Prime Minister in 1964, only to be gobbled up again in 1967, on the demise of the even shorter-lived Ministry of Land and Natural Resources.

This interplay of distaste for new ideas, Departmental jealousies and conservatism; political prejudice against assumption of almost any new function by government; and Whitehall's capacity to do any new imaginative task so badly that it is clearly not worth continuing, can be seen functioning with systematic regularity, and most frequently with success, over the whole of the past half-century. The Cabinet proposes, but Whitehall disposes, and the disposal bin is capacious.

Certain types of innovation and measures of reconstruction get done in Britain early and well, others only after long delay and often in an emasculated form, others make no headway at all decade after decade. This peculiarly selective pattern is often supposed to be fortuitous, but that is a misconception. It is enduring and systematic, as analysis of its results shows. It operates through built-in blocks either in the administrative or the political levels of the System, the most effective being those administrative blocks which are more or less duplicated by an unrelated political block, acting for quite different reasons but having a decisively reinforcing result. For example, the block against relaxing puritanical restrictions on activities to be permitted on Sundays has been almost entirely political, based on a fanatical religious minority view, enforced through political pressures, and has had no serious administrative support. On the other hand, the block against any serious move towards economic planning has been mainly administrative, and has continued with unabated rigor even after all political parties have learned better. The blocks against abolishing capital punishment, and against restraining inflationary rises in wages and prices, were both administrative and political, but once the political balance changed decisively the administrative resistances could be overruled, because politicians and the public were so deeply and personally interested.

In only a small minority of cases does the impulse and concept for a reform originate in one of the political parties, or in Parliament, or in the Civil Service. Their role tends to be one of strangling at birth many projects good, bad and indifferent, testing the viability and support of others by keeping them in suspense for longish periods, and giving a green light, and even practical assistance, to others which chime in acceptably with current Whitehall and Westminster views of timeliness and promise. Conversely, the number of proposals which are dropped, through either general lack of interest or broad and convinced objection, may not be as great as the category of those at least potentially acceptable to the majority but vetoed by a resolute minority.

The civil servant destined for promotion is he who can instantly recognize an OUT suggestion whenever it comes his way, and can preserve and consummate its OUT status through whatever processes and ramifications it may need to pass in order to satisfy public or Parliamentary opinion, or to silence its initiators. The flaw is that OUT suggestions include not only those which on merits would be rejected by any competent administration as half-baked and unworkable, but also a number which would be found acceptable and practical by administrators in Paris, Washington and Stockholm, but which are OUT in Whitehall on grounds peculiar to itself, and to the outlook and prejudices of those who run the machine.

One of the most important categories affected by this process in modern times is that of alternative models for performing public services, other than in Civil Service terms. In Britain, unhappily, the technical and managerial argument how necessary public service agencies are best structured, staffed and operated has been hopelessly mixed up and bedeviled with political arguments about nationalization and about extensions of state control. These conflicts derive on one side from passionate commitment to, and on the other from lack of confidence in, or downright hostility to free enterprise. In glaring contradiction to the allegedly pragmatic and commonsense bent of British leadership the issue has been clouded by interminable, tedious and half-baked theoretical vaporings on both sides, in preference to practical test and experiment. By chance, however, and largely for the wrong reasons, the Attlee administration was launched with the power and authority and also with the consensus among its supporters to undertake a massive transfer of economic functions to newly-created, more or less autonomous public concerns. Some of these were formed at the expense not only of privately-owned utilities (including the Bank of England) but of municipal socialism, especially in the fields of transport, gas and electricity, and the hospital services. The program of nationalization, starting with the Bank of England, coal mines, and national health services in 1946, extended by 1948 to include also railways, electricity distribution and gas. For all these, informed non-party opinion had found a good case. This basis of consent did not, however, exist for the unwise extension of nationalization to iron and steel in 1949, which was dictated predominantly by party political pressure, against the better judgment of senior Ministers. The British Overseas Airways Corporation, although technically established in 1939 by the Chamberlain administration, was in effect a post-war development, and was complemented on the shorter hauls by British European Airways. Cable and Wireless Ltd., although remaining an ordinary company, was acquired by the UK government in 1947 and a Colonial (now Commonwealth) Development Corporation was created in 1948. Others were to follow, among which the United Kingdom Atomic Energy Authority (1954) and the British Airports Authority (1965) were significant as representing transfers wholly from Departments to a public concern of the modern type.

It is an astonishing commentary on the workings of misgovernment that, despite the output of verbiage to which these and related changes gave rise, and the real and substantial advance which they formed, at no time was there any authoritative and coherent attempt to study, digest and formulate any body of principles and experience as an authoritative guide for the nation to the appropriate division of function and the preferable basis of organization as between conventional government departments and the various modern alternatives which had been developed. It has all been done by groping through a fog, and one must go back through the fog to find out why. The fog is composed of two blended vapors, of which the more acrid and strongly colored is political, but the more blinding is administrative. In the chronic confusion of British politics, the men who understood the need for and the means of creating efficient public concerns were largely managers and technologists, to whom no one listened, or members of the Conservative and Liberal parties who were heavily out-numbered and talked down by their more politically-minded brethren. The Labour Party, which politically would have preferred some syndicalist or Marxist pattern, alone had the steam within it to adopt and implement, not always straightforwardly or adroitly, the ideas of the frustrated technocrats. The record of the Civil Service in thinking out the great underlying issues and in developing the significant new patterns is extraordinarily thin. The bulk of what is in the statutes, as well as the techniques of management and other elements which have made success possible, are known to have been supplied from elsewhere.

A number of these new bodies—the United Kingdom Atomic Energy Authority, the British Electricity Authority, the Gas Council, the National Coal Board, and British European Airways for example —have in many respects achieved records of performance which are by world standards good, and in some aspects outstanding. In the case of the railways it is clear that failure to unify the system after World War I, as was clearly necessary and was definitely contemplated until party politics dictated otherwise, led to crippling handicaps for the eventual nationalized concern. It was launched far too late to command the services of the leading railwaymen of high caliber, who were still available in the 'twenties, and inherited a run-down, shabby, demoralized batch of obsolescent or obsolete assets, at a time of immense difficulty for reconstruction. Nevertheless, compared with the German, French, Japanese and other war-worn systems, the management of British Railways was painfully slow off the mark and ineffective in the planning and execution of the necessary program, which has even now only belatedly and partially achieved what had been seen to be needed nearly half a century ago. One has only to compare the caliber of the Polytechnicians imported to reconstruct the French railway system with the education and training of their British opposite numbers to find the explanation. The contrast, in timing and development, with electricity is also instructive.

Had even half the economic reconstruction which was pushed through without undue difficulty during 1946–49 been done, as it should have been, in 1919–22, modern British history would have been very different, and many sufferings and humiliations could have been avoided. One of the most striking recurrent themes of the British system of misgovernment is its capacity to make mountains out of molehills, and to spend decades in messing about and failing to do things which, when they can be postponed no longer, get done with no great trouble in a matter of weeks, or at most months. Probably something of the order of 90 percent of the difficulties which have been solemnly explained to the British public as preventing or delaying measures of reconstruction during the past century have been sham difficulties, which could readily have been surmounted had the electorate insisted on replacing those who thought them up by more competent or less ill-disposed successors. The public should learn to ask quite toughly not only what is the difficulty but who is the difficulty.

One lesson which Britain had entirely failed to learn from the Crimean War, the Boer War and World War I, but took pretty much to heart from World War II, was the vital importance for Britain's future of much more and better education and training, especially in science and technology, accompanied by a growing and better integrated effort in research. The English had long believed deeply in the value of training, for horses. The alien, theoretical, and ungentlemanly suggestion of the Prince Consort, in the mid-nineteenth century, that they should also try applying it to themselves was firmly rejected in ruling circles at the time. But, after reflecting at intervals over the next hundred years on the inconvenience of competing and struggling with foreigners unsporting enough to take the other view, they began reluctantly and confusedly in the mid-twentieth century to accept that there must be something in it after all.

Under the wartime coalition government, R. A. Butler's Education Act of 1944 had recognized public responsibility for enabling every child to have the education appropriate to his age, aptitude and ability, and had reorganized state-aided education into primary, secondary and further stages, with a lowest permissible school-leaving age of fifteen. Once this came to be implemented it was clear that the cost would increase by a process which was only later identified as escalation. Fortunately the initial post-war stages fell into good hands, and the risk that realization of this cost would lead to a cancellation or crippling of the program was averted. One of the most significant and successful achievements of the new Ministry was to bring together a joint working party of architects, builders, teachers, educationists and administrators to design and arrange for production of largely prefabricated new school buildings, of the highest possible standard and at the lowest possible cost. By this simple device, counter to all the conventional principles and practices of Whitehall, British school design and construction achieved a leading position in Europe. The human material was unhappily more intractable, and less easily upgraded. Large numbers of teachers had had only a most inadequate, substandard, non-university training before returning to run the same schools in the same areas of which they were often themselves recent products. Any encouragement of graduate entry by differential salaries met strong and blind resistance, and this for a time largely nullified attempts to expand and improve, in particular, school teaching of science. As a body, the molders of the new generation proved hardly less bigoted and backward-looking regarding their own interests than the manual workers. Only after years of pressure and persuasion was the new approach given a chance. Here, government was on the whole, under all administrations, on the side of the angels, but the handling of the problem was not always inspired, and progress was disappointingly slow.

Total expenditure on education, at constant prices, had risen from an index of 76 in 1937–39 to 83 in 1946, and 122 in 1959, and by former standards educational expenditure was quite generously increased in the 1950s and 1960s. But arrears from past neglect were so immense, increases in the school population so rapid and acceptable minimum standards so much higher that performance in relation to need remained poor.

Education, in Britain, tends to be looked at rather as a specialist activity than as one of the most essential elements in the main-stream of national life, and is therefore rarely viewed in perspective with full regard to its peculiar heritage from the past, its vast future potential and its many implications, for example for the study of government. The importance of the past as a shadow over the present can readily be seen by comparing the Scottish system with the very different one in England. In Scotland the Presbyterian tradition derived from Knox, like the Lutheran tradition in Germany and neighboring lands, strongly favored a broad-based education based on opportunity and encouragement, irrespective of income group or social class. Scotland thus found a ready outlet, in England and the Empire, for a large body of almost penniless but relatively well-educated students who became doctors, especially in public health, engineers, administrators, and teachers, for example, while most of the corresponding types in England were denied any such chance until quite recent years. By contrast the Anglican Church, in combination with the tighter class system, imposed, south of the Border, distortions and restrictions so odd and deep that this century will undoubtedly have ended before their influence ceases.

Amateurs among the English gentry formed the main body of pioneers of modern science. It has been calculated that of eminent British scientists born in roughly the first half of the seventeenth century, some two-thirds were educated at Oxford and Cambridge. With creditable public spirit, many of them and their successors attended especially to applying science to practical use. They met such embarrassing success that by the late eighteenth century these applications came to be widely regarded as virtually the whole end of science, which therefore ceased to rate as a fit occupation for a gentleman, who should not lay himself open to the suspicion of being anything else but a classicist. This was the period when the nobly-born and scientifically gifted Smithson decided to cut the loss here, and to bequeath his entire fortune for promoting American science, as he most successfully did, by founding the Smithsonian Institution in Washington. He did not feel it necessary before reaching this momentous decision actually to visit North America: to have got to know what went on in England was enough. When Thomas Arnold set out in the 'thirties and 'forties of the nineteenth century to educate the sons of the middle classes into model Christian gentlemen he could therefore hardly do otherwise than follow this anti-scientific trend, which his astonishing success managed, as we have seen, to fasten firmly on the Civil Service and other vital areas of national life to this day.

Meanwhile the odd doctrine sprang up that while, in the words of the Bishop of London in 1803, "it is safest for both the Government and the religion of the country to let the lower classes remain in that state of ignorance in which nature has originally placed them", an exception might safely be made for teaching them science, which might help them to do their work better.

In principle, therefore, through much of the nineteenth century the ruling classes in England wanted their own children to be taught nothing about science, but were quite favorable in theory to the workers learning it. As however the financial and other provision made for this was negligible, little came of it, especially since the manufacturers strongly objected to any teaching of applied science which might trespass on vocational training or lead to discussion of trade secrets. Until as recently as a century ago, religious veto and squabbling between churches, combined with parsimony, prejudice and lack of understanding, held back the provision of even general elementary education. England has thus so far only experienced it for three generations, and secondary education on a national scale only for two. It thus came about that while on the Continent and in America, institutions of the highest status long since took up education and research in technology, in Britain the task was left largely to a Cinderella movement of non-conformist-backed evening schools, polytechnics and a few new university colleges, whose efforts were statistically a drop in the bucket, and, owing to financial starvation, were in many cases qualitatively unsatisfactory as well.

Almost throughout the past century a triple split has developed in British higher education between those, overwhelmingly dominant in the public schools and most of the universities, who wished to see science and technology admitted, if at all, as not more than an inferior adjunct to education in the arts; those who wished to secure much more and better higher education and research in technology by upgrading the existing technical colleges and other non-university institutions; and those who pressed for a showdown within the university world, and insisted on the need for new technological universities at the highest post-graduate level. Oddly enough, in their last years, this last was the one subject on which there was full agreement in principle between Sir Henry Tizard and F. A. Lindemann (Lord Cherwell). This was undoubtedly due to their both having been compelled to go to Germany for their own post-graduate studies because Oxford could not supply the need.

This ostensibly academic argument, with its deep class and religious roots, came to a head, rather astonishingly, only in the early second half of the twentieth century when it afforded the extraordinary spectacle of one top body, the Advisory Council on Scientific Policy, advising the Lord President in one sense while another, the National Advisory Council on Education for Industry and Commerce, was advising the Ministry of Education in the other. No one, ostensibly, was advising the government to maintain the arts hegemony as it then stood, but both university and Civil Service opinion leaned strongly in that direction. In principle, neither the Advisory Council nor the National Advisory Council was wrong, nor were the developments they favored really incompatible, as the partial fulfillment of both has since demonstrated. The argument was rather about priorities and tactics, and about the best means of reversing quickly the low status of science, and especially of technology, in the established peck-order within the British academic chicken-run. In substance both battles have been won, not so much on merits as because the Russian sputniks and inter-continental ballistic missiles brought, at the critical moment, strong reinforcement to those who considered it unwise to embark upon a second century of gross neglect of technology by a technological nation in a technological age.

The grossly overrated British educational system, with its built-in distortions, tabus, inhibitions and blind spots, its undertrained and miscellaneous army of overburdened and often underpaid teachers, its frequently obsolete buildings and its unscientific and backward-looking approach to the great problems of the learning process, has thus found itself flung at last into the central arena of national contro-versy. No longer the largely irrelevant rights and privileges of reli-gious minority schools but the real choices between different types of school, as a way of bringing up different types of citizen who will form a different type of Britain, are becoming the focus of controversy. Even if this controversy could be conducted with a clean slate, the choice would be intensely difficult. The questions how to multiply quality, and how to preserve the best from the past, give it agonizing overtones, but at least the long-postponed debate is at last getting un-derway.

Education hitherto has been one of the chief examples of the pecu-liar English theory that something can be "kept outside politics" by putting a discreet political veto on its evolution in certain directions, by rigging matters so that effective ultimate supervision and control is in the hands of holders of a particular but cryptic political attitude, and by discouraging inquiry and discussion about it as much as pos-sible. We are now at the stage where a somewhat half-baked collection of new ideas is locked in conflict with older traditions, and where the size of public funds centrally committed has become so great that, coupled with the growing public interest and concern, it must inev-itably make education a central issue in politics for a long time to come. This is healthy and constructive, because the recasting of educa-tion is inseparably entangled with the necessary recasting of govern-ment and of so many other parts of the national social and economic system. The new generation which has emerged from the schools and universities and technical colleges since 1950 is already becoming a force in national evolution of quite a new type. The current plowing back into the educational world of most of its brightest products is a particularly encouraging feature, even though the nature and structure of the education provided still leaves so much to be desired.

The character of Parliament is already being much altered by this new stream, and the same is true of industry and commerce, and many especially of the newer professions. Only Whitehall, so far, remains largely unaffected, but Whitehall is now doubly outflanked, both by finding itself the last first-class stronghold of demand on the general pool Oxbridge-type Arts graduate without higher degree or professional qualification, and by the fact that so many of its recruits still have to be drawn from the diminishing Oxbridge fraction of the educated population, in default of willing takers from other quarters. Even if reasons of misgovernment did not urgently call for drastic change, the writing is therefore on the wall for the present type of Administrative Class of the Civil Service, and for its already diluted priesthood in the Treasury. The moral and intellectual sanction for regarding this kind of academic product as a defensible basis for a governing élite has melted away.

Indeed one of the most remarkable events of the past twenty years in Britain, as G. K. Chesterton would have put it, has been the reconstruction of the machinery of government which never occurred. All the way from Calais to Vladivostok and on to Tokyo we travel through lands whose professional administration has been thoroughly, and in many cases fundamentally, remolded since 1945. In Washington, too, there have been great changes. Only in London could some new Rip van Winkle, awakened from twenty years of slumber, return to his desk in the Treasury, the Board of Trade or the Home Office and find the old place itself not changed, although the nature of the problems in his in-tray would no doubt give him a shock.

In no field are this stability and its results more clearly visible than in the management of the national economy. The evident aim of the Treasury, readily traceable since 1951, has been to return as nearly as practicable to the pre-war set-up completed by Sir Warren Fisher forty years ago. That was where the Treasury had for many decades wanted to get to, and it was to that, with the return of Conservative rule in 1951, that they sought to get back. A younger Churchill would have soon dealt with such an ambition, since as we have seen he now knew too much. Unfortunately, being old and unwell, and unable to command the help of Sir John Anderson and others whom he sought to enlist in the task, he had to give up and let the Treasury have its way.

It would require a whole book to itself to trace even in outline the complex and subtle effects of the structure and practice of central government upon the chronic and often acute difficulties of the British economy in the 'fifties and its emergence as a grave world problem in the 'sixties. In modern conditions the adaptation and strategic management of an economy is inevitably the responsibility of the government concerned. If the economy does not succeed, and, above all, if it drifts out of control or undergoes violent and unexpected crises, the finger points to failures and weaknesses in government. It may be also that industry is efficient, or that workers are not working well enough, or that the economic or political climate is unfavorable, but none of these or similar factors can be accepted as an alibi for government. The contention, which was so widely relied on in the 'twenties, that it is not desirable or practicable for governments so to manage the economy that the fruits of steadily advancing knowledge can be won in steadily advancing standards of life, has long been disproved, not only in theory but by the practice of numerous other countries. If such advances do not happen, government is responsible to an overwhelming degree, and the key is usually to be found in professional administrative incapacity, in political backwardness and ineptitude, or in a basic insincerity of purpose which purports to will the end but refuses to will the means necessary to achieve it. In Britain all three of these factors have been traceable, but the third, perhaps, has been the most pervasive and the most disastrous. It is indeed the equivalent in British government to British hypocrisy in British morals. At the time of writing the ill-starred Ombudsman is the latest human sacrifice to it.

Since to restate what occurred on the surface would not be very enlightening, it may be more helpful to illustrate some of the basic governmental failures in relation to economic planning by a comparison with a more tangible and limited wartime example. In World War II, as head of Allocation of Tonnage in the Ministry of War Transport, I was responsible to the Anglo-American Combined Shipping Adjustment Board (jointly with my American colleagues) for advising on the potentialities and limitations of dry cargo shipping in relation to wartime requirements, and for preparing and implementing the necessary programs to fulfill these requirements so far as practicable. These programs were, during the latter part of the war, agreed at the high-level Conferences, such as Cairo, Quebec and Yalta, sometimes only during an all-night sitting at the very end. Before the Conference met the other Combined Boards and civil authorities had submitted their requirements to the shipping authorities, which had fully discussed them with the applicants and in many cases reduced them to realistic levels. These discussions usually revealed that there was an inflation in the requirements, not only in order to add margins as an insurance against possible cuts, and to try to fasten upon shipping shortage the responsibility for inadequacies of any kind, but also because there was over-optimism regarding dates when cargo would be ready or when recipients would be ready to use it. Only when this inflation was, so far as practicable, squeezed out of the figures, was it possible to strike a true balance between the prospective carrying capacity of the allied merchant fleets and the quantities, origins, destinations and timings of the world-wide cargo programs. It then usually emerged that on paper there was still some deficit to be faced, but, in the light of operating experience of delays and changes of plan on the supply side, the shipping authorities usually accepted this difference as being "not unmanageable". This system was made to work and to maintain the flow of military and civil supplies, by a series of essential measures. Among these, the first was universal acceptance that physical considerations should prevail over financial, and thus that the Treasury should not be permitted to dictate any course involving a waste of shipping resources. This had been so plainly laid down that it never needed to be argued. The second was that the entire management responsibility for programing and meeting requirements on shipping should rest with the civil shipping authorities—a principle which was asserted with increasing effectiveness in face of attempted encroachment by Lindemann in London and by the admirals and some of the generals in Washington. The third was the combination, at one point within the organization, of responsibility for intelligence, planning and strategic supervision of operations. Early in the war, under the original regular Civil Service structure, these functions were divided, with the result that shipping intelligence came in from an evacuated branch at the back end of Lancashire so belatedly and in such an unwieldy form that its value was little more than historical, while the calculation of carrying capacity and prospective imports and deliveries were entrusted entirely to actuaries and statisticians whose superb technical competence within their own field could not overcome the error imported by numerous variables and uncertainties outside their ken, in the processes of shipping operations within a daily changing context.

Before a mature pattern was developed, forecasts were going as badly astray as recently over the British economy. This was eventually remedied late in the war only by a series of adjustments and adaptations. Among the most important of these were intensive briefing of, and constant liaison with, all the main users, through officers able to speak their own language and to win their full confidence; the devising of a system of rapid intelligence rapidly analyzed and made instantly available at the point of control of allocations; and the enforcement of day-to-day priority adjustments in order to ensure that no accident or setback could have repercussions on programs of the highest urgency, while other programs were so managed that the overall result over the period was attained more opportunistically, with fluctuations according to tonnage supply, to port and other conditions and to rises or falls in pressure of need.

Thus the objectives and policies were plainly laid down at regular and fairly frequent intervals from the highest level, and were expressed in approved programs. The management and realization of these programs by the immediately responsible officers was subject to no further interference, provided that the job was done.

Soon after the war it became apparent that no account whatever of wartime experience was to be taken by the Treasury, who indeed through the mercy of Providence to Britain had had almost nothing to do with the conduct of the war. Contrary principles were not followed in almost every instance. The frequent systematic, technical and operational adjustments, by which a number of the more important high-level wartime decisions had been subsequently caused, against all probability, to come out right in the end, were evidently not appreciated at the center of the Whitehall machine. Here it was fondly supposed, by both politicians and high administrators, that a fiat hastily prepared and issued with a minimum of consultation through hierarchical channels to a series of agencies without any real grasp of what was meant or sought, but with a profound knowledge of numerous reasons why it must be impracticable, would be a feasible means of embarking on economic planning. If it proved a fiasco, the mourning at the top of the Civil Service would be exceedingly brief. This was the situation when the long-awaited change of government in 1951 gave ministerial approval to the anachronistic conclusion that Britain should not and need not plan.

Confused and conflicting as the direction of the national economy had been during the immediate post-war years, it could have offered a basis for development of more successful subsequent planning, on the part of a resolute and open-minded government served by a professionally competent machine. As, unfortunately, neither of these conditions were satisfied the modest impetus achieved with so much effort was allowed to run down. Figures compiled for the Economic Survey of Europe show that during 1947–50 the United Kingdom increase of 29 percent in industrial production much exceeded that of Sweden and Belgium, and was slightly more than that of Italy and Denmark, but rather less than that of France and Norway, which reached 31 percent. During 1950–56, however, the British percentage increase slipped back to 21, while Sweden rose 10 points to 27, France 18 points to 49, Belgium 23 points to 36, and Italy more than doubled its increase to 63; Germany, a unique case, actually doubled total production, in these years of European recovery from which the British government had opted out. Even worse was to follow during 1957–59, as the Common Market got into its stride. British industrial production increased by only 17 percent while French rose by 51, German by 53 and Italian by 46. Trends in productivity followed a similar course. Far from lamenting the disastrous state of economic inferiority into which it had led the country, the government, under Prime Minister Harold Macmillan, basked in complacency matched only by that of Stanley Baldwin in the corresponding inter-war fool's paradise over defense. Relying, as he confessed with Baldwinian candor, on "last year's Bradshaw", the Prime Minister told his countrymen: "You never had it so good!" The fact that he claimed at the same time to be a planner stands as an index of the political confusion and impracticality of the 'fifties.

Just as inter-war British government had left it to the German *Wehrmacht* to make rings round them with tank designs and strategy and tactics borrowed from neglected British pioneers, so after 1950 France went right ahead with the aid of planning concepts and methods largely originating in, but discarded by, Britain. The main architect of the French plan, Jean Monnet, had worked throughout the war in the inter-allied planning organization, and such devices as the short-lived working parties set up for seventeen industries during 1946–48 served as partial prototypes for the far-reaching mechanism of consultation with industry on which the success of the French planning was based.

Countless words have been written on the relatively poor economic performance of Britain since 1951, and on where the blame for it lies. While many alternative explanations are possible one central feature stands out. Up to 1951, the government was, however gropingly and feebly, directing the economy on a coherent course towards expanding production, and production was expanding at least as fast as that of most comparable European countries. After 1951, government policy was reversed, direction was dismantled and for a decade Britain consistently lost ground. Clearly this could not go on indefinitely and in July 1961 the Chancellor of the Exchequer, then struggling with the unpopular burden of what became known as the Selwyn Lloyd freeze, uttered some critical comments on the inadequacy of the "various bodies" on whom the Conservative government had for years doggedly persisted upon relying:

> I say frankly to the House that I want something more purposeful than that. I envisage a joint examination of the economic prospects of the country stretching five or more years into the future. It would cover the growth of national production and distribution of our resources between the main uses, consumption, government expenditure, investment and so on. Above all it would try to establish what are the essential conditions for realising potential growth.

This sickness in the economy thus drove Selwyn Lloyd just beyond the point reached by his Conservative predecessor Balfour thirty-six years earlier, during which every step taken in this direction had invariably been reversed and eventually abandoned by some succeeding British government.

The pattern was not to be long in repeating itself. The moribund Economic Planning Board and the new Council on Prices, Productivity and Incomes were quietly dispatched, and a National Economic Development Council was formed early in 1962. It quickly became known to its many intimates as Neddy, and acquired a talented staff, but its terms of reference omitted those matters vital to the health of the economy but potentially embarrassing either to the government or to the trade unions.

As an acute foreign observer remarked (Hans Daalder in *Cabinet Reform in Britain,* p. 234):

> the first conversations between the Chancellor and the two sides of industry (on 22 and 23 August, 1961) were held on the thirtieth anniversary of the debacle of Ramsay Macdonald's Labour Government, which, if anything, had excelled in improvising machinery for economic policy.

Moreover, as Daalder pointed out, shortly afterwards there were other features "warranting a somewhat pessimistic outlook". The Chancellor's role as chairman of NEDC and as head of the Treasury was anomalous. "No difficulties need occur on that score if prevailing opinions in the Treasury and the new Council are virtually identical. Things will run equally smoothly as long as the NEDC is willing to function mainly as a passive sounding-board for the Chancellor in power. Neither assumption seems realistic, however." What would happen if the Chancellor could not steer the Council's thoughts in ways congenial to him and the Treasury? If they disagreed, could he publish reports in effect critical of Treasury policy? Would not government Departments be profoundly skeptical and unco-operative? Had the staff sufficient authority, as non-civil servants, to extract all the necessary information? If, as seemed likely, the Council alone should employ more high-class economists than the government as a whole, "The Treasury is not likely to look favorably on any sign of the (presumably highly competent) NEDC staff's becoming an effective alternative source of economic advice."

These and other decisive weaknesses were plainly visible at the outset to an observer in the Netherlands, but they were evidently too subtle, or perhaps too embarrassing, to be grasped in Whitehall and in Downing Street. Neddy's growth target of 4 percent per annum diverged sharply from the Treasury view of a maximum 2–2½ percent. In the Douglas-Home administration, a window-dressing change was made by renaming the President of the Board of Trade the Secretary of State for Industry, Trade and Regional Development, but the moment of truth was approaching, and with the crisis of 1964–66 the jerry-built features of the new economic policy structure made its collapse inevitable.

All kinds of excuses and interpretations were produced, but no one in Whitehall or Downing Street seemed aware that the exact nature of the inevitable breakdown could have been and was forecast, even by a foreign observer, simply on the basis of the experience of the Economic Advisory Council of 1930 and the Economic Planning Board of 1947.

Owing to the scrupulously repetitive nature of the British system of misgovernment, students can identify with a high degree of precision which dishonest and shoddy expedient will be revived in which types of political or economic stress, and how it will break down. The most important persons to whom this wisdom is not vouchsafed are those who operate the System, to whom its consequences come always as fresh surprises. It is not really necessary, in the circumstances, to do more than merely note that the Treasury did not fail to produce with a flourish of trumpets in 1962 a far-reaching scheme of reorganization which left its role and its competence to perform it essentially as they had been before. Daalder concluded in 1963 that "only time will tell whether the traditional role of the Treasury and the new approaches to economic planning and modernisation will be compatible." Time has told.

CHAPTER 17

The Imperial Legacy

During the 1950s and 1960s it was not only the economic, administrative and educational chickens which showed an urge to come home to roost in Britain; the imperialist chickens were even more clamorous. By a quirk which would have seemed odd anywhere else, the Treasury signaled this event at the end of the 1940s by insisting, in a rare burst of generosity, on providing a magnificent new headquarters for the Colonial Office, facing Westminster Abbey. On planning and amenity grounds a government Department at this point would have been even more disastrous than the ill-sited new Juxon House marring the façade of St. Paul's. Fortunately, Whitehall being what it is, the colonies were lost before any start was made on the building whose site remains to this day more elegantly and acceptably laid out as a large hole in the ground.

That the colonies should have become self-governing was, and in principle had long been widely recognized to be, desirable and inevitable. During the inter-war years and afterwards much devoted and fruitful work in that direction had been done by British colonial administrators, by a number of political leaders and by many others, including professional men and scientists, among whom the founders and sustainers of new universities, such as Sir Alexander Carr-Saunders, rendered outstanding service. Unfortunately this fine record was distorted and often marred by reincarnations of the men who caused the Boston tea-party, whose niggling, reactionary and ungenerous attitudes gave a wrong impression that Britain looked with an ill grace on the natural consequences for the colonies of exposure to British ideas and British ways of life. In too many cases armed revolt was required before the authorities in Westminster and in Whitehall became reconciled to the necessity for granting self-government. The serving of terms of British imprisonment by several of those who were afterwards to become official national leaders was perhaps in a different class, since it proved an immense political asset to those who had undergone that preparation for the summit, and a serious handicap to those who had missed it.

In the process of disbanding the colonial Empire the muddled thinking which had led us there in the first place was given new prominence. In which areas were there significant British interests? What were these interests, and to what extent, if at all, did they depend upon continuing British rule or on British military presence? What costs were involved for Britain in overseas expenditure and in overheads at home, and what was the benefit/cost ratio for Britain of the system in each of the territories to which it applied? What were the implications of a continuing Imperial role in indirect terms, throughout a world which increasingly disapproved of imperialism? These and other obvious questions were neither asked nor answered by the framers of British policy. Many British lives, much British money and property and vast amounts of goodwill, prestige and other intangible assets were squandered through the refusal to take realistic views based on a sound political, economic and military appreciation.

It is fortunately unnecessary to cover the ground in any detail, as this task has just been admirably performed by Christopher Mayhew MP in *Britain's Role To-morrow,* with the analysis and conclusions of which I am in full agreement. As Minister of Defence of the Navy until his resignation over a major policy disagreement in 1966 he is fully informed.

Mayhew shows that "In 1938 when we ruled a great empire, and were in the front rank of great powers, the foreign exchange cost of our public expenditure overseas *of all kinds* was no more than £16 million." Defense estimates for 1966–67 show that *on defense alone* net foreign exchange expenditure is now running at £239 million ($669 million) annually. "This is almost equal by itself to our average balance of payments deficit over the last five years. We need look no further to understand why the pound has been weaker in recent years than the deutschmark or the franc." Mayhew estimates that withdrawal from the Persian Gulf, Malaysia and Singapore would save at least £300 million a year from 1969–70 onwards, of which at least £100 million would be a saving in foreign exchange.

One of the systematic extravagances built into recent imperial defense policy has been the habit of building up immensely costly bases and stocks, in precarious situations, where it is necessary successively to cut the loss on them. As Mayhew stresses:

> when the time for withdrawal arrives, perhaps quite suddenly, we find we have spent large sums of money on resources which have never been used.
>
> "This has happened several times before, When we left the Suez base hurriedly, we wasted huge resources, and spent large sums building up in Kenya instead. When we left Kenya hurriedly, we again wasted resources, and spent heavily on alternative facilities in Aden. In 1968, when we leave Aden, we shall again leave valuable facilities behind. Untaught by experience, we are now spending large sums in building up our military presence in the Persian Gulf.

Once again an authoritative witness testifies, not only to the wrongness of British policy and to the gravity of the waste of resources involved, but to the almost incredibly systematic repetition of the same blunders, entirely irrespective of changes of government. Indeed, as he demonstrates, the only solid opposition to the commonsense view which he presents is to be found in "the Labour and Conservative leadership". There is one common source which these two supposedly antagonistic groups have for their views, unshared by their parties at large and by the public, and that is Whitehall. There can be no clearer indication of the way to trace the British system of misgovernment back to its fountainhead.

Ministers themselves have sometimes, perhaps unconsciously, recognized the shortcomings of Whitehall by ignoring the normal channels of the System. The consequences of replacing bad advice, not by good advice, but by no advice, have been disastrous. One example was the pre-war appeasement policy; another, equal in its importance but very different in its nature, was the policy pursued over Nasser's nationalization of the Suez Canal.

Towards the end of July 1956, Egypt nationalized the Suez Canal Company. Britain owned 45 percent of the company's shares and transported three-quarters of her oil supplies through the canal. An immediate Anglo-French reply to Nasser's action was ruled out for military reasons. But the plans for such a reply—Operation Musketeer, as it was called—were ready by August 14 and disembarkment was planned for September 15. Meanwhile, intense diplomatic activity, on the part of the United States in particular, attempted to avert a military clash. In the middle of September, Eden postponed Musketeer when Dulles proposed a scheme for an international Suez Canal Users' Association (SCUA) to operate the Canal. The British and French later decided that the proposal was inadequate and resumed their military plans.

It was hoped that the Israelis would provide an excuse for the implementation of Operation Musketeer, by launching an attack on Egypt. On October 22 and 23, Ben Gurion met the French secretly at Sèvres. The meeting remains something of a mystery to this day, the participants being sworn to secrecy. According to Professor Hugh Thomas, in his recently published *The Suez Affair,* Ben Gurion demanded a written Anglo-French assurance of support before Israel moved, because only Great Britain had the aircraft to maintain a watch over Egyptian airfields. On the evening of October 23 an unnamed British minister (probably Selwyn Lloyd) went to Sèvres and gave the necessary British assurances.

The military activity began on October 29, when the Israelis attacked Egypt. The British and French governments issued an ultimatum to both sides. The House of Commons and the United States Ambassador were informed only *after* it had been issued. Israel, of course, accepted; Egypt refused. On October 31, the ultimatum expired and British bombing and aero-psychological warfare against Egypt was launched. The British landing-force was unable to follow up immediately because the distances involved were too great.

In reply to the British attack, Nasser ordered the blocking of the Canal and Syria blew up three pumping stations on the Iraq pipeline. This was the first time that British oil supplies were threatened. Throughout the previous three months, no ships (other than Israeli) had been denied passage through the Canal.

The United States introduced a cease-fire resolution, with Canada's support, into the Security Council. Britain and France aimed to capture the Canal Zone but, by November 4, Israel had achieved all her objectives. She, therefore, wished to accept the UN cease-fire. The British and French governments dissuaded her.

Hence, on November 5, British paratroops landed at Port Said and, the following day, a naval bombardment began. Shortly afterwards, Port Said surrendered and a British armored column set off for Suez. It was still eighty miles from the Canal when it heard that the government had ordered a cease-fire for midnight.

The reasons for the cease-fire are still somewhat unclear. They were probably diverse: the realization that the Israelis could not be persuaded to fight any longer; fear of Russian intervention; the Prime Minister's health and feelings; strong opposition in Britain; and, perhaps most important of all, the weakness of sterling. Uppermost in Macmillan's mind was a US warning that it would not back an IMF loan to support sterling unless there were a cease-fire.

The immediate results of the Suez Operation were that Israel retired to her former frontiers and the British and French governments gave place to a UN force. The following month, Britain experienced petrol rationing and a balance of payments crisis.

Some of the most bitter controversy over Suez has centered around charges that there was prior collusion between Britain and Israel. The Americans were among those with suspicions. On October 29, Dulles told Eisenhower:

> . . . we must expect British and French intervention. In fact, they appear to be ready for it and may even have concerted their action with the Israelis.

Since 1956, a number of books have been written, making the charges in more detail. Erskine B. Childers in *The Road to Suez* (1962) has listed and weighed the evidence (pp. 225–80). Professor Thomas, whose investigation is certainly the most thorough yet undertaken, strongly confirms the charges, and refers to the denials by Selwyn Lloyd and Eden as "straight-forward lies". In his *Memoirs*, Eden himself avoids comment. Indeed, he never even uses the word "collusion" and completely ignores the charges made against him. But his account suggests that "he had definite foreknowledge of all that occurred from October 16 onward" (Herman Finer: *Dulles over Suez*, 1964, p. 347). The latest piece of evidence is the diary of the Israeli Chief of Staff, General Dayan. At one point, he talks of planning his campaign on the assumption that an Anglo-French attack would take place. A few lines later, however, he talks of "the Anglo-French action which, *we hope,* will indeed take place." (My italics.)

No more conclusive judgment on collusion can be reached until the British government either publishes the documents relating to the crisis or institutes a Parliamentary inquiry. The sovereign electorate has a right to see the evidence and nothing is to be gained by hiding it. The secrecy and mystery surrounding Sèvres has only magnified its importance.

Unfortunately, it is a characteristic feature of the Suez affair that normal democratic and governmental procedures should have been brushed aside. The Suez operation is one of the few, perhaps the only twentieth-century instance of a partisan (as distinct from a bi-partisan, non-partisan or extra-partisan) foreign policy, involving a substantial military adventure. A force was assembled, larger than that under Wellington's command at Waterloo, without the support or even the knowledge of the Opposition. (It should be noted that in France, apart from the Communists, only Mendes-France and Monnet opposed the operation.) Not since 1709 had Britain taken military action on such a scale in face of open disagreement between the leading parties in the nation. In the latter half of 1956 the number of citizens indicated as in disagreement with the British policy over Suez never dropped below 32 percent. A poll taken on November 1–2 indicated that 44 percent disapproved of the military action against Egypt. That war should be gratuitously initiated without consultation and with such a large slice of the sovereign electorate opposed to it appears constitutionally reprehensible. Her Majesty's Opposition, which had the nominal support of 46·4 percent of the voting electorate, was not consulted, in even the most cursory manner, by the government.

Information, as well as consultation, was sadly lacking. Gaitskell did not learn until mid-August of the scale of the forces being assembled, and then only from the Maltese Prime Minister. The flow of information to the Press, and ultimately to the people, almost dried up in late October. The House of Commons was not kept properly abreast of events. Members of the government hinted, as they often do in such circumstances, that the information they were withholding would strengthen their case. On November 8 for example, one member of the Cabinet remarked that the decision to attack had been made "in the full knowledge of all the considerations, a great many of which are not known to honourable Members opposite . . ." On the basis of such facts, an American political scientist, Leon D. Epstein, has written (in *British Politics in the Suez Crisis,* 1964, p. 204):

> There is . . . some doubt about the efficiency of the debating and criticizing function of the British parliamentary process . . . It is worth asking how suitable the British parliamentary style is for clarifying government policy. The much-cherished Question period never succeeded in obtaining for MPs the crucial information on British military plans before the commitment was made, or any confidential reports after the event . . . Therefore, from the standpoint of an effective opposition at least, there might be more to be said for the American legislative committee. It does provide,

especially in Congress, an independent opposition to press the executive both before and after commitments are made.

The usual consultative processes and flows of information came to a standstill even within the Cabinet and the machinery of government itself. The Cabinet, at this time, was dominated to an almost unprecedented degree by the Prime Minister. This was clear even at the time. The *Manchester Guardian Weekly* of October 25, for example, commented that Eden had assumed personal responsibility for British policy:

> probably to an even greater degree than is usual in a country with Cabinet Government. Sir Anthony seems to have been acting rather in the manner of Sir Winston Churchill at critical periods of the war.

Eden restlessly meddled in departmental affairs, especially foreign affairs, in which he considered himself a professional. The Foreign Secretary, Selwyn Lloyd, like Halifax before him, offered no protest. Like Halifax again, he had reservations about his master's policies which he failed to press.

The Civil Service was largely bypassed during the crisis. At the outset, the Foreign Office timidly pressed for a peaceful line, mainly in the interests of the "special relationship" with the US. The view was presented most forcefully by the Minister of State, Anthony Nutting. For the most part, the Foreign Office was inclined to bow to Eden; in diplomatic affairs, it had faith in his "antennae". Towards the end of September, Eden, although keeping Kirkpatrick, the permanent head of the Foreign Office, Patrick Dean, its Deputy Under Secretary of State, and the Secretary of the Cabinet fully informed, began to ignore the civil servants completely. French and British Premiers and Foreign Ministers held their discussions alone. Professor Thomas (p. 92) aptly remarks that their techniques of planning:

> though doubtless effective when blowing up a train in the Resistance, had certain disadvantages when it was a question of committing 100,000 men to a conventional war.

When the Cabinet discussed Suez no minutes were kept, thus avoiding the need to let the Civil Service into the secret. Macmillan and Eden were clearly "intoxicated" with the sense of adventure: hence their unconcern for "legal quibbles" and other details. The law officers placed on record the fact that they had not been consulted. Professor Thomas concludes (pp. 163–64):

> The bizarre aspect of this whole affair is that with a few exceptions nearly all the British Ministers seem to have been hostile or dubious about the use of force by the end of October; but they were caught up in a whirlpool . . . and, transfixed by Eden's superior reputation, were apparently unable to act . . . To embark on an offensive of this size without bringing in the normal Civil Service made many British officials, particularly abroad, look foolish or dishonest, and damaged the Government machine when it was most needed.

The failure to consult and inform was not merely an internal aspect of the government's policy. Its relations with its allies were also bedeviled by this shortcoming. In the House of Commons, Gaitskell told the government:

> . . . we are not satisfied with the degree of consultation which appears to have taken place either with other countries in the Commonwealth or with the United States of America.

The Americans were naturally more detached from the situation than the British—only 15 percent of their oil imports came through the Suez Canal. One of the most important factors was that Eisenhower was standing for a second Presidential term, as the Prince of Peace. Doubts about the validity of the Anglo-French legal position were uppermost in Eisenhower's mind. In his memoirs, he recalls:

> My conviction was that the Western world had gotten into a lot of difficulty by selecting the wrong issue about which to be tough. To choose a situation in which Nasser had legal and sovereign rights and in which world opinion was largely on his side was not in my opinion a good one on which to make a stand.

The split in the Anglo-American Alliance began to emerge when, at the end of September, the British and French decided to take the Suez issue to the UN without consulting Washington. The rift widened when, after October 16, there was something of a diplomatic "blackout" between London and Washington. Eisenhower testifies that "we had the uneasy feeling that we were cut off from our allies".

At a Cabinet meeting on October 25, Selwyn Lloyd's suggestion that the Americans be informed of the British plans was rejected by Eden and Macmillan. Lloyd subsequently told his officials that, as far as the US and the Commonwealth were concerned, "it's all very awkward". Hence, the October 29 ultimatum was issued without prior consultation with Washington. The US considered that it had been double-crossed by Eden, especially when the evidence pointed to British collusion. The Anglo-French action could also be interpreted as a breach of treaty obligations. Under a tri-partite Declaration of 1950, the British, French and Americans were pledged to take joint action to prevent any violation of the Egyptian–Israeli frontiers and armistice lines. Eden once remarked: "I know very few international commitments if any which carry so strong a commitment as that one." Eisenhower was referring to the tri-partite declaration, when he cabled to Eden (October 30):

> . . . I feel very seriously that whenever any agreement or pact of this kind is in spirit renounced by one of its signatories, it is only fair that the other signatories should be notified.
>
> It seems to me of first importance that the UK and the US quickly and clearly lay out their present views and intentions before each other, and that . . . we find some way of concerting our ideas and plans so that we may not, in any real crisis, be powerless to act in concert because of misunderstanding . . .

Professor Finer, in an account of the crisis generally favorable to Eden, concludes:

> Suez tore NATO apart and it has never been possible fully to restore its corporate morale.

This conclusion has been endorsed by many other authorities. Kirkpatrick, too, considered Anglo-American disunity to be the most important consequence of the Suez Crisis.

The consequences of the failure to win even tacit American support quickly became clear. As Thomas points out (pp. 154–55), Britain was forced to withdraw from Egypt not because she was militarily incapable of maintaining her position but because she was too dependent on the US in other respects. Above all, she maintained a reserve currency, vulnerable to overseas pressure—a matter which troubled neither Mollet, the French Premier, nor the franc.

In the long run, the failure to consult the Commonwealth probably did even more harm. Although Menzies played a large part in the diplomatic activity of September, British policy, throughout the Crisis, seemed to ignore the very existence of the Commonwealth. A Commonwealth Prime Ministers' Conference was held only a few weeks before Nasser's action. In view of the withdrawal of Western aid to the

Aswan Dam and repeated threats by Nasser (and, indeed, by most other Egyptian leaders since 1920) to nationalize the company, the Suez Canal was at least a prospective problem at that time. Yet the matter was not even discussed.

Canada, concerned that the Commonwealth might cease to be a bridge between the West and Asia, was hostile to British action. In India, Nasser was admired as the Nehru of Arab nationalism. South African and Pakistani attitudes were ambivalent. Only Australia and New Zealand were unreservedly favorable to Eden's policy, though the former's Foreign Minister offered some opposition.

After the ultimatum, Pearson told the Canadian House of Commons:

> There was no consultation with other members of the Commonwealth . . . and no advance information that this very important action, for better or for worse, was about to be taken.

Yet Selwyn Lloyd claimed that the Anglo-French operation had taken place because:

> The Suez Canal, the main artery to and from the Commonwealth between Europe and Asia, was in imminent danger.

In fact, even if the Canal was in "imminent danger", there is only slight evidence that it constituted a threat to the economic survival of either Britain or the Commonwealth. In a close study of this question, two Australian economists (W. Woodruff and L. MacGregor in *The Suez Canal and the Australian Economy,* 1957, p. 20) concluded that:

> . . . The Suez Canal is not vital to the Australian economy.

Even the Treasury suggested, in August, that the blocking of the Canal would not have an unduly serious effect on our oil supplies.

The government's insistence that there was no time for consultations can be dismissed as special pleading. Quite apart from the evidence of collusion, Eden's *Memoirs* admit that, at the October 25 Cabinet meeting, the terms of the ultimatum and the subsequent Anglo-French action were "decided in principle".

Thus Eden, bypassing all the normal channels of consultation and communication, went ahead with his plans. The ghost of Munich presided, in a very real sense, over this new British debacle. Eden insisted on seeing parallels between appeasement of Germany and Italy and appeasement of Egypt. He compared the nationalization of the Canal to Hitler's occupation of the Rhineland. In a broadcast to the nation on August 8 Eden said of Nasser's actions:

> The pattern is familiar to many of us . . . We all know this is how fascist governments behave and we all remember, only too well, what the cost can be in giving in to fascism.

Long after other men, like Hugh Gaitskell, had recognized the inaptness of the analogy, Eden continued to compare Nasser to the pre-war dictators. When he came to write his memoirs, Eden still held to this view. It was this delusion of the Prime Minister which led to the "failure to make that political and diplomatic preparation for war which all nineteenth century statesmen would automatically have ensured". (Thomas, *op. cit.,* p. 159.)

Eden's obsession was linked with the illusion of Imperial grandeur. Macmillan told Dulles that he would rather pawn the pictures in the National Gallery than submit to Nasser. The Suez Crisis was part of the death pangs of French imperialism too. France believed that Nasser was behind the Algerian Resistance. Thus, by a strange irony of history, these former imperial rivals, Britain and France, were to join forces and to meet jointly, in one catastrophic week, the moment of truth which destroyed the grand illusions of two centuries.

Britain was attempting, and still attempts, to sustain her illusory imperial role by a colossal military expenditure. Yet, at this crucial hour in 1956, no base in the Mediterranean was big enough to take the ships necessary for the Suez operation. Cyprus could accommodate only a few minesweepers and no tank landing craft; Malta was too distant and too small. Nor would the bases further east have been much use had the conflict escalated. In the middle of September, Bandaranaike successfully asked Eden for a guarantee that, if war came, British bases in Ceylon would not be used. Of the defense estimates for 1956–57, Eden writes:

> The action which the British Government could take was circumscribed by international considerations. First came the strategic value [of Cyprus] . . . Our military advisers regarded it as an essential staging point for the maintenance of our position in the Middle East . . .

The lack of suitable bases and of a large and well-equipped mobile reserve had two results. First, instead of an immediate riposte to Nasser's action, it took weeks "to gather the necessary resources". (A. J. Barker: *Suez: The Seven Day War,* 1964, p. 194.) Secondly, it took over six days, from the start of the eventual operation, to get the British invasion force to Egypt. As Barker points out (p. 196):

> From its earliest conception the plan for 'Musketeer' had envisaged an armoured force moving quickly down the Canal to secure the vital areas . . . Yet when the time came, only the armoured regiment that had moved with the assault force was available, the rest of the armoured group being afloat in Southampton . . .

The British Army's lack of mobility was thus one of the most glaring features of the Suez operation. But, even later, there was no attempt to develop "short take off and landing", "vertical take off" and transport aircraft—all of which would have made a contribution to solving the problem.

The cost, in actual military expenditure, must have been at least £100 million ($280 million). In his *Memoirs*, Eden recalls:

> The Treasury had felt satisfied that these outlays could be borne without undue stress, though if the canal were blocked and our pipelines cut indefinitely, our balance of payments would be endangered.

Suez was a politician's blunder, for which administrators and diplomats bear no blame. In this they are fortunate, for the blame of history is likely to rest very heavily indeed on those few men who involved Britain in an ethical, political, diplomatic, military, logistic, economic and constitutional catastrophe of such appalling magnitude.

Just as the mistakes of Munich gave rise to the mistakes of Suez, so the humiliation of Suez gave rise to an urge not to tolerate British freedom of action being handicapped by a dependence on the American nuclear umbrella, and thus intensified the expensive and illusory policy of creating an "independent" British nuclear "deterrent".

The story of the independent deterrent—its adoption by the Attlee government, its elevation to an article of faith in the late 1950s and its virtual disappearance since 1964—is amply documented by David Divine in *The Broken Wing* (1966). He remarks (pp. 276–77):

> The first V-2 rocket detonated in Chiswick, five miles from Westminster. The actual echoes . . . were heard in Whitehall. It is impossible to discover that the echoes of their implications reached it

then or after . . . No serious studies were begun, no committees set up to examine effectively the implications of missiles to the British defence system: no senior officer emerged to advocate an interest in a new and expanding sector of the art of war.

Hence, curious timelags appear again and again in British post-war defense policy. British awareness of new developments in weaponry lingers several years behind the Russians and the Americans; weapons are adopted without any clear awareness of how, in what context and against whom they might be deployed; models become obsolescent before they are operational; final costs bear not the remotest resemblance to original estimates.

Seaslug, a Navy missile, was initially estimated to cost between £1 and £1½ million. In 1960, the Auditor General announced that the estimates had increased to £70 million ($196,000,000). It is certain that the final cost was rather more. By the time the weapon had emerged, it was so large and so complex that a new class of ships had to be built to use it. By the time they had been built, the first mark of Seaslug was obsolescent. When the second mark was completed, the new ships had to be substantially modified to use it. By then, the Russians had perfected anti-ship missiles which left Seaslug with only a limited defensive value.

The Army's Thunderbird, the first mark of which was also obsolescent by the time it was operational, escalated from £2½ million to £40 million. The Fireflash/Firestreak air missile development escalated from £4 million to £53 million. Estimates for the RAF Bloodhound, again obsolescent on its first mark, doubled during its production. Divine concludes (p. 317):

> The net result was Gilbertian. By the time the missile deployment had been completed at a cost . . . of substantially more than £100 million . . . the plan provided that there would be effectively no deterrent bombers to protect. By its provisions the majority were scheduled for dispersal to areas remote from and uncovered by the East Coast defence zone. Those still nominally covered by the defences were intended to be off the ground minutes before the arrival of a missile attack.

Meanwhile, Britain depended for attack on the manned strategic bomber, whose role in total war was steadily declining. The 1957 White Paper on Defence declared that a British megaton bomb had been developed and that ballistic rockets would be acquired, as means of delivery which would supersede the V-bombers. It was on this basis that the decision to develop Blue Streak had been taken. The 1958 White Paper, however, announced that a manned aircraft, TSR-2, would also be developed. The 1960 White Paper announced that:

> The V-bomber force remains the United Kingdom's main contribution to the strategic nuclear power of the West . . .

Thus, similar mistakes were being systematically repeated. Before and during the war, the British overestimated the value of the bomber. The lessons were not learned: the government continued to rely unduly on the bomber in the 1960s. In the case of TSR-2 the persistent neglect of research had disastrous results. the rigid-winged model was preferred to the pivoting F-111-type wings because, quite simply, Britain had insufficient data on the latter although its original invention was British.

In April 1960, Blue Streak was canceled. In 1955, its cost had been estimated at £50 million, in 1957 at £160 million–£200 million, in 1960 at £280 million–£310 million. Militarily, it was too vulnerable to the Russian IRBM system. Yet the US had already reached such conclusions about the Russian system in 1955. Blue Streak was to be replaced by the American Skybolt which, requiring the manned bomber as a primary stage, would indefinitely prolong the life of the V-bombers. These two decisions—to cancel Blue Streak and to adopt Skybolt—were, according to the Minister of Defence, complementary. In fact, one was taken five years too late, the other three years too early. The defects of Blue Streak, both economic and military, were plainly visible in 1955; the feasibility of Skybolt would not be proved, by testing, until 1963. Richard Worcester, a leading aviation consultant, has remarked in *Roots of British Air Policy* (1966, p. 193):

> The Government cannot just cancel a weapon, they operate on the theory that 'The King is dead: long live the King.' Thus until a new weapon is ready, the old one cannot be withdrawn. Accordingly money may have to be spent prolonging an old one until a dual announcement is possible, by which time the new project must appear to be mature enough to fit in with the demise of the old system. In this case the cost of a second fiasco of £27 million was balanced against the cost of the first fiasco—officially set at £84 million, but in fact considerably more.

As it happened Skybolt never reached the testing stage: the Americans canceled it in 1961.

The TSR-2, along with the P1154 and HS681, were canceled in Labour's first "Hundred Days". Shortly, however, variable-sweep aircraft and P1127s, a rejuvenated Concord program and proposals for a European "air bus" appeared. The cycle of blunders may well have begun yet again, except that this time the overall strategy for the aircraft industry and the defense system is, if anything, less clear. The cost of Concord has already climbed from a 1962 estimate of £150–£170 million to £500 million. Only one-third of the costs of research and development are expected to be recovered from the sales of the aircraft. The Committee of Public Accounts expressed doubts about the Ministry of Aviation's cost control procedures, as indeed it had done five years previously when faced with a fivefold increase in the cost of Blue Steel. The estimates for the new Anglo-French swing-wing aircraft have already been criticized by reputable experts, including Mr. Worcester, as too low. It is not due to become operational for eight years. It is not clear whether it will be required to operate east of Suez or even east of Margate. The export market for such an aircraft, especially in view of the high cost per individual machine, is of doubtful size.

The effect of British air policy since 1945 has been, despite the vast expenditures of money, to leave the United Kingdom without an adequate defense system at any stage and to plunge the aircraft industry into a state of constant uncertainty and near-collapse. The latter is one of the main sources of the brain drain—1,300 qualified aerospace specialists emigrated in 1966. Its plight has been described by the Report of the Plowden Committee.

The total cost of the "deterrent" since 1948 was estimated by Mr. Watkinson, in 1960, at half a billion pounds and by Mr. Thorneycroft, in 1963, without explanation for the discrepancy, at one billion pounds. These were only the direct costs. The cost in the waste of resources and manpower that could profitably have been deployed elsewhere was equally immense. As the *Sunday Times* has recently remarked: "There are lies, damned lies, and aircraft estimates."

Blaming the blunders of twenty years on "the Air Marshals and the Air Establishment", Divine writes (p. 367):

> The causes of failure are distressingly obvious; traditionalism . . . failure of imagination, inflexibility of mind, inability to keep pace with an evolving technology, a smugly arrogant distrust of the American point of view, and indecision at least as lamentable as that of the politicians.

For the financial aspects of these failures, the Treasury must also bear a large share of the blame. Parliament, too, must shoulder some of the blame for failing to keep a searching eye on the government. Select Committees have often done good work in investigating aviation failures, but their reports are all too rarely followed up on the floor of the House. Often, as in the case of TSR-2, Parliament did not even concern itself with a project until it was already far advanced. During the 1960 Debate on Blue Streak and Skybolt, the House of Commons, as Mr. Airey Neave ruefully observed, was almost empty. Worcester (p. 33) sums up Parliament's attitude as:

> a disastrous lack of proper concern. It is too naïve, and too ready to take the easy way out. It will accept any old story—or indeed no story at all—rather than find itself forced to probe too deeply into embarrassing matters.

In retracing the dismal trail through the later 'twenties and the 'thirties into World War II, the record gave an uncompromising and astringent reply. The British bumbled ineptly through these critical years without knowing, and without seriously attempting to discover what was hitting them, and what challenge they would have to meet. Their measures for dealing with it were accordingly grossly inadequate, and only in limited areas well-conceived. Only over a minor part of the field were they well executed and successful, and in almost every case where this occurred it was due to some exceptional or lucky initiative evading or overcoming the built-in tendency of the System to come up with the wrong answer, or with no answer at all. Although disappointed and often dismayed at this record, the British people at the time did nothing in any way effective to insist upon improving it. A clear majority of those in a position to influence national policy were accessories, before or after the fact, to nearly all the neglects and omissions, and most of the blunders and crimes of their chosen System of misgovernment. The minority who protested and proposed alternatives, including some very distinguished citizens, were on the whole unheeded, and the suffering majority of wage-earners, housewives and children in general left to stew in their own juice. If it were profitable to try to assign more blame, it would be hard to decide whether the largest share should go to the politicians, the Civil Service, employers, trade unions or the general citizenry. In terms of cause and effect, however, it appears that the Civil Service, by leaving so largely unused its powers of inquiry, warning and advice on emergency problems, blocked at an early stage the nation's opportunities for adapting itself.

Inheriting the unhappy results of the cardinal errors of judgment which were saddled on the nation around the 1860s, the various mal-administrations of the 1920s and 1930s broke faith with those who had given their lives in World War I for a better world, missed the great opportunity for making a new start, and made a quite inadequate contribution to solving the major inherited weaknesses in technology and education, in economics, in administration and in the evolution of the Commonwealth. Thanks to Lord Balfour and others it was perhaps in this last sphere that most progress was made, but owing to the obdurate resistance of Winston Churchill and many others to progress towards self-government, above all in India, a legacy of bitterness and strain was handed on to the post-World War II period, and the opportunity of floating off the new Commonwealth ship of state with goodwill and with honor was thrown away. In economics and administration the doors were firmly closed against adaptation through foresight and intelligence, and the choice was stubbornly made that each step of adaptation must be dictated and forced through in disaster and in misery, such that they would brook obstruction no longer.

The series of valuable break-throughs made in broadcasting, electricity, agriculture, London transport, military aviation and other sectors hardly affected the growing obsolescence of the central machine, whose blind spots and wrong decisions so gravely aggravated the already chronic problems of modernizing the nation and its economy, and of equipping Britain with some solid power and authority to pursue with impetus and success the kind of realistic policies which might so easily have averted the tragedies of the slump and of the outbreak of World War II. But those with whom the choice rested chose otherwise. At the very time when the country was being so copiously and tastelessly embellished with toy British lions from Wembley, the genuine victorious British lion of 1918 was being quickly converted into the British paper tiger of the 'thirties.

World War II brought about an interesting experiment in a partial suspension of the System and the improvising of a quite distinct type of government, crude and faulty in many ways, but demonstrating at least that it is possible to govern Britain effectively on very different lines and with very different personnel.

Since peace again broke out, the System has resumed its sway with consequences which are only too near and familiar to all. In the following pages an attempt will be made to draw some conclusions and to suggest how a more sane, rewarding and human successor to the System might be created, once people are agreed that they have had enough.

PART SIX

THE BRITISH ROLE: BASIS FOR A NEW LOOK

CHAPTER 18

Britain in the World

It is now four years since Dean Acheson so shocked our native ostrich population by remarking that Britain had lost an Empire but not yet found a role. It would be equally true to say that a century ago Britain had abandoned a perfectly good role, which had brought her world success and prestige, and had rashly substituted for it a mirage of an Empire, with its pompous trappings and posturings, its liabilities and hatreds, and its predestined doom. Goodbye to all that; now the time has come to face Dean Acheson's question, which in a less misgoverned country would have been resolved by the leadership long before he got round to asking it.

The task of finding a new role calls for a thorough assessment of the potentialities and capabilities which Britain still enjoys. A second requirement is a reasoned forecast of the world conditions within which the British state and the British economy and society will have to function in future.

We are moving into an age when everything will need to be weighed, measured, tested and justified, and not least those ancient and often bogus institutions the nation-states, among which Britain is currently the one most open to challenge. The slipshod, long-winded, amateurish national debates by which these matters were handled in the past will no longer serve. Adequate research and professional work to uncover and present the main relevant material; high-level seminars and appraisals of the issues and alternatives emerging; public discussions at all levels concerning the national policies and programs which are indicated must be provided for if Britain is to deserve, and to have any prospect of achieving, a new place among world leaders in the coming century. "Muddling through" is through.

The cards Britain still holds are not so poor as in themselves to condemn Britain to an inferior role in future, yet neither are they strong enough to save her from it, in the absence of drastic adaptation and much fresh effort. Britain still commands vast reserves of talent, of training, of vigor, of cultural and political maturity and of almost every other form of human resource. Geographically she is ideally placed for the age of air travel. Economically, although by a sadly narrowed margin, she still has a foundation for leadership in many industries and trades. Technically she has great gifts and assets if she could find governmental and industrial leaders competent and trained to make proper use of them. Perhaps above all, in an ever more internationally-minded world, there are British people who know their way about better and feel more at home in more places and in more activities than any other nation has yet produced.

Only the most hopeless incompetence or the most paralyzing complacency can deprive the British of their obvious heritage as the natural catalysts and integrators in many of the most important processes of international growth. Yet in view of the level of stupidity and incompetence which has recently been demonstrated in playing Britain's hand and in shaping Britain's future it would be extremely rash to bank upon assets, however promising and numerous, not being neglected, misused or simply thrown away by the normal processes of the System so long as it is allowed to continue. Until genuine reason can be shown to the contrary, bitter experience teaches us that pessimism over Britain's future must still be the order of the day. Never is this more true than when a few encouraging reports and statistics are heralded as marking a turning-point, and are interpreted as meaning that soon everybody can stop worrying and go to sleep again.

Accustomed as we are in Britain to bumbling along in a perpetual dense fog in place of a strategic or a foreign policy, it is difficult to measure or interpret the immense and fairly rapid changes which have occurred in the structure of world affairs and world power during the past quarter of a century. In terms of rate and degree of change Hitler is already nearly half-way back to William the Conqueror.

Setting aside such incidental stereotypes as colonies, conquests, Empire and Commonwealth, Great Britain has experienced historically four main distinguishable organized administrative relationships with other parts of the world. In the first, under Rome, Britain, at least south of the Wall, was herself a province of a much wider political grouping. In the second, under the Normans, England, and eventually Wales, came under a dynastic link with large parts of what is now France, and was involved for some four centuries in an abortive series of campaigns to achieve some sort of State straddling both sides of the English Channel. In the third, during the sixteenth to late eighteenth centuries, a series of colonies of settlement, thinly populated by emigrants from the British Isles, evolved to a point where the issue of their relative rights and powers in relation to the mother country became critical. The most important group, in eastern North America, then broke away, leaving a miscellaneous series of possessions acquired and administered largely for the negative reason that it would be harmful to British strategic and trading interests if they fell into the hands of any hostile power. In the fourth, the frankly and often aggressively competitive imperialist expansion of the late nineteenth century, and during its attempted consolidation and defense during the first half of the twentieth, Britain emerged as a deliberately empire-building power. Unfortunately no substantial advance justification for the British deviation into imperialism appears to have been prepared or discussed. The nation was, in the main, committed to it unknowingly and through piecemeal measures, which were said to have one intention and actually had an opposite one.

D. K. Fieldhouse, Beit Lecturer in the History of the Commonwealth at Oxford University, has summed it up in *The Colonial Empires* (1965):

> These prizes have dazzled the eyes of many observers, giving the impression that colonial empires were so many Eldorados. They were not. The selectivity of colonial expansion before 1883 reflected in part the knowledge that much of what was rejected was not worth the taking. The indiscriminate partition of the next thirty years was a lucky dip in which there were few prizes, and those mostly well hidden when the draw was made. Most participants, in fact, acquired only white elephants to which their most enthusiastic efforts could give little future value.

Yet informed observers both before and during the deviation described with great clarity what it would mean. Here for instance is the Liberal economist J. A. Hobson's summary, written in 1902, in his often reprinted *Imperialism: A Study:*

> Imperialism is the very antithesis of this free wholesome colonial connection, making, as it ever does, for greater complications of

foreign policy, greater centralisation of power and a congestion of business which ever threatens to absorb and overtax the capacity of parliamentary government. The true political nature of Imperialism is best seen by confronting it with the watchwords of progress accepted in the middle of the nineteenth century by moderate men of both great parties in the State, though with interpretations, varying in degree—peace, economy, reform and popular self-government. Even now we find no formal abandonment of the principles of government these terms express, and a large section of professed Liberals believe or assert that Liberalism is consistent with the maintenance of all these virtues.

This contention, however, is belied by the facts. The decades of Imperialism have been prolific in wars; most of these wars have been directly motivated by aggression of white races on 'lower races', and have issued with the forcible seizure of territory. Every one of the steps of expansion in Africa, Asia and the Pacific has been accompanied by bloodshed: each Imperialist power keeps an increasing army available for foreign service. . . . Peace as a general policy is antagonized not merely by war but by militarism, an even graver injury. Apart from the enmity of France and Germany the main cause of the armaments which have drained the resources of most European countries is their conflicting interests in territorial expansion.

If leaders of the Left in British politics, from William Ewart Gladstone to Harold Wilson inclusive, had not allowed themselves to be blinded to the social and domestic implications of the seductions of imperialism, and had adopted a more modern-minded political approach, vast progress in many other directions need not have been forfeited by Britain. The question therefore now is: how are the inheritors of the shambles in foreign and strategic policy resulting from the collapse of the imperialist deviation going to pick up the bits and produce a realistic external policy and posture which will enable Britain to get back on a sound course again in world affairs?

Stated in other terms, is Britain to revert to a degree of formal separation from the rest of the world which has not been attempted since the last failure to assert it in 1066, or are we now to begin a fifth pattern of organized relationships, and if so, what choices have we over the nature of that pattern? As reversion to pure isolationism is obviously a non-starter we are left with a discussion of the second of these alternatives.

There is still a tendency from force of habit to drift towards or into policies or actions deriving from now vanished or insignificant imperial interests, or from a desire to please in some costly manner some member of the Commonwealth who may or may not give thanks for it. What were the supposed benefits of possessing colonial and dependent territories? Some, like parts of Kenya, for example, had been settled by British "kith and kin" who expected that the old country would and could protect their lives, property and interests in perpetuity, regardless of trouble and expense. Military provision had therefore to be made, and diplomatic attitudes adopted in the United Nations and elsewhere, which would cover such commitments. Similarly, dispositions had to be made which would in foreseeable circumstances hold open lines of communication by sea, cable and later also by air, for making clear our ability and intention to defend these territories to the uttermost against any aggression or undue pressure. As two of the Dominions in question, Australia and New Zealand, were almost at the opposite pole to Britain, and could only practically be reached either by the Mediterranean or the Cape Route, a concept emerged of a lifeline of Empire along those paths, and thus of antagonism to almost any significant disturbance of the *status quo* across half the world. Certain fortresses, harbors, depots and fuelling stations such as Gibraltar, Malta, Suez, Aden and Singapore emerged as of critical importance. Other territories were equally important as tried sources of supply of some vital strategic commodity such as oil, copper or rubber. Many parts of the Empire were without serious importance of any of these types, or of others, but had to be looked after partly on account of prestige considerations or for some economic interest which might later expand, or simply because acquiring and administering colonies had become a British habit, like pursuing foxes or hitting balls, and had thus come to be regarded as worth doing for its own sake.

While typical British families at all social levels were likely to have relatives in the settled Dominions, the dependent Empire was never a living reality except to some smallish minority groups, mostly of middling or fairly high social status, who looked to it for interesting and well-paid career jobs, civil and military, and in certain cases for rewarding opportunities of investment, commerce or settlement. To the man in the street it never meant anything much, despite the almost continuous and at times emotional campaigns to brainwash him on the subject.

Yet, surprising as it may seem, it is difficult to resist the conclusion that, however feeble and unreal the British Empire remained as a part of the national consciousness of the mother country, this was its least ineffectual aspect. Evidence of major requirements previously met, or of outlets afforded by the Empire whose disappearance now creates some obvious problem for the United Kingdom, is singularly elusive. No one seems to have been noticeably inconvenienced by its liquidation, except a number of those who actually had homes, jobs or property in some ex-dependent territory, and by no means all even of these. Moreover, Britain's recent economic and other difficulties would not at all obviously have been eased had all these territories continued dependent and the map gone on being so flatteringly red. It is indeed arguable that, in that event, the present difficulties could well have been aggravated, since burdens would have been heavier and freedom of action more restricted. The indications are that the coincidence in time between the loss of colonies and the British economic crisis has been largely accidental, except that having lately been a great colonial Power still saddles Britain with customary military and financial obligations which, if terminated earlier, might have greatly mitigated the overstrain on the British balance of payments.

It also seems that to a remarkable extent the Empire was a self-canceling system, which lived by taking in its own washing. If it was always a net liability to Britain, as is almost certainly the case, it also carried a large proportion of the burdens implicit in it. Costly strategic bases and substantial armed forces were maintained for its protection, which in turn was supposed in some mystic, or at best unproven, manner to contribute to the defense of the United Kingdom. Yet the maximum peacetime strength of these British forces, deployed right across the globe, barely exceeded the armed manpower which during the past twenty years Chiang Kai-shek has maintained (by American aid) on the relatively small offshore Asiatic island of Taiwan, without making any direct difference to the world military situation. They amounted to less than 7 percent of the forces mobilized by Germany in World War I, and less than 25 percent of the German military *dead* in World War II. The great reductions in British territorial responsibilities have not correspondingly, if at all, reduced the strength thought necessary for the British armed forces. Nor has the cessation of this protection resulted in hell being let loose in the ex-British dependencies. That stands in sharp contrast to the bloody havoc which succeeded the end of Belgian rule in the Congo, or of French rule in Indo-China. Indeed, some of the worst bloodshed within the British colonial Empire has been occasioned by British forces being directed from London to outstay their welcome in order to enforce contested political settlements, as in Cyprus and Aden. The great apparent exception was the bloodshed accompanying the partition of India and Pakistan, but in this region it had long been the Indian, not the British army which had the task of maintaining peace and order.

At its peak in 1933 the British Empire covered some 12·2 million square miles, or nearly 24 percent of the earth's land surface—a block larger than all Africa—populated by some 500 million people, forming nearly one quarter of all mankind. It included more than half the area, and more than two-thirds of the population, of all colonial or colonized territories combined. Colored maps, books and newspapers, films and exhibitions and other media, not forgetting the speeches of politicians, incessantly reiterated the splendor and dominating importance of this British Raj. Yet those most closely concerned were always troubled that the message had not really got across to the British people as a whole. When the Empire eventually broke loose it left behind not any practical yawning gap but merely a disturbing and persistent after-image, like the smile of the Cheshire Cat. Unimpressed and even frankly bored with it as the nation had tended to be while it lasted, its loss removed not only a source of worry and a load on the conscience, but also a prize status symbol and source of comfort and of pride, especially to traveling British. Many people were left with a vague feeling of deprivation and frustration, mitigated for a time by the device of free association within the Commonwealth, until this came to be recognized as a hollow substitute for a hollow institution. So this odd, immensely unwieldy, and fundamentally unconvincing contraption vanished from the political scene, leaving the British people, who had never really been told plainly what it was all about, in a state of greater bewilderment and of greater disillusionment with their rulers than ever. We were owed an explanation, but THEY never gave us one. Nor did THEY appear to have any clear idea where to go from here.

Perhaps the most basic British external interest is freedom of access to all other countries, and of communication with any of their citizens. In conflict with this interest are the closure of large tracts of China, the Soviet Union and their satellite countries, and less rigid and complete restrictions in parts of the Middle East, Africa and elsewhere. It is worth noting that, when the British Empire was at its greatest extent, political restriction on the movement of British citizens within areas under British control or influence was practiced from London, and passports stamped accordingly. Indeed those who acquiesced in the then policy of the Passport Office were, until quite recently, illegally denied British passports entitling them to move freely wherever they pleased in the world, and were fobbed off with substitutes valid for certain countries only.

This requirement for open access and communication is therefore not one on which a British Empire was in practice entirely helpful to ordinary British citizens. It is essentially one best dealt with by stronger bargaining through United Nations and diplomatic channels. The only obvious aspect where Empire bargaining power may have helped has been against lobbies seeking to bar reasonable rights of overflying and landing by recognized civil airlines. Even here, notably in the case of the American Pacific routes, it proved a feeble instrument.

Next to freedom of access comes freedom of trade. One of the greatest and best features of the British Empire, and that which most enabled it to be so widely expanded and to survive so long, was the concept of the Open Door. This was, however, anathema to many of the keenest imperialists. The later days of the Empire saw a gradual surrender to such pressures, and the recent tough and gradual but not unsuccessful campaign for greater trading freedom in the world has coincided with the loss of colonial territories. Clearly then possession of an Empire is not an asset from this standpoint; indeed as a main obstacle to Britain entering the Common Market in time to be an original signatory of the Treaty of Rome it was a calamitous liability. It was not, as was so strongly urged at the time, an effective alternative to the European Common Market, but merely a means of ensuring that by 1967 Britain was excluded from enjoying any possible advantages of either.

A more intimate and complex problem is that of outlets for employment and settlement overseas. On an individual level the British peoples throw up perhaps as high a proportion as any of men and women who are ready and eager to uproot themselves for years, or even decades or a whole lifetime, and to work or settle in some more or less distant land. Name at random any obscure valley, forest, mountain range, or island on the planet, and there will be someone in Britain who knows it well. The "presumed" Dr. Livingstone was only the best-known among many thousands of like-minded compatriots, whose traces and whose graves are scattered through every continent. Lone British sailors dot the remotest oceans, and even British typists and mothers' helps work their way adventurously round the world. Quite a few eventual additions to the Empire originated from some wild escapist impulse, and Sarawak was able to keep its independent British rajahs for generations before Whitehall laid hands on it.

The urge for going abroad in search of a better life has evidently weakened in recent decades, and the vast streams of emigration from the British Isles have largely dried up, even to destinations where they would still be welcome. Probably not less than seventeen million people left the British Isles in the century between Waterloo and World War I. By an odd coincidence the Colonial Land and Emigration Department, created to promote emigration to Australia and New Zealand, was closed in 1878, just as the policy of imperialism was gathering its fullest strength. Between 1847 and 1869 some 340,000 assisted emigrants had been sent out. Unassisted migration to the United States reached its peak at this time, with a total of 807,000 immigrants from Great Britain alone (and 655,000 more from Ireland) during the decade 1881–90. Without this massive influx, and an equal volume from Germany, the vast expansion of the American economy would not have been possible.

After World War I there was a belatedly renewed effort to encourage emigration from Britain to the Dominions, and during the ten years 1922–31 nearly one and a half million British left the United Kingdom, of whom 880,000 went to Canada, Australia or New Zealand. It remains, however, a mystery why under imperialism more was not done to pay the British emigrant stream to populate the emptier regions of the Empire.

The current position is somewhat confused. Emigration continues on a substantial scale to Australia and Canada, in accordance with immigration policies adopted by their governments for domestic reasons. Emigration to such territories as Kenya is virtually at an end, and there has been some return movement, although less than was often predicted to follow independence. A country such as Rhodesia, resulting from spontaneous British migration to a territory mainly populated by Africans, has given rise to international problems of the utmost gravity, and has caused disproportionate trouble to Britain, on account of some 200,000 "white"—about equal to the population of Portsmouth.

A comparable amount of internal trouble has been caused by the stubborn maintenance until recently by the Home Office of the principle of freedom to settle in the UK for all Commonwealth citizens, which in view of the Welfare State was clearly impossible to continue. This has imported grave racial problems destined to plague Britain for a very long time to come. To have invited mass immigration, from any quarter, in the situation of Britain in the 'fifties was one of the crassest byproducts of the system of misgovernment, which showed itself too prejudiced and too ignorant to face the obvious need for a national population policy, brought authoritatively to its attention nearly twenty years ago. The excuse for this blunder was provided by the same sacred cow, the Empire, which thus added once more to the burdens it had already inflicted on the ordinary citizen of Britain. Economically the labor-wasting features of British industry were largely responsible for encouraging mass immigration of unskilled labor.

A quantitatively much smaller, but qualitatively most important movement, apparently gathering strength, is the so-called brain drain from Britain, much of it to the United States. Since it is so much entangled with transatlantic movements in search of higher education and training, which have been normal in view of the failure to keep corresponding British facilities abreast of the times, it is difficult to assess its eventual scale or to evaluate its implications. Nor is it easy to determine the relative importance as causes of lower gross or net salaries in Britain, the desire for better facilities and more freedom for scientific and technical work, disillusionment with prevalent attitudes in Britain, hard-selling recruitment by American organizations or mere desire for a change.

Whatever the answers, there can be no question that if there were in Britain today a strong and widespread sense of being wanted and appreciated, above all by officials, in the minds of the younger scientists and other professional men and women, the problem would not have attained such proportions. In view of this psychological element it is most unfortunate that government spokesmen should have been so ill-advised as to issue pious exhortations on the duty of the straying sheep to return to the fold where they have been so expensively reared. All the indications are that this duty is not far from their minds, but they nevertheless feel torn in other directions for reasons sometimes no less cogent than those which moved the Pilgrim Fathers in the same direction, under the different brand of British misgovernment associated with the Stuart Monarchs. That so many of the most talented and the best educated young Britons should find themselves compelled to feel this way about continuing to live in Britain is primarily a condemnation not of them but of those who have governed Britain in recent years. It is THEY who should heed the warning, see the red light and change course accordingly. To suggest to the emigrants that they are not acting like gentlemen invites the retort that those who have forced them to consider such a course have not been acting like gentlemen either. Experts, they told each other with a complacent smile, should be on tap not on top. But what if the experts choose instead to take a trip, with a one-way ticket? Where then, in the modern world, is the bright graduate classicist, who can administer absolutely anything or anybody? And where too are the millions of workers who have been misled into a fixed belief that the world owes them a living as good as that of those few who take the main strain and responsibility of keeping Britain abreast of the world? How many can ride for how long on the backs of how few, before the few can take it no longer? The right to many things is loudly insisted on in Britain, but among those rights is the right to quit, and it is well that the announcers of other rights should be reminded of it. It is their selfishness, their thoughtlessness, and their irresponsibility which have made this an issue.

It is perhaps significant that the brain drain should be so little directed towards other parts of the Commonwealth, and so much to the United States. But for the coincidence of the Vietnam war and the American army draft there is little doubt that the permanent losses would be much larger. There is much evidence that, but for a number of specific conditions at home, which are viewed as intolerable, many of those concerned would not dream of emigrating. As one such academic has aptly said: "America wastes things: Britain wastes people." The demand is for conditions and an atmosphere in which modern trained people can be permitted to work rewardingly in a modern way without being forced to quit their native land.

Supposing the opportunity recurred, as it did after George III, to make good the loss of one Empire by assembling another, what would Britain do with it and what use would it be? Only by being able to answer such a question is it possible to assess what it is that has actually been lost. Whether through infertility of imagination or otherwise the present writer is entirely incapable of finding any plausible answer. There is no evident need of the British nation which now calls for anything remotely resembling an Empire, or which could not be better met in other ways, always provided that the trauma inflicted by its liquidation can be healed and that some satisfying alternative British image and role can be created in its stead.

Applying this conclusion to the present situation, where should

Britain go from here? Of the remaining non-sovereign territories in the world at the outset of 1967 twelve were American, ten French, seven Portuguese, five Spanish, two Dutch, two Danish, one Norwegian, one South African, plus thirty-five British, eight Australian and four New Zealand, all still within the Commonwealth. Thus more than half the world's remaining colonies are still under a British flag, even allowing for double counting in the case of the New Hebrides (also under the French tricolor), and the still smaller condominium of Canton and Enderbury Islands, over which the Stars and Stripes also fly. For practical purposes, however, we should exclude the three Antarctic territories, claims to which are frozen under the Antarctic Treaty, and we must note that Rhodesia is currently in revolt and subject to United Nations sanctions. The numbers are artificially inflated by some recent subdivisions, and the remaining colonies are small islands or island groups, with only six exceptions, including Aden, Gibraltar and Hong Kong. This last (if Rhodesia is excepted) is much the most populous remaining British colony, and no one, not even Chairman Mao, seems anxious that it should receive independence just now. Aden, British Honduras on the Central American mainland, Gibraltar on the European mainland, Brunei, enveloped by Malaysia, and, among the island groups, Fiji and the Falkland Islands (claimed by Argentina) are the only obvious sources of controversy. The future of such small possessions, often incapable of standing on their own feet and deeply committed culturally and economically to one historic source of support, is a difficult problem. If Britain is to avoid retaining all the political and psychological liabilities of an imperialist-colonialist power and none of the advantages, it appears that some form of trusteeship should be devised, and that the status of crown colony should be terminated as soon as possible.

That would leave Britain as the center and potential leader of a self-governing Commonwealth of Nations still covering about 13·7 million square miles and including at mid-1966 an estimated 843 million people, or over 25 percent of total world population. How much is this Commonwealth worth? The mere fact that it has continued to hang together as a grouping, however loose, and that its members, in more senses than one, tend to speak the same language internationally, has undoubtedly been a factor making for peace and a political testimonial and benefit to Britain, just as the failure to keep the Republic of Ireland and Burma within the Commonwealth represented defeats.

Few in Britain or overseas still believe that the Commonwealth is, or is likely again to become, anything in the nature of a world power or an economic asset. Its links seem sometimes as light as gossamer and little more dependable. Yet it does mean something, and having at such cost and through so much effort created it Britain would be unwise lightly to let it die. Already, in face of tremendous strains and changes, it has been transformed by strenuous effort into something very different from the Empire of forty years ago. The next forty years could see further changes which would enhance its significance, and bring fuller credit and co-operation to Britain. But if this approach is to be adopted Britain must learn and pay the necessary price, which is to cease pursuing "British interests" and seeking to throw weight about in the world irrespective of, or counter to, the collective interests of the Commonwealth. The role of a mature, responsible parent and grandparent, with a diverse and growing family, is notoriously exacting, but it can also be rewarding and worthwhile. It cannot, however, in any circumstances be doubled with the role of *enfant terrible,* as the Eden government sought to do in the Suez episode. A case can be made out for retaining and further developing the Commonwealth, but for this a sound and consistent British lead is essential, and the tone and content of this lead are within close limits dictated by external circumstances, not by domestic sentiments or ambitions.

There are many uncontroversial fields of great importance within which such a lead could be, and to some extent already is, helpful and welcome. Science, technology, education (especially university education), professional services, health, family planning, and many kinds of cultural activity, recreation, and sport are obvious examples. If part of the effort and resources misguidedly put into trying to make the Commonwealth into an economic entity or a Great Power could have been channeled in those directions, the Commonwealth would now be a much more effective and respected group. But a realistic distinction must be made between those family affairs and matters of mutual aid which can best be tackled on a Commonwealth basis and the many others where an international approach, either global or regional, makes more sense. There is sometimes a disturbing tendency to try to handle things as Commonwealth business where the nature of the subject makes nonsense of that conception.

Although it is only to be expected that special links and agreements will continue between particular complementary Commonwealth countries such as Britain and New Zealand, it is now accepted that the concept of any Commonwealth economic unit as such is a dead duck.

In the management of sterling, however, there has always been a hankering after the promotion of imperial unity through monetary and banking links. It is here, perhaps, that fresh straight thinking about the nature of Britain's interests in relation to world economic interests is most needed. Indications of readiness to discuss such matters have been welcome in many quarters, even though progress is temporarily blocked, here as elsewhere, by contrary views in Paris. It is to be hoped that the immense opportunities for developing a fresh role for London in money matters, which will provide a firm base bridging the Channel, and thus reaffirm and adapt London's worldwide functions, will not be let slip, as was the original chance of joining the Common Market. A determined and thorough British initiative here could have far-reaching consequences, while there is still no real rival in sight.

As a world political grouping the Commonwealth must of course depend for its importance on its power. After so many crude and spectacular displays of naked force the modern world perhaps tends to underrate what can, in many conditions but not in all, be achieved by other means, such as diplomacy. Force also fascinates many minds into attributing to it far greater effectiveness than it normally possesses. The spectacle of the entire might of the United States failing year after year to defeat the eleventh largest state in Asia should be instructive, but it probably will not be. Be that as it may, a virtue must in any case be made of the economic and political necessity of operating the Commonwealth on something quite other than a Great Power basis. This is far from being such a crippling handicap as it may at first appear.

CHAPTER 19

The Limits of Power

Parading as a Great Power immediately brings three big debits. First it makes enemies, creates jealousies and stimulates counterploys. Second it costs a lot—so much that even the largest and most resolute powers such as USA and USSR are unable to afford defensive equipment which their Chiefs of Staff tell them is essential. And as defense expenditure is so rigid and tends so often to grow by escalation year by year, it leaves little margin for flexibility and for even modest initiatives in other directions. Third, a state possessing Great Power capabilities without Great Power armaments and "interests" immediately becomes a natural leader of the great group of uncommitted or smaller countries, whose collective voice, although negligible up to World War II, is increasingly powerful in the emerging world. A state, on the other hand, which continues to pretend as nearly as possible to Great Power status and to pursue Great Power interests without having the necessary resources makes the worst of all possible worlds, and is as little respected in world affairs as is the United Kingdom today.

War, as Clausewitz remarked, is the pursuit of policy by other means, and every war, as many others have remarked, is entered by generals on the mistaken assumption that it will be the same as the last except that it will be over much more quickly. In order to make sense, even in the most hard-boiled circles, as a continuance of policy by other means, a war needs to be predictable, limited in scope, brief, decisive and as economical as possible in men, material and money. The only serious possible exception is a war designed, regardless of cost and suffering, to bring down existing social structures and to create a revolutionary situation for a desperate conspiratorial band. Such a band, however, is most unlikely in modern conditions to be able to start such a war unless it already forms or controls the government of some sizeable state. The obvious possible case of this currently is China. With that notable and grave exception it seems that the combination of successive military disappointments and stalemates, and of the development of the many articulate nations which have votes but virtually no arms, is producing a radically new world power situation, in which only a rogue power can act with the ruthless self-regard and crudity which used to be the hallmark of any Great Power. Short of taking up a rogue-outlaw posture even the largest and strongest powers must listen assiduously to "world opinion". That is no longer mainly the voice of more or less impotent liberal minorities within advanced states, but is the largest effective voting block in the United Nations. It can at least wield immense worldwide nuisance value against those who seek to ignore it. With quite secondary exceptions the generals, admirals, and air marshals are now plainly impotent to deliver the goods which their backers would normally expect of them. With an average cost of £134,000 ($375,200) to the United States for killing each Viet Cong soldier the business is patently uneconomic. Technology and Professor Parkinson have been more successful than centuries of moral persuasion in convincing an increasing number of governments, and the vast majority of mankind, that war doesn't pay. The entrance fee and the subscription are becoming prohibitive.

But British governments already drew a similar conclusion, and practiced its implications with triumphant success, during the forty years between Waterloo and the Crimean War. Armed forces were then reduced to the barest minimum and the Concert of Europe maintained international order diplomatically, throughout a period of intense social stresses, and of not infrequent revolutions on the Continent. While it would be impossible to draw any useful analogy between that time and this they may prove to have one factor in common —namely a widespread disillusionment with war as an effective way of settling international disputes, and a strong general opinion in favor of applying available resources to objects other than armaments.

This was made possible by an early nineteenth-century interruption in the wars of containment which have overshadowed civilization for the past four centuries. The process seriously began with the wars for the containment of France from around 1660 to 1815, and, after this interval, continued with wars for the containment of Germany between about 1860 and 1945, and with the Cold War for the containment of Russia immediately thereafter, now slowly giving place to the wars for the containment of China, which started in Korea in 1950. How will the containment of China be achieved? How long will it take? How much will it cost, especially in terms of death and destruction? Who will achieve it and by what means? These are the big current questions.

The fact that since World War II wars have been either "hot", localized and conventional, or "cold" and potentially nuclear, creates an entirely new power situation. Just as in the sphere of mass communications mankind reels under the diverse and conflicting impacts of radio, television, cinema, photographs in color and in black and white, newsprint, public amplifiers and other media, so in international relations the proliferation not only of different types and levels of military equipment, but of different unwarlike means of pressing home policies and objectives, has outrun the power to digest, marshal and choose between them. The way is wide open for revolutionary new approaches to the achievement of political aims by novel combinations of means. Some of these might, in terms of cost-effectiveness, enormously improve upon the unwieldy and ineffective loads of modern weaponry.

Given the adoption of a thorough-going, non-warlike and non-imperialist international posture, Britain could, with readily available ingenuity, do much to forge from existing, often frustrated international groupings, including the Commonwealth, an immense power for sanity and peace in the world. There is plenty of reason to suppose that the cold war for the containment of Russia has now virtually succeeded in its aims. With the massive and well-placed reinforcement which the Russians must, as a matter of survival, bring to the containment of China it should be quite practicable for the United States, otherwise militarily unaided, to win this additional cold war. It is in any case not nearly so menacing or so apt to unloose a world conflagration as the cold war with Russia looked a dozen or so years ago. Britain, situated most remotely from the Pacific, and saddled there with responsibility for the essentially neutral territory of Hong Kong, is much better able to play in that theater, above all, a militarily inactive but positive and helpful role in the common interest of all peace-loving nations.

Such a British role could transform the status and effectiveness of the United Nations, which at present is like a Parliament with a fairly good if miniature civil service, but only primitive and immature substitutes for political parties, and no adequately organized and skilfully led grouping able to sustain and develop policies carrying the support of a stable majority of the Assembly. The time is overdue for such a development. To have left the Assembly with a choice only between crude negative lobbies, such an the Afro-Asian bloc on the one hand and the tied clients of Great Powers on the other, is a negation of statesmanship. That can only, as it does, go far to nullify the value and the healthy growth of the United Nations as a world representative body.

Britain, uniquely qualified by an unmatched experience of developing and even of exporting Parliamentary institutions, and with the ready-made Commonwealth club amounting to around one-sixth of the UN membership, should cease frittering away such opportunities in largely backward-looking activities. The constructive alternative is to launch out boldly as the sponsor and guide of a world peace and development party, committed to the more rapid building up of the United Nations. The natural line for a healthy "party" division within UN would be between those who wish to strengthen it to the utmost and those who wish to keep it weak or limited. Britain, although among the foremost in launching UN, has too often lately wobbled between these two views, at times with a clear bias towards the second. Given such a lead a substantial number of other nations, and possibly a clear majority of all, could be brought to work consistently and effectively for the achievement of a series of obvious UN objectives. These might include the consolidation and development of its peace-keeping role through increased availability of earmarked national contingents, the reconstruction of its finances, and an expanded program of world education in world common tasks and interests, including technical aid and, above all, the containment of the world population explosion.

By simultaneously making large savings in national overseas expenditure, especially in defense and in some diplomatic fields, Britain could contribute a decisive share of the necessary additional resources, while still reducing, in the interests of the balance of payments, British overall expenditure abroad. In particular, once she had adopted a plain and permanent posture excluding the risk of conflicting "national interests" of a separate and controversial nature, Britain could herself acceptably make available a much increased standing military contribution to UN peacekeeping forces. That would go far to overcome the frustration and enfeeblement of UN which the lack of adequate available trained forces and resources to carry through peacekeeping commitments has entailed.

There is every reason to expect that the adoption of such a role by

Britain would command the enthusiastic support of the Commonwealth, certain members of which, such as Canada, have currently to do more than their fair share in this way, partly on account of the disqualification of British aid by hangovers of imperialism. Many newer members would regard something on these lines as probably the only legitimate excuse and reason for Britain to continue to play a worldwide role. General de Gaulle's policy initiatives, although even more vitiated than Britain's by clinging to anachronistic attitudes at certain points, have amply demonstrated how great an opening exists for a large power to clean the slate and exercise this kind of leadership. Unlike de Gaulle, the British people would clearly prefer operating under UN, as has been outlined, to seeking to play a lone hand. Also unlike de Gaulle, they would wish their hand to be played in the closest friendship and understanding with the United States.

This, however, does not imply either continuing subservience to Washington or seeking to do the same things in exactly the same way on a much smaller scale—two of the greatest faults of British postwar policy. On the contrary, Britain, as the independent leader of a great peace movement of uncommitted and positively unwarlike nations, would for the first time become diplomatically free and competent to develop a converging and complementary campaign towards a peaceful world order. In this the United States, as far as possible in collaboration with USSR, would have the nuclear responsibility and wield the ultimate deterrent, while Britain, no longer entangled in conflicting obligations of a military or imperialist nature, would be responsible for bringing world public opinion, supported by strengthened UN forces, to bear effectively on the common long-term interest. British membership of the European Common Market would fit well with this new conception of the British world political role. Incidentally it would go far to meet recent French objections, which have largely been well founded.

British acquisition of some of the privileges of a dominant Great Power during the early nineteenth century was due to the accidental coincidence of a lull between the wars of containment of France and of Germany and a temporary British lead in technology and capital formation. That lead is now held by the United States. It is American organizations which command the superior earning power and resources to enable them to start great new enterprises overseas, and to make successful takeover bids for leading foreign industries. Some very odd things have been happening recently to the theory and practice of free enterprise and competition. One of the most compelling forces making for economic integration in Europe is the urgent necessity to construct, by vast mergers, firms large enough to take on their American opposite numbers on more level terms. European industry has been conclusively shown to be too fragmented, too confused and complicated in its commercial aims, and too little conscious of costs and of profits in relation to capital employed, to hold its own with American. Mr. Richard Barker of Harvard, formerly of the US Department of Commerce, has in a recent study concluded that by the end of the century some 75 percent of the industrial assets of the "free world" will be in the hands of some 300 major firms. According to the Business News editor of the *Sunday Times* about 175 of these are likely to be American, while Britain has currently only about 30 possibles for the remaining 125 places, and few of these have emerged during the last quarter-century.

The political fragmentation of Europe, and all that goes with it in marketing terms, is simply another handicap among many. Given a policy reorientation which would make possible uninhibited British integration within a wider European economy, there is still no reason why a European match for America should not be constructed, but every further year's delay makes success more difficult and less probable. The Treasury's incorrect first assessment that the European Common Market was doomed to failure, and that Britain should steer clear of it, may almost be ranked with the Treasury's assessment in 1773 that there was no need to consult the Colonial Secretary about so trivial a matter as the Tea Act, which resulted in the loss of the American colonies.

It is an irony of history that surplus British capital seeking an outlet should have done so much to construct modern America a century ago, while surplus American capital looking for an outlet threatens to convert Britain and Europe into something resembling an American colony now. In the interim, diversion of British capital to investment overseas did much to involve Britain in ruinous and short-lived imperial commitments, and to leave undercapitalized and undermodernized British industry in a state highly vulnerable to American invasion, and too backward to awaken in time to the need for closer links with Europe.

Blunders in national policy as frequent, as huge, and as long sustained as have been committed by Britain almost uninterruptedly during the past hundred years cannot be made good quickly, or simply by changing course. If the Foreign Office has discovered that its chief role in the shaping of external policy has been usurped by the Treasury and the Ministry of Defence, the Foreign Office should blame itself for failing to think out and uphold a coherent and realistic basis of policy to keep Britain in the lead in world affairs. Radically new policies must be thought out with the utmost care, not only in the abstract, but in the measure and timing of their adoption and in the reciprocal repercussions of each upon others. Drastic reconstruction of institutions and correspondingly sweeping changes in personnel must be made simultaneously in order to command success. The same types of person working through the same patterns of mind and of institutions which have brought calamity in the past will readily repeat it in the future, even if they pursue policies sound in themselves. Conversely, however, there are plenty of examples where a radical modernization of institutions, accompanied by well-judged infusions of new blood into the vital organs of government, can produce surprisingly quick results in following through policies well adjusted to current conditions. We need look no farther than across the Channel to check this.

The possibilities are much improved at those rare moments when several countries have themselves made bad mistakes or got into severe difficulties. Regrettable as the fact is, United States policy in Vietnam has gravely compromised American prestige and capacity for world leadership, and has much strengthened the prospects of pursuing with success the sort of independent British line sketched earlier. Such things are apt to happen from time to time in world affairs, and not only in international interests, but in those of both Britain and the United States, it is highly desirable that when one of the great English-speaking democracies finds itself temporarily in the doghouse the other should be well placed to carry on and to keep world opinion on an even keel. Something like last century's Concert of Europe on a world scale could before long become practical politics, with the diplomats taking over where the generals have failed, if diplomats of the required caliber now exist.

Fond as we are of remarking how fast situations change nowadays, we are very slow to learn that the pace of policy obsolescence and of institutional obsolescence has correspondingly speeded up. Worn-out policies and dowdy institutions need no less critical and frequent attention than dated fashions or superseded models of machine-tools.

Earnest exhortations for modernization come ill from government departments which in essentials have learned nothing and forgotten nothing for decades. Not only a widespread readiness to criticize and to change practices and institutions, but an awareness of modern means of doing so, are vital if recurrent failures are to be avoided. Nothing could be more wrong than to regard exhortation, or the adoption merely on paper of new methods, as solving any of our problems; that is why so many remedies hailed at the time as decisive prove merely to have added to the problems. Change for the sake of change, and without a clear working purpose, is equally futile. The political leader, like the doctor, must treat the patient as well as the disease. Hence the attempt in this book to bring out the interrelations between institutions, policies and practices on the one hand and the human qualities and capacities of both government and governed on the other. The attempt may be judged inadequate, but nothing less can be more than a palliative.

Britain has got into a blind alley, and can only regain a road which leads somewhere by retracing her steps and striking out afresh. Some of the obvious measures are to abandon all policies and practices arising from the imperial past, and to assume an open and progressive role of leadership for the Commonwealth countries, and for such others as will be willing to accept it on merits, provided that it gets results, and that it has no hidden or inconsistent strings attached to it. One such inconsistent string is colonial possessions, and those which cannot be given independence will need to be converted into some type of trusteeship in order to terminate British extra-territorial ownerships. This should present no great difficulty. British territorial claims to Antarctica should be renounced, and Britain's status there should be like that of the United States, as a signatory of the Antarctic Treaty. Given a firm policy declaration on these lines there need be no rush about completing transfer arrangements, such as unhappily occurred over the independence of Pakistan. The important thing is that Britain should achieve the recognized status of a post-colonial power, and be able to enjoy the moral and political strength which this would confer.

A second inconsistent string is the so-called "special relationship" with the United States. Many British people dislike and feel humiliated by the toadying to Washington which this highly artificial and futile pretense increasingly involves. Many friends of America equally feel pained at the obvious embarrassment which this charade causes to the friendly and helpful leaders in Washington who are expected to suffer it gladly. Its perpetuation is one of the least rewarding and most objectionable of the fruits of the British System, and it should be publicly recognized as having long since served its purpose. The question has been fully and frankly analyzed by the Washington Correspondent of *The Times* in an article on Janury 4, 1967, entitled "Why so little remains of the special relationship". This well-informed account amply confirms the incapacity of those who have been shaping British external policy to tell what time it is in the world beyond our complacent shores. The abandonment of the "special relationship" in no way inhibits the continuance and development of the many exceptionally close and warm ties between Britain and the United States at a non-political level. Indeed it might facilitate the process.

A third inconsistent string is Britain's tenuous status as a sovereign nuclear power. Admittedly the Attlee government's original decision on this had to be taken in some haste, in circumstances when it was peculiarly difficult to judge the strategic future. Since then it has been the usual British story of hanging on doggedly to a fragment of an asset which makes no sense as it stands, or as it has any prospect of becoming. The economic and moral loss should be cut in such a way, however, as to maximize the prospect of successfully restraining nuclear proliferation.

The fourth item is different, in that it represents something which has proved a success but which threatens to outlive its usefulness — the North Atlantic Treaty Organization. France has withdrawn, and it has become clear that the threat of Soviet overrunning of continental Europe has receded. Hence the arguments for maintaining NATO seem to be outweighed by the advantages of renegotiating a wider New Concert of Europe, liquidating the Iron Curtain, and paving the way for reunification of Germany under joint European defense arrangements, guaranteed both by the United States and the USSR. A Declaration of Intent on these lines should not be impossible to negotiate; its fulfillment would evidently take a number of years, during which, however, relaxations of tension and dismantling of particular barriers could already proceed. Thus disembarrassed of the clutter of past pretensions and commitments, which no longer make sense, Britain would be outstandingly well placed to enter the fifth great period of her external relations. (See pp. 320–21.)

Institutionally the new pattern would be based on making the most of the Commonwealth as a club of free nations, and making the most of Britain's leading role in the United Nations, especially as a permanent member of the Security Council. On the basis that colonialism, imperialism, material "special interests", nuclear armaments and membership of exclusive alliances would be excluded, Britain might occupy a role neither "neutralist" nor militarily activist, using her unrivaled diplomatic and other experience and resources to marshal and consolidate the immense potential forces for world peace and development. A bloc of countries committed to similar objectives, and working closely in concert, could do much to realize such a policy through UN and its special agencies, as well as through their own channels, and their fraternal or regional connections.

One of the early practical objectives might be to develop strong compact groups of neighboring uncommitted or neutral countries to limit and minimize world tensions. Perhaps the top priority for such a group would be one based on Malaysia, Indonesia and the Philippines. It would represent an extension of the successful and creditable preparation and launching by Britain of the Federation of Malaysia. The decisive, although bloody, repulse of Communist encroachment in Indonesia, following its military defeat in Malaya and Borneo by British forces, gives a promising opening for such a neighborly grouping. Given strong and sustained economic assistance this could rapidly become one of the most important exporters in the world, able to sustain a quickly rising standard of living, and to make a buffer between China and Australasia, thus facilitating an eventual peaceful settlement for SE Asia.

A second such region of high priority would be East Africa, from Ethiopia to the border of Mozambique and the Zambesi. Contrary to many gloomy prophecies a few years ago, this great region has, under African rule, been able to maintain an adequate degree of order and progress. The investment of more effort of appropriate kinds in its future would appear to be the most promising way towards eventual solution of the grave tensions which must inevitably continue for a long period south of the Zambesi. The objective of multiracial evolution demands that a resounding success should be made of the growth and progress of this critical and promising East African region. The right kinds of aid, not least in highly trained personnel and in building on the already excellent start made in higher education, could transform the outlook for Africa.

A similar effort might perhaps in time be developed jointly with France and Belgium, and with European Common Market backing, in

West and Central Africa between Dakar and the Congo. There might be some advantage in France acting as the senior partner here.

Another obvious sphere for such an initiative is the Caribbean. American attempts to settle the future of Cuba and of the Dominican Republic have not been conspicuously successful, and, although previous more limited and biased moves towards Caribbean regional organization have given only thin results, such a grouping seems historically and geographically inevitable. The Commonwealth is well placed to resume the effort on a long-haul basis. The United Kingdom is especially concerned in view of the repercussions of demographic pressures from the Caribbean, and the bloodties of so many inhabitants of the region with immigrants living in Britain.

A final example would be the replacement of the shadowy CENTO by a grouping based on Turkey, Iran, Afghanistan and Pakistan, if possible also including Cyprus. Here again Commonwealth diplomacy and aid might promote a structure of closer relationships which would help to alleviate tensions and to pacify the Middle East.

The general aim for such neighbor groupings would be to develop along the sort of lines so well pioneered in Europe by the five Nordic States—Denmark, Sweden, Norway, Finland and Iceland. While speaking different languages, and developing diversely, these states have contrived to make a reality of their concerted arrangements and politics and to achieve an intimate and continuous communication from which great social and economic benefits and a valuable example of relaxed tensions have flowed. There seems no ground to be pessimistic about the prospects of eventually developing comparable patterns in the regions above named, and possibly in others. The European Common Market is of course a much larger example of the same trend, but as it is in so many ways unique, and as the needs for British participation in it have already been discussed almost *ad nauseam,* it is not further reviewed here.

British participation in such a range of new initiatives would, it is suggested, amply fill the hiatus left in so many respects by the collapse of imperialism and colonialism. It need not cost more in overseas expenditure than has been required for the maintenance of British bases and armed forces in recent years, plus some of the more overblown of the diplomatic missions and their ancillaries. Above all it would give the British people a new role in which they could believe, and which would bring them credit and friends, and form a realistic investment in the world's future, rather than a hidebound clinging to Britain's somewhat shabby past. A long-term policy which does not win the support of the young is out, and the young clearly are massively opposed to many of the features of British external policy proposed here for elimination. What is more, the young are right.

It will no doubt be said that such a reshaping of British external policy would leave Britain militarily defenseless. The honest answer is that this is just what Britain already is, and must continue to be in modern conditions of strategy and armaments. The difference is not between those who leave Britain defenseless and those who would provide adequate defenses, which no one recently has done or could do. It is between those who would leave Britain friendless and despised, as she is uncomfortably close to becoming, and those who would win her the friendship of a majority of the nations, and the merited enmity of none.

In any case, by persisting in striking old irrelevant postures before a bored and irreverent world public, Britain would be most likely to bring about a recurrence of past reactions which could only be disastrous for her, and to miss the fine but fleeting opportunity which now exists for a renewed role of world leadership in modern dress. By the standards used for the "ten year rule" over military preparedness it is now possible to exclude the prospect of a major war involving Britain before 1978 unless Britain chose to be drawn into a possible war with China.

Such a war, however, would inevitably involve the USSR and the United States on a scale which would render any possible British participation insignificant and pointless from the standpoint of her potential allies. It could only lead to a repetition of the immense waste and humiliation of the Fleet Train, which, on Churchill's orders, became such a crippling toll on our urgently needed shipping at the end of World War II, and which yielded no military or political benefits whatever.

From a British standpoint it is fortunate that China should have emerged as the only great potential aggressor. It means that threats of conventional war have receded farther from this island than for a very long period indeed, and thus offers the British a welcome and immediate opportunity of shifting from their prolonged soldierly posture to their more civilized and civilizing posture, with a minimum of recrimination and disruption. By so doing, and only by so doing, as the repeated abortive initiatives with Peking and Hanoi have shown, Britain might be able to establish an independent authority sufficient to lead in time to some diplomatic bargaining power with Peking and the Chinese satellites, and a capacity to counter Chinese cultural, economic and political infiltration in other countries.

Throughout the world young people, singly and in groups, watch with growing dismay the anachronistic antics of the Powers, and of the great conflicting propaganda fronts. In the United States, as in Europe and elsewhere, many such thoughtful young citizens have had about as much as they can stand of this, but the United States administration, in particular, has got itself into a position from which disengagement is acutely difficult. Only a great new initiative opening up new lines of resolving tensions and offering a focus for the highest human aspirations can offer a tolerable way out. Britain, and probably Britain alone, could quite quickly and without insuperable difficulties give such a lead, and create the conditions for tolerable and acceptable settlements in SE Asia and in Europe.

That is why the continuance of the System as it stands today is a tragedy not only for Britain but for the whole world. Whitehall fiddles while Rome burns. Given a reorientation which would make British attitudes and policies widely acceptable, and enable Britain to become once again regarded as a second home of all who care for liberty and human progress, many doors which have lately been closed, or merely ajar, would be wide open to British personnel, British trade and British investment. The brain drain, instead of merely adding to American dominance, would partly be diverted to providing much-needed scientific and technical or medical reinforcements for countries desperately short of such expertise. The perennial problem of finding constructive outlets for the energies of those who, if bottled up too much at home, become frustrated and turn to making trouble, would become less serious. Easier, more welcome and more frequent interchange, not just of tourists but of working personnel, would help in modernizing Britain, and in bringing Britain better abreast of what is being thought and done in other parts of the world, thus incidentally strengthening Britain's position within the European Common Market. Through such wider and more numerous contacts the ideas and designs of the talented creative young people in Britain would influence the whole world. Even despite all current obstacles and hostile attitudes, world centers such as Paris and New York are becoming increasingly Anglophile in their cultural and leisure life. This process could be greatly stimulated and extended. As the bogus Roman façade of Britain is stripped away the genuine Greek-type contributions would be able to emerge again.

In terms of technical aid perhaps the greatest opening, and the most urgent and immense problem, is that of assisting many nations to bring under control their share of the population explosion. It is deeply discreditable to Britain that, through sheer prejudice and timidity, the precise and well-founded warnings which were clearly given on this subject should so long have been utterly disregarded. Britain is in many ways the country best fitted to provide a large share of the outside aid which is so badly needed in Asia, Africa and Latin America, and one of the necessary reversals of policy is to begin to tackle this problem on an adequate scale. The human misery and degradation, and the probable breakdowns in administration and health services resulting from failure to face the population explosion over the past twenty years, will cost Britain and other advanced nations very dear. The longer effective action is postponed the higher will be the cost, and the longer the more ugly repercussions will continue, as they now must, during the twenty-first century.

We are moving into an age when most previous political, social and economic concepts are becoming increasingly unserviceable. We have in Britain people who are quite capable of the necessary new thinking and new planning once the fixed habit of never listening to them can be broken. It must now be apparent to all that most of the traditional alleged antitheses or choices, such as that between socialism or capitalism, tariffs or free trade, full employment or the Gold Standard, planning or freedom, were quite misconceived. No people preens itself more than the British on practicality, yet probably none has wasted more time during the whole of the past century in bandying around verbiage on half-baked political and economic theories, none of which were properly thought out and hardly any of which were rigorously tested by experiment. There is nothing much wrong with the British except that they have got themselves into a most appalling and chronic muddle about who they are, what they really want, and how to set about achieving it. Most of their inadequate efforts to get out of this muddle have been frustrated from the outset by the same mental laziness and confusion of aim which got them into it in the first place. If the "English sickness" is not, as some foreign observers may be too apt to assume, an incurable and eventually lethal malady, neither is it, as far too many British authorities assume, some temporary and localized affliction largely due to bad luck or the errors or unhelpfulness of others, and thus to be remedied by some simple, partial, short-term devices or techniques involving no basic reorientation or adaptation to the world of tomorrow.

In the next part discussion will hinge on what Edmund Burke, in reviewing British administration 187 years ago, identified as "the grand radical fault: the apparatus is not fitted to the object, nor the workmen to the work". Proposals will there be outlined which, in the event of their being adopted, might enable the bicentenary of Burke's speech to be celebrated by a review of how this grand radical fault had at last been tackled and put right. The nation can on this subject fairly say to its rulers in the words of a later statesman: "Give us the tools and we will finish the job."

Yet no mechanism, however streamlined and efficient, will prove satisfactory unless it fits in smoothly with the complex and diverse nature, and the age-old but ever fresh aspirations and aims, of the British peoples, so often grossly misunderstood, not merely across the Channel and the oceans, but right at the center of their own governmental organs. One of the greatest and best features of the British way of life is its perennial and inspired blending of the new with the old, leading to increased variety, harmonized into a unity through tolerance and perception. One of the crassest, and historically the most resented, features of successive models of British misgovernment has been the repetition of political and administrative attempts to freeze out or extirpate parts of this diversity, and to cram the remainder into some more or less rigid mold according to the current prejudices of those who happen to have managed to lay hold of the levers of power. This is something which the British peoples are bad at analyzing but quick to sense and to react against, whether in terms of the insurrections under the Plantagenets and Tudors, the civil war, the Chartists or the General Strike of 1926, or of the Pilgrim Fathers and other disillusioned emigrants right down to the current brain drain.

For centuries there was widespread and successful resistance to any but the sketchiest development of government, in the partly mistaken belief that it would afford a bulwark against such interference being pushed too far. Now that at last the nation can no longer get along with a mentally retarded administration, whose development has been arrested for the past hundred years, the great issue is how to harmonize a new model administration, not only with the need for effective progress, but with the full diversity and maturity of the British peoples.

The sheer technical task of devising and constructing such an administration is perhaps the least difficult part of it. The more difficult is to
heal the breach between US and THEM, and to ensure that the new
model reflects, and keeps reflecting, what the nation is and wants,
growing and adapting itself as times change. For certain privileged
groups have over many years built up a remarkably close relationship
with certain organs of government. Regiments in the army have been
almost as much the preserve of particular social circles as their clubs
in St. James's Street. A large, although slowly diminishing, part of the
diplomatic service has been drawn from highly specific sections of the
total population. It would be wrong to condemn this absolutely. The
same applies to, say, the Lifeboat Service, where the reasons are obvious and generally acceptable. The abuses arise when well-placed
groups, whoever they may be, exert their power to exclude or prejudice others from areas where free competition would give better results, which is no doubt the rule, but is not without valid exceptions.

Apart from such abuses it is important that every group or element
which wants and is able to contribute towards the operative as well as
the representative aspects of government should be encouraged and
enabled to do so to the limits of its capacity. This is another reason for
breaking up the archaic Civil Service hierarchies, and redistributing
many functions to differently recruited and differently organized
branches of a wider public service. For example, just after World War
II there was a much esteemed radio service called Weather London,
through which those who cared could hear the detailed state of the
weather at many points throughout Britain at various hours of the day.
This involved for the first time broadcasting direct bulletins read by
the actual technicians working hour by hour on the job, whose accents
were regarded as terrible not only by the BBC and the higher Civil
Service but by a section of the listening public. Had the weather been
willing to oblige by not changing so intricately and so continually these
men would have been put off the air as unsuitable, and replaced by
much more ignorant fellows with much more polish and much better
accents. Except where such physical circumstances forbid it, that is
just what happens. Why? The men who carried Britain to world leadership in the industrial revolution must often have had shocking accents. Later in the nineteenth century, the more refined the voice of
Britain became the more Britain fell behind. The time when any of
those who understand and contribute to technology and the sciences
and arts can be allowed to be looked down upon and pushed into the

background by well-bred ignoramuses should by now be long past. The young, happily, appear to be fast losing this particular type of snobbery. A modern Britain, making full use of its human resources, will speak confidently and effectively with far more voices and accents than in the recent past, and, let us face it, many of them will not be good accents. However much a good accent may be worth, a good man with a bad accent is worth more.

The truth of this is readily seen in activities where talent is in short supply and is a matter of life and death in competitive success, as in producing films, plays and television programs, in sculpture, in popular music, fashion and other branches of design, mountaineering, and various forms of racing, sport, and record-breaking. It is in such fields that, even in Britain, humble origins count for less and less as a handicap, as does being young, and that British performance tends to be well abreast and not infrequently ahead of other nations. By an odd coincidence these are among the activities most remote from and least influenced by government. Unhappily modern misgovernment has tended to harass, economically undermine and then take over even these last strongholds of individual and team excellence. It is for that reason, above all, that the whole pattern and fiber of government must be remade before the present system can impose its own dreary mediocrity on the creative springs of Britain.

At the present stage in social evolution mankind is ready for a great step forward in the quality of living, and in the fulfillment of human potentialities. No nation is better placed to play a leading part in this than Britain, but four great obstacles stand in the way. The first, and the most stubborn, is the System. The second is a worldwide state of illiteracy in the right uses of economics and technology, emergence from which is barely coming within sight yet. The third is the absurd and tragic population explosion, which threatens literally to trample underfoot every prospect of civilized advance. The fourth is the continuing risk of nuclear war, fed by the hatreds, suspicions and distortions arising from long periods of abuse of power, above all by the larger nations of Europe, including Britain.

Of these four great obstacles only the first is purely domestic, and its removal is within the power of the British and of nobody else. If it is not removed, quickly and in full, Britain is destined to count for less and less in world affairs. If it is removed, then Britain is as well placed as any nation to take a leading part in tackling the other three, none of which presents insuperable difficulties, although all are grim and will inflict much more damage before they are mastered. Concentration upon the main object of fulfilling the human potentialities of Britain by the unrestricted and intelligent use of Britain's human resources is the key. The British role now is to show just how governments can be made to stop trying to use their nations as blunt instruments in order to achieve some imposed and often immoral purpose, and to demonstrate how a government can be reshaped to become simply the practical instrument by which the nation expresses and puts into practice the sum of its aspirations and capacities, translated into manageable programs.

PART SEVEN

TOWARDS AN UP-TO-DATE GOVERNMENT

CHAPTER 20

Proposals for Reform

British governmental institutions now have to function in conditions differing fundamentally from those for which they were designed, and further immense changes are in prospect. It is extraordinary in view of these changes that the need for a comprehensive recasting of the institutions has not yet been generally recognized. It is all the more extraordinary in view of the dismal record of misgovernment, of failures and of catastrophes, which have dominated recent British history, and which have made life a misery for so many, from top Ministers to the citizens who are merely toads beneath the harrow. No prudent investor would keep his money in a concern whose management had adapted itself so little during the past century, yet the lives and livelihood of all the British are willy-nilly in the hands of just such a management. Every time it falls down it is we who get bruised.

No reasonable man can any longer question that reform is urgent, and that it must be comprehensive and drastic. Such reform must combine the thorough correction of deep-seated defects which have already revealed themselves in practice with the development of a balanced and adequate structure of government. While these two requirements are distinct it is possible to meet them in combination, and thus to remedy past faults while preparing to lead rather than to lag in the future. A satisfactory basis of management, practice and manning, to meet the needs of a great nation approaching the problems of the twenty-first century, can be combined with preserving desirable historical continuity.

To produce what amounts to an indictment of many present practices and organizations without having the courage or the capacity to offer any concrete alternative would not be helpful at the present time.

On the other hand, anyone faced with such a task must be keenly conscious of his own limitations and weaknesses. Whether successfully or not this book has, however, aimed to distill from the British record something of the essence of British aspirations and requirements, and to relate these to present-day conditions. In exposing the unconformity of existing government structure and outlook to these requirements it attempts, not to argue what the British ought to be or ought to want, but to establish who they are and what they do want. If this has been truly done, although the particular formulation is no doubt controversial and in parts faulty, the concept behind it, of harmonizing the structure of their state to the wishes of the British people, should prove less disputable.

While it would have been over-optimistic until very recently to discuss comprehensive systematic rearrangements and radical changes in practice, such an approach is perfectly realistic now, subject to one proviso, that too many stick-in-the-muds do not too stubbornly insist that it is not, and thereby make it not so. Rousseau, unfortunately, lacked the necessary social science technicians to ascertain what the General Will was, and to devise means for fulfilling it. We are better off in such respects, and we can therefore begin, tentatively and in due humility, to edge forwards towards the satisfaction of concepts of human polity developed for us by great men of the past, who in that sense were born before their time.

In doing so it is also possible to resume the recurrent popular movement in England for something which is not just shoddy and squalid and second best, but which achieves the quality and the fulfillment of human possibilities sensed by people from time to time however dimly, as a latent promise within them: the spirit of the Arthurian legends, of *Piers Plowman,* of Shakespeare's *Henry V,* of Cromwell's Commonwealth, and of the Battle of Britain. Such fulfillment must remain a dream until it can be married with the will to achieve it and with the technical means for the task, both of which are no longer beyond the realm of possibility.

At the beginning of last century the functions of government were virtually limited to foreign relations in peace and war, and to keeping order at home. The great majority of the electorate at that time did not want to see these expanded. Now they extend into virtually every

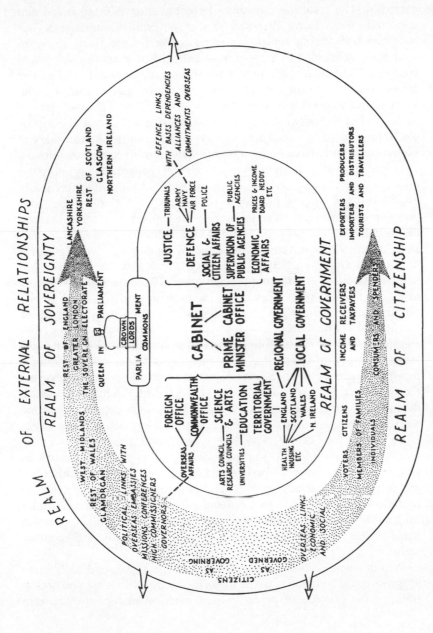

THE UNITED KINGDOM BODY POLITIC
A SCHEMATIC OUTLINE OF THE PROPOSALS

aspect of human life and there are still demands for them to be further extended. The resulting growth and complication is often noted and deplored. What is rarely noted is that government in essence has switched from being something imposed on people from above to something demanded by people from below. Unfortunately the whole tradition and bias of government tends to make it cling to the earlier image, and thus to frustrate and antagonize the mass of citizens who want it, but who want to feel that it is "Ours," not "Theirs." Just as nationalizing the railways gave the passengers not the least comfort or joy as owners, so universal suffrage has failed to shift the machinery of government away from being a blunt instrument to coerce the citizen.

If government is shorn of its mystique and recognized as simply the greatest of common services of the nation, a frame of reference is established for judging its degree of success in this role. The basic problem is seen to consist of improving the capacity and strengthening the incentive of a larger proportion of citizens to take up active citizenship; of providing convenient and effective channels of two-way communication and of participation through which this can be given life and can function; of adapting the activities of Members of Parliament to enable them to play a key role in expressing and educating public opinion and in bringing it effectively to bear upon the executive; of freeing the Cabinet from enslavement to the problems arising from conflicting or half-baked policies, and from decisions taken in the absence of adequate knowledge, and enabling it to exercise a strategic top-level guidance over the development of public policy: of freeing the public service from the clutter of outdated hierarchies and castes, departmentalism, amateurism in high circles and excess of routine work, and enabling a small number of compact key departments to exercise, under the Cabinet, a modern type of top management over the nation's business; of restoring the judiciary to its full historic role as guardian of the citizen's liberties and overhauling administrative law and justice to fit that requirement; and of greatly increasing delegation to national, functional, regional, local and other bodies which, under safeguards and supervision, are more apt than Whitehall to perform many of the tasks of government acceptably, efficiently and economically.

Within such a frame of reference more rapid and deliberate progress could be made with the historic process of sharing and decentralizing the exercise of power, which, often in disregard of current theory, has been under way in Britain for more than three centuries. Greater dispersal of power would be in the interests both of political evolution and of managerial efficiency. Attempts to hog power on the part of one element in the body politic—the grossest current offender being the Treasury—are undesirable in principle and intolerable in practice, and no reform worthy of the name can fail to come down on such usurpations with firm hand. Intimately linked with greater dispersal of power is greater fluidity of communication and mobility of persons within, into, and out of the public service. A contemporary structure of government should have fewer and less pronounced discontinuities between the various parts of the whole, central and local, and should be capable of carrying much more rapidly a much larger volume of messages and responses of all kinds right from one end to the other, and of ensuring quicker, more sympathetic and better coordinated action wherever action is called for.

One of the great fallacies of the existing system is to suppose that failure to gather, analyze and disseminate facts, failure to forecast and to check progress systematically, and failure to give authority to people who are trained to use such aids in planning and administration, can be compensated for by endless committee work, where too many officials who are too complacent about too much ignorance merely sit round a large table to exchange its arid fruits.

The key to co ordination and to getting the best results with the highest morale is a clearly thought-out plan, based on a complete and sound appreciation of the assembled facts, fully and simply explained to all whose efforts are essential to its fulfillment. Field-Marshal Montgomery and Admiral Nelson were among those who have grasped and brilliantly applied these basic principles for Britain's good, but of course neither of them would have been admitted to the Civil Service or, had this accidentally occurred, they would soon have been extruded, with large black marks against them.

It cannot be too strongly emphasized that the shorter the political and economic perspective, the dimmer and more confusing the model in our minds of where we stand and where we are going, and the fewer the people who are, and feel themselves, in the picture, the more frustration will be experienced, the more energy will be dissipated and the less useful result will be achieved. Since this is roughly the existing situation the right course is in approximately the opposite direction to that hitherto followed by those ruling the destinies of Britain. Fortunately a large and growing number of citizens have begun to recognize that this is so. This book is intended to encourage and assist them in their meditations. As Disraeli wrote:

> A political institution is a machine; the motive power is the national character. With that it rests, whether the machine will benefit society, or destroy it. Society in this country is perplexed, almost paralysed; in time it will move, and it will devise. How are the elements of the nation to be blended again together?

This task of blending again together cannot be shirked or bypassed simply by a reorganization of the machinery of government, however excellent. The essential elements and partners in government include the governed, not merely because they are in Britain the ultimate sovereign as electors, but because their awareness of their own identity, their readiness to release and bend their energies to a common task and their sense of its value and its compatability with their human dignity and well-being are the required driving force without which the programs and policies of government will be of no avail.

Nor is a short cut to be found in exhortation, or in the smooth devices and magic spells of public relations. These can promote sound policies already fully thought out and organized through effective and competent executive agencies, and needing only added public understanding and good will for their successful realization. They cannot compensate for shoddy thinking and neglected homework in high places, nor can they retrieve or salvage policies and programs which are foundering, through their own built-in unseaworthiness, in the stormy oceans of economics and politics.

It is for this reason that what may appear to some an undue emphasis has been laid in earlier chapters on historical and background factors underlying the present mood and predicament of Britain. For those who still have not learnt that gimmicks and short-cuts offer no solution such fundamentals may still seem irrelevant, but to fail to grasp and to build on them would simply be to add one more dreary chapter to the century of evasions, of illusions and of wanderings into blind alleys which makes up British history since about 1855.

Enabling and encouraging all citizens to take up some form of personal and direct participation in some aspect of government according to their own tastes and resources is clearly a long-dated undertaking. For that very reason it is important to make an early start. Such a start, once widely perceptible even on a token scale, will subtly improve the atmosphere, siphoning off a part of pent-up frustration, harnessing extra energies to undermanned or handicapped efforts by volunteers or officials, and offering a basis on which plans and hopes for the future can gradually take shape. But this cannot be achieved by half-baked measures dribbled out in penny packets in the normal British way.

A beginning naturally presents itself with the electoral roll and the right to vote. By this means it is possible at least to know who and where all the citizens are, while they know that they are voters and have certain minimum civic duties expected of them in Parliamentary and local elections at longish intervals. How can a warmer and more satisfying dwelling be built on this cold and almost barren ground, a structure in which the forgotten citizen can begin to feel remembered, wanted and in the game?

One of the first needs is somewhere for citizens to meet, and something significant for them to meet about. Almost everywhere, however poor, except in the most remote and scattered country districts, there are already existing buildings where all the citizens can assemble, either owned by local authorities, or by community organizations. Many of these buildings are standing empty day after day, and are crying out to be more fully used. Whatever inhibits active citizens from getting together it cannot be physical lack of accommodation. Where nothing else exists schools, churches and chapels are never far away.

Despite the publicized growth of leisure, volunteer man-hours and leadership are commonly in short supply. Where such situations are fully probed it is not the potential which is lacking, but the capacity to realize it. A proper modesty in coming forward to take up responsibility often masks an apathy and inertia, a timidity about perhaps stirring up personal jealousies, or a reluctance to learn about and embark upon something novel, but all these can be overcome without insuperable difficulty in most cases. It seems therefore reasonable to suppose that the development of active democracy need not be barred either by lack of basic facilities or by lack of suitable manpower if really worthwhile ways for citizens to participate more actively can be found. But can they?

Self-evidently any program of active democracy should hinge at its national-international end on Parliament, and at its local end on the local authority and the local community organizations.

Taking the Parliamentary end first, should it not be possible to marry the citizen's unsatisfied hunger for status and participation with

Parliament's unsatisfied hunger for information and support? This could not be solidly and continuously achieved without an organized regular channel, prototypes of which were in fact successfully developed during World War II in the shape of the Hansard Society and the Army Bureau of Current Affairs (later, before its untimely abolition, converted into the civic Bureau of Current Affairs).

The obvious need is for an attractive, authoritative impartial service of information and explanation about the nature and current activities of both Houses of Parliament, in suitable form for use by all interested citizens wishing to keep up to date with public affairs either generally or on any particular subject. This implies that general and summary communications could be reinforced by more detailed and specialized material on demand. The preparation and issue of such material should be under the authority of the House of Commons, although its execution might be delegated to a sponsored unofficial body of suitable composition and expertise. For purposes of distribution, and to supplement this Parliamentary material with much else from United Nations and other appropriate international sources, from local government and from responsible public bodies, there should be constituted once more something roughly equivalent to the Bureau of Current Affairs. This would also arrange for lecturers or debaters, films, visiting discussion teams and many other forms of communication, including attractive and concrete suggestions for profitable and practical programs of meetings or events at the local level. At this level local elected members, including the local Member of Parliament, together with local representatives and officials would be *ex officio* members of a panel to advise and foster the local citizen groups in their area, each of which, however, would have its own elected voluntary officers, who should change at fairly frequent intervals. The agenda in each case would vary widely according to local conditions and interests, but running through each should be the common thread of elucidating the impact on the community of events and new thinking at national or international level and of assessing, digesting, and making known to the center the doings, aspirations, problems and grievances of the local community and its minority elements.

Each of these citizens' groups should be given the services mentioned above without charge. They should however be required to affiliate to a national council of citizen groups, which should have power under the terms of membership to guard against serious abuses, such as refusal to admit or give a fair hearing to minorities, or seizure of control and monopolization of the agenda or facilities by particular interests or parties. Subject to such broad ultimate disciplinary powers for holding the ring, the freest discussion and controversy should be in order.

Many existing bodies such as political parties, Rotary Clubs, Women's Institutes or Townswomen's Guilds, trade union or co-operative branches, church organizations, civic societies or trusts and charitable bodies should be encouraged to belong actively and to explain their aims and work, if possible by such means as organizing trips or visits of inspection, which should embrace also all publicly operated services. Active membership in such citizen groups would thus not only be in itself a means of status and communication, but would be a doorway to many other more specialized opportunities and invitations. This in itself would be an encouragement to those devoted to any particular interest to pass through the right doorway rather than to try to use the citizen group itself as an arena beyond the limit appropriate to its role as serving all interests of all citizens.

Obviously it would not be desirable or practicable to try to set up such citizen groups everywhere at once. Perhaps the best approach would be, after full consultation with knowledgeable and interested persons of all kinds, to select something of the order of a hundred places scattered throughout the United Kingdom where promising nuclei are in existence, and where sufficiently keen and sustained support seems probable. With the aid of such a national sample the right lines for further development could be arrived at by investigation, experiment and discussion. Eventually it could be hoped to reach a stage where becoming a citizen would automatically mean becoming a member of a visible, lively, and friendly neighborhood club, itself belonging to a national family of similar clubs. The more active of these might promote or engage in any competitive, exchange or social activities, as well as forming a firm and recognized element in the national polity, and a means of two-way communication between government and governed, with an open-ended remit and agenda. No doubt a number of the clubs would fail through apathy, through misbehavior of unruly or self-centered intransigents or on other grounds, but even if 10 percent or 15 percent of communities had such fully functioning citizen groups they would go far to transform relations between government and governed, and to convert from fiction to fact the ultimate sovereignty of the electorate.

The natural next step is to the House of Commons, which is currently under severe and widespread criticism. Not all that criticism is necessarily well-founded and just, but to expect justice in politics would be looking too far into the future, and the criticism is certainly a fact of which a note must be taken. How long has Parliament still got to mend its ways and improve its image before anti-Parliamentary opinion gathers dangerous strength? Opinions will differ on the answer, but he would be an optimist who could suggest anything longer than three years at most. In one sense Parliamentarians are entitled to sympathy. After all, they now exercise at most times little real power and yet they receive a big share of the kicks and reproaches for all that goes wrong. On the other hand Parliament is still the one body which, if fully convinced of the need, has the undoubted authority and duty to insist on changes, however drastic, throughout all other branches of government. In so far as it should do just that, and has entirely failed to, Parliament is entitled to perhaps even less sympathy and exculpation than is commonly accorded to it. At this time, in particular, the sovereign but frozen electorate is vividly aware that those gainfully occupied as Members of Parliament have given themselves one of the heftiest wage increases of recent times, and the electorate wonders what the Members are going to do to justify it.

One of the main dilemmas of Members is that they are situated at a point in the constitutional flow of business between, on the one hand, the electorate, an inchoate, inarticulate mass whose sole formal act of communication at quinquennial intervals is hardly more meaningful than signals picked up by radar from outer space, and on the other the tightly organized power-hungry ranks of Ministers and their Departments. These would clearly like to treat Members with about as much consideration as Members themselves might sometimes be tempted to show to the electorate. A reassertion of Parliamentary authority is clearly dependent on finding two remedies to this unbalanced state of affairs. On the one hand the electorate, and the Member of Parliament who serves as its guide, voice and conscience, need to be given greater credibility and substance, so that the executive will really have something to regard with a certain degree of awe and apprehension, singularly remote from its thoughts at the present time. On the other hand the concentration of power which has so inopportunely slipped out of Parliament's hands and become lodged next door in No. 10 must in future be shared afresh, if Parliament is ever again to rule. This however would not be enough, and it certainly would not be desirable, unless simultaneously the capacity of the House of Commons to hold the reins of government can be greatly improved. The urgency of this need would be heightened by televising Parliamentary proceedings, an innovation calculated to give sleepless nights, if not to Members, at any rate to many lovers of democracy. Let the dog see the rabbit is a healthy English maxim, but it does presuppose that the rabbit can run. The dog is lethargic enough already.

Television programs on current affairs in which leading figures in public life have discussed such problems as incomes and prices policy played a considerable part in the events of 1966, and were ably complemented by a series of revealing interviews with men and women in the street on their opinions and reactions to government decisions and to other developments. It seems possible that a stage has lately been reached at which television has made a breakthrough as a serious medium of communication comparable with that achieved by radio broadcasting during the General Strike of 1926. In any reassessment of the future role of Parliament the part which can be played by television confrontations and discussion needs to be fully considered, along with the televising of the proceedings of Parliament itself. The latter may well not prove the most important aspect of the relationship.

At the center of the complex of problems revolving round Parliament is the issue of improving the quality of Members and of their work. How can this be achieved? The recent pay increases, although they seem likely to change the educational and vocational composition of the House in a somewhat favorable sense, cannot in themselves do much. Anything which would enable Members to speak more authoritatively for more representative and mature public opinion would help, as has been suggested above. What else?

Innumerable possible reforms of Parliament are under discussion, of which quite a number sound promising, and they cannot all be reviewed here. One point which seems not to have been given enough attention is the numerical size of the House of Commons. In its great days during the eighteenth century it rose from just over 500 members to nearly 550 after the union with Scotland, but throughout the nineteenth century, until as recently as the partition of Ireland after 1920, it was larger than its present strength of 630. As population has risen (in England and Wales) about six times since 1800 and the electorate has been expanded to form a much larger part of it, it appears that the present size of the House of Commons represents rather the practicable maximum than the optimum ratio to voters. But why, especially now that Members cost so much and are so overcrowded, should the House be kept at such a ceiling level? Might not some 400 members representing some 60,000 electors each, with better accommodation and staff support, do a better job than 630 representing some 40,000 each? Either way the number is far too large to permit widespread individual contact, and unless the individual is to be a permanent cipher some mediating device, such as has been proposed in the citizen groups, is in any event essential.

The Government of Ireland Act in 1920 not only greatly reduced the size of the House of Commons, by eliminating no less than ninety-two Irish MPs; it also for the first time in the history of the United Kingdom set up a subordinate regional Parliament at Stormont for Northern Ireland, with a House of Commons fifty-two members strong and a Senate of half its size. There was also a continued representation by twelve MPs at Westminster.

The political conditions of Northern Ireland are peculiar, having fortunately no counterpart in Great Britain. Yet the Northern Ireland Parliamentary experiment appears to have worked pretty well, insofar as it has enabled much legislation to be enacted and administration to be conducted on lines quite distinct from those across the Irish Sea, and in certain cases more advanced, while maintaining the Westminster Parliament's unchallenged sovereignty and handling of external affairs, finance and the armed forces. At least in this case, it has proved possible to delegate wide governmental powers to a region comprising less than 3 percent of the United Kingdom's population without the experiment involving Parliament in any serious trouble, and indeed with the result that Northern Ireland's problems take up proportionately very little time at Westminster, serious though they are. The fact that another Parliament and government rule the rest of Ireland affords an independent yardstick for judging performance. There is no evidence for doubting the capacity of the regional Parliament to compete in terms of efficiency and achievement. Yet, but for a narrow strip of sea, it would never have been created.

There has as yet been no serious and substantial demand for a resumption of the Scottish Parliament, or for the establishment of one in Wales. The true significance of this is uncertain, in view of the stranglehold exercised over Scots and Welsh political representation by party machines which give every appearance of being totally subservient to direction from Smith Square, London S.W.1. The oddest case is that of Scotland, perhaps the only advanced nation to possess its own law, and in effect its own government, without having retained its own Parliament. It is difficult to resist the conclusion that at least some of the notorious faults and deficiencies of St. Andrew's House are due to this peculiarity in being responsible, as virtually a national government, to a Parliament four hundred miles away in what for many purposes is quite a different country. Decentralization of Scottish affairs to Scotland has been so gradual that the virtual completion of the process passes almost unremarked, and its logical implications in terms of political structure have been largely ignored except by extremists. If, as there is strong reason to believe, the future is with delegation and decentralization from Whitehall and Westminster, the question of resuming a Scottish Parliament within the ambit of the Act of Union cannot much longer be ignored. Such a Parliament, judging by the Northern Irish model, could do much for Scottish development, and in terms of numbers and resources within its jurisdiction it would be more than three times as strong.

Such a move in Scotland would do much to facilitate and encourage adequate decentralization in England and Wales. Wales is especially unfortunate in its centrifugal pattern of geographic units, the absence of any obvious functional national capital around which to rally, the lack of such distinctive and robust features as Scots law, and the arbitrary incorporation in England for the past four centuries of its second most populous county, Monmouthshire. Compared with Northern Ireland, and most of northern England, Wales has received a pretty adequate share of new economic development ever since World War II, and even earlier. But prosperity, such as it is, does not necessarily bring fulfillment, especially as an accelerated rate of invasion by English people and by alien culture has been the price which Wales has had to pay for it.

There seems no doubt that, if existing trends continue, most of the surviving elements of the culture existing in Britain since before the Anglo-Saxon invasions will be smothered and killed by the end of this century. Unfortunately most Welshmen simply recognize and occasionally bemoan this impending fate while others seek to avert or postpone it by acts of violence, neither of which is markedly constructive or likely to help. A joint Anglo-Welsh study of the ramifications of the problem and the possible means of handling it as an issue concerning the preservation of Britain's heritage seems overdue. It is not good enough for the English, having helped themselves to most of the best land on the island, to shrug off the final extinction of their smaller neighbor's national identity as being no concern of theirs.

Greater London, like Wales, suffers from chronic meddling by

Whitehall in such affairs as its traffic and police. The latter through Scotland Yard has certainly carried some national interest, although in constitutional theory the central government is not supposed to control police forces. On the other hand London, especially the City of Westminster, has long enjoyed certain unfair advantages over other local authorities, such as having most of its admirable central parks handsomely maintained at the expense of the national taxpayer. The new structure of thirty-two London Boroughs embraced within Greater London with its co-ordinating Council creates an administrative unit larger in population than nearly half the countries in Europe, being only just smaller than Portugal, Greece and Bulgaria, and a great deal more prosperous. There are already signs that this Council is thinking in more strategic terms than the much narrower although already huge, London County Council which preceded it. That Council was already able on occasion successfully to defy Whitehall and Westminster. With the rapid growth in partial autonomy of, for example, the Northeast, the distribution and center of gravity of power over internal affairs in Britain is visibly changing. There is scope for relieving Parliament of much regional and local detail, as in Northern Ireland, without leaving responsibility for dealing with it in limbo. Bolder and more positive delegation is the answer.

If Parliament is to regain its lost control over other political institutions it must learn quickly to delegate under proper safeguards in other directions. The Select Committee on Nationalised Industries shows the way, and its success should not be left without follow-up. There is clearly a need for a corresponding but even more powerful Select Committee on the Public Service in all its ramifications. This might possibly be created by reconstituting on a wider basis the Public Accounts Committee, and, as will be proposed later, giving it teeth by developing the Comptroller and Auditor-General into a Comptroller-General of Accountable Services with a much strengthened staff.

A further badly needed tightening-up and return to sound constitutional principles and practice lies in the field of administrative tribunals and administrative law. It has been a clear dereliction of duty by Parliament to have allowed these pervasive and potentially despotic powers to fall so largely into the hands of Ministers and the Civil Service. This blunder must be corrected. It stems in large part from the mistake of the great Dicey, who felt so horrified at the idea of the French *Droit Administratif* that until nearly the end of his life he never bothered to find out what it was. He therefore bequeathed a wholly misleading account of the issue to students and practitioners of politics in Britain down to this day. So badly was the pitch queered that the correct and comprehensive studies by subsequent scholars have been largely disregarded. The great opportunity presented in 1929–30 to the Committee on Ministers' Powers for taking a new look at this matter in the light of Lord Chief Justice Hewart's spirited but one-sided presentation in *The New Despotism* was muffed. As Professor W. A. Robson sadly recorded (in *British Government Since 1918*), although its report was "sane and temperate . . .":

> . . . the Committee was so restricted by its own narrow ideas about rule of law that it failed to make any practicable proposals, except on matters of procedure, for the reform of administrative justice. It failed to produce a practicable criterion by which judicial functions should be entrusted to Ministers and administrative tribunals . . . it allowed itself to be hamstrung by the illusory distinction between judicial and quasi-judicial decisions which was contained in the Committee's terms of reference and introduced in many different forms by several witnesses, notably the Treasury Solicitor. The Committee's purpose in pursuing this chimerical distinction was to recommend that judicial decisions should normally be confided to the Courts while quasi-judicial decisions can properly be entrusted to administrative tribunals.

This clear and gentlemanly exposition of a characteristic piece of British Civil Service thimble-rigging shows where the rats got in. The record of Crichel Down, the Chalk Pit case, Stansted Airport and other notorious Departmental malpractices illustrates what was bound to happen afterwards.

To complete the usual story we have the stock gambit of the largely impotent Council of Tribunals being created in 1958 to silence the more tiresomely pertinacious critics of these malpractices, and, when that failed, the resort to the yet further device of a Parliamentary Commissioner or Ombudsman, who, if the Civil Service has any say in it, will share the same fate. If the drowsy watchdogs of British liberties have not learned the game by now they never will.

What is needed is in outline clear enough. Civil servants and others in similar positions should not be permitted to continue to hide beneath the woolly folds of the Prerogative, but should be brought within the bounds of a clear and comprehensive Statute of Administration, in which all administrative law, and major practice which has the force of law, should be reviewed, modernized and codified, in clear and understandable terms, eliminating all quasi-judicial quasi-gibberish and other forms of Whitehall doubletalk. The citizen is entitled to know where he stands *vis-à-vis* Ministers and the public service, and also *vice versa,* for the victims of the present state of this branch of misgovernment are by no means all on one side. The head which rolled after Crichel Down was that of a well-liked Minister of Agriculture who never knew anything about it until the mischief had been done. Civil servants themselves are not infrequently deprived of their rightful due by chicanery in the Treasury and elsewhere which could be much reduced, if not eliminated, by giving a modern and businesslike legal form to their terms of service. Even Estacode, probably the most important managerial document in the country, is so far as possible concealed from the public.

An essential part of such a Statute of Administration would be comprehensive provisions for administrative courts which would wholly and finally relieve Departmental Ministers of any kind of judicial function. The new courts would both hear aggrieved citizens on any judicial aspects of administration and assess and decide due compensation where a citizen is damnified by administrative action within some area where provision for compensation has been made by Parliament. On certain types of issue which closely touch civic liberties there should be a right of appeal to the regular Courts of Justice, for which, as well as for Parliament, these administrative courts would in effect be exercising delegated jurisdiction. It is especially important that cases where the administration is suspected of exceeding its legal powers should be tested in this way, and should not be in effect left, as they too often are now, to be determined by the administrators themselves as judges in their own cause. The healthy fear of an adverse judicial decision has been allowed to become much too remote from the thoughts of Ministers and their civil servants. But Parliament also should be equipped fully to resume its watchdog role through a Select Committee on Administrative Law, reviewing at frequent intervals the work of all bodies which exercise delegated judicial powers in any degree, shape or form. Such a Select Committee might be advised by the Council on Tribunals, whose findings should be regularly referred to it, and by the Parliamentary Commissioner or Ombudsman. It should from time to time promote sample field inquiries, with the help of the national council of citizen groups, whose membership should have a direct line of communication with it through the appropriate Member of Parliament. In such ways a transition, inevitably somewhat gradual, might be made from today's misgovernment towards self-government in the future.

A distinct but equally important issue is the right of the government to promulgate, and the duty of the citizen to follow, "guidelines". Such virtual directives, which have no basis in law, may in practice prove necessary if things have been allowed to get in enough of a mess. In principle, however, they are objectionable and should whenever possible be curbed by Parliament.

One further area in which Parliament needs to be specially equipped to watch the performance and evolution of delegated functions is the world overseas, in which membership of the United Nations, of other international groupings and alliances and prospectively of the Common Market passes over the line between delegation of function and actual transfer or sharing of the rights and acts of sovereignty itself. However welcome such a process may be, it is essentially one which ought to be continuously watched and reviewed at the highest level, not only by the executive but by Parliament as trustee for the nation. Some kind of Select Committee or similar body, not to be confused with a Foreign Affairs Committee, but concentrating on all that relates to the development of an international political structure embracing Britain, appears the obvious answer.

Finally there is the important duty and function of looking forward, for which the Estimates Committee, suitably adapted, might possibly provide the House of Commons with an instrument. Such a Committee should particularly satisfy itself that the duty of organizing foresight, and of providing it with the necessary tools, is understood and fulfilled throughout the machinery of government, and that the assumptions and objectives adopted are in turn thoroughly known to Parliament so that their implications and tendencies can be discussed, whenever necessary, with Ministers concerned. (Since this was written it has been officially proposed to set up new Parliamentary Committees on agriculture and on science and technology. These may do no harm but they do not seem likely to do much good. Unlike the organs here proposed, they are not clearly designed to help the House to perform its own inherent constitutional responsibilities.)

In this part of the discussion, in addition to the possibilities of regional Parliaments or other decentralized bodies, and to noting the success of the existing Select Committee on Nationalised Industries, suggestions have been put forward for possible new committees on the Public Service, on Administrative Law and Justice, on International Political Structure and on Forecasting and Planning. It should be noted that none of these is purely financial, since that is the business of the whole House, and that none of them is concerned with a field or subject in which the House might appear to overstep its constitutional limits and to invade those of the executive. For the House to delegate, and to create from among its own Members, organs for watching and reporting on such delegation is a very different matter, inseparable from the conscientious exercise of its constitutional responsibilities. There are good precedents for developing the powers and procedure of such committees, on the basis of the Public Accounts committee. Allowing for the number of members holding ministerial offices and for those who would prefer to occupy themselves more with legislation and other functions, five high-level standing committees of this sort would give a challenging and worthwhile outlet for the energies of a high proportion of the abler members; and would greatly strengthen the capacity of Parliament to maintain its status and prestige by better fulfilling its essential functions and responsibilities in relation to the electorate on the one hand and the executive and judiciary on the other.

Given a capability for laying off much case-work of a "welfare officer" nature to better staffed and consumer-oriented public services, kept up to the mark by Ombudsmen centrally and locally, the Member of Parliament should find opening before him a much more significant and responsible role as one of a top team chosen to watch, defend, and expand the rights and opportunities of citizens, to keep in closer touch with them on more important issues, to be sufficiently informed to be a searching but constructive critic of executive acts and practices, and to be better informed about the performance, experience and plans of the outside world, in so far as they bear upon this problem of keeping Britain abreast of the times.

For good or ill the nation is now committed to a corps of paid professional politicians. The worst possible outcome of this trend would be to leave the constitutional control of the professionals in the hands of a band of ill-informed, untrained, miscast full-time amateurs, doing a little of everything without any coherent pattern. A clear and realistic appreciation of those functions which essentially flow from Parliament's constitutional role in modern Britain is fundamental to any sound reform of Parliament. The sovereign electorate is entitled to look to every Member of Parliament as a personification and efficient agent of the collective needs of the nation and of the individual needs of each person and family, watching to ensure that the right tasks are correctly envisaged and are acceptably and effectively performed by every arm of government at every point. If the agenda and procedure of Parliament can be better harmonized with this conception, which has always been implicit in it and is not impossibly far from realization today, then it can be confidently hoped that the right men and women will be found to join the cast and to play their appropriate parts.

It is a misconception to argue that Parliament should "do" this or that. Parliament's role is to see that modern competent mechanisms exist to cover all national needs and to keep these mechanisms up to the mark in their standards, programs and performance by continuous, well-informed, constructive criticism.

If Members individually can measure up to this role, then they will automatically cease to be the sort of people whom Ministers and party leaders can herd through the division lobbies without ceremony or adequate explanation. The fiber of the House will have been stiffened and the MP will no longer rate quite so low in the political peck-order compared with a Minister.

As always, much will depend on the process of selection and training. The political parties have a fairly good recent record in weeding out the playboys and adventurers, the axe-grinders and cranks and even a good many of the deserving but dim or plain stupid party stalwarts from the constituencies. There is little reason to doubt that, if the House of Commons can be made into a more demanding and rewarding vocation, the quality of volunteers coming forward will improve considerably and the party selection committees by and large will not fail to take advantage of it. But much also depends on the quality and scale of the opportunities presented by local and regional government for bridging the gap between the parish pump and Westminster, and for bringing on a steady stream of younger, vigorous, experienced and articulate men who are in really close touch with the electorate, and especially with the younger sections of it. For many such men and women membership of the House of Commons will be the crown of a career already rewarding and distinguished in regional or local government. If these are frustrating, old-fashioned and ineffective, then this major source of recruits to Parliament will suffer accordingly. It is time therefore to soften the hitherto over-rigid lines between central and local government, both at the elected and official levels, and to facilitate and encourage a flow between them, in both directions.

It is impracticable in a treatment such as this, and would in any case be confusing and exhausting for the reader, to cover the innumerable detailed reforms and improvements which have recently been under discussion in relation to Parliament, some at least of which appear sound and desirable. The object here must be simply to indicate an approach and a series of broad guidelines for achieving the main purpose of getting Parliament back on course and enabling it once more, in terms of the impending twenty-first century, to fulfill its historic and essential role as the nurse of British political evolution and the guardian of British liberties and opportunities.

By reducing the number of MPs, by shedding some of the burden of detail from them to Ombudsmen, to welfare officers and to subordinate legislatures or councils, by reinforcing safeguards for the liberties of the citizen against administrative misrule, by improving channels and sources of independent information and specialist advice, and by providing more high-level focal points for serious exercise of Parliamentary control, it should be possible to make a start on correspondingly reforming the Executive. More men and women of Ministerial quality should thus be attracted into the House. While serving as Members they would have much better opportunities to gain the necessary experience to fit them for office as Ministers. Considering all the handicaps and frustrations which now beset the path to Ministerial office, and the irreconcilable demands which it is allowed to entail, it is on the whole remarkable that the level of intelligence, experience and integrity among Ministers should be as high as on the whole it recently has been. There are always weak points which stick out, but even parties long denied political power have already proved tolerably successful in deploying Ministerial teams able to put up a reasonable performance after a brief period of induction in face of formidable problems and of the attacks of a highly informed and experienced Opposition. Nevertheless it is incontestable that a larger supply of better-qualified potential Ministers would do much to strengthen British governments, not least by enabling new blood to be brought in when it is wanted rather than when it can be obtained. If the individual MP in his own peculiar role enjoyed more of the status, participation and interesting opportunities now largely monopolized by Ministers, the size and quality of the pool of nationally-tested political talent would benefit. There should be more opportunity for making a national political reputation otherwise than on the front bench at Westminster. Incidentally some of those so trained would be invaluable in providing a backbone for Scottish and Welsh Parliaments if these are constituted, and for elected regional councils in England. On the political as well as the administrative plane too much power should no longer be monopolized by so few at the expense of so many.

It seems neither necessary nor desirable to maintain so many Ministerial posts of Cabinet status as we have got into the habit of expecting. Except during World Wars I and II, when War Cabinets of as few as five to seven members were substituted, modern Cabinets have grown from fourteen to fifteen in the mid-nineteenth century and above seventeen at its end to often even higher figures, up to twenty-three in 1966. It has often been cogently argued that such levels are much too high for efficient working, but the contrary view has strongly tended to prevail. Why is this? Probably two main factors have been responsible, and have overlapped. First, under the party system it is probably essential that the widest practicable group of political leaders having potentially dissident followings should be fully committed to taking responsibility for government policies and decisions. Sharing the collective responsibility of the Cabinet achieves this result as nothing else can. The status it confers induces potential troublemakers, rebels, rivals or embarrassing lone wolves to toe the party line at least for long periods, although, like Frank Cousins in 1966, they may eventually refuse to stay the course. Secondly, Departments whose political chiefs are not in the Cabinet are widely regarded, and what is more, regard themselves, as having been relegated to an inferior status, against which they jib.

Lobbies and pressure groups conducting business with such Departments are particularly concerned that their efforts may be frustrated by the Department itself failing to carry its objectives with the Treasury and the government, and their continual demands for righting the wrong are by no means unwelcome to the Department. It is therefore difficult in present conditions to exclude from the Cabinet Ministers responsible for Departments unless these are either of a purely common service nature, or are in effect sub-departments of some more powerful Minister. Current examples of the first are the Post Office, and Public Building and Works. Recent examples of the second are the Ministers of Defence for the Army, Royal Navy and Royal Air Force, the Minister of Aviation and the Minister of Land and Natural Resources.

At the beginning of 1967 the Cabinet consisted of the Prime Minister, the Lord Chancellor, Lord President of the Council, Chancellor of the Exchequer and President of the Board of Trade, Lord Privy Seal, nine Secretaries of State (for Foreign Affairs, Economic Affairs, Defence, Home, Commonwealth, Colonial Affairs, Scotland, Education and Science and Wales) and eight Ministers (Labour, Housing and Local Government, Agriculture and Food, Transport, Power, Technology, Overseas Development, and Without Portfolio).

As at times other holders of the title "Minister" were outside the Cabinet, while all the Secretaries of State were in it and all the Ministers of State were omitted, it is clear that "Ministers" are the marginal element.

Since 1929, however, the Prime Minister and Foreign Secretary have been the only ones unfailingly included in every Cabinet. The Lord Chancellor, Lord President, Chancellor of the Exchequer and the civil Secretaries of State have had a seat in every peacetime Cabinet, except for a temporary lapse in 1931 in respect of the Secretary of State for Scotland. Certain Departments, such as Health, Transport and Works (recently Public Building and Works) have achieved Cabinet rank intermittently, while two (Labour and Education) appear to have fully established their claims to it in the post-war period.

The famous Haldane Report of the Machinery of Government Committee in 1918 recommended that "the Cabinet should be small in number—preferably ten or, at most twelve". The failure to achieve this reduction must be attributed to the two factors already mentioned, and unless they can be adequately dealt with it is idle to expect any progress in this direction. How might it be achieved? As regards political representation and pacification it appears that the recent trend towards a more dominant "Presidential" role for the Prime Minister, and the development of mass-communications and especially television, have weakened the bargaining power of rebel barons in British political parties, and strengthened the hold of the machine, provided it is used with reasonable commonsense and competence. The failure of Frank Cousins, even with the most powerful trade union in Britain at his disposal, and the backing of very widespread restiveness among the workers, to shake the Wilson administration by his resignation in July 1966 is an indication of this.

A smaller Cabinet, though painful to some, now looks feasible. This however is entirely dependent on ensuring that the political resistances are no longer, as at present, reinforced by powerful Departmental resistances, reinforced in turn by associated lobbies and pressure groups.

The argument for retaining Departmental Ministers as such in the Cabinet boils down to three main points—knowledge of and participation in broad policy formation and decisions, support in pursuing departmental objectives on a wider front, and sheer status. Consultation over, and participation in, decisions affecting his Department directly are omitted, since it is standard practice to call in a Minister on such occasions whether he is a Member of the Cabinet or not. Taking the three points in order, the first has importance in so far as the Cabinet tends to reach decisions, especially when in haste, without consulting Cabinet Committees or other appropriate sifting bodies, and without keeping Ministers who may be indirectly affected fully informed. In the past this has often happened, but the growing development of the Cabinet Commitee and Cabinet Secretariat systems has reduced its significance recently. Given efficient co-ordination, and a reasonable attitude towards calling in Ministers who may be affected, there seems no reason why a substantial reduction in Cabinet size should not be compatible with the operation of even the present Departmental pattern. This however can and should be very much streamlined. The second point is essentially one of power politics, hinging mainly on two sensitive issues. The first is the natural ambition of the Minister to rise not only by doing a good job but by letting his senior colleagues know it, and perhaps winning their support by playing up to them in suitable ways. The second is the struggle for increased resources, which can be affected by knowledge on the part of the Treasury that cuts or paring of estimates will lead to repercussions at Ministerial level. While these considerations must always persist in some form, it is possible to minimize their force by the reforms discussed below. Much the same applies to the status argument in its naked form. It should not be politically or administratively impracticable in future, given such reforms, to reduce the size of the Cabinet to about the level recommended by Haldane, which would unquestionably make possible a higher level of performance. Indeed the practical value of membership for the more specialized Ministers is to some extent illusory, since they must usually in any case be seen but not heard, and the glamor attaching to their Cabinet status arises largely from the decent cloak of secrecy thrown over their often very modest actual contribution to the proceedings.

The Haldane Report, as has been emphasized by Professor Mackenzie in *British Government since 1918,* and by Sir Charles Wilson in his Haldane Memorial Lecture in 1956, was based largely on administrative arguments. "It contains no hint of recognition that the Cabinet's first problem is to *run* Parliament" says Sir Charles, who in turn, however, gives no real evidence for his contention that "In normal times the combination of parliamentary, administrative and political skills in the Cabinet enforces a body of roughly twice the size envisaged by the Haldane Committee." What are "normal times" — 1850, 1899, 1929, or 1966? The Cabinet size at these dates ranged from just above the Haldane level to about ten more.

It appears also from history that political skills in a Cabinet can be mutually discordant, and that as they tend to be associated with strong and vocal personalities one can easily have too much of a good thing, unless the negative and defensive line is taken that they may be less of a nuisance inside than if let loose outside. While in the particular pattern of "normality" prevalent since 1920 pressures of this type have been felt to be conclusive, the most certain fact about the future is that its pattern of "normality" will be very different.

It seems more probable that the decisive element will be the pattern of administration. Even in the recent past political arguments in favor of a larger Cabinet, although powerful, may have been less strong than the administrative vested interests inherent in the number and nature of the separate Departments which have been maintained. Each Department must have a Minister, and each Department but the humblest will move heaven and earth to secure Cabinet status for its Minister, by methods which no Department will admit but which every Department knows. Let us therefore at least suspend judgment whether the political considerations are overriding, and study what might be done on the administrative plane to remedy at this late hour the unfortunate defeat of Haldane, remembering that (as Field-Marshal Sir Douglas Haig testified after the Armistice in 1918) Britain could not have been a victor in World War I had Haldane's earlier reform measures for the War Office and the Army suffered the same fate. "Where would we be today without the Imperial General Staff which was your creation and the Field Service Regulations which you forced through in spite of opposition from Army Council and Treasury?" Where are we today, one might add, without the corresponding genuine reform of the machinery of government to which the Haldane Report, however imperfectly, pointed? Where might we by now have been had he succeeded in fighting through such reforms also against Treasury opposition?

One of the main obstacles to reconstruction of the machinery of government is the claim that what have once been Ministerial offices should continue as Ministerial offices, and what have once been Departments staffed by civil servants should always so continue. Neither commonsense, nor management research nor even history lend support to either of these propositions. In Walpole's government of 1740 the Archbishop of Canterbury, the Lord Steward, the Master of the Horse and the Groom of the Stole were all Ministers, but these posts soon ceased to be Ministerial while the Lord President, the Lord Privy Seal and the Chancellor of the Exchequer have remained Ministerial, although the first two of these three have no Department. Some former Departments, such as the India and Irish Offices, have vanished with their jurisdiction. Others such as Works and the Post Office have remained (although the Post Office is at last on the point of being converted into a Public Agency) but have lost all claim to Cabinet rank. There have been many amalgamations, the most important being that of the Admiralty, War Department and Air Ministry in the new Ministry of Defence. It is significant that this last case is the one in which the needs to work closely with the Pentagon and to measure up to international standards provided some external imperative for reform, to offset the Treasury veto on anything more serious than a palliative.

The basic fact to be fully faced is that organization of a governmental function within a Department staffed by civil servants and presided over by Ministers is only one, and not necessarily the best, of several alternatives, among which a conscious and careful choice should in every case be made. In an earlier chapter of this book we looked at the main categories as they have developed in the past. Among the effective choice of alternatives which they present us for the future are:

> Organization as a Commission or other non-Departmental agency, based on statute, or charter of incorporation, financed by fees, charges or grant-in-aid rather than a straight vote, and staffed only partly, or not at all, from the Civil Service. The success of this pat-

tern has been amply demonstrated by bodies such as the British Broadcasting Corporation, and the Research Councils. It is notable that the one body in this latter field which was constituted as a conventional Civil Service Department—the Department of Scientific and Industrial Research—was as a result of comparative experience abolished in 1965 and replaced largely by a new body, the Science Research Council, created outside the Civil Service under Royal Charter. Many sectors of Departmental work might with advantage follow a similar path.

Organization as a trading or economic concern—a course now belatedly promised for the Post Office, which might also be considered for a number of other services. A useful variant of this is the non-Departmental government purchasing agency, such as the former Crown Agents for the Colonies (now Crown Agents for Overseas Governments and Administration), and the non-Departmental banking and technical service agency, such as the Commonwealth Development Corporation. Another variant is the state-owned firm, such as Cable and Wireless Ltd. which arose from the Imperial Wireless and Cable Conference of 1928.

Organization as a public regulatory or supervisory commission or tribunal. These range from the National Board for Prices and Incomes, the Monopolies Commission, the Industrial Court and the National Insurance Commissioner to the highly successful Gas Council, which has supervised among other things the development of North Sea gas as a domestic fuel.

Organization as a regional or local public service, such as the Highlands and Islands Development Commission, the North of Scotland Hydro-Electric Board, the Commissioners of Northern Lighthouses, the Port of London Authority, the Thames Conservancy and the various New Town Development Corporations.

Organization on a decentralized basis by regional or major local authorities.

Delegation to recognized non-official bodies having some statutory or similar status, such as the National Trusts for England, Wales, and Northern Ireland, and for Scotland, the Royal National Lifeboat Institution and the Women's Voluntary Services and Red Cross.

Between them these alternative models offer such immense opportunities for advantageous transfer of functions outside the Civil Service that it would not be unduly difficult, if they were fully utilized, to cut the Civil Service by more than half, with great gains in efficiency and flexibility for the functions transferred and with great benefits to the healthier and slimmer Civil Service remaining. Such a "cut" has of course nothing in common with proposals for simply discontinuing the performance of essential functions: it relates simply to the best means of organizing, staffing and financing them.

Under such a reorganization three Ministers would become responsible for any necessary government supervision of, or contact with, the hived-off agencies. These would be: for tribunals and all other bodies engaged in administrative law or exercising functions of a judicial nature, the Lord Chancellor; for all public concerns of an economic or trading nature, a new Minister of Public Agencies, who might also occupy some traditional office such as Paymaster-General. He should, initially, be a Minister of Cabinet rank but later, after the launching of the new System, a non-Cabinet Minister working under the supervision of the Minister of Economic Affairs might be sufficient. The third Minister would be the appropriate Secretary of State for English, Scottish or Welsh Affairs, who would handle everything of a regional and local character within the three national territories.

Under such a reorganization only small higher policy and top administrative functions of such Ministries as Transport, Power and Public Building and Works would remain within the Civil Service. These would be brigaded together within a new consolidated Ministry of Public Agencies, somewhat as has been done recently for the armed services departments within the Ministry of Defence, but on a much more streamlined and less overblown scale. The rest would be taken over by, for example, a National Highways Board, a Road Safety Commission, a Shipping Commission, and similarly in the case of public works, Ancient Monuments, Royal Parks and development of building methods.

The criterion would be to retain in the Departmental structure only the strictly governmental functions for which *direct* Ministerial responsibility to Parliament is *essential,* and to make that responsibility a reality by ensuring that everything included in it can be and is watched, reviewed and adjusted day to day to the standards of the best top managements. Above all the choice and terms of service of the men at the top, and the maintenance of their authority and confidence, would be the Minister's special concern. He should be able to apply lessons learned in one field to others widely different. All else, whether routine payments, technical or specialist services, trading and economic services, judicial and equity administration, or regionalized and localized services, would be entirely freed from Departmental structures and from Civil Service staffing conditions. There would thus be a family of public services, among which the Civil Service would not necessarily be the largest, each having its own appropriate terms of service, without regard to those possibly essential in Whitehall itself but unnecessary and detrimental elsewhere.

All these public services, central and local, would come under the ultimate supervision, although with much delegated authority, of a new Public Service Commission, which would be a body of the highest importance, reporting directly to the House of Commons through a Select Committee exclusively concerned with these matters. The existing Civil Service Commission, which has been hamstrung through being made a creature of the Treasury, would be superseded. All powers relating to public service recruitment, training, personnel management, organization and methods and establishments would pass to the new Public Service Commission, which would be required to delegate, subject to proper inspection, to the managements concerned in each case. All patronage over appointments and nominations to public bodies, or to bodies in which the Crown has a voice over appointments, would also pass to a Crown Appointments and Nominations Commission, either forming part of, or twinned with, the Public Service Commission, and reporting annually to Parliament. Among its other duties this Commission would be required to maintain a full national appointments availability register compiled from a wide variety of sources, and to ensure that it was properly used and considered in relation to all public appointments. The Comptroller and Auditor-General, appointed by and solely responsible to Parliament, would become answerable for the inspection of both the Public Service and the Appointments and Nominations work, all of which would be wholly removed from Civil Service, and in particular from Treasury, control.

The next point to tackle would be the muddle between United Kingdom, Great Britain, English, Scottish, Welsh and Northern Irish, and English-regional functions, which have so long been hopelessly mixed up, and have contributed so much to swamping the central mechanism. The guiding principle here would be to perform every governmental function and service as near to rather than as far from the eventual consumer, user or subject as the employment of modern techniques and devices allows. While giant industrial concerns find it possible and efficient to delegate more and more to divisions and subsidiaries, or even to semi-autonomous, owned undertakings, the British system of misgovernment persists in more and more senseless centralization, compensated, in the eyes of its rulers, by a carefree willingness to expel from the metropolis any small service in which they themselves do not happen to be interested, regardless of the merits of the case.

The time has come to recognize that half-hearted, piecemeal and half-baked measures of decentralization are no good at all, and that instead of weakening and circumscribing every office outside Whitehall such offices should be strengthened and encouraged to take on all they properly can. Now that half the world has shaken off Whitehall administration it is too late to tell the Welsh, the northern English and the Midlanders, for example, that they are the only ones left who are not yet fit for self-government, and must still be ruled almost as Crown Colonies by the gentlemen who know best. Certain Ministries have already had to hand over certain powers such as Transport to the Scottish Development Department, but the concept of decentralization has been woolly and its fulfillment often nebulous.

A starting-point for reform would be to recognize that any function which is already decentralized from Whitehall to St. Andrew's House in Edinburgh, or to Stormont near Belfast, should in principle also be decentralized to Cardiff and to one or more points in England, as being *ex hypothesi* not an essential function for United Kingdom government. It has been suggested in the *Economist* and elsewhere that the whole British administration should be removed from London to Yorkshire or somewhere else central for Great Britain, but this appears outside practical politics and economics. A more realistic approach might be to develop York, or somewhere near it, as a specifically English sub-capital, acting as an equivalent for Edinburgh, Cardiff and Belfast in a national pattern of decentralization involving all local and regional services and functions, including planning, police, housing, fire, education, parks and recreation, traffic, roads and environmental services.

Before such a step could be taken however it would first be essential to define the scope and powers of a modernized local government system. That system is now under review by the Maud Commission, in whose members and terms of reference it is possible to feel some confidence. It seems clear that the course is now set for fewer, larger, stronger, more comprehensive basic units of local government, in which the traditional separation between urban and rural authorities

UNITED KINGDOM STRUCTURE OF GOVERNMENT *(as proposed)*

LEGISLATURE

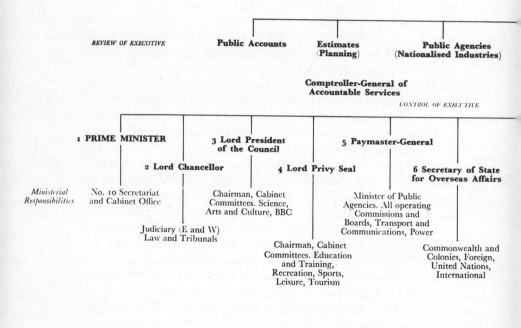

REVIEW OF EXECUTIVE

Public Accounts **Estimates (Planning)** **Public Agencies (Nationalised Industries)**

Comptroller-General of Accountable Services

CONTROL OF EXECUTIVE

Ministerial Responsibilities

1 PRIME MINISTER **3 Lord President of the Council** **5 Paymaster-General**

2 Lord Chancellor **4 Lord Privy Seal** **6 Secretary of State for Overseas Affairs**

No. 10 Secretariat and Cabinet Office

Chairman, Cabinet Committees. Science, Arts and Culture, BBC

Minister of Public Agencies. All operating Commissions and Boards, Transport and Communications, Power

Judiciary (E and W) Law and Tribunals

Chairman, Cabinet Committees. Education and Training, Recreation, Sports, Leisure, Tourism

Commonwealth and Colonies, Foreign, United Nations, International

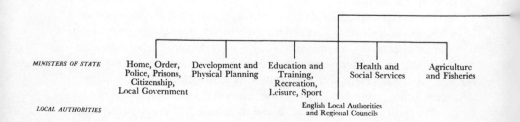

MINISTERS OF STATE

Home, Order, Police, Prisons, Citizenship, Local Government

Development and Physical Planning

Education and Training, Recreation, Leisure, Sport

Health and Social Services

Agriculture and Fisheries

LOCAL AUTHORITIES

English Local Authorities and Regional Councils

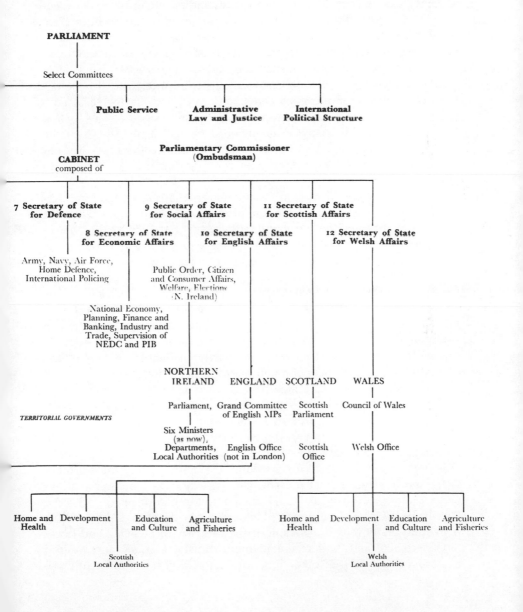

PARLIAMENT

Select Committees

Public Service **Administrative Law and Justice** **International Political Structure**

Parliamentary Commissioner (Ombudsman)

CABINET composed of

7 Secretary of State for Defence **9 Secretary of State for Social Affairs** **11 Secretary of State for Scottish Affairs**

8 Secretary of State for Economic Affairs **10 Secretary of State for English Affairs** **12 Secretary of State for Welsh Affairs**

Army, Navy, Air Force, Home Defence, International Policing

Public Order, Citizen and Consumer Affairs, Welfare, Elections (N. Ireland)

National Economy, Planning, Finance and Banking, Industry and Trade, Supervision of NEDC and PIB

NORTHERN IRELAND   ENGLAND   SCOTLAND   WALES

Parliament, Grand Committee of English MPs   Scottish Parliament   Council of Wales

TERRITORIAL GOVERNMENTS

Six Ministers (as now), Departments, Local Authorities   English Office (not in London)   Scottish Office   Welsh Office

Home and Health Development   Education and Culture   Agriculture and Fisheries   Home and Health   Development   Education and Culture   Agriculture and Fisheries

Scottish Local Authorities   Welsh Local Authorities

will be largely replaced by more balanced hybrid urban regions stretching as far round the great urban clusters as their effective spheres of influence extend for purposes of distribution, management and leisure activities. On this basis, normal main units of local government should have the financial resources and the administrative capacity to handle within their jurisdiction all services and functions not subject to overriding considerations of national policy and standardized treatment. Where necessary Regional Councils, without executive or operating functions, should be able to mediate between central and local government sufficiently to harmonize inconsistent or potentially conflicting approaches and practices in neighboring local government areas. It must, however, be clearly understood that the extent of delegation will be partly determined by the degree to which the holders of delegated powers are willing to ensure the necessary coordination themselves, rather than force the central government to impose it on them.

This part of the field is at the moment perhaps more fluid and obscure than at any previous point in history, with the possible exception of the 'eighties of the last century. It seems, however, reasonable to assume that the trend will be as outlined above, and that action for comprehensive reform will not be much longer deferred. On such assumptions a major relief to central government business from the local government quarter may be expected not only by transfer of functions —such as the absurd interference by the National Ministry of Transport in the internal traffic problems of Greater London, which it has so abysmally failed to solve—but by a general abatement of interference from Whitehall in local affairs, partly justified in the past by the smallness and feebleness of a number of local authorities.

On this basis the time may well have come to pursue to its logical conclusion the trend set by maintaining separate agricultural departments for Scotland, Northern Ireland and England and Wales. This implies organizing all central government functions of an essentially localized or regional nature under groups of offices pulled together at national territorial level for Scotland in Edinburgh and for Northern Ireland in Belfast, as at present, complemented by similar groupings for Wales in Cardiff, and for England possibly in or near York. The only new Department required would be an English Office, taking over all the powers in England of the Ministry of Housing and Local Government and the late unlamented Ministry of Land and Natural Resources, as well as other functions capable of being efficiently administered at this level and not requiring much co-ordination or standardized treatment on a Great Britain basis. The corresponding functions for Wales would go to the Welsh Office in Cardiff. Thus each national territory within the United Kingdom would run its own internal affairs, and while London would remain the UK capital it would renounce the role of capital of England to a northern city. The territorial Secretaries of State would thus become the only Ministers in the United Kingdom Cabinet or government whose functions did not extend to the whole of Great Britain, although in some cases part or all of the functions of Great Britain or United Kingdom Ministers might be co-ordinating and supervisory, the administration and operation being also delegated territorially. The effects of such a change would be far-reaching, both in bringing the level of governmental decision-making nearer the area of operation in all practicable cases, and in relieving the reformed United Kingdom government in Whitehall of a vast unwieldy mass of regional and local detail and case-work. Fortunately accidents of history and politics provide us with nearly half a century of experience of the working of a regional "Whitehall" and a regional Parliament at Stormont for Northern Ireland, and a long period also of experience of running a regional "Whitehall" under a Secretary of State and sub-Ministers, but without a Parliament, at St. Andrew's House in Edinburgh. Both these experiments show serious faults, which no one would wish to imitate, but in both cases there is good reason to regard the faults as due to particular circumstances which need not arise elsewhere, and which are in no way inherent in the structure. It would therefore hardly be a rash leap in the dark to advance Scotland now to the constitutional stage reached by Northern Ireland under the Government of Ireland Act 1920, by means of a Government of Scotland Act setting up a Scottish Parliament on comparable lines and entrusting it with the full oversight of St. Andrew's House, which badly needs such overseeing. Excellent as the correspondence column of *The Scotsman* is, it cannot form an adequate channel either for conveying all the available guidance, or for expressing all the exasperation, which the Scots justly feel about their central administration, nor can this role possibly be fulfilled by an overburdened and uninterested Parliament at Westminster.

At the same time Wales might be permitted to catch up, belatedly, with the stage in evolution and devolution already attained by Scotland, supplemented by a provisional substitute for a Parliament in a reconstituted Council for Wales, including all Welsh Members of Parliament *ex officio*. This body might meet, say, twice a year to hear and advise the Secretary of State and to receive the regular annual Report of Welsh Affairs in draft before transmission by the Secretary of State to the United Kingdom Parliament. The opportunity should also be taken to rectify the historical blunder of including Monmouthshire for certain official purposes in England, which has gone on 400 years too long.

In many ways the most complex and difficult operation will be the extrication of England, at once the main victim and the main despot, from its hopeless entanglement with the broader affairs of the United Kingdom, and to create an integral national mechanism of government which the English nation has not possessed since at least the time of the first Queen Elizabeth. Such an unscrambling operation clearly cannot be achieved in a single drastic act of surgery, but must be spread over about a generation. The rump functions left to Housing and Local Government, Transport, and Education, following the take-over of the Welsh parts of these duties by the Welsh Office, form the core of a potential English Office. To this must be added the agricultural and fisheries functions of the existing England and Wales Ministry, the police and law enforcement functions of the Home Office, and the administration in England of the National Health Service and other social services, making in all five English Departments — Home, Development and Physical Planning, Social Services and Health, Education, and Agriculture and Fisheries.

England, in common with Wales, Scotland and Northern Ireland, could benefit from having its own national Ombudsman, working in close concert with the United Kingdom Parliamentary Commissioner at Westminster. Unlike Scotland and Northern Ireland, England would hardly within the foreseeable future be likely to wish or be ready to maintain a distinct national Parliament, but by setting up a Scottish Parliament the way would be left clear for an English Grand Committee at Westminster in which all the English MPs would have opportunities to pursue English affairs with the Secretary of State and his Ministers of State for each of the English Departments. (In Scotland, as in Northern Ireland, the distinct Departments would have their own Departmental Ministers in the territorial Parliament; in England and in Wales only Ministers of State would be appropriate, in the absence of separate Parliaments.)

One factor peculiar to England would be the number and importance of the Regions, forming an intermediate tier for some purposes between the territorial and the local governments. The eight English economic planning regions can be brought together in three groups, the Northern trio, the Midland pair and the Southern trio of Southeast, Southwest and East Anglia. Probably only trial and error can determine what regional grouping is best for which purposes, under a new territorial administration with new and larger units of local government, but it seems likely that for a population of over forty-five million in England alone, some subdivision will be essential for some purposes. The concentration of the English Departments at a new capital specially built, probably near York, would facilitate the necessary new start, although clearly a long transitional stage would be necessary. It should however be possible at an early point to secure a massive relief of the burden of English affairs on a United Kingdom government by appointing the Secretary of State and his Ministers of State and progressively transferring to the English Office, under its Permanent Secretary, the constitutional and administrative responsibilities outlined above.

A comparable and perhaps even larger early relief could be obtained by transforming not only the Post Office as already decided, but major sections of the Ministries of Transport, Public Building and Works, Social Security, Health, the Ordnance Survey, Stationery Office and others into non-Departmental agencies under Commissions or Boards, subject only to supervision at the highest level by a Minister of Public Agencies who might also be Paymaster-General.

A further very significant relief would be provided by a Statute of Administration under which the Lord Chancellor would take over all responsibility for Administrative Law and Justice through something like the existing network of Tribunals and Commissions suitably supplemented where necessary.

Thus the United Kingdom Cabinet and Civil Service would be relieved of three large blocks of current direct functions in respect of territorial and local, utility and service and judicial and legal aspects of government, all of which would however continue to be answerable to Parliament through appropriate United Kingdom Ministers of the highest supervisory level. A case can be made out on these lines for the proposition that it *is* possible to reduce the Cabinet to what is generally accepted as the optimum size for human and working efficiency, namely around a dozen members. This can moreover be done without depriving the offices concerned in any case of their own Ministerial champion, guide, and spokesman at United Kingdom Cabinet level, although owing to the degree of devolution proposed, and the mutation of so many Civil Service departments into more modern types of public service agency, the frequency with which such issues may be expected to arise should be much less. But it would be wrong to look at the subject simply in quantitative and structural terms. Quality is even more important. Experience gives us no justification for supposing that the United Kingdom can produce or maintain an effective first line of top Ministers or Permanent Secretaries much in excess of ten. Men of the necessary caliber are simply not available for such tasks on a larger scale, and, as we can see only too plainly, more means worse. If we are serious in demanding the highest quality for the highest responsibilities we simply delude and frustrate ourselves by settling for any such figures as twenty-three Cabinet Ministers and thirty-one Permanent Secretaries. The dangerous visionaries who support such figures should know by now that they are preaching not only the chronic cluttering up of the highest channels but the grave dilution of standards of the office-holders, by men of insufficient caliber, who cannot look ahead, cannot form sound judgments on broad policy, and cannot combine the human and the technical with the administrative aspects of a question.

So far we have gone over the possibilities of devolution, decentralization and conversion of Departments on a basis implying, besides the Prime Minister, a Lord Chancellor and a Paymaster-General/ Minister of Public Agencies to supervise broad groups of no longer Departmental functions, and three territorial Secretaries of State, only one of whom, for England, would be new. Of the remainder one, the Secretary of State for Defence, has as already mentioned been developed as a result of recent reforms which implement, although still most imperfectly at executive level, the principles on which these proposals are based. Clearly there must be such a Secretary for Defence in the Cabinet, and one can only hope that in God's good time he will come out on top of the almost farcical Parkinsonian propensities of the civil servants whom he has inherited. Meanwhile we must do our best to live with the idea that it makes sense that there should be more *non-*

industrial civil servants in the Ministry of Defence than sailors in the Navy.

A second partly reformed area of government is Overseas Affairs, a single Secretary of State for which, assisted by Ministers and later by Ministers of State for United Nations, Foreign, Commonwealth and Colonial Affairs appears within reach in the tolerably near future, supported by the recently unified HM Diplomatic Service, which is quite distinct from the Home Civil Service.

A much less discussed and digested series of problems revolve round the archaic and almost totally unreformed Home Office. Although the fact is often overlooked, this hoary and whiskered Department has lost jurisdiction in Scotland, and if the logical consequences of devolution are followed out, as proposed above, it should be also relieved of jurisdiction over the police and fire and certain other services in England and Wales. This would give a much-needed opportunity for creating what the Home Office has always aspired to be and has in its best moments fitfully and imperfectly become, an office genuinely standing up for the rights and human dignity of the citizen, and shielding him from the undue pressure of administrative necessity. There should be in the Cabinet a full Secretary of State who has time and backing to watch over and stand up for the broad interests of the citizen. He should not only exercise a broad supervisory role, but should keep directly under his control those functions of government which bear most tenderly and critically on the quality and freedom of the citizen's life—elections, immigration and nationality, criminal affairs and prisons, child welfare, racial discrimination, consumer protection, Ministerial responsibility for law and order and for social services at the United Kingdom level, and so forth. The devolution of such large, expensive, and routine services as police and fire to territorial administrations would help such an evolution. Moreover, insofar as greater integration of police forces is inevitable, it is desirable for the safeguard of individual liberties that they should be buffered from Whitehall and the Cabinet by the territorial layer of administration and of representative bodies. The new-style United Kingdom Home Secretary would also fulfill the role of a Secretary of State in respect of Northern Ireland affairs, and undertake any other duties germane to his role. He should and would be a less harassed and overburdened man than his recent predecessors, whose task has become impossible. His Department, however, is among the most important and most in need of help from a thorough overhaul of the Civil Service.

Recent attempts to reform the administration of education and science have been far from happy. Too many of the better scientists have voted with their feet against the resulting conditions. Science is not suitable for devolution below the United Kingdom level, and under a reformed layout there is much to be said for reverting to the successful arrangement under which science was taken care of by a Lord President of the Council also acting as a Chairman of Cabinet Committees. He might fulfil a similar role for the arts and cultural matters generally, possibly including the supervision of the British Council and certainly that of the British Broadcasting Corporation and the Independent Television Authority. Another high-level non-departmental Minister, the Lord Privy Seal, could exercise at the Great Britain level a similar set of functions in respect of Education, Training, Recreation, Amenity and Tourism.

It is in the field of finance and economic affairs that the thorniest and most complex problems of reconstruction lie, and here the unadulterated principle of organizing government according to "functions" is most full of pitfalls. One of the commonest modern errors is to suppose that by changing governmental labels you change the character of the business to which the labels apply, instead of merely advertising a change of subjective attitude in your approach to this business. A twin error is to imagine that inseparably entangled problems can be converted into two distinct groups capable of being managed independently merely by entrusting them to different Ministers under different names. Unfortunately politics, like ecology, is not all that tractable.

At the highest level the great perennial and interlocked problems of the British economy are indivisible. Many thousands of millions of pounds have been thrown away through the stubborn refusal within government to face the obvious implications of this simple fact. It must be realized first that the allocation of various of the key elements which are continually interacting to different Cabinet Ministers and their rival Departments pulling in different directions without any clear unified guidance, as is the case with the Treasury, Board of Trade, Ministry of Labour and Ministry of Economic Affairs, is a totally unworkable arrangement. A second is that the only basis for a single effective guiding and supervising Department for the whole field is one which is not committed to any particular approach or instrument more than to any other which may be more appropriate. In other words the conception that the Treasury as a basically financial

Department must be the dominant partner no longer makes sense in contemporary terms. It belongs to the horse-and-buggy age of government organization.

The problem then is to reconstruct the economic machinery of government in such a way that all the main elements in the management of the economy can be equally closely reviewed and, where and when necessary, manipulated in coherent relationship to one another. This goes for the expansion of production, the stimulation and direction of investment, the control of prices and incomes, the restraint of inflation, the limitation and deployment of public spending, the balance of payments, overseas investment and aid, resource aspects of defense commitments present and future, wise use of manpower—in fact the lot. Clearly the scale, complexity and rate of change of this group of problems are comparable to those involved in the higher control of a major war, and need to be taken no less seriously, even though they can and should be managed with a far less heavy hand. The first essential is to bring all the main threads effectively together; the second is to make quite sure that the point in government where they are brought together is freed from all other burdens whatever, especially those of routine, and indeed all executive work which is capable of devolution. Only thus can the task be made manageable, and the new organization be saved from the Parkinsonian fate of the Ministry of Defence.

We need therefore to envisage a Secretary of State for the National Economy served by an Office of the National Economy of, by Whitehall standards, quite modest size—say, around 1,500 staff, whose work would center on the problems mentioned in the previous paragraph, and would be expressed in terms of the shape, direction and fulfillment of the National Plan, of the Budget, of the Balance of Payments, of the cost of living and the prevention of inflation, all allocations for public expenditure, national and local, and their enforcement, and of a manpower budget. While the Office and its Ministers would be the final arbiter on all these matters, it would in each case receive considered recommendations and schemes on them from a series of specialist and highly responsible ancillary departments. The first of these would be a Public Finance Office which, unlike the present Treasury, would deal with the whole of public finance and nothing but public finance. It would therefore be much larger than the existing Treasury, because it would include the staffs—already answerable to Treasury Ministers—of the Boards of Inland Revenue and of Customs and Excise and of smaller units such as the Public Works Loan

Board. It would also have oversight over local government finance, which is currently being allowed to get completely out of hand, while the Treasury busies itself with the affairs of everybody else in government. Under the new arrangements the purposes and programs to be served by the Budget within the National Economy would be laid down in advance and kept continually under review. Within these purposes it would be for the Public Finance Office to recommend taxation levels, to estimate yields and to make provision for covering governmentally-approved levels of public expenditure of all kinds, at home and abroad. But the responsibility for determining the broad content and limits of economic policy within which the Budget would be prepared and administered would rest with the Secretary of State, not with his lieutenant the ministerial head of the Public Finance Office.

Somewhat similarly the preparation and control of the National Plan would be delegated to a National Planning Office, constituted under the supervision of the highest representatives of employers (including public concerns) and trade unions, with representatives of government as a third party, somewhat on the lines of Neddy and the "little Neddies" but much strengthened. A strengthened Central Statistical Office and an Economic Research and Advisory Office would work closely alongside.

A further Office would be concerned with territorial and regional aspects, including national oversight of land use planning and town and country planning, the entire administration of which would be delegated within England, Scotland and Wales under the respective Secretaries of State. This Office would be responsible for research, surveys, statistics and central co-ordination.

A much larger Office would be needed to handle all government policy matters affecting industry and trade, including their overseas relations, e.g. within the Common Market. Basically this would be a recast Board of Trade, without functions regarding Shipping, Films, Exhibitions, Consumer Standards, and other extraneous matters.

The National Board for Prices and Incomes would, as at present, be associated as an autonomous body.

Finally an Office of National Manpower, transmuted from the Ministry of Labour but with more emphasis on development of a modern fully decentralized structure of industrial relations and conciliation and on a long-term manpower program, would complete the series of supporting Offices—three largish and five smaller—under the wing of the Secretary of State for the National Economy. He would clearly need to be buttressed by a strong team of ministerial lieutenants, three of whom, as was recently the case at the Ministry of Defence, should be senior and experienced politicians, with about half a dozen more junior Ministers of State and Parliamentary Secretaries.

In effect therefore the Secretary of State would become a kind of Deputy Prime Minister for the National Economy. This, rather than a series of rival Departmental Ministers, is what is needed in that field, if the Prime Minister is to be given a chance to do his own unique overall job, and to command a ship of state which has some steering way to allow him to steer a course. All other Ministers in the economic field, experienced and capable as they must be, would be quite plainly and unequivocally under the Secretary of State's direction and no one else's. His immediate Office would be large enough and high-powered enough to ensure his being kept fully informed, and able both to devise practicable and timely policies and to ensure their prompt and effective execution.

In Britain today the relationship between nation and state has degenerated into that of an unhappy marriage. The state has muddled the nation into situations of the utmost danger, discomfort and humiliation without being able to show any acceptable way out of them; hence the general lack of confidence and even of interest in the government which is reflected in the morale of its political supporters of either party, and in its public servants.

It is quite unnecessary and quite unacceptable that so much of the power in Britain should be so highly concentrated and so far divorced from sovereignty, from accountable responsibility for its exercise and from the homes and work-places of those over whom it is exercised. This is not democracy, it is not efficiency, and it is not sense. In fact it is a nonsense of the first order. For many centuries Englishmen fought against the building of an efficient central administration because they feared that it would spell tyranny. Now they sweat under a central administration which in many ways is, and in some ways has to be, more tyrannous than the worst nightmares of our ancestors, and which has not even the saving grace of being efficient. Fortunately the day when only centralized government could be efficient is past; decentralized government is now inherently the more efficient pattern, and it is much more compatible with all that the British people have fought for and have come perilously near to losing today. The more widely power within the United Kingdom is decentralized and dispersed, the more the central government will find itself compelled to concentrate on doing well the things which can only be done at the center, and adjusting its structure and practices accordingly. And this above all means radical changes in the type of recruit enlisted in the higher ranks of the public service. It cannot be said too often that the existing basis of the Administrative Class in Whitehall derives virtually unchanged from that devised, oddly enough with Gladstone's connivance, to ensure that the central mechanism of British government should rest permanently in the hands of a particular privileged class, carefully trained to despise professional competence and to exalt a cult of high-minded amateurism, dedicated to opportunism as against planning, to aloofness from everything felt or done by the vast majority of their fellow-citizens, and to the self-satisfied assurance that THEY know what is best for US.

Although the man at the desk in Whitehall may know better than the man at the desk in Leeds he certainly does not know better merely *because* he sits in Whitehall, and he may well know a lot worse. The onus of proof is on him. The ghost of Benjamin Jowett, who first chose and persuaded a willing Treasury that Britain should be governed by this peculiar type of human being, needs to be publicly exorcised from haunting, as it still does, the corridors of power.

Two quotations are needed to illustrate the outlook to which these comments apply. The first is from that quintessential work *The Spirit of British Administration,* by a highly placed and evidently representative member of the Administrative Class named C. H. Sisson, published in 1966. It reads:

> A good idea is no good unless it fits into the context of the time, has a place in the universe of discourse within which, by consensus, the discussion of public affairs is conducted.

The second, from the same source, relates to training or the absence thereof:

> "This practice" to quote an authoritative Treasury source "is in accordance with the long-established tradition of regarding members of the Administrative Class as intelligent amateurs who form their judgments on the basis of experience rather than as a result of a prescribed course of theoretical training."

Rather than comment on these sentiments it may be best to follow our author by falling back on quotation of words written long ago in a similar case by the distinguished Colonial civil servant Tom Harrison:

> I leave you to brood over their muddle, reality, sincerity, sense, significance and universal *jenesaisquoi*. My view is: bullshit.

All judgments and estimates on the value of particular types of organization for British government depend on whether we are to have another hundred years of Jowettocracy. The view adopted here is quite plain; one century of it is enough. How such a picked group of intelligent, educated, agreeable, high-principled and hardworking people can be quite so disastrous for their nation as the record clearly shows the British higher Civil Service to have been certainly calls for explanation.

CHAPTER 21

Eliminating Amateurism

The Civil Service New Deal of 1855 onwards was deliberately based on a rejection of the national demand to which it purported to respond. The nation, so far as it was articulate on the matter, wanted to supersede the old gang of largely incompetent placemen, employed through patronage, by a professionally-trained corps of administrators selected and promoted on merit. The Treasury, on the advice of Jowett and others, specified instead a requirement for recruits just as amateurish and unqualified as their predecessors, who although in many cases indolent and corrupt did include some of the finest public servants whom Britain has had until this day, such as Edwin Chadwick, the founder of public health services. This new type was to be chosen without fear or favor by a competitive examination, but in fact the examination conditions barred entry to a very high percentage of the ablest young men in Britain, including for several decades practically all who were not sufficiently well-to-do to gain a place and to complete a course at Oxford or Cambridge Universities. Even to this day, to the embarrassment of the Civil Service Commission, relatively few others surmount these cunningly designed hurdles. The subject was discussed at length, and in the light of varied experience and standpoints, by the Estimates Committee of the House of Commons in their Sixth Report, Session 1964–65. (It is also currently being examined more fully by the Fulton Committee.)

According to this Report it can be assumed that of 16,435 students graduating with honors from British universities in 1962–63 some 4,600 obtained the First or good Second Class qualifying them for the Administrative Class and its allies. Vacancies in these totaled 105, or 2·3 percent of the presumed supply, of which 61, epresenting 1·5 percent of it, were filled. In 1963 the Home Civil Service recruited 51 Assistant Principals (against 80 required) out of a pool of 869 applicants. During 1957–63 out of 1,673 candidates for the Administrative Class educated at State schools only 140 were chosen, against 173 out of 1,152 from boarding "Public" schools. During this latter period 395 successes came from "Oxbridge" out of 2,272 competitors, against 68 out of 1,318 from all other sources. One thing which is practically certain is that the easy assumption of class or other bias by the selectors is groundless. The built-in bias is much more subtle and intractable, and is defeating the genuine and conscientious efforts of the Civil Service Commission to correct it. (Actually the Oxford and Cambridge percentage of successes, which was only 82 percent in 1905–14, and fell to 78 percent between 1925 and 1956, rose again to a peak of 85 percent in 1957–63.)

The ghost of Benjamin Jowett proved too strong. As Professor W. J. M. Mackenzie pointed out to the Committee, it was Jowett who reformed the Oxford examination system almost simultaneously with the initiation of the Civil Service Commission in 1855 on lines largely influenced by him. Not unnaturally, therefore, Oxford in particular has ever since had a strong advantage in turning out the very type who would happen to satisfy the Commission, and there is very little that the Commission can do about it, pending drastic reforms of a much wider scope. Moreover, other universities, even including Cambridge, have never shared to the same extent the intense bias against specialist branches of learning which was clamped on Oxford in the early and mid-nineteenth century, and which has only recently begun to be corrected there. Students of high ability but no coherent bent of mind are thus welcomed and catered for at Oxford more than anywhere else. The University thus attracts a high proportion of the national "general pool" eligible and interested in the Administrative Class. As in 1950 78 percent of higher civil servants came from social classes I and II, and Oxford and Cambridge are still so preponderantly occupied by the middle and upper classes, it is not surprising that many in the redbrick universities believe, erroneously, that recruitment of administrators is influenced by class bias. There is a good deal of evidence that many of the most able students from other universities are opposed to joining the administrative class for quite other reasons. While Oxbridge graduates are *ex hypothesi* already mobile or in the metropolitan orbit many students in other universities are not. The virtual monopoly of Administrative Class posts in London, and to a much less extent Edinburgh, puts them off. The masquerade about the all-round administrator who is not really expected to know what he is administering leaves cold those who are not heavily doped in advance with the peculiar Oxbridge mystique which holds everyone else to be out of step on this matter. As the scientifically-trained Secretary of Manchester University Appointments Board stated to the Committee:

> The concept of the administrator as such, who could as well administer the Ministry of Defence as the Post Office, is one which is entirely foreign to the training of the scientist. He sees it as a nineteenth-century outpost-of-Empire idea which has nothing to offer to the decision-making processes of the 1960s.

There is substance in this criticism. The present basis of recruitment for the higher Civil Service was partly modeled on that found successful in India just before the Indian Mutiny. Even in India that model showed grave weaknesses. Above all the failure to differentiate between such different types of administration as large-scale managerial and operational tasks, political advice to Ministers, public control and economic forecasting and planning made nonsense of the basic conception of the all-rounder. Very few men indeed have such versatility as that.

Another strong reason given by non-Oxbridge students for not wishing to join the administrative class is their keen desire for a "high degree of personal freedom in carrying out the job", which is placed easily top among eight desirable job attributes by students in Arts, Science and in Social Science sampled by the Acton Society Trust. It is suggested that these students are misinformed, but I would say they are right both in their rating of this factor and in their suspicion as to how they would fare in the lower orders of the Administrative Class. At the behest, therefore, of a long-dead Master of Balliol we continue to restrict the Administrative Class not much less narrowly than in 1870.

Although, for obvious reasons, every effort is made to disguise the fact, it is perfectly plain that the unwillingness of so many able young people to compete for entry into the Administrative Class has resulted not only in failure to fill many vacancies but also in some lowering of the standards of those who are now appointed. There is no ground for believing that a soundly conceived up-to-date public service would have any difficulty in attracting all the able recruits it would need. What many vote against with their feet is not the public service in principle, but the Victorian higher Civil Service as a surviving anachronism. The luckless Civil Service Commissioners are stuck with the job of finding a type of candidate who is gradually becoming extinct to man a type of Service which is assisting to make Britain itself extinct as a great force in world affairs. Despite broad Treasury hints to Parliament about the time not yet being ripe, it is none too soon that the Fulton Committee has been set up to consider at least part of this problem, and to say as much about it as the Treasury will let them.

In contrast to the great Continental public services of Germany and France, the concept foisted on Britain in 1855 and eventually consolidated from 1870 onwards was unique in its almost morbid mistrust of the possession of knowledge, expertise and research bearing on the subject of government. The higher civil servant was, and is, painstakingly selected as one who doesn't know and is unwilling to learn about his chosen profession. Eccentric as it was even in 1855 this concept has grown increasingly preposterous. It is arguable that the unreformed Civil Service up to 1855 was in a number of important respects more in touch, less out-of-date in relation to national needs and little if any poorer in first-rate administrators than the Civil Service of 1967. Who now in Whitehall will go down in history on a par with Edwin Chadwick?

Martin Cooper, reviewing in the *Daily Telegraph* of October 10, 1966, *The Public Schools* by Graham Kalton wrote:

> I cannot imagine anyone reading Dr Lambert's Introduction without coming to the conclusion that the unique value of the public schools has been ethical rather than intellectual, and has shown itself in the production of a governing class efficient and morally responsible but severely restricted intellectually and emotionally.

He stressed the need for replacing this pattern by a coherent new ethical ideal accepted by the nation. That pinpoints one of the basic faults built in to the higher Civil Service. Its cadets are selected from the picked products of Victorian approach to life which is about as relevant to today's world as the Pre-Raphaelite School of painting, and a good deal less relevant than Lewis Carroll's also contemporary *Alice in Wonderland*. Vindication of the paramount value of ethics and ideals by the new middle classes against their more lax and cynical aristocratic predecessors was no doubt rightly regarded as of crucial importance in the 1860s but the battle now is against inefficiency, not against corruption. The fact that a number of the recruits now come from maintained schools makes little difference, since, as we have already seen, these also are largely imitators of the Arnold tradition of the public schools. It is not so much that they come from such schools but that they are expected to be among their prime products, and thus exemplars of their defects as well as of their virtues. Adding to this criticisms made of many university courses, of which most taken by Civil Service entrants show only the sketchiest concern with research, the conclusion must be that both in personality and training the higher Civil Service is seeking and finding types who will perpetuate the worst of its blind spots.

Whatever the nation may demand, and Ministers may instruct to be done, can only be faithfully performed within the mental capacity and limitations of approach of the Civil Service administration. If such limitations exclude or distort part of the message it is just too bad for the nation—the message will to that extent with the best will in the world remain unheeded in Whitehall, as it often is. Adding the number and magnitude of the decisions which, as is common knowledge, higher civil servants themselves make on behalf of a Minister who is not even informed of them, it is clear that any systematic selection of peculiarities in Civil Service entry will be reflected in certain types of governmental decision being reached and others not. To choose the wrong choosers is indeed the worst type of wrong choice.

It has been said that in order to qualify as a top leader of one of our great industrial unions, and thus hold the nation's industrial peace in his hands, a lad must achieve a run of four decisive failures in succession. He must first fail at eleven-plus to gain a place at a grammar school or some equivalent which would put him in the white-collar class from the outset. He must next fail to continue his schooling beyond the minimum leaving age, and thus get on to the shop floor at the lowest level rather than acquire any embarrassing excess of education beyond the compulsory minimum. He must then fail to be selected by his firm as a tolerably bright lad worth sending on to part-time further education, which would lead him to the bottom rungs of the management ladder. And as a budding trade unionist he must fail to attract notice as worth sending on a scholarship on behalf of the movement to some university, whence he would probably emerge as a back-room boy in Transport House. If he does not fail to fail at all these stages he may, with luck, gain enough of the ballots of his ballot-shy colleagues to send him on a minority vote to one of the highest posts in the British national economy.

What is not often appreciated however is that a similar negative process is at work on the selection of civil servants. As schoolboys they must fail to show enough individuality and initiative to fall foul of the powers that be, as a fair minority of the ablest boys do. As undergraduates at university they must fail to show the type of keen interest in any learned subject leading them into one of the degree courses which frown on, because they were long frowned on by, the Civil Service. They must equally fail to show promise for a higher degree, which would probably lead to their staying on as university teachers or researchers, or would at best handicap them by having to arrange a long deferment of their Civil Service entry behind their more carefree contemporaries who join immediately on graduating. They must, too, fail to attract the insistent notice of the countless talent scouts of large industry who comb the universities first for much the same levels of ability sought by the Civil Service, but with more accent on enterprise and leadership. They must then fail to recognize, as many of the brighter undergraduates do, that entering the present-day Civil Service can prove more frustrating than several alternative choices. Having thus reached the qualifying score they present themselves as candidates to the Civil Service Commission, who, in accepting them for the profession of public administration, will sanctify by a cocked-hat certificate their failure to acquire any professional qualification and their admission to a profession which indeed looks up to leaders glorying in the conviction that no such profession exists.

It is impossible to begin to understand the true workings of the system of misgovernment without appreciating the role played by the painstakingly selected members of this devotedly negative nonprofession, wrapped as they are in an ample cloak of non-responsibility, non-publicity and at best virtual non-existence by their interpretation of the British constitution, tamely accepted by successive generations of ministers and by the Official Secrets Acts (God bless it!). That they may be the wrong people tackling the wrong task in the wrong way is the last thought that would ever occur to them.

The Administrative Class could be, like its French counterpart, a highly trained élite, but quite ostentatiously prefers the role of Gentlemen (versus Players). It is, at our expense, the last and most obsessive stronghold of amateurism. It could be a compact close-knit band able to respond instantly and smoothly to every challenge. Instead, although stubbornly metropolitan, it is dissipated over too many, too unwieldy and too woollily-conceived Departments and sub-Departments to retain any effective coherence. It could be, like the late Indian Civil Service, a body imbued with a high sense of mission and *esprit de corps* as a Service, but apart from a vague tendency to administer Britain like almost the last remaining Crown Colony in an otherwise vanished Empire it has no real coherence or commanding level of morale commensurate with its indubitable power. It prefers to present to the outer world a self-deprecating, appeasing image, without having anything much more definite even for its internal functioning. Oddly enough, although this is now evaporating too, one of the most marked characteristics until recently of this supposedly apolitical service was its nostalgic attachment to its peculiar brands of moribund liberalism, for which the Reform Club served as a discreet shrine. Contemplating the Service in relation to almost any other aspect of British national life the impression which it gives is above all of not belonging. Indeed analysis suggests that it is not merely a misfit, but a multiple misfit.

How in such circumstances can it have survived for a century? First it was an ideal job outlet for the influential and fast expanding professional middle classes, without capital or personal connections for placing their sons. Secondly, its capacity for pretending not to exist and for keeping out of the way of all kinds of trouble has a survival value which any animal organism might envy. No one should underestimate, even at this late hour, its powers of evasive action.

Even to learn about it is usually intensely difficult, since as a Silent Service it can easily make the Navy look garrulous. Recently, however, the Estimates Committee of the House of Commons under Dr. Jeremy Bray managed to get the Service talking about itself, with results which are enshrined in 1,108 printed questions and answers and a number of enlightened memoranda in the invaluable Sixth Report for the Session 1964–65 (Paper 308). First-hand, up-to-date, authentic and informal, it is of singular importance for students of this aspect of the subject, and it often demonstrates or explains features which otherwise could only be inferred or guessed at. Nothing could be more gentlemanly and agreeable; almost nothing could be more disastrous for Britain than what is spelled out here.

It is difficult briefly to convey the nature of the amateurism of which the Administrative Class itself is so conscious and on the whole so proud (although there are of course some dissident voices). This amateurism, which is so frustrating for professionals working alongside or below, has consequences much more pervasive than is usually recognized. The very word "professional" takes on a double meaning, covering the highly-trained lawyer, chemist or chartered accountant and the completely untrained administrator who is only a professional in the sense that he is permanently and highly paid as if he were one.

The mentality which declines to admit the basically professional nature of public administration, and to accept the discipline and training for it which all reputable professions except perhaps journalism adopt, not only makes the average higher civil servant woefully ignorant of many principles and techniques which he should professionally have mastered in order to do his job properly, but also gives rise to many other shortcomings. Not understanding or valuing professional status, he tends to misuse or underuse the services of other professions, and to incur their often merited dislike and distrust, with unhappy consequences. He expects them also personally to undertake paper-work which any member of the Administrative Class would himself promptly delegate to lower forms of life which exist in the Department but not in normal professional offices.

Typical professional journals, especially their correspondence columns, demonstrate a lively and often intense professional self-criticism which is strangely muted and generally lacking in the higher Civil Service. Indeed, but for the successive Royal Commissions and other outside inquiries inflicted upon a reluctant Service at intervals, and a handful of books by individuals or from academic sources, the literature about basic administrative problems and methods over the past century would be very thin. Even when evidence is given its significance is mainly negative. Take this, for example, from the Secretary-General of the Civil Service National Whitley Council Staff Side before the Estimates Committee on 12 April, 1965:

> I do not think people recruiting outside are recruiting in the same way as we are recruiting inside. A view expressed about the administrative machine is that one can move in and out of it and do all sorts of jobs. I should take a quite opposite view and say that one ought to recruit Arts people from universities who have been trained in a number of disciplines and who then become specialists in administration . . . administration is really an expert part of the operation . . . The Government has, I think, paid more than one

tribute to the fact that there is a Service which works: which produces papers and briefs for Ministers, sets up Ministries and so on. I believe this occurs because you have experts in administration.

I said that this is a rarefied atmosphere, and people find themselves in the Private offices of Ministers at an early age, never having had contact with the public as I had when I served at a post office counter. This has been accepted. I think we shall see more people having to spend a number of years meeting the public . . .

The Secretary of the Staff Side artlessly added:

We think the solution lies somewhere between breaking it [the distinction between the Administrative and Executive Classes] down and letting anyone come in and going all French and sending people away for four years. We should do roughly what we are doing today but we must be ready to take people from elsewhere and create opportunities for advancement in the Service. Broadly, however we are not far off the mark at the present stage.

This, translated out of the Civil Service language, means "I'm all right Jack!"

These verbatim quotations will perhaps assist the reader to judge the characteristic mentality of the Service and the astonishingly loose, slipshod, opinionated and unsupported statements which the Service is accustomed to get away with, even when summoned to give an account of itself before Parliament. The extraordinary myth that a newly-fledged Oxbridge Arts student will through some mystical laying on of hands by some surrogate Whitehall bishop mysteriously become "an expert in administration" is rather repeated as a creed than explained or substantiated. Any serious professional training is crushingly dismissed as "going all French and sending people away for four years". The fact that France under her trained administrators surges right ahead while Britain under her so mutually admired Whitehall paragons slips back towards the bottom of the league does not mean a thing to these men. If the French do it, it must be wrong.

It is, however, brightly conceded, as happens in the Civil Service at intervals of thirty or forty years, that it really would be better if the chaps could refrain from so completely avoiding ever meeting "the public" even when they are young. It looks bad, and in the interests of the Civil Service "image" some chaps will in future have "to spend a number of years meeting the public". But will the day never come, one wonders, when the public, whose money they are living on and whose livelihoods they are compromising, insists upon meeting *them?* It would be an educational experience for both.

The Estimates Committee, in their covering Report on recruitment to the Civil Service, suavely reviewed the evidence presented to them in terms leaving no doubt as to their own judgment on it. The Committee point out that the Order in Council setting up the Civil Service Commission in 1855 required it to apply "fixed rules" and that these, plus open competition, "underlie the work of the Civil Service Commission as it is at present organised". They quote the impression recorded by Professor W. J. M. Mackenzie that "what was good enough for Sir Charles Trevelyan is good enough for us". The Joint Permanent Secretary to the Treasury himself commented to the Committee: "It is very often apparent that a Principal who is extremely intelligent knows very little about life other than what he gets out of the files".

An equally revealing reply was given in respect of a question where research is "actively taking place in government as distinct from outside." "Everyone talks," remarked the sub-Committee Chairman Dr. Jeremy Bray, MP, "of the percentage of net output of an industry which is devoted to research. What is the percentage of staff inside a government department which can be devoted to research in the sense which you have just described? . . . Very small. We have now nineteen economists; at any given time I should think the work of one could be devoted to it." (This refers to the Treasury.)

The Report stated:

> Your Committee are disturbed to learn that through lack of staff in the Civil Service Commission there has been no attempt to follow up the performance of people recruited to the Executive Class, to discover either the effectiveness of selection procedures or to measure the extent of dissatisfaction with the work provided (Q.29). That the latter is a real issue is demonstrated by figures supplied to the Sub-Committee by the Staff Side showing a 21% wastage of male Executive Officers under thirty, as well as by their more general remarks concerning the impression that is created 'that in many cases square pegs are being squeezed into round holes'.

Among many other penetrating criticisms the Committee referred to the new opportunities for recruitment to many occupations opened up by expanding higher education and the related change in the character of "the wider community of which the Civil Service is a part . . . Though changes have been made there has been no adaptation of the structure of the Services to meet either the demands of the first or the opportunities of the second." "There is need for research and public discussion of these important developments, to contribute to 'the shaping of a public doctrine about the place of the Civil Service in modern Britain'." This Part is itself offered as such a contribution.

Enough authoritative recent evidence has been cited to give some indication that documentation is not lacking to support a strongly critical judgment of the British Civil Service as it exists today. Indeed this has virtually been conceded by the setting up of the Fulton Committee, and by the change of front already apparent in the Treasury's evidence to it. The issue now, however, is whether the expected reform, which will unquestionably come too late, will also be too little. If the Civil Service has any voice in it this will obviously happen. That is why it is so essential at this moment that public-spirited citizens should not turn their eyes away from this subject, however dismal and boring it may be made to appear, but should insist that he who pays the piper calls the tune.

To say that the Civil Service today is characterized by shoddiness of thinking, feebleness of imagination and foresight, intellectual inertia, distaste for and distrust of research, technical and scientific illiteracy, reluctance to admit mistakes and proficiency in covering them up as far as possible, timidity in venturing beyond past precedent and routine, caste consciousness and Departmental pettiness is merely to recapitulate some among the defects which the Service itself has placed on the record. Despite the lessons of World War I, and the alleged inter-war reforms, World War II could run only for a few weeks before blindingly demonstrating the low quality and operational inefficiency of the regular Civil Service. Many of its key wartime posts had to be hurriedly taken over by "temporaries" recruited (like myself) from outside activities affording a more adequate training and experience, although in quite different fields.

While authorities on top management have their differences most, if not all, would agree upon as essential a number of factors and acts which the Civil Service disregards, or even deliberately excludes, or pretends to perform as an exercise in eyewash. The education and training of higher civil servants often makes them prone to practice logic in a factual vacuum, and thus to postulate a version of the situation which has no objective validity, and can only lead to a wrong decision and an unsatisfactory result. The decision-making sequence of framing the correct initial questions, finding the facts, analyzing and interpreting them, consulting on the conclusions to be drawn, reaching a decision, giving instructions for action, embodying such instructions in integrated programs, chasing and checking progress, detecting and investigating points needing review, and so forth, is quite unfamiliar, except to such uncharacteristic and specialist branches as the Cabinet Office. This, like, in their very different ways, the Export Credits Guarantee Department, the Meteorological Office (now in the Ministry of Defence), the Overseas Trade Fairs Directorate of the Board of Trade, the Exhibitions Division of the Central Office of Information and the National Lending Library for Science and Technology, now of the Department of Education and Science, should be mentioned as among smallish and fairly self-contained branches of central government whose performance is readily measurable and is widely regarded as having nothing to fear from current international comparisons. It may be significant that all these agencies are presented with clear and sophisticated demands, from a source external to them, which have to be met according to high professional standards and to an exacting timetable. It may also be significant that in all these named cases the selection of staff diverges substantially from the criteria normally considered sufficient in the Civil Service. The verification of Civil Service claims regarding adequacy of selection and training methods by a thorough comparative efficiency audit of different government offices in relation to the origins, training and experience of their staffs would be an instructive exercise.

The last comprehensive Royal Commission on the Civil Service, which produced the Tomlin Report of 1931 (Cmd 3909) showed that the Civil Service structure at that time, as now, represented basically the Victorian model as reviewed in 1912–14, and (that review having been overtaken by World War I) slightly amended in 1920. Each of these belated exercises was promptly knocked sideways by a national emergency before it could be fully carried into effect, so we must go back as far as the Ridley Commission of 1886–90 for a general inquiry into the Civil Service not promptly overtaken by events. Although some lip-service was paid to management in the Tomlin Report it was still regarded as a secondary and subordinate aspect. The Report indicated that the layout and functions of Departments have never been examined in terms of the staffing and management of the Service.

The report already criticized the tendency to over-extend the number of steps in the hierarchy, and indicated that the need up to that time for an Executive Class had been based partly on educational arrangements which no longer determine recruitment, and partly on the peculiar needs of certain large Departments. The Tomlin Commission, although set up by the 1929 Labour Government, was as usual heavily rigged by the Treasury, and was not able to undertake any serious fundamental review of the subject such as its predecessor the Macdonell Commission had toiled to produce before World War I.

Has the Civil Service simply failed to adapt itself to new conditions and to rise to new challenges, or has it also deteriorated within its pre-existing limits? There is reason to believe that both forms of deterioration have occurred and are still in progress, possibly even at an accelerating pace. The growing strength of the demand for bringing non-civil servants in at relatively senior levels, and the concessions which the Civil Service has already been compelled to make to this long-obstructed recommendation (made by the Reorganisation Committee as far back as February 1920), are an indication that the inadequacy of the Service for its present tasks can no longer be disputed. The cessation, over a long period, of sufficient competition for entry on the part of sufficiently able graduates from the general pool (as the undecided residue of the university population are euphemistically styled) is hard to reconcile with anything but some deterioration of the Service, not only quantitatively but qualitatively, within its own arbitrary and misguided specifications.

As the Civil Service never looks critically at itself unless compelled to do so by outside pressure direct data are naturally lacking. Reference to Civil Service minutes from the past, however, often conveys a refreshing and impressive sense of lucidity and elegance, even when the substance is questionable. There are strong indications of a pronounced and largely unremarked falling off in intellectual and literary standards, even at the top of the Administrative Class. Even a workmanlike précis of a situation is increasingly hard to obtain, and the standard of minuting, except in the Cabinet Office where it is superlative, has become in many branches of the Service so poor as to be a critical weakness. Many Departments do not even circulate the minutes of an official meeting within a week or in some cases a month of holding it, and it is not unknown for every single office represented to have to correct the record in some material particular. During the war Winston Churchill, as Prime Minister, frowned on the practice of "hunting in couples," but it would now be a great economy to get back even to this. Parkinsonian inflation has gone so far, and anarchy has so developed that it is by no means unknown, on inviting a Department to discuss some simple business, to find as many as half a dozen of its officers turning up, as no branch will trust any other out of its sight, and no one can convey adequately to anyone else what was said or what action was recommended. For similar reasons much that could and should be done by telephone with a brief record is flogged out in writing on voluminous files filled with wordy and inconclusive essays. In the frequent absence of adequate training and expertise to appreciate the main aspects of the problem, adequate information to describe and analyze it and adequate knowledge of the public to assess requirements and response, it is small wonder that the Civil Service has become heavily and dangerously dependent on material and advice emanating from outside pressure groups. There is often no practical alternative to simply swallowing these substances and regurgitating them to Ministers, after sufficient delay and digestion to disguise their origin.

What can be done to remedy this sad state of affairs? The first short answer is—"abolish the Administrative Class." It is an entirely obsolete idea that the manning of the higher ranks of the public service should or can be based on the recruitment of raw graduates who take no higher degree or serious professional training. Except for the rather narrow clique for which it has long served as a protected source of jobs, this would cause little inconvenience and would bring much benefit. By all means let some cadets continue to be taken from the universities, provided that they are then required to carry out an adequate course of higher studies or professional training suited to their capacities and to Service needs, for example courses in resource economics, town and country or regional planning, management studies or certain branches of law. The practice of learning the job by "sitting by Nellie", which has been abandoned in all serious training schemes, should be forbidden as a waste of public money.

One possible approach would be to handle the higher manning of Whitehall in three "streams", to borrow a term from the comprehensive school. The first stream would consist of a broad basic general service class, replacing the existing Administrative and Executive Classes, which would in principle be a straight graduate entry, with suitable exceptions, and would have an open channel of merit promotion to the top. The second would be a much smaller higher degree or equivalent entry at a comparable age and level to the existing Scientific

Civil Service. The third would be a much larger entry from local and regional government, the universities and schools, industry and elsewhere at age thirty-two upwards to about forty-two. To balance this there should be a substantial exodus, similar to that which has long prevailed in the Navy between Lieutenant-Commander and Captain level in the late 'thirties. This could stiffen up other main areas of national activity with a minority element of officers trained in the public service who might either benefit by a change, or have proved more suitable for non-Whitehall functions. It would also eliminate those unable to qualify for promotion in Whitehall to a level justifying their retention throughout their career. As not more than about a third of the senior men would be permitted to serve in Whitehall uninterruptedly throughout their service the atmosphere would be much more favorable to mobility, as it already is in the Diplomatic and Defence Services, which handle their personnel responsibilities far better. The insistence on choosing and promoting only men and women capable of working peaceably and innocuously together for some forty years is too costly in the kinds of talents and skills which it excludes from Whitehall, and is no longer necessary in terms of career planning. This proposal bears a considerable resemblance to that advanced by such an eminent and independent authority as Professor W. J. M. Mackenzie, before the Estimates Committee (Paper 308, pp. 128 ff). He incidentally observed: "One could obliterate the Administrative Class overnight, and able men could be found within a month to keep our top administration going (we could not similarly make good the disappearance of the Executives). But the present 'style' of the administrators is part of our whole system, and will not change without wider changes." That is profoundly true, and it is what this Part is about. He also adds the important technical point that the "Superannuation Acts, the foundation on which the Victorian civil service was built, are now largely out of date . . . they need a drastic overhaul, relating them to the whole problem of 'middle class' superannuation in all varieties of public service and in big private organisations."

This leads on to the question of how to get away from the monastic isolationism of the British Civil Service and to make it simply the chief of a family of public and semi-public services, with much closer mutual contacts and interchange. Even if the Superannuation Acts, which have considerable merits, are retained, there seems no reason why they should not be supplemented by a clearing house for personnel, initiated by the Public Service Commission. This would "value" each officer's superannuation rights at intervals on some kind of points system such as was imposed on the Treasury in World War II for taxation under Pay As You Earn (PAYE). Interchange could be freely permitted at the appropriate "price" and the respective liabilities to contribute could be finally resolved on this basis when the officer actually retires, rather than being the subject of expensive and time-consuming transfer deals on each change of employment.

As an essential accompanying measure there should be established a national profession of Public Administration with its defined professional standards, both substantive and ethical, and its own professional discipline, training and progressive activities. This profession should have statutory recognition such that in due course the higher and middle officers of central, regional and local governments, and of public concerns and other similar bodies should be encouraged to join it. Thus the identity of the public administrator as such, his assumption of professional responsibilities for his performance and his community of interest with those working in other branches of the public service would be clearly established. It would, for instance, be desirable that, as in medical practice, any charges of professional misconduct or departure from ethical standards should be referred to the appropriate professional disciplinary body, rather than to a Civil Service or other authority. Professional qualifications should be so defined and administered as to be readily acceptable worldwide, thus facilitating temporary or longer postings overseas whenever desired.

There would clearly have to be a carefully-discussed relationship between such a newly-established profession of public administration and the employers of public servants, central, territorial, regional, local and functional. As a profession consisting entirely of employees, public administration would be unable itself to adopt restrictive practices and in so far as numbers are correctly regulated through the Civil Service mechanism, the reforms here proposed would take care of that. Despite the objections of the Treasury to an independent Civil Service Commission on grounds of the undesirability of divorcing it from "managerial control", the view is maintained here that there should, in total replacement of the existing 1855 system, be a new Public Service Commission working directly under Parliament and entirely free of control or direction by any part of the Civil Service.

The apparent difficulty over management only arises through the Treasury which, wishing to preserve its own monopoly of power, has progressively usurped the proper management responsibilities of each Head of Department, who alone can efficiently discharge them in everything pertaining to his own Department. The increasing encroachment of the Treasury, in defense of its own privileges, into the essential and even day-to-day management not only of Departments but even of grant-aided bodies has to be seen to be believed, and is one of the greatest sources of inefficiency and waste of the taxpayers' money at the present time. Parliament should insist on managers being permitted and required to manage without interference, and on their being fired if they prove to have managed too badly. It is true that there is a central interest in management research, organization and methods, and in management consultancy, but this can and should be attached to a Public Service Commission. There is no ground whatever for tying it to national finance.

The Treasury in a new Britain has no role. It belongs to the dead past, and its influence has been, is, and will be a dead loss for Britain as long as Britain goes on tolerating it.

In the Royal Institute of Public Administration's authoritative Study Group report on *The Organisation of British Central Government 1914–1956* this issue is skated over with the utmost delicacy:

> The Treasury is at once more and less than a Ministry of Finance. Partly because the Prime Minister is the nominal head of the 'Treasury Board', partly because of a British conviction that the authority responsible for raising public funds should also have a say in how these funds are spent, and partly for other reasons of historical development, the Treasury has a unique constitutional position . . . Moreover, it is not easy to say exactly what the Treasury comprises: because of its miscellaneous interests and its numerous subordinate departments, its boundaries may be drawn in a number of different places to suit different purposes.

Returning to the subject in considering the central co-ordination of government the Study Group aptly comments:

> The Treasury is, however, itself only a department, and it is in the last resort only as strong as the desire of the Government as a whole to put financial considerations first, or the man who holds the office of Chancellor of the Exchequer. But the Treasury is responsible, under the Cabinet, for controlling expenditure, and it is on this that its influence and its position as a 'central' department is primarily based . . . Whatever the full reasons may be, the Treasury was— and has remained throughout our period—at least *primus inter*

pares in Whitehall. This status, impossible to define precisely, had long enabled the Treasury to take an interest in matters of general structure and organisation.

This delicate account, produced by a Study Group including half a dozen heads or former heads of government offices, says plenty between the lines of the solidity of the case on which the Treasury's almost mystical and almost unlimited authority rests.

An earlier collective work under the same auspices, *British Government since 1918,* contains, in a contribution by Professor W. A. Robson, a more specific reference:

> The primacy of the Treasury is emphasised by designating the Permanent Secretary to the Treasury as the official head of the Civil Service. The precise origin of this position is by no means clear. In 1926 Sir Henry Craik, MP, himself a former civil servant, declared in the House of Commons that the Government of the day had caused a constitutional revolution by placing the Secretary of the Treasury at the summit of the Civil Service and 'assigning to him certain functions which are arbitrarily to be attached to the newly minted office'. The Financial Secretary of the Treasury stated in reply that by 1872 the Permanent Secretary to the Treasury had become definitely established as head of the Civil Service. The post is said to have been created by Treasury Minute in 1867, but the Minute disappeared for more than fifty years so that, as Sir Henry Craik remarked, 'its historical value is appreciably impaired'. Be that as it may, in 1920 the Government of the day formulated the principle of requiring the consent of the Prime Minister to the appointment of Permanent Heads of Departments, their deputies, Principal Financial Officers and Principal Establishment Officers. The duty was laid on the Permanent Secretary to the Treasury, on a vacancy occurring in any of these posts, of submitting advice to the Prime Minister . . .

Thus the Treasury achieved a power of life and death over the career of any senior civil servant who might be rash enough to differ from it. The whole story, which some day ought to be told in full, reeks of sharp practice and improper influence. It shows quite clearly that, by biding its time sometimes for decades, the Treasury has repeatedly been able to inveigle some naïve or harassed senior Minister into signing some piece of paper which is then used as an instrument for discreetly coercing Departments or individual civil servants into doing the Treasury's will.

Some Ministers have lived to rue their complaisance, as did Winston Churchill, who as Chancellor of the Exchequer in 1926 was actually the Minister responsible for the issue of the directive to which, as recounted above, Sir Henry Craik, MP, took such exception. Alone among the main periods of his life, his career while responsible for the Treasury was never written up in detail. When he became Prime Minister in 1940 he showed his views by omitting the Chancellor of the Exchequer from his War Cabinet. Even in 1942, when a majority of the enlarged War Cabinet were Departmental Ministers the Chancellor of the Exchequer was not among them, and only the accident of Sir Kingsley Wood's death in 1943 resulting in his being succeeded by an existing Cabinet member, Sir John Anderson, restored the normal position. On again becoming Prime Minister in 1951 Churchill was evidently displeased at the extent to which the Treasury had reconquered its pre-war empire over Whitehall. The steps which he took to check this were ineffective, once Sir John Anderson had declined his extraordinary offer of the post of Chancellor of the Duchy of Lancaster with supervisory functions over the Treasury, the Board of Trade and the Ministry of Supply. While World War II had been won without the Treasury, which remained almost totally in eclipse throughout the decisive years, the continuance of such a situation in peacetime would only have been possible on the basis of a drastic reorganization of the whole central machinery of government.

What the Treasury lacks in open and straightforward statutory or constitutional authority it cunningly makes good in giving itself an air of immense antiquity and divine right, illustrated by the lavish employment of the spurious title HM Treasury. So far as history goes it is a bogus antique, although in terms of contemporary management and administrative techniques the antique element is only too genuine. The lives of successive generations of higher civil servants in other Departments have often been clouded by the predicaments in which they have been placed in resisting with due gentlemanliness and discretion the improper encroachments and interferences of the Treasury. As was lately said to me by a public servant of outstanding reputation and achievement, "In order to cope with the Treasury you must behave like an absolute swine and just hope you don't become an absolute swine in the process!"

These are some of the reasons why it is essential that the Treasury should be abolished. Do not be misled into some plausible compromise; if you are feeble enough to settle for less the Treasury will soon be up to its tricks once more. It will co-operate loyally with any government which will preserve and enhance its monopoly of power. It will suffer, if it must, any temporary abridgement or suspension of its power which, as in World War II, may be irresistibly dictated by circumstances. But as long as it exists it is going to get that power back before long, because it is, in essence, a power-seekers' club sitting in the best strategic situation in Britain.

If I have spoken strongly on the faults of the Civil Service and on the misdeeds of the Treasury it is because they constitute the main and central intellectual and institutional strongholds of the System in Britain. Buckingham Palace, the House of Lords, even the universities and perhaps even the trade unions undergo with more or less good grace a process of regeneration which enables them to adapt to changing circumstances, but fundamentally, in everything that matters, the higher Civil Service, and the Treasury which is its master, will not change because to change would be suicide for them. A new start is thus the only way open. Like so many inheritors of an *ancien régime,* the present heads of the Treasury and their senior colleagues in the Service deserve a great deal of sympathy in their well-meaning but hopeless efforts to deal with the mess that has been bequeathed to them and to grope their way towards modernization. The fact that it has been necessary recently to split the headship of the Civil Service from the effective headship of the Treasury, and that even so the burdens are excessive, indicates that nemesis is overtaking the present incumbents who were not the authors of the System they are compelled to try to sustain. Once again it is striking how the built-in vices of the System repeat themselves, and how plainly it is the System which uses and manipulates the individuals rather than *vice versa.* The tenacity and dominance of systems of misgovernment have often been demonstrated in the past, and here we can see it again before our own eyes, all the more disturbingly in view of the high principles animating so many of its servants.

Until some thirty years ago the City of London dominated British business as the Treasury now dominates the British machinery of government. The City exalted finance, as understood by the City, into the main criterion of British prosperity and welfare, and the deciding voice over the growth and evolution of the whole economy, commercial, industrial and agricultural. Finally through the shambles of 1931 the City dragged Britain down into such a morass that its peculiar and usurped powers had to go. The parallel is clear. Through its inability to break loose from the Stop-Go cycle, and its chronic mismanagement of the national economy and the national finances, the Treasury has reduced Britain to begging alms and has compelled, as a condition of immediate economic survival, the reversal of most of the worthwhile programs and projects through the whole field of economic and social policy. Successive Chancellors who trusted to Treasury advice have withdrawn from politics as discredited and disillusioned men, as indeed Winston Churchill would have remained but for the extraordinary circumstances of World War II.

Although this case for abolishing the Treasury seems overwhelming, it is not the only case. As was indicated earlier any rational grouping of the nation's official business which can make sense for the future implies a type of redistribution of function quite incompatible with the retention of such a unique and functionally confused entity as HM Treasury. Even if its retention were on all other grounds desirable there would still be no place for it on that account.

The new deal which I have proposed hangs on a drastic redistribution and decentralization both of power and of powers in the United Kingdom. It envisages the creation of distinct territorial administrations and representative bodies for England, Wales and Scotland, as well as Northern Ireland, and the hiving off of many other present functions of central Civil Service Departments to commissions or tribunals under the supervision of the judiciary and of Parliament or to public concerns of an operational character, under the indirect supervision of Ministers and of the House of Commons. It thus looks forward to a drastically reduced United Kingdom Cabinet and series of Departments, staffed by professional public administrators drawn largely from one pool with the officers of territorial, regional and local government, and of the commissions and public concerns, and to some extent also from private commerce and industries and from the universities and schools. It thus looks to a career open to talent on a much larger and more flexible scale than hitherto, complemented by a more real and effective Parliamentary supervision and control with much more two-way communication with and guidance from the electorate. The current steps to establish a Parliamentary Commissioner, to associate employers and workers more closely with planning and towards reform of the Civil Service and local government, are in this context steps in the right direction as far as they go, but are not nearly far-reaching or comprehensive enough to meet modern requirements.

Conclusion

The British are great myth-addicts, and their leaders tend therefore to be master myth-makers who saddle them with a load of half-truths, destined to outlive their occasion and their usefulness. These myths are in their way facts, but the main fact about them is that they are myths, and should be treated as such and no more. We cannot dispense with myths, and in learning to enjoy living with them we need to be observant and discriminating about their continuous tendency to throw dust in our eyes, and to cling on after they have deserved to be discarded. We ourselves will not get far without creating fresh myths of our own, and of them we should be especially wary, since these must be the myths most fitted to seduce us, and most dear to us because they are best tuned to our moods and outlook.

Stripped so far as possible of myth, Britain is seen as an immensely complex living organism, at times and in parts strikingly successful, at other times and in other parts sluggish, dull and inert, or tangled in tension and conflict. Often tiresome and frustrating for those who experience it from within, and bafflingly incomprehensible to those who regard it from outside, Britain remains full of promise, with flashes of brilliant fulfillment and longer stretches of tedious eclipse. Richly diverse in its human resources, continuously throwing up talents and new ideas which collide with deeply rooted beliefs, feelings and habits of mind, Britain has for centuries been troubled by the difficulty of ensuring freedom from persecution, or crude discrimination, for its teeming and lively minorities, who create such incessant discomfort and stress for the settled and complacent majority. The point that such boasted tolerance is not enough, and that the talents and vigor of uncomfortable minorities are among Britain's most precious national resources, to be fostered and stimulated, is still a shocking new concept to the majority, who feel they have been jolly decent in not being more beastly to the minorities, and that for them to expect even more is unreasonable. The right to waste people, and the right of people to insist upon not being wasted, is central to the muddled, tacit, decisive controversy about the future of Britain which is raging in Britain today.

Rightly or wrongly it seems that more people feel more wasted than ever before. Perhaps nowhere in the world is the gap between readily realizable potential and total actual performance more pronounced than in Britain. Over a wide field there is reason to believe that first-class potential exists, but first-class performance is so restricted that few have ever actually experienced it, and even second-class performance is uncommon compared with third- and fourth-class. This applies perhaps most in administration, in production and in distribution, and least in the arts and sciences. Its results are most serious in areas dependent upon teamwork between different types of skill and capability. Unhappily, too, they are greatest where they most affect Britain's international economic and political welfare.

Something is throttling down the national effort and crippling the performance. If this were not so the native vigor and talent still manifestly available might confidently be expected to produce immensely greater results. There is no good ground to suppose that the British will not give a fair performance without being exhorted and driven, or that they need anything beyond a modicum of good management and effective leadership. If the nation has become crusted over with cynicism, frustration and self-mockery we need not look beyond the souring disillusionment created by a System which cannot and will not lead, and which brazenly refuses to allow anyone else to.

Commentators on Britain today often speak of The Establishment. That term, which has not been used in this book, is defined in the Penguin Dictionary as an "Ill-defined grouping of upperclass conservative persons and organisations wielding influence in the background of public life". Charles Arnold-Baker in *The 5,000 and the Power Tangle* (London, 1967) has recently argued that some 5,000 people, whom he classifies by occupation, have an identifiable part in the management of the nation. He contends that they are not an "Establishment" because they differ strongly among themselves. Like-mindedness is assumed to be a feature of a true Establishment. This dilemma can however be resolved. The System is not to be viewed primarily as a set of people but as a series of principles, aims, policies, practices and codes of conduct handed down through a group of allied institutions since the System was devised and imposed in mid-Victorian times. These institutions included Parliament, the higher Civil Service, the older universities and public schools, the City, the legal profession, the Anglican church and to some extent the Services. Through the erosion of recent events the task of sustaining the System has recently been dropped, or less keenly pursued, by most of these, except the higher Civil Service and certain parts of the university and public school world, which now constitute the hard core of its support, sometimes more from inherited tradition than from conviction. Since The Establishment as such is held to have no coherent opinion or common belief the upholders of the System remain as the only element enjoying its prestige and contacts who are able to dominate it by reason of their group solidarity, their clear-cut if obsolete ideas and their continuing command of the mechanism of central government. There is, however, a growing rift within the so-called Establishment between that priesthood still dedicated to the System and the looser band of heretics who think they see through it. Eyes are at last opening. The duality of the ostensibly normal government and of the highly peculiar System which has annexed it and which operates it begins to be understood.

Many more years might have passed without this occurring, but for the spectacular unsuccess of the British government's operations, and the frustration which this has created throughout Britain. After attributing this for years to ill-luck or to normal bureaucratic inefficiency the nation begins to perceive that something more systematic is behind such a course of misgovernment. The first reaction is to resort in despair to something like a sitdown strike against it. Although understandable and natural this response is not constructive or helpful. Where there is something so badly wrong the way to recovery is through searching diagnosis and appropriate treatment. The governed cannot undertake this, because the System is so strongly dug in, with its intense secretiveness, its front of misleading pretenses, and its craftiness in meeting demands for fundamental investigation and reform by measures which leave intact its power and its capacity for mischief.

Constitutionally the System is the servant of the sovereign nation; practically it has been allowed to become the master, up to this time.

Britain is at last at the moment of truth. Either the allegedly free and sovereign nation will so express itself that the sectional vested interests of the System must give way to it and the System itself be radically recast, or the British liberties which have been so valiantly and triumphantly vindicated on so many fields of past struggle must be reckoned now at an end. In that case a period of slow Byzantine decline, under a strangling bureaucracy, awaits the next generations. We recall, perhaps too often, the military and moral troubles of the declining Roman Empire. It all led to Byzantium.

As Bagehot delighted in showing, the British constitution is, above all, a confidence trick. In the foreground, a stately band of persons, gorgeously robed, moves in solemn procession to traditional music, dazzling the populace in time-honored ceremonies. In the background, another band, unobtrusively attired in dark suits, scurries along the corridors from the offices where the Ministers and the knights of the large carpets labor to the austere rooms sacred to the Cabinet and its committees, running affairs very much as they happen to think best.

Let us grant that there is nothing to be said against confidence tricks, but on one condition only—that they work. That, after all, is the test most deeply enshrined in British tradition. It was often feared in Bagehot's day that the show would sometime have to stop because the performance of the foreground band would begin to bore a more modern and sophisticated public. So far this gives no sign of happening, and our diagnosis has found no serious fault either in the direction or script of the front spectacle, nor in the performance put up by the players and their capacity to hold an audience. Other nations do these things in other ways, or try to manage without them altogether. Superficial critics often manage both to overrate their importance in current affairs and to underrate their enduring social psychological role.

Unfortunately, Bagehot was wrong in postulating that these theatrical "dignified parts" serve to conceal "a simple efficient part" which "*can* work more simply and easily, and better, than any instrument of government that has yet been tried". The stately actors find the show being stolen from them by the ill-concealed clumsy antics of the men in the dark suits, who keep on dropping things and tripping over one another, or pressing the wrong buttons so that all the lights go out or the curtain comes down in the middle of some important act. The theater has been modernized, but the scene-shifters and electricians have not awakened to the fact, or learned how to manage it, and as they are supposed to be invisible the embarrassed audience does not know how to react. As this is a play within a play, and is essentially about power, it cannot be understood without securing a seat in the corridors or committee rooms as well as in the public auditorium.

Here one observes clearly that the cast of the real play includes the audience and the scene-shifters, and the head scene-shifter is its anti-hero, supported by his henchmen, of whom all the others in the know are abjectly but secretly afraid. Conversely, on the other hand, there is an intense fear of being caught in the spotlight or out of cover, and a paradoxical belief in the genuineness of the front show, which functionally is only meant to deceive the main audience. The rule that those who most successfully manipulate propaganda become themselves its most credulous dupes is nowhere better illustrated.

A hundred years ago Bagehot and his sophisticated contemporaries viewed the addition to the British electorate of millions of uneducated inexperienced voters as a grave, unwelcome risk, only to be surmounted by flattering and deceiving the newcomers into entrusting all the real power and authority to their betters. The still unpaid membership of Parliament, the new professionally manned, interest-financed, political parties, and the new Arnold-Jowett-molded, competitively recruited Civil Service were all devices skilfully shaped to that end. To serve it these Victorian liberal classical philosophers consciously rejected purposeful advance in public education, in technology and in economic productivity as being too risky for the System. They resolved that Britain should enter the modern age dragging its feet, rather than imperil the constitution as they understood it and desired it to be.

It was an open conspiracy of some of the most high-minded men who have ever graced British public life, inspired by humane and civilized principles. As tends to happen in such cases, its results for Britain have proved even more disastrous than might have been expected if they had been a greedy band of scoundrels. Spectators of this tragi-comedy must spare some sympathy also for the present directors and operators of the System, who have inherited and are expected until further notice to carry on a set-up whose structure and methods no longer work, in aid of tacit objectives which are recognized as both misconceived and inapplicable. Although thus deprived of its *raison d'être,* and operated by men who have no responsibility for or understanding of its origins and purpose, the System grinds mindlessly on, incapable of preserving Britain in the safe hands of classically trained Christian gentlemen, but well able still to ensure that no one else can take over and start picking up the bits.

How can the System prove so disastrous, when so many of those who have served and developed it have personally been so good? The answer can be given in one word—Fear. In its inmost heart the System is a bundle of chronic nervous dreads and mistrusts. It is held together and driven by a triple fear—fear of facing new facts, fear of facing the people and fear of facing the future. All that it does, all its evasions and esoteric practices, its mystique and its morbid love of secrecy derive from that triple fear.

The System hates the thought of what the British people will choose to do if they are allowed to be themselves. After the shocks of the 1832 Reform Act, of Chartism and of the wave of enthusiastic continental revolutions in 1848 a frightened determination was formed at the heart of Britain's affairs to stop the clock just there, but without ever admitting it. Successive generations of trusty hand-picked Janissaries of the then established social order must strictly regulate future progress. Faced with the regrettable necessity of entering at last a century after the nineteenth, and with the anticipated dangerous thoughts of future British generations, the custodians of the System have become increasingly ill-at-ease, more estranged from public opinion, and more obsessed with clinging to their authority by hidden or indirect means. Inheriting a divine mandate to save US from ourselves, but troubled that the magic formula for doing this is ceasing to work as it ought to, THEY are increasingly troubled to find how little WE appreciate the purity and rightness of their mission.

One reason for this great affliction is contained in the maxim that every nation gets the government it deserves. In Britain, where so much of public affairs has been viewed and handled politically, there has been a resolute neglect of the entire history, art and science of administration. Bagehot himself recognized, yet openly shared, this blind spot.

"Why is it," he asked, "that our English Government, which is beyond comparison the best of Parliamentary governments, is not celebrated through the world for its administrative efficiency? . . . Why, according to popular belief is it rather characterised by the very contrary? . . . no man would select the cadets of an aristocratic house as desirable administrators. They have peculiar disadvantages in the acquisition of business knowledge, business training, and business habits . . .

"Our middle class, too, is very unfit to give us the administrators we ought to have . . . The sort of education which fits a man for the higher posts of practical life is still very rare; there is not even a good agreement as to what it is. Our public officers cannot be as good as the corresponding officers of some foreign nations till our business education is as good as theirs."

As an afterthought he adds a footnote that this evil is much diminishing, but this was optimistic in the context; what he wrote in 1867 is not far from the mark in 1967. Until Britain can develop a strong and critical group of independent people who really take an interest in the managerial and administrative aspects of government, as is now at last done for industry and commerce, the effective professional base on which sustained and thorough improvement can be developed will be lacking.

One of the objects of this book has been to try to show that government administration and management form a larger and more essential part of history and of life than is commonly supposed, and that to give more attention to them would be rewarding, while to go on neglecting them will cost us dear. If it is felt that the administrative aspects of British government have been more critically and drastically treated than others, this is the reason. We need to emancipate ourselves from the dreadful blend of ancestral piety, mental indolence and intolerable complacency with which the constitution and government of Britain are so often treated. Nowhere are these evils more serious and indefensible than when, under cover of quite unnecessary secrecy, the mystique is extended to government Departments and to the Civil Service.

Modern principles and techniques of organization and management are potentially liberating influences. By contrast the now obsolescent forms have been rigid and fettering, prolific in sterile paperwork, and in the pursuit of action by laws and regulations. When we see a public service unafraid of finding the facts, unafraid to study and face the future, unafraid to trust the British people and ready to put its cards on the table face upwards, we will be able to feel that we are making progress. The need now is to look at what the nation requires and wants, in all its human diversity, and to match it with a basically integrated but generously diversified and responsive new system, helping and encouraging the sovereign people to do their sovereign will, and to find the means to achieve the ends on which they are resolved. Wooden government means a dull sullen nation. Imaginative, resourceful modern government can mean a lively contented nation, moving forward fast.

It is necessary to think in terms of a triple harmony among a healthy satisfying environment, an uninhibited free people actively pursuing human fulfillment in all its aspects, and an informal unstuffy, highly trained and professionally resourceful government which can earn the right to be regarded no longer as just THEM but as really part of US. Sobering as it is to reflect that four and a half centuries ago Sir Thomas More wrote his *Utopia* close by where these words are being written now, they are not intended to relate to "an impossibly ideal society", but to something which could happen here and soon.

It could happen, not, however, as a new prescription artificially imposed from outside, but as something which the British have long had it vaguely in mind to do some day. Not only poets and story-tellers, but political writers and leaders and popular tradition, have kept alive in many forms the aim and conception of achieving some deeply satisfying harmony, order, and human fulfillment under a more civilized political pattern. In many respects the barriers in the way of realizing such a break-through have recently either been removed or reduced to more manageable proportions. Yet, as the objective difficulties have lessened, the subjective have proliferated. People have relapsed into a muddle about who they are, what they want to do, and how it might be done. The mainspring of this muddle (if a muddle can have a mainspring) is the warped relation between government and governed. Once this is corrected, even without any clear preconception about future purposes, the rest can follow.

Having themselves been overrun by successive invaders throughout the first millennium after Christ, and having devoted much of the second millennium now ending to overrunning other countries, it is time for the British to settle down in the world and to find a more civilized basis for their human relationships during the third. For this they are admirably fitted by their talents, interests and experience, while the sudden closing in of the rest of the world in terms of journey time around their central position in global air travel puts the ball once more at their feet.

There is no good ground in history, or in current analysis, for doubting that the British themselves will rise to the occasion if they are freed from the fetters which the System has drawn tightly around them. They are a resourceful, responsive, lively people, when they are allowed to be themselves. It will be a great experience for them and a great inspiration and help for others when this happens, as it now must. The gloomy spectacle of a great nation lost in the political deserts of Gladstraelia has held the stage long enough. The British are ready for a new role, and they deserve it.

How will they liberate themselves from the System? The first obvious step is to identify it, and to recognize its workings. This in itself will come as a shock to many, but it will be a healthy shock. As the curtains of woven fog are drawn aside, and the light and air streams in to the sickroom, the patient will at once begin to feel better. There is after all nothing in the nature of the disease that cannot readily be cured by a change of doctor, or, better still, by dispensing with a doctor altogether, and letting the task ahead be itself the treatment.

Who will stand in the way of liberation? Politicians of all parties would be behaving contrary to their own obvious interests in doing so. Year after year they have been forced to eat their words, default on their solemn promises and retire as frustrated men for lack of a governmental machine able and willing to perform what in modern times should reasonably be expected of it. The impossibility of running a successful Labour administration on such lines has been abundantly demonstrated. The Conservative ministers in the 'fifties probably put in as much constructive hard thinking as any political team in British history, but their administration ended in confusion and discredit through the same great defect. Conservatives will recognize the System as basically a product of mid-Victorian liberal thought, and will perceive that if it continues to spread disillusionment and to defy replacement, sooner or later it may well drag down with it the entire constitution. How the System will go is still anybody's guess, but that the British nation will sweep it away sooner or later is as certain as anything can be. The British are not a people to cling to their chains.

Notes on Sources

In a work covering such a broad field and involving so many difficult condensations and generalizations of fact and opinion it would be impracticable to aim at a detailed list of first-hand sources.

In these circumstances the principle adopted has been to provide a selective guide to the further reading likely to be of most value to those students or general readers who may wish to go more deeply into particular subjects, or to review the treatment and presentation of some of the many debatable issues. In selection, preference has been given to the most up-to-date and readily accessible works, and to those which are reasonably comprehensive, except where more technical or detailed treatments have to be cited because of their decisive significance to the argument. In cases, however, where such works have been quoted and acknowledged in the text (see entries in Index) it has not usually been found necessary to repeat the reference in this bibliographic section.

Anyone attempting any such book must constantly be aware of an immense debt to many who have previously worked over parts of the ground. In freely acknowledging that it must be emphasized that omission from the present list in no way implies any reflection on many other publications, some of which are in any case cited in one or other of the works here listed.

Wherever possible, American publishers and publication dates are noted.

PART ONE

Probably the best conspectus of the environmental background of human pre-history and history is *Man's Role in Changing the Face of the Earth,* the record of the Wenner-Gren Foundation's International Symposium in 1956, edited by William A. Thomas, Jr. (University of Chicago Press, 1956). Further research and new interpretations have modified to some extent the accounts therein provided, but there is no single more up-to-date review.

The geographic and biological background for Britain are well presented in *Britain's Structure and Scenery* by Dudley Stamp (Collins, 1946), and *Climate and the British Scene* by Gordon Manley (Collins, 1952), and in Harry Godwin's *The History of the British Flora* (Cambridge University Press, 1956).

The Oxford Atlas of Britain and Northern Ireland (Oxford University Press, 1963) contains a wealth of useful material. Many interesting presentations of results of recent extensive studies are given in the *Reader's Digest Complete Atlas of the British Isles* (Funk and Wagnalls, 1965).

G. M. Trevelyan's *History of England* (Doubleday, Anchor), though forty years old, still provides a most valuable perspective of pre-conquest relationships between the various human races in Britain and their environment. Subsequent studies have, however, much expanded our detailed knowledge, and have enabled early relationships between Britain and Europe to be reinterpreted. A stimulating and suggestive review published after this book was written is Beram Saklatvala's *Arthur: Roman Britain's Last Champion* (Taplinger, 1967).

Another recent work throwing considerable light on the successful integration of the British is Doris M. Stenton's *English Justice between the Norman Conquest and the Great Charter 1066–1215* (American Philosophical Society, 1964). *The Medieval Foundations of England* by G. O. Sayles (Barnes and Noble, 1950) is also valuable.

Two wide-ranging imaginative works by Esme Wingfield-Stratford must also be cited here—*The History of British Civilisation* (1928) and *The Foundations of British Patriotism* (1939).

For two particularly critical periods of administrative adjustment we have the invaluable illumination of G. R. Elton's *The Tudor Revolution in Government* (Cambridge University Press, 1959) and of G. E. Aylmer's *The King's Servants: The Civil Service of Charles I 1625–1642* (Columbia University Press, 1961). Sir Lewis Namier's *England in the Age of the American Revolution* (St. Martin's Press, 1961) is of key importance for its period. A useful view of British technical development is given by W. H. Chaloner and A. E. Musson in *Industrial Technology* in *A Visual History of Britain* (Dufour, 1963).

A thorough and comprehensive comparative review of the modern development of political institutions and administrative organization in western countries will be found in the two volumes of *The Theory and Practice of Modern Government* by Herman Finer (Barnes and Noble, 1961), which also provides a valuable corrective to conventional insular approaches to the subject in Britain.

The most important direct evidence on the mid-nineteenth-century reforms of the Civil Service is contained in the *Report on the Organisation of the Permanent Civil Service*, with letter from the Rev. B. Jowett (1854), C. 1713 and the accompanying *Papers relating to the Reorganisation of the Civil Service* (1855), C. 1870 and in the *Reports of the Civil Service Inquiry Commission* (1875), Cd. 113, 1226, 1317. Reference should also be made to Edward Hughes's article, "Civil Service Reform, 1853–55" in *History*, Vol. XXVII (June, 1942).

Two works in the New Whitehall Series, *The Treasury* by Lord Bridges (Oxford University Press, 1964), and *The Home Office* by Sir Frank Newsam (Oxford University Press, 1954), present the record from the standpoint of the two key Departments.

On the political and Parliamentary plane *The Growth of the British Party System* (Humanities, 1965), by Ivor Bulmer-Thomas, although questionable for the earlier period, is valuable on the astonishingly complex nineteenth-century evolution. R. B. MacCallum's *The Liberal Party from Earl Grey to Asquith* (Humanities, 1963), gives a terse and penetrating analysis, while John Vincent in *The Formation of the Liberal Party 1857–1868* (Charles Scribner's Sons, 1967) breaks entirely new ground at the grassroots level of Victorian politics. He also gives illuminating portraits of political leaders, notably Gladstone. His great rival, Disraeli, has been devastatingly dissected in Robert Blake's new biography *Disraeli* (St. Martin's Press, 1966), which is an eye-opener on the influence of the talented mythmaker even when dead and buried.

On economic history a most valuable conspectus is provided by *British Economic Growth 1688–1959* by Phyllis Deane and W. A. Cole (Cambridge University Press, 1962). *The Migration of British Capital to 1875* by L. H. Jenks (Thomas Nelson & Sons, 1963), and *Home and Foreign Investment 1870–1913* by Sir A. K. Cairncross (1953) are basic sources for the outcome of the City's activities, on which direct documentation is fragmentary and inadequate. On education, extracts from the most important primary documents can be found in J. Stuart Maclure, *Educational Documents* (Barnes and Noble, 1965).

The best critical account of Imperialism is still J. A. Hobson, *Imperialism: A Study* (University of Michigan, Ann Arbor Paperbacks, 1965). A. P. Thornton has written brilliantly, though untidily, of *The Imperial Idea and Its Enemies* (St. Martin's Press, 1959). George Bennett, *The Concept of Empire, Burke to Atlee 1774–1947* (Barnes and Noble, 1962), is a collection of quotations which illustrate the essential consistency of British political attitudes to Imperialism. Esme Wingfield-Stratford's *Beyond Empire* (1964), ending with the Boer War, discusses the imperialist chapter against the background of British history as a whole.

PART TWO

At the level of human economic and social studies there appears to be no more up-to-date comprehensive appraisal of recent development than *World Population and Production: Trends and Outlook* by W. S. and E. S. Woytinsky (Twentieth Century Fund, 1955). There have, however, been many excellent more recent reviews and statistical presentations of many parts of the field, a number of which have been used especially in this Part.

On population problems basic reliance has been placed on the two PEP Reports, *Population Policy in Great Britain* (1948) and *World Population and Resources* (1955), in which I was closely concerned. As both these are now somewhat out of date in certain respects they have been supplemented by later sources, including the excellent *Population Bulletins* issued by the Population Reference Bureau, Inc., 1755 Massachusetts Ave., N.W., Washington, D.C. 20036, which also issues a regular World Population Data Sheet for over 130 countries.

For comparative statistics generally sources consulted include *British Political Facts 1900–1960* by David Butler and Jennie Freeman (St. Martin's Press, 1967) and *Britain: An Official Handbook* (Central Office of Information, 1967).

Numerous more specialized works have been consulted on particular issues, and special mention should be made of the following: *Modern Capitalism* by Andrew Schonfield (Oxford University Press, 1965), *Comparative Productivity in British and American Industry* by L. Rostas (1948), *The Stagnant Society* by Michael Shanks (Peter Smith, 1961), and *Britain and the World Economy* by J. M. Livingstone (Penguin, 1966).

PART THREE

W. A. Robson, *The Governors and the Governed* (Louisiana State University Press, 1964) is a useful short introduction to the problems discussed in this Part. A. M. Carr-Saunders, D. Caradog-Jones and C. Moser, *Social Conditions in England and Wales* (revised ed., 1958) is an excellent introduction to the governed, as is G. Gorer, *Exploring English Character* (S. G. Phillips, 1955). Ronald Frankenburg, *Communities in Britain* (Penguin, 1966) refers to the results of several social surveys of specific communities and has a very comprehensive bibliography.

Alienation

There has been very little study of this growing aspect of contemporary Britain. Christopher Driver gives a useful portrait of one recent alienated group in *The Disarmers: A Study in Protest* (Verry, 1964). For less obvious forms of alienation, the best sources are literary: Alan Sillitoe's novel *Saturday Night and Sunday Morning* (New American Library, Signet, 1960) and two plays, John Osborne's *Look Back in Anger* (S. G. Phillips, 1957) and Arnold Wesker's *Roots* (1959) have particular value.

Politicians and the Governed

Richard Rose, *Influencing Voters* (St. Martin's Press, 1967) is an important study of politicians' attitudes to market research techniques in campaigning. Lord Windlesham, *Communication and Political Power* (1966) has a similar theme, but is somewhat different in its approach. Both books make comparisons between Britain and the United States. G. Almond and S. Vebra, *The Civic Culture* (Princeton University Press, 1963) is a fascinating comparative study of political attitudes and democracy in five nations. A. P. Thornton in *The Habit of Authority: Paternalism in British History* (University of Toronto Press, 1966) fails to define his theme clearly enough to make it a coherent and satisfactory study but it is, nevertheless, a useful survey of the relations between governors and governed throughout British history, refreshingly free from illusions. R. Williams-Thompson, *Was I Really Necessary?* (1951) contains the personal reflections of one who served as a public relations officer under the 1945–50 Labour Government.

The Individual and the Law

Viscount Hewart, *The New Despotism* (1929) was the pioneering work in this field. Harry Street's *Freedom, the Individual and the Law* (Peter Smith, 1963) is claimed as the first attempt to define the content of British civil liberty.

PART FOUR

Anthony Sampson, *Anatomy of Britain* (Harper and Row, 1965) describes most of the sources of power in modern Britain, ranging from Buckingham Palace to the offices of J. Walter Thompson. Jean Blondel, *Voters, Parties and Leaders* (Penguin, 1964) discusses, as the subtitle puts it, the social fabric of British politics.

Richard Rose, *Politics in England* (Little, Brown, 1964) and Samuel H. Beer, *British Politics in the Collectivist Age* (Alfred A. Knopf, 1965) are two recent works of great importance.

Sovereignty and the Constitution

Three classic sources are still of great value: Sir William Blackstone, *Commentaries on the Laws of England* (1765–1769) (Beacon, 1962),

A. V. Dicey, *Introduction to the Law of the Constitution* (1885) (St. Martin's Press) and, of course, Walter Bagehot, *The English Constitution* (Doubleday Dolphin). The most up-to-date commentaries on this subject are Francis Hinsley, *Sovereignty* (Basic Books, 1966) and Sir Ivor Jennings, *The British Constitution* (Cambridge University Press, 1966). D. L. Keir, *Constitutional History of Modern Britain* (Van Nostrand, 1966) provides historical perspective.

Geoffrey Marshall and Graeme C. Moodie's modestly titled *Some Problems of the Constitution* (Hillary, 1961) is distinctly a contribution to the new problem-oriented school of constitutional studies.

Electorate

Most of the discussion in this section is based on Angus Campbell *et al.*, *The American Voter* (John Wiley, 1960). In Great Britain, we must, for the moment, rely on individual constituency surveys, as did A. J. Allen in *The British Voter* (1964). But David Butler and Donald E. Stokes are working on a comprehensive survey of the British voter, sponsored by Nuffield College, which was published late in 1967.

Parliament

Eric Taylor, *The House of Commons at Work* (1965) is a solid basic account. Erskine May, *Treatise on the Law, Privilege, Proceedings and Usages of Parliament* (ed. by Sir Barnett Cocks, 1964) is the most authoritative source. H. V. Wiseman, *Parliament and the Executive: An Analysis with Readings* (Humanities, 1966) is an excellent introduction to a wide range of distinguished thought on the role of Parliament. Herbert Morrison, *Government and Parliament* (Oxford University Press, 1964) is a most useful work by a statesman and political organizer who played a key role in the war and post-war governments. Nigel Nicholson, *People and Parliament* (1958), whose political career was curtailed as a result of his opposition to the Suez operation, gives the back-bencher's view.

On Parliamentary reform, there is a useful study by the Hansard Society for Parliamentary Government, *Parliamentary Reform, 1933–58, A Survey of Suggested Reforms* (1961). Bernard Crick, *The Reform of Parliament* (Doubleday Anchor, 1965), and *Parliament as an Export*, edited by Sir Alan Burns (Barnes and Noble, 1966) are also valuable.

On the Upper House, there is P. A. Bromhead, *The House of Lords and Contemporary Politics* (Hillary, 1957) which, unfortunately, preceded the introduction of life peerages and is, therefore, in some respects out of date.

Finally, there is H. J. Palmer's *Government and Parliament: A Bibliography* (1964).

The Crown

Kingsley Martin, *The Crown and the Establishment* (Penguin, 1962) and Lord Altrincham (John Grigg) *et al.*, *Is the Monarchy Perfect?* (1958) are two well-written, critical accounts.

Political Parties

In this field we have two classic expositions in Sir Ivor Jennings' exhaustive *Party Politics,* comprising three volumes, *Appeal to the People* (1960), *The Growth of Parties* (1961) and *The Stuff of Politics* (1962), all published by the Cambridge University Press, and R. T. Mackenzie, *British Political Parties* (Praeger, 1964).

Pressure Groups

S. E. Finer, *Anonymous Empire* (Humanities, 1966) is a clear and concise analysis of British pressure groups. J. O. Stewart, *British Pressure Groups* (Oxford University Press, 1958) is a well-documented and vivid account. Allen Potter, *Organized Groups in British National Politics* (Hillary, 1961) is more concerned with the internal mechanisms of, and relationships between, the pressure groups themselves.

On the agricultural pressure group, there is a valuable study by P. Self and H. Storing, *The State and the Farmer* (1962). PEP's *Industrial Trade Associations* (1957) provides much information on a number of other pressure groups.

The Cabinet

For the history and performance of the Cabinet since the beginning of the First World War, Hans Daalder has provided an illuminating and well-documented account in *Cabinet Reform in Britain 1914–1963* (Stanford University Press, 1963). Two other useful studies of the Cabinet are Sir Ivor Jennings, *Cabinet Government* (Cambridge University Press, 1959) and John P. Mackintosh, *The British Cabinet* (University of Toronto Press, 1962).

The Machinery of Government and the Civil Service

On the financial and economic side of the Treasury's dual functions, there is S. H. Beer, *Treasury Control* (Oxford University Press, 1957) and the *Report of the Plowden Committee on Control of Public Expenditure,* Cmd. 1432 (1961). For a broader perspective, it is essential to look at the Treasury's partner in financial management, namely the City, entertainingly portrayed by Paul Ferris in *The City* (1960). The (Radcliffe) *Committee on the Working of the Monetary System,* Cmd. 827 (1959) unearthed a great deal of fascinating information.

PART FIVE

There are three brief works covering the whole of the period discussed in this Part: David Thomson, *England in the Twentieth Century* (Penguin, 1965), E. E. Reynolds and M. H. Brasher, *Britain in the Twentieth Century* (Cambridge University Press, 1966), and L. C. B. Seaman, *Post-Victorian Britain* (Barnes and Noble, 1966).

On the earlier part of the period, there are a number of more detailed studies. C. L. Mowat, *Britain Between the Wars 1918–40* (University of Chicago Press, 1955) is particularly strong on economic and social affairs. On the political aspects, A. J. P. Taylor, *English History 1914–1945* (Oxford University Press, 1965) is often very penetrating. It is also important, not least for its unorthodox conclusions, on foreign affairs and defense. The best economic history is S. Pollard, *The Development of the British Economy 1914–1950* (St. Martin's Press, 1962).

The General Strike

W. H. Crook, *The General Strike* (1931) is a well-documented account. Julian Symonds, *The General Strike* (1957) is livelier. George Glasgow, *General Strikes and Road Transport* (1926) deals with the Government's emergency machinery. The documentary evidence has been collected by the *British Library of Political and Economic Science* and is listed, in its catalogue, under *General Strike*.

The Samuel Commission's Report (*Royal Commission on the Coal Industry, 1925: Volume One: Report,* Cmnd. 2600, 1926) is the crucial document for the coal industry.

The Gold Standard and British Financial Policy

The Report of the Macmillan Committee (*Committee on Finance and Industry: Report* [1931], Cmnd. 3897) is of great importance. J. M. Keynes, *The Economic Consequences of Mr. Churchill* (1925) criticizes the return to the Gold Standard. M. S. Sayer's essay in L. S. Pressnell (ed.), *Studies in the Industrial Revolution* (Oxford University Press, 1960) presents a contrary view. E. Nevin, *The Mechanism of Cheap Money* (1955) traces the new policy which was ushered in with the suspension of the Gold Standard. The Macmillan Committee's *Minutes of Evidence* (2 vols., 1931) casts much light on the City's relations, or lack of them, with British industry. Sir Henry Clay, *Lord Norman* (1957) is a useful, but rather too indulgent account of the Governor of the Bank of England in this period.

The 1931 Crisis

D. Lloyd George, *We Can Conquer Unemployment* (1929), a Liberal manifesto in the 1929 Election campaign, is the best illustration of Keynes-ian and Liberal solutions for Britain's economic difficulties. *Memoranda on Certain Proposals relating to Unemployment* (1929), Cmd. 3331 embodied the Government's views. R. Bassett, *1931: Political Crisis* (Verry, 1958) is, to a large extent, a polemical and rather heated defense of MacDonald but is a fairly reliable account of the political events of that year. *Committee on National Expenditure: Report* (1931), Cmd. 3920—the May Report—is the crucial document.

Roads

Rees Jeffreys, *The King's Highway* (1949), despite its elusive prose, is a damning and well-documented indictment of the Government's policy. Royal Commission on Transport: *Final Report: The Co-ordination and Development of Transport* (1930), Cmd. 3751 marks the origin of the decision to neglect the construction of new roads. Ministry of Transport, *Highway Development Survey, 1937 (Greater London)* (1938) was a report by Sir Charles Bressey, the Buchanan of the 1930's. The Alness Committee (*Report by the Select Committee of the House of Lords on the Prevention of Road Accidents,* HL. Papers 2, 52, 1938–9) drew attention to the failure to ensure safety on the roads.

The Public Corporations

W. A. Robson (ed.), *Public Enterprise* (1937), Lincoln Gordon, *Public Corporation in Great Britain* (1938), T. H. O'Brien, *British Experiments in Public Ownership and Control* (1937) all deal with the BBC, CEB and LPTB. Gordon's work is marginally the most thorough and well-documented of the three.

W. A. Robson, *Nationalised Industry and Public Ownership* (1962) and A. H. Hanson, *Parliament and Public Ownership* (Oxford University Press, 1961) discuss public ownership in all its aspects as it appeared after the postwar additions and changes.

Four Reports on Electricity Supply in the post-war reconstruction period indicate much uncertainty in the official mind. Two were published under the aegis of the Ministry of Reconstruction: Cd. 8880 (1917) and Cmd. 93 (1919). The Board of Trade contributed two other committees which reported in Cd. 9062 (1918) and Cd. 9072 (1918). The Weir Report—Ministry of Transport, *Report of the Committee appointed to review the National Problem of the Supply of Electrical Energy* (1926)—preceded the creation of the CEB. The story of the BBC up to the Second World War is told reverently by Asa Briggs, *The History of Broadcasting in the United Kingdom* (2 vols., Oxford University Press, 1961 and 1965). The Reports of three Broadcasting Committees, Sykes Cmd. 1951 (1923), Crawford, Cmd. 2599 (1925), Ullswater, Cmd. 5091 (1935) add up to a fascinating picture of how the public service concept developed and survived. The influence of Lord (J.C.W.) Reith on broadcasting was immeasurable. His *Into the Wind*

(1949) is an important historical document. Briggs deals adequately with the first television service. *Report of the Television Committee,* Cmd. 4793 (1935) recommended the inauguration of the service.

For the LPTB, Herbert Morrison, *Socialisation and Transport* (1933) contains many interesting observations by one who had a hand in its creation.

Government Trading Estates and Special Areas

Ministry of Labour, *Reports of Investigations into the Industrial Conditions in Certain Depressed Areas,* Cmd. 4728 (1934) are accounts of the problems of the Special Areas. The Reports of the Commissioners in England and Wales—Cmd. 4957 (1935), Cmd. 5090 (1936), Cmd. 5303 (1936), Cmd. 5595 (1937), Cmd. 5896 (1938)—and Scotland—Cmd. 4958 (1935), Cmd. 5089 (1936), Cmd. 5245 (1936), Cmd. 5604 (1937), Cmd. 5905 (1938)—are accounts of what was done about the problems.

Appeasement and Rearmament

A. J. P. Taylor, *The Origins of the Second World War* (Fawcett, 1964) incorporates the results of the latest research. It is controversial for its interpretation of Hitler but is nearly always right on the British side. Mr. Taylor casts much light on the experts' miscalculations in the formulation of foreign and defense policy. We now have an excellent history of foreign policy between the Wars in F. S. Northedge, *The Troubled Giant: Britain Among the Great Powers 1916–39* (Praeger, 1966). It is thoroughly competent on appeasement. An essay in D. C. Watt, *Personalities and Policies* (1965) has a few important points.

The documentation can be found among the numerous volumes of E. L. Woodward and Rohan Butler, *Documents on British Foreign Policy 1919–1939* (1946—).

The field is rich in memoirs, some of them more informative than others. Lord Avon, *The Eden Memoirs: Facing the Dictators* (Houghton Mifflin, 1962) and *The Reckoning* (Houghton Mifflin, 1965) are mines of information, most of it reflecting the author in an unduly favorable light. Lord (Sir Robert) Vansittart, *The Mist Procession* (1955) takes the story only as far as 1937, although it is still important. Ian Colvin, *Vansittart in Office* (1965) uses the Vansittart Papers to fill the gaps. Lord Strang, *Home and Abroad* (1956) has some shrewd comments.

On rearmament, R. J. Minney, *The Private Papers of Hore-Belisha* (1948) is of crucial importance for the Army. M. M. Postan, *British War Production* (1952) includes a reliable account of rearmament. There is a biography of *Tizard* by Ronald Clark (MIT Press, 1965).

The Economy

Liberal Industrial Inquiry, *Britain's Industrial Future* (1928) (The Liberal Yellow Book) anticipated many later developments in British policy. A number of policy-makers in the 1930's acknowledged their debt to this work. Two collaborative works by a Research Committee of the Economic Science and Statistics Section of the British Association for the Advancement of Science, *Britain in Depression* (1935) and *Britain in Recovery* (1938) contain valuable information on the state of the economy and individual industries. The latter particularly informative on the effects of the completion of the Grid. R. F. Harrod, *Life of John Maynard Keynes* (St. Martin's Press paperback, 1963) is the story of a voice crying in the wilderness throughout the pre-war period.

R. Lekachman in *The Age of Keynes* (Random House, 1966) reviews the slow process by which Keynes's views became generally acceptable in Britain and in America.

For general discussion, there is D. N. Chester (ed.), *Lessons of the British War Economy* (1951), a collection of essays by wartime "temporaries"; J. C. R. Dow, *The Management of the British Economy 1945–60* (Cambridge University Press, 1963), which combines discussion for the general reader and for the technical expert; and two works edited by G. D. N. Worswick and P. H. Ady, *The British Economy 1945–50* (Oxford University Press, 1952) and *The British Economy in the 1950's* (Oxford University Press, 1962).

Samuel Brittan, *The Treasury under the Tories 1951–64* (1964) contains a useful discussion of the Treasury and its place in the machinery of government, as well as a critical historical narrative. PEP, *French Planning: Some Lessons for Britain* (1963) is of great importance.

For more recent events, there is Henry Brandon's behind-the-scenes account of *In the Red: The Struggle for Sterling 1964–66* (Houghton Mifflin, 1966) and, on the ill-fated National Plan, the PEP Broadsheet (*Planning* Vol. XXXII, No. 499, January, 1967), "Inquest on Planning in Britain," written by Samuel Brittan.

Education

Stephen Cotgrove, *Technical Education and Social Change* (Hillary, 1958) has considerable value. Among recent educational reports, the most important are Ministry of Education, *15 to 18: A Report of the Central Advisory Council for Education (England)*, Vol. I, *Report* (1959) known as the Crowther Report, and Committee on Higher Education, *Report* (1963), Cmd. 2154, known as the Robbins Report.

Suez

The first serious historical attempt to deal with the Crisis from the British angle is Hugh Thomas, *The Suez Affair* (Harper and Row, 1967).

Very few of the main participants in the drama have given us their thoughts and recollections. Sir Anthony Eden (Lord Avon) has published his memoirs for the period in *Full Circle* (Houghton Mifflin, 1960). It need hardly be added that they should be consulted in a critical frame of mind. Anthony Nutting's *No End of a Lesson* (Clarkson Potter, 1967) had not been published when this book went to press, but the advance extracts in *The Times* were revealing. From the United States there is Dwight D. Eisenhower, *The White House Years: Waging Peace 1956–61* (Doubleday, 1966) and Robert Murphy, *Diplomat Among Warriors* (Doubleday, 1964). James Eayrs, *The Commonwealth and Suez: A Documentary Survey* (Oxford University Press,1964) is a thoroughly competent study of British and Commonwealth reactions to the Operation.

PART SEVEN

The *Annual Reports of the Civil Service Commissioners*—published as Parliamentary Papers—yield a great deal of important information. Recent Civil Service recruitment has been analyzed by C. H. Dodd in "Recruitment to the Administrative Class 1960–64" in *Public Administration,* Spring, 1967, Vol. 45. R. K. Kelsall, *Higher Civil Servants in Britain* (Humanities, 1955) is a good introduction. Lord Salter, who served as a British and as an international civil servant and as a minister, has given us his thoughts in *Memoirs of a Public Servant* (1961). Comparisons with the Continent are of great importance in this field. W. A. Robson has compared and contrasted *The Civil Servant in Britain and France* (1956). Brian Chapman has described the European Civil Service in *The Profession of Government* (Humanities, 1959) and contrasted it with Britain's in *British Government Observed* (1963).

Index

Index

Edward Max Nicholson is one of
Great Britain's leading planners and conservation-
ists. Born in Ireland of English parents, he read modern history at Oxford and then worked as a journalist
on *The Weekend Review*. He has twice accepted invitations for government service, in wartime for shipping control and after World War II for national economic planning.

Mr. Nicholson attended the Cairo, Quebec, Yalta,
and Potsdam conferences as senior advisor of the
Anglo-American Combined Shipping Adjustment
Board. From 1945 to 1952 he was senior official advisor to the then Deputy Prime Minister, Herbert
Morrison, and to his successors as Lord President
down to Lord Woolton.

From 1952 Mr. Nicholson was responsible for building up the official organization for conservation in
Great Britain, traveling widely within the country
and overseas. In this and several other capacities he
has had extensive opportunities for both study and
practice of modern relationships between government and governed, on which his book is hinged.